Scharmel Bolling
771-6128
224-7681
501-221-1932

ORGANIZATIONAL COMMUNICATION
Theory and Practice

Gary L. Kreps
Rutgers University

Longman
New York & London

Developed under the
advisory editorship of
Thomas W. Bohn, Dean,
School of Communications,
Ithaca College

Executive Editor: Gordon T. R. Anderson
Text Design: Nina Tallarico
Cover Design: Steven August Krastin
Text Art: J & R Services, Inc.
Compositor: TCSystems
Printer and Binder: The Alpine Press, Inc.

Organizational Communication

Longman Inc., 95 Church Street, White Plains, N.Y. 10601

Associated companies: Longman Group Ltd., London; Longman Chesire Pty., Melbourne; Longman Paul Pty., Auckland; Copp Clark Pitman, Toronto; Copp Clark Publishing Inc., Boston

Library of Congress Cataloging-in-Publication Data

Kreps, Gary L.
Organizational communication.

Includes index.
1. Communication in organizations. 2. Communication in management. I. Title.
HD30.3.K75 1986 658.4′5 85-23818
ISBN 0-582-28573-9

86 87 88 89 9 8 7 6 5 4 3 2 1

Contents

Preface

Organizational communication is an important theoretical and applied field of study and has developed as a popular and active academic area in recent years. The development of organizational communication has been evidenced by:

1. a steady increase in the publication of books, monographs, and articles dealing with the subject over the last 20 years
2. the installment of undergraduate and graduate courses on organizational communication in communication programs at many universities and colleges
3. the introduction of major and minor emphases in undergraduate and graduate degree programs in organizational communication in communication, management, and business programs at many universities and colleges
4. the growth and increasing influence of organizational communication divisions within international, national, and regional professional and academic societies (International Communication Association, Academy of Management, Industrial Communication Council, American Business Communication Association, Speech Communication Association, International Association of Business Communicators, Public Relations Society of America, American Society for Training and Development, Eastern Communication Association)

There has been a consistent thematic pattern presented in the organizational communication textbooks. First, these books have presented three primary historical perspectives on organizational behavior—scientific management, human relations, and systems theory. But these three perspectives, although important, do not represent a comprehensive survey of key approaches to organizational communication developed from current research and theory in organizational communication. Second, the textbooks have concentrated primarily on the internal (administrative) functions of organizational communication, while neglecting to develop fully the external functions of organizational communication. This thematic pattern has limited the comprehensiveness of these books' presentation of organizational communication scholarship and application, presenting a limited and fragmented picture of the discipline.

This book is designed to increase the scope of current representations of organizational communication knowledge by addressing a broader range of theoretical perspectives on organizing and explaining internal and external organizational communication functions and applications. Moreover, it attempts to integrate current knowledge about organizational communication in a clear, theoretically sound, and convivial manner. To accomplish these goals, this book introduces an integrating perspective of organizational communication that emphasizes the role of information and communication in the organizational process. Additionally, I have tried to avoid the use of sexist language and have endeavored to explain complex academic and professional jargon wherever they appear. The use of figures, diagrams, and case studies should also help clarify complex concepts in the book.

The first part of the book provides an introduction to organizations, as well as to communication. Chapter 1 begins by exploring the nature and functions of organization in the modern world. Connections between information and the organizing process are examined, leading to the claims that information helps direct organizational behavior, elicits subunit cooperation, and enables organizational adaptation. Internal and external channels of communication are delineated, and the information functions of these message systems are described. The first chapter ends with the introduction of an integrating model of organizational communication that emphasizes the balance between internal and external information systems in organizations.

Chapter 2 presents a full examination of the nature of human communication, identifying relevant communication theory and research. A full range of progressively more complex yet interdependent levels of human communication—from intrapersonal to interpersonal to small-group to multigroup—are presented and discussed. Human perceptual processes are described. Verbal and nonverbal modes of communication are explored. The overlap between human communication and information processing is explained and applied to the organizational context.

The second part of the book presents a comprehensive view of five major theoretical perspectives on organizational behavior and communication, interpreting and analyzing each approach. Chapter 3 introduces the mechanistic model of classical theory; Chapter 4 examines the humanistic model of human-relations theory; Chapter 5 explores the integrative model of systems theory; Chapter 6 examines the information-processing model of Weick's theory of organizing; and Chapter 7 explores the symbolic model of organizational-culture theory. These five different perspectives on organization are presented, compared, contrasted, and integrated into the book's information-based model of organizational communication. Part II makes this book unique, for it is the first book that combines, articulates, and integrates these five perspectives on organizational behavior.

The third part of the book examines the use of communication channels in organizing. Chapter 8 applies the information-processing model of organizational communication to human communication behaviors in organizations. The functions of communication and information in organizational relationship development are explored. Interpersonal relationships are presented as the functional unit of analysis of all human organization, the level on which all organizations are built. Key aspects of interpersonal communication in organizations are examined, including communication reciprocity, leadership and relational influence, conflict management, power politics, and the development of therapeutic communication relationships in organizations. Chapter 9 provides a fully conceptualized examination of internal communication systems in organizations. The administrative functions of internal message systems are explained. Formal and informal channels of organizational communication are described. The reciprocal impact of organizational structure on communication and communication patterns on organizational structure is explored. Motivation, control, and communication climate are examined as crucial aspects of the internal information system within organizations. Chapter 10 presents the external organizational communication system. Open systems theory is presented as an explanatory model for describing the interdependent relationships that organizations have with other organizations within their relevant environments. Organizations are represented as existing within a suprasystem interorganizational field, where they must be able to coordinate their activities and outputs with interdependent organizations. The use of external message systems, such as public relations, marketing, advertising, lobbying, recruitment, management information networks, market research, and long-range planning, are examined as message strategies used to elicit interorganizational coordination. Ethical constraints on external message systems are examined and external communication abuses are discussed, in light of organizational responsibility for external accountability.

In Part IV of the book, the information-based model of organizational communication, introduced earlier, is fully articulated and related to organizational effectiveness. Chapter 11 explores organizational effectiveness and how it can be accomplished only through the coordination of internal and external message systems, enabling organization members to maintain a balance between stability and innovation in their organizations. The process of organizational innovation is explored, and strategies for organizational development and proactive management are suggested. The book concludes with a summarizing discussion of how organizational effectiveness can be established and maintained through the enlightened use of information to maintain the quality of input, process, and output of organizational communication.

To help readers analyze and apply the concepts presented in the book, each chapter contains several case histories, each of which represents specific principles of organizational communication presented in the chapter. These case histories will help readers apply the chapter content to their understanding of organizational practice. Instructors can use the case histories to stimulate class discussion or as assignments, by having the students analyze the cases in case-study reports. (See the Appendix, at the end of the book, for an examination of specific functions and implementation strategies for case-study analysis in organizational communication instruction.)

In writing the book I attempted to present a comprehensive, theory-based, yet pragmatic view of organizational communication. The information-based perspective used in the book, which draws largely from Weick's model of organizing, is designed to provide a fresh orientation to organizational communication. The coordinating role of information as the central ingredient of human organization and organizational communication activities are highlighted. The book examines the interrelationships among information, human information processing, and the organizing process. Information seeking, selection, processing, sending, and retention are described as crucial communication activities that organization members must engage in in order to accomplish organizational goals. The book progresses toward the development of an integrated model of the organizing process that emphasizes coordinating information-processing activities at internal (management) and external (public relations) levels of the organization to establish and maintain a productive balance between organizational stability and innovation.

In developing the information-based model of organizing used in the book, I trace the contributions of several theories of organizational behavior and communication. Thus, the book extends the theoretical foundations of organizational communication beyond the currently presented perspectives of scientific management, human relations, and systems theories to include a presentation of Weick's model of organizing and organizational culture perspectives on organizational communication. Additionally, the book explores the interdependent communication functions of both internal and external organizational message systems, expanding the traditional organizational communication focus on internal administrative message systems. I attempt to provide a balanced presentation of the administrative and public relations functions of organizational communication.

I am grateful for the help of many individuals in the development of this book. My colleagues at Rutgers University have provided me with valuable feedback about the ideas presented. Special thanks go to two colleagues: Brent Ruben, who encouraged me to pursue an information-based approach to organizational communication; and Lea Stewart, who shared her expertise with me to help make sense out of early drafts.

I am grateful to the insightful analyses of organizing processes by Professor Karl Weick, which helped liberate my thinking about the nature of organization, especially in his classic volume *The Social Psychology of Organizing*. My thanks to Chuck Bantz and Harrell Allen for encouraging me to study carefully Weick's model of organizing.

My thanks to Mike Pacanowsky and Linda Putnam, the organizers of the ICA/SCA Summer Conferences on the Interpretive Approach to the Study of Organization, and all of the participants of the first three conferences (1981, 1982, 1983), who helped me explore and make sense of the cultural aspects of organizational life.

I appreciate the confidence, respect, and encouragement shown me by Tren Anderson, executive editor at Longman, and by Tom Bohn, dean of the School of Communications at Ithaca College and editorial advisor to Longman. My thanks to the reviewers: Phil Tompkins of Purdue University, Don Faules of the University of Utah, and Joe Chilberg of Ithaca College. They all provided me with excellent criticism, encouragement, and ideas for improvement of the text.

Additionally, I am grateful for the meaningful and often spirited interaction my students, past and present, have provided me, which helped me develop and refine many of the ideas and examples I have presented in this book.

On a more personal note, I sincerely appreciate the love, support, and patience shown to me in the preparation of this manuscript by my wife, Stephanie, and the rest of my family. Special thanks to Sid Kreps, the epitome of an effective organizational communicator, for his inspiration and guidance, as well as to the omnipresent guiding spirit of my grandfather, Julius Cohen, which fostered my interest in human communication. Most of all, I dedicate this book to the miracle of Rebecca Michele Kreps.

Gary L. Kreps

PART I

INTRODUCTION

In this book we explore the ways that communication is used to create and utilize information to facilitate coordination and organization. Chapter 1 introduces and defines several basic concepts and themes that are utilized throughout the book. We wrestle with two opposing conceptualizations of the nature of human organization and tie together these seemingly unrelated points of view into a unifying framework. We trace the basic relationships among communication, information, and organization, describing the pervasive, adaptive organizational functions of communication in the modern world. Two different, yet functionally related, channels of communication in organizational contexts—internal and external message systems—are introduced and developed into an integrating model of organizing that will be used again in Chapter 11 to summarize, illustrate, and apply many concepts and theories presented throughout the book. In Chapter 2, the key elements of the communication process are described and explained. Both chapters elaborate on the overly simple and stereotypic views that most people have of organizational and communication processes. By expanding and clarifying traditional perspectives on organizational phenomena, we are setting the stage for our exploration of organizational communication.

CHAPTER 1

Communicating and Organizing

THE NATURE OF ORGANIZATION

Human beings have learned to work together to accomplish tasks in a complex and challenging world. In early prehistory, cave dwellers learned that it was more productive to hunt in groups than to hunt alone. Together, the hunters could effectively trap and surround their prey, sharing the quarry that they had captured. These prehistoric people also found that by banding together in tribes to withstand the threats to their survival posed by carnivorous animals and an inhospitable climate, they could better provide for their safety and shelter than they could individually. Thus our prehistoric ancestors precipitated the birth of the first human organizations and the beginnings of organizational life. The powerful lessons about interpersonal cooperation learned by prehistoric men and women have helped later generations of human beings develop organized activities to accomplish their objectives.

The shift in prehistory from nomadic to communal society reflects the growing role of organization in human development, as people began to grow food and gather resources, as well as hunt game. As prehistory progressed into antiquity, the ancient Egyptians established social organization with a highly structured society under the strict rule of the pharoahs, two of the legacies of which are the incredible pyramids and the Sphinx, which the Egyptian people were directed to painstakingly build as tombs for and monuments to the royal family. The Egyptians, who established military organizations to protect and expand their empires, both lived and died by the sword. Egyptian dynasties were conquered by the Assyrians and the Persians, introducing the organizational structure of the Egyptians to Greek and, later, Roman society. The Greeks and Romans created a wide range of human organizations to serve their societies. These organizations helped to stimulate the development of science, government, trade, industry, philosophy, education, religion, architecture, art, and the military.

The social organizations of the Romans and their Germanic conquerors evolved into a feudal society, which was based on a hierarchical, interorganizational system of fiefdoms, ruled by kings, emperors, and lesser nobles. These militaristic fiefdoms fought for power and glory on fields of battle. "The feudal virtues were faith, courage, and blind loyalty to peer and superior. . . ." (Fleming, 1975, p. 121). The blind loyalty of organizational life during the Middle Ages was eventually replaced by the enlightened individualism of the Renaissance, during which people were encouraged to develop their talents and knowledge. Patrons supported the arts, architecture, science, and invention. Commerce and industry were encouraged. Craft, merchant, and trade guilds taught and promoted high-quality standards in handiwork and increased the production, procurement, and discovery of specialized goods and services. The combined growth of business and science during the Renaissance sowed the seeds for the Industrial Revolution and mechanized production, which flowered in the nineteenth century. Mechanization and the Industrial Revolution firmly established the role of business organizations in society and had a strong influence on the development of modern organizationally based industrial society.

The seeds of social organization have come to fruition in the myriad coordinated networks of relationships that help make our modern world work. Our organizationally based society depends on interpersonal and intergroup cooperation and coordination, which are an inherent part of our lives. It is through a wide range of cooperative activities that we are able to resist environmental threats, such as pollution and nuclear war, to achieve our goals.

People coordinating activities with one another to achieve their goals and ultimately to survive is the primary activity of organization, which is based on cooperation. Coordination is not always easily accomplished, however. People must be persuaded to cooperate, and communication is the tool that elicits cooperation. Through communication, people gather information from others and provide others with information. It is information that can determine whether people will cooperate.

Networks of individuals coordinating with one another over time appear to us as well-established, stable social systems commonly known as organizations. This image of organization is a bit of an overgeneralization, since human organization is an adaptive, ongoing process that is seldom stable and is usually quite hectic (Weick, 1979). Indeed, a major theme of this book is that effective organizations are never totally stable; a primary goal of organization is to strive for a productive balance between stability (order) and change (disorder). Yet the notion of organization as a fairly static structure, although not completely accurate and somewhat stereotypic, provides us with a useful handle for recognizing, examining, and discussing organizational activities. For the moment, let us examine the social phenomena we call organizations. Later in this chapter, we will explore in more depth some of the process aspects of organization, contrasting the active, emergent process view of organizing (verb) with the more structured entity view of organization (noun). Although the conceptualizations differ from each other, both are useful and correct. As Casteneda (1971) points out, there is always more than one correct perspective on reality.

The structurally oriented definition of organization, which also recognizes and respects the operational activities of organizing, describes *organizations* as *social collectives in which people develop ritualized patterns of interaction in an attempt to coordinate their activities and efforts in the ongoing accomplishment of personal and group goals.* Well, that is a mouthful. Let us examine and evaluate this definition for a moment. What is a "social collective"? A social collective is a gathering or grouping (the "collective" aspect of the definition) of human beings (the "social" aspect of the definition). Why are these people gathering? In organizational life, people gather to join efforts to achieve their individual and collective "goals," such as financial goals, affiliative goals, educational goals, production goals, and cultural-promotion and -development goals. The "ongoing" part of the definition recognizes that people never totally fulfill all their goals and continually establish new ones. This indicates that organizing is not a one-time effort, but a repetitive activity. Well, you might ask, how are these goals achieved? They are achieved through the efforts and activities of people working together through organization. The key question is: How are individual efforts joined toward goal attainment? A brief answer is that communication is the social force that enables individuals to work cooperatively toward achieving mutually recognized goals. As Johnson (1977) has so aptly pointed out, "Communication is the process of organizing" (p. 3). The ways that people communicate to coordinate efforts and exhibit organization is a major theme that will be addressed in this book and a subject that we will be discussing in depth.

Communication is the process that enables people to co-orient their behaviors. Communication empowers people to establish functional interpersonal relationships that allow them to work together toward goal attainment. More specifically, people in social collectives establish mutually acceptable relational agreements through ritualized patterns of communication with each other. These relational agreements direct interdependent relational partners to coordinate their efforts toward common objectives. Relationship development is the key to interpersonal coordination, and human communication is the tool people use to establish and maintain effective relationships (Chapter 8).

Organizations seem to be everywhere. Each of us has many organizational affiliations. We not only belong to a wide range of organizations, but also interact with and seek the services of an even broader range of organizations every day of our lives. For example, you may belong to one or more business organizations, perhaps as a worker, a supervisor, an executive, an owner, an investor, or an intern. Since you are reading this book, you are very likely to be a member of an academic organization in at least one of the following roles: student, staff member, research assistant, research subject, patron, alumnus, faculty member, or even administrator. Furthermore, if you are a member of a college or a university, you may belong to organizations that operate within the boundaries of this academic organization, such as fraternities, sororities, sports teams, clubs, special committees, governing bodies, or academic departments. You are inescapably a member of state- and federal-government organizations, as a resident, a "law-abiding" citizen, a taxpayer, an activist, a lobbyist, a politician, or a voter. It is a good bet that you are part of many social and cultural organizations, the most basic of which is your family. Other social organizations you may hold memberships in include religious congregations, sports leagues, health clubs, art-appreciation groups, sporting-event-ticket-holder groups, self-help groups, therapy groups, dating clubs, travel groups, and on and on.

As you begin to reflect on the different organizations to which you belong, you will realize that it is virtually impossible to escape organizational membership in modern society. The very fabric of our social, cultural, and economic worlds are inextricably organizationally based. In Case 1.1, a typical modern family, the Smith family, is presented. In the brief breakfast scene depicted in the case, the family members allude to their organizational affiliations. As you read the case, see how many organizations you can identify that influence the lives of different members of the Smith family.

1. To which organizations do all the family members belong?
2. To which organizations do one or more of the family members belong?
3. How do these organizational affiliations affect the lives of the Smith family members?
4. What functions do these organizations provide for them?

Case 1.1

The Smith Family and Organizational Reality

It was a bright sunny Monday morning in Pleasantville, and the Smith family was sitting around the kitchen table eating breakfast and preparing for the new day. Bob Smith, the father of the clan, was dressed in a dark business suit and was leafing through the appointment book in his gray attaché case. "Let's see, budget meeting at 9:00, sales call to the new clients at 10:00, lunch at noon with the accountants, staff meetings at 2:00, and interviews with job applicants the rest of the afternoon; it's going to be another busy day for me," he mumbled. "It's my turn to drive the guys to the train station. I hope Baxter is ready early for a change. I can't miss the 8:19 this morning."

Sue, Bob's wife, asked, "What's your rush? You'd better not rush to the station and get another traffic ticket. You had to pay a $60 fine at traffic court for that maneuver. Why can't you just take the 8:30 train into the city?" Bob shot Sue an impatient glance and responded in an irritated voice, "Don't you remember? Today is the day for the company blood drive, and I have to stop off at the clinic before work to give those medical vampires a donation. If I don't go there today, I'll have to reschedule, and who knows when I'll have time later. If I don't donate, I might lose my medical-insurance coverage. I never realized how many hassles there would be when I signed up for the darn blood-replacement program."

Little Sally, Bob and Sue's precocious 8-year-old daughter, chirped in, "Don't be afraid of the doctor, Daddy. She's real nice. When I got my booster shot, it didn't hurt, and she gave me a lollipop!" Jimmy, Sally's 14-year-old brother, smirked at his little sister's foolishness, "Dad doesn't go to the same doctor as you, dummy. Besides, they give lollipops only to shrimps like you." Sue glared at her son. "Instead of teasing your sister, Jimmy, you'd better finish eating, put your plate and spoon in the dishwasher, and get ready for your school bus. If you miss the bus again, you're going to be in big trouble. The junior-high-school vice principal warned that you've been late to school too many times already. I can't drive you. I'm taking Sally to the elementary school, which is in the other direction," Sue said sharply. Turning to her husband, she explained, "I'm due at the shop at 9:00 this morning. We're getting in a new delivery of books, and I have to sign the invoices, price the books, and get the books on the shelves before the people from the book club overrun us at 10:00."

"If you miss the early train, you can always stop off at the clinic after work, Bob," Sue suggested. "Oh no I can't; I have to go to the bank to open our IRA account today before the tax deadline, and then I have an Elks meeting. Today is the election, and I'm up for office," Bob replied. "Oh, right, I forgot about that. Good luck! I just hope you're home by 7:30, Bob. We're supposed to go to the church fund-raising dinner tonight, and we have to drop Sally off at the baby-sitter's house and Jimmy off at his Boy Scout meeting," Sue said. "I'll be there, honey. Got to get going. You all have a nice day. Daddy loves you!"

5. What roles do the family members perform in each of the organizations?

You probably have to write a list of all the organizations that each of the Smith family members belongs to if you want to keep them straight. The number of organizational relationships exhibited in this brief scene is amazing when you recognize that the case mentions only a meager sample of the many organizations that each family member will encounter during his or her busy day. Organizational activities will occupy a huge percentage of the time and energy of each member of the Smith clan. Each of the four family members is influenced by and influences many organizations.

The Smith family illustrates the pervasiveness of organizational influence in modern society. They are members of a very important, yet often overlooked, organization—the Smith family. The family is an excellent organization to identify and discuss first, because it will help liberate our thinking about the nature of organizations. People often think only of businesses, industries, or corporations when asked to identify organizations. Where is it written that "large," "profit making," or "production oriented" are defining characteristics of organization? In this book, we will consider many types of organizations, including profit-making businesses. But the traditional view of organizations should not narrow our thinking about organizational life. The family is by no means a trivial organization; on the contrary, it is an extremely important social organization that provides its members with educational, emotional, spiritual, and economic guidance and support.

In Case 1.1, all the family members are coordinating their activities to help one another prepare for a busy day. They help one another cook, serve, and clean up after breakfast; plan hectic schedules; plot business strategies; provide and coordinate transportation; counsel and discipline one another; and offer suggestions, moral support, and encouragement. It is amazing how successfully the family members can coordinate these important activities in the brief scene described. They obviously have practiced their roles and routines. The case illustrates some of the ways that they use interpersonal communication to direct one another and coordinate their activities.

The family is certainly not the only organization to which each of the Smiths belongs. All probably are members of the church that is hosting a fund-raising dinner that the parents are planning to attend. The family's membership in such a religious organization helps to provide a common organizational frame of reference and enables the family members to participate together in social networks. Another organizational affiliation the Smith family shares is their insurance company. The family is covered by a medical-insurance plan mentioned by Bob Smith, and the coverage makes the family members constituents of that organization. In times of medical emergency, when a family member might become hospitalized or seek medical services, the family's constituency in this organization will provide significant financial benefits that will help the family meet the economic costs of health-case treatment.

The Smith children are affiliated with several organizations. Both Sally and Jimmy attend public schools. Sally attends elementary school, and Jimmy goes to junior high school. Each is a student member of an academic organization. Educational organizations play a significant role in our lives. Schools impart important information and training. By directing the children to participate in organizationally designated activities, the educational organizations provide Sally and Jimmy with social and educational stimulation and indoctrinate them into behaving in accordance with the rules of the larger society. The case identifies additional organizational contexts in which the Smith children participate. Sally speaks of her experience getting a booster shot from her family physician, indicating her participation as a health-care consumer in a medical organization. Jimmy is a member of a local Boy Scout pack, a social organization, whose meeting he plans to attend that evening.

Bob and Sue Smith are employees in different business organizations. Sue works in a bookshop, and Bob works for a company in the city. Bob, likewise, mentions his involvement with a medical organization when he gripes about having to stop off at the clinic in the city. He also mentions his participation in a blood-drive program, sponsored by the medical-insurance company to which he subscribes. Unhappily, Sue tells us that Bob has encountered the local police force and the court system, when he received a ticket for speeding to the train station.

Bob and Sue depend on a baby-sitting operation to take care of Sally while they are out to dinner. Bob is a member of the Elks Club, a social organization. He mentions having to go to the bank to open a retirement account, before tax deadlines, indicating membership as a taxpayer in state and federal government, as well as being a customer of a bank in the city. Bob also is a member of a car pool that transports its members to the train station. Once at the train station, Bob participates in a public mass-transportation system. Sue works not only with a book club that frequents the bookshop, but also with a delivery company that ships books to the shop.

Whew! We probably can identify even more Smith family organizational affiliations, but you get the point that modern life is inextricably organizationally oriented. We depend on our connections with other individuals within organizational networks to achieve our goals. It might be interesting for you to try to identify how many organizational affiliations influence your life in any given day. What goals do these organizations help you to accomplish? How do these organizational affiliations affect your life and constrain or liberate your activities? When you couple your recognition of the powerful impact of organizational affiliations on your life with the fact that communication is your primary tool to influence organizations and to gain access to organizational resources, you will begin to realize the importance of organizational communication not only to you, but also in the modern world.

Talcott Parsons (1963) provides an interesting functional classification of organizational types. His classification is based on the ways organizations help create and maintain modern society. He identifies four primary functions that different organizations are developed to perform in society. The four-function classification system is instructive because it helps us differentiate among some of the primary purposes for organizing and developing organization within society. The functions are not always mutually exclusive, and some organizations may seem to perform more than one of these functions in society. Yet we usually can identify most organizational classifications based on the organization's most basic and primary social service (Tompkins, 1982).

Organizations oriented to economic production are the typical profit-making business organizations, which manufacture products and/or offer services for consumers. These organizations are economically self-sufficient, surviving or failing to survive based on their ability to recoup their expenses through the sale of their products and/or services. Most organizations from which we purchase goods or services fall into this category.

Organizations oriented to political goals are those designed to generate and distribute power and control within society. These organizations are generally funded and empowered by federal and local governments, and include government offices, legislative bodies, police and military forces, and even financial institutions (such as banks), since "the banking system creates and allocates power in a business economy" (Tompkins, 1982, p. 165).

Organizations oriented to integration goals are those that help mediate and resolve discord among groups and individual members of society. Organizations that are designed to help solve social problems, such as legal offices, the court system, public-interest groups, consumer-advocacy organizations, and even political parties, are integration oriented.

Organizations oriented to pattern-maintenance goals are those that promote cultural and educational regularity and development within society. Organizations that help to socialize the public into learning and following the norm structure of a given society, such as families, schools, and religious organizations, promote pattern maintenance. Even many health-care organizations are oriented toward pattern-maintenance functions, to the extent that they help preserve society by reducing health problems and morbidity, thereby helping the ill to return to their proper and normal functioning within society.

In Case 1.1, we can identify organizations that represent each of the four categories established by Parsons. The most commonly referred to organization type is the pattern-maintenance organization. The Smith family itself is a pattern-maintenance organization that helps the family members cope with the difficulties of their social worlds and teaches them to act in accordance with societal norms. Other pattern-maintenance organizations include their church, the children's schools, Jimmy's Boy Scout troop, and Bob's Elks Club chapter. Both Sue and Bob work for economic-production organizations. They help these organizations develop, market, and sell goods and services, enabling these companies to make profits and, in turn, remunerate Sue and Bob with money and other benefits. Bob mentions his need to purchase an IRA account before tax time, referring to two politically oriented organizations, his bank and the Internal Revenue Service. Sue mentions another politically oriented organization, the police force, one member of which gave Bob a speeding ticket. To pay his traffic fine, Bob had to go to court, which is an integration organization that rules on societal problems and disputes.

Not only are organizations an inescapable part of modern life, but organizational life has become exceedingly complex. We are expected to perform unique and varied roles in each of the many organizations to which we belong. There are distinctly different goals, rules, responsibilities, and communication networks associated with membership in different organizations. For example, the various classes (organizations) you attend as a college student require you to perform different activities to accomplish the course objectives. Course-leadership styles vary from one class to another. Course content and class lectures are different. You probably will not take the same exam, read the same book, or write the same term paper in two different courses. Some classes encourage students to take an active role in the discussions. Other classes discourage student communication. Still other classes assign student presentations about course topics. The roles and activities that may make you a successful member of one class, may not help you at all in another class. To be effective within any organization, you must be able to identify and accomplish the activities and objectives of that organization.

To make organizational life even more complicated, every organization is a living, growing, adapting social system, subject to continual change. Every organization is in a state of flux, developing and instituting new activities, guidelines, and directions in an attempt to adapt to changes in environmental constraints. This means that the roles and activities we perform as organization members are potentially under constant revision. For example, workers in business organizations are often promoted, demoted, reclassified, transferred, or given new job responsibilities. Products may be redesigned, discontinued, or distributed to new markets. Departments may be abolished, revamped, or restructured. Standard operating procedures may be reworked and altered to fit new knowledge or changing personnel, technologies, and goals.

How do we know what changes are going to occur within organizations and what influences these imminent changes will have on our roles and responsibilities as organization members? To be aware and effective, organization members need clear, pertinent, and full information, which is an extremely powerful commodity in organizational life. Armed with timely and relevant information, a member can interpret some of the complexities of organizational phenomena, evaluate different courses of action, and plot strategies for adapting to changing organizational conditions. Effective organizational communicators attempt to gather relevant information about the changing constraints, problems, and goals that are part of organizational life. Information empowers organization members by enabling them to understand and predict changes and adapt their behaviors to these new developments within the organization.

Communication, Information, and Organization

Organizational communication is the process whereby members gather pertinent information about their organization and the changes occurring within it. Communication helps organization members by ena-

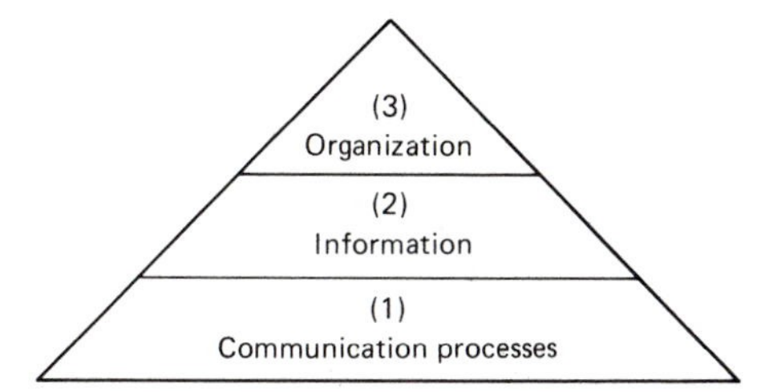

Figure 1.1 The relationship between communication, information, and organization.

bling them to discuss critical organizational experiences and develop relevant information which demystifies complex organizational activities and organizational change. Communication helps organization members accomplish both individual and organizational goals by enabling them to interpret organizational change and ultimately enabling them to coordinate their fulfillment of personal needs with their accomplishment of their evolving organizational responsibilities. Organizational communication serves a crucial data-gathering function for organization members by providing them with sense-making information. Human communication is also the primary vehicle by which organization members can help direct organizational changes by influencing the activities of other individuals within the organization.

Communicating and organizing are closely related human activities. Information is the mediating variable that connects communication to organization. Communication is a message-gathering, -sending, and -interpreting process that enables people to understand information. Information is used to constrain and coordinate the activities of individuals to establish organization. Figure 1.1 depicts the relationship among information, communication, and organization.

Communication is a symbolic activity that people engage in to help them interpret and influence their social worlds. Through communication, they gather raw data from their environments and process these data into information, an interpretive outcome of communication that helps them understand diverse phenomena and increase the predictability of life. By communicating, people create, exchange, and respond to messages by creating meanings. Information is relevant data that is gained from the meanings that people create.

Information provides predictability in human endeavors by reducing uncertainty about the choices that individuals must make to accomplish their goals. People can demonstrate organization as an outcome of effective communication and information use. They can coordinate their activities to achieve commonly recognized goals only to the extent that they have relevant information that influences their behavior. The performance of cooperative coordinated activities, in turn, enables human beings to develop and exhibit organization.

Organizing and Organization

Organization is an important and encompassing concept. The word *organize* is commonly used as a verb (to organize), while the word *organization* is typically used as a noun (the organization) (Weick, 1979). The process of organization refers to both an activity that people engage in and the successful outcome of that activity. Organizing (as a verb) refers to the process of developing coordinated activities. People may engage in organizing intrapersonally as well as interpersonally. For example, I might attempt to get myself organized by trying to coordinate my many (often diverse and seemingly unrelated) ideas and thoughts into a coherent whole, to establish a sense of order and direction in my activities and life. Similarly, two or more students might organize their different ideas, information, and talents toward working cooperatively in the preparation of a term project. If attempts at organizing are successful, individuals will achieve a state of organization, or coordinated activity. In this manner, the active process of organizing can lead to a relatively stable (at least temporarily) state of organization, in which people demonstrate coordination of their activities in the accomplishment of individual and collective goals.

The term *organization* is also used as a noun, to describe a specific context. As such, the word identifies structural entities, such as businesses, industries, hospitals, and government agencies. Organizations are typically regarded as specific contexts, buildings, or places where people work, such as major corporations like AT&T (American Telephone & Telegraph), RCA (Radio Corporation of America), P. & G. (Proctor & Gamble), J & J (Johnson & Johnson), or IBM (International Business Machines). (Why is it that so many large business organizations are known by multiletter acronyms? We will discuss the importance of organizational symbols in connection with organizational cultures in Chapter 7.) These large corporate organizations appear to be stable structural entities because we tend to view the organizing behaviors of their members only briefly and usually from a distance. When viewing organizations as static structures, we fail to notice the ongoing organizational processes. When viewing them up close and over time, we can see that these corporations only seem to be static entities because their members are effectively coordinating their behaviors and exhibiting successful organizing activities. Organizations are organized only as long as their members are cooperating. We can recognize the outcome of organization (noun) only when the process of organizing (verb) is being accomplished.

Organization members are continually engaged in a process of organizing and reorganizing. As they interlock their behaviors, they begin to exhibit organization. Human communication is the process these organization members use to facilitate the performance of coordinated activities.

Information and Organizational Behavior

Information, as mentioned earlier, is a product (outcome) of communication and meaning creation that serves to help people understand and predict the world around them. As such, information is an extremely important and useful outcome of communication. Obviously, the clearer, fuller, and more accurate the information an individual possesses, the better he or she is able to interpret confusing phenomena and identify effective strategies for responding to these phenomena. Information is a powerful commodity in organizational life because individuals who possess relevant knowledge can help their organizational partners interpret and respond appropriately to different organizational tasks, problems, and endeavors.

Information helps direct behavior in organizations by indicating the most fruitful way to interpret and accomplish tasks. Here is a simple example of the way that information helps direct behavior. Let us say that you are working as a salesperson for a large insurance firm, and your supervisor requests that you make a sales call on a potential client. You will use the information you possess to help you accomplish this task. If you have detailed knowledge of and experience with the types of insurance your company offers, the rates available, and the specific insurance needs of the potential client, you possess relevant organizational information. This information will direct your use of the particular communication strategies available to you to sell insurance to the client. If you do not have such relevant information, you probably will not be able to make a convincing sales pitch to the client and will have a very difficult time making the sale. (This lack of relevant organizational information is evident in a story about a public school teacher who was directed to clean the heads on a new videotape recorder purchased by the school. The teacher, who knew very little about video equipment, attempted to clean the videorecorder heads with steel-wool pads, which resulted in almost destroying the machine.) Thus information directs organizational behavior by providing members with insight and knowledge about how they can best accomplish their jobs. Lack of job-related information can lead to disastrous results.

Information also helps elicit subunit cooperation in organizations. As we will discuss more fully in Chapter 5, organizations are generally composed of different functional subunits, each of which performs specialized activities for the organization. At the same time, however, the activities of each subunit are closely related to and interdependent with the activities and functions of other subunits. To get these organizational subunits to work in concert, members of each subunit must share information with representatives of related subunits.

In many large, complex organizations, information systems are designed and implemented to help coordinate the organizations' varied information needs. For example, management information systems are used to help coordinate the activities of interdependent organizational subunits by providing each with information and directions about organizational activities. Information systems also are used to furnish salespeople with customer leads, to suggest product and production innovations, to evaluate the strengths and weaknesses of the organization, and to give organization planners information about relevant changes in the organization's environment. Information-system functions are performed by a wide range of organizational subunits, including departments of records management, research and development, public relations, community relations, government relations, customer relations, personnel, quality control, inventory control, corporate libraries, corporate archives, accounting, and strategic planning. To accomplish their information-related goals, all these departments depend not only on communication, but also on modern information-storage and -retrieval technologies, such as computer systems and microfilm, as well as more traditional information-storage units, such as file cabinets, ledgers, and books. Information systems, such as these departments, use communication to collect, interpret, evaluate, and make available relevant organizational information.

The way information is used to promote subunit cooperation can be easily seen in a manufacturing organization. For instance, if the sales department (a functional subunit of the organization) has committed 500 widgets (a mythical product) to a customer, the organization had better be able to produce and deliver the widgets to the customer by the specified date. To accomplish this, the production department (another functional subunit of the organization) must possess relevant information about the increased product demand. This information can be conveyed to the production department either directly by representatives of the sales department or indirectly by representatives of an organizational information system who convey the information about product demand. It is the provision of relevant interdepartmental information, derived through communication, that helps to elicit cooperative action between these subunits in the manufacturing company.

Case 1.2 further illustrates the information needs of modern organizations by identifying some of the information needs and processes of a health-care organization, a hospital. Hospitals are an excellent example of organizations that depend mightily on timely and accurate information. Any slight information delay or distortion can have life-threatening repercussions for health-care consumers (Kreps and Thornton, 1984). The case describes a potentially dangerous organizational situation in which the hospital information system breaks down, causing a serious dilemma for hospital employees and patients.

Based on the information in the case, answer the following questions.

1. What is meant when this hospital is characterized as an information system? Identify the key elements of this hospital information system.
2. What are the communication functions of this hospital information system? Are these information functions typical of health-care organizations? Are they typical of other organizations?
3. Think of examples of the ways that different organizations use information. Identify some of the primary sources of information in this hospital. How is the information gathered from these sources and later processed and stored in the hospital information system? How can the information be retrieved by hospital members?
4. What role does communication play in the hospital information system? How has this relationship between communication and information led to organizational problems?
5. Identify some of the communication problems evident in this hospital. What could be done to improve the communication and information system in this organization? Optimally, how should this system work?
6. Do you believe the hospital spokesperson's claim that the information breakdown had no relation to Pawelski's death? How do you think this experience may have affected Pawelski? What implications does this suggest about the importance of accurate and timely information in organizations, especially health-care organizations?

This case clearly illustrates the importance of gathering, interpreting, preserving, and making available relevant information in organizations. Information is the resource that directs organizational activities. Human communication is the process by which information is generated and shared. Effective human communication is crucially important in organizing activities.

Organizational Communication and Adaptation

Communication has developed as an adaptive mechanism for humanity. An *adaptive mechanism* is a tool people use to help them recognize

Case 1.2

The Hospital as an Information System*

A perceptive visitor to a hospital would observe that a great deal of staff activity is devoted to information processing activities.

At the nursing station are several nurses filling out patient record forms, talking on the telephone, or discussing the coordination of their day's schedule. A doctor is being paged on a P. A. system. Food trays are being wheeled down the corridor to patients' rooms, each tray supposedly assigned to a specific patient on the basis of particular dietary needs, as indicated on a form that was sent previously to the hospital kitchen. At bedside, a doctor is obtaining information from a patient about symptoms, information that will then be entered in the patient's record file.

It would be hard to overestimate the importance of this file to the hospital. If the record file were ever lost or misplaced, as sometimes happens, the hospital would be at almost a complete loss as to how to treat the patient. The file is begun when the patient enters the hospital's door, and it must accompany the patient wherever he or she goes: to X-ray or to surgery, for example. Upon discharge, the file, by this time an inch or two thick with forms, charts, and notes (and representing hundreds of hours of skilled expertise worth thousands of dollars), goes permanently to the hospital records department. The record file is so sacred to the hospital that the patient is not allowed to see it, except in very unusual cases, and then only with the permission of the doctor. The file can be so thick that it represents an information overload problem. One solution is to computerize the file data; another approach is to utilize a "problem-oriented" record system, in which essential data are isolated and instantly accessible.

Great effort is expended by the hospital to ensure that the patient record file contains adequate and accurate information. Each entry in the file must be signed and initialed, so that responsibility for it is precisely fixed. Every bit of information about the patient must be recorded: every bowel movement, every medication that is administered, every rise in temperature. The cost of an error in the patient file is awesome: each year one or more patients' lives in a typical hospital

* *This case is reprinted from* Communication in Organizations *by Everett M. Rogers and Rekha Agarwala-Rogers. New York: Free Press, 1976, pp. 8–9; by permission of the publisher.*

may be lost owing to errors in information processing or transmittal. Because of the cost of such errors, most hospitals expend great effort on continually redesigning their communication system, on training and retraining the hospital staff to use it properly, and on checking on its accuracy and adequacy through various feedback devices.

Despite such extensive precautions, however, embarrassing communication breakdowns still occur. One spectacular example is the case of a patient in the Chicago-area Veterans Administration hospital, Erwin Pawelski, who was "lost" for twenty-seven hours.

Pawelski, a patient who could not speak, was strapped onto a wheelchair by an attendant and wheeled out of his ward to receive occupational therapy at 9:30 A.M. on May 1, 1975. What happened next is anybody's guess. The patient record file shows a twenty-seven hour blank. A hospital spokesman later told newspaper reporters: "There's a presumption that he arrived in the basement for therapy. But we are not positive."

At 7:00 A.M. on May 2nd, Pawelski's wife was called by the hospital to ask if she had removed him from the hospital. When she rushed to the hospital, she found that another patient had moved into his bed. Pawelski's effects had been shoved into a closet.

Pawelski was found by a therapy supervisor who stepped into an elevator in the hospital basement at 1:10 P.M. on May 2nd. The hospital has 3,000 employees, 1,295 patients, and about 700 visitors daily. Pawelski was in one of the main banks of elevators, ridden each day by hundreds of doctors, nurses, attendants, patients, and visitors. "It's unbelievable that there wouldn't be one person during those twenty-seven hours offering to help this man slumped over in a wheelchair. It's a mystery what happened," stated the hospital spokesman.

Twenty days after Pawelski was "misplaced" for twenty-seven hours, he died from cerebral hemorrhage after undergoing brain surgery. The hospital claimed the death was not connected with any ill effects sustained from the incident.

A hospital can best be viewed, then, as an organization that devotes much of its activity to processing information. So, in fact, do most other types of organizations.

and respond to threats to their existence. Communication helps people survive by providing them with information about impending threats and by helping them avoid or overcome these threats. For example, if you were crossing a street and looked up to see a large truck hurtling down a hill toward you, you would be facing a serious threat to your survival. Your ability to perceive and comprehend this threat would certainly be a significant piece of information aiding your survival. By gathering pertinent environmental messages through your eyes and ears (sight and hearing) and by interpreting these messages as useful information through intrapersonal communication, you could adapt to your environment and avoid this threat to your survival. You probably would use the information you gained from communication to respond to this threat, perhaps by directing yourself to jump out of the path of the truck, thereby averting injury. Communication served as an adaptive mechanism by helping you survive a serious threat to your survival.

We also use communication to elicit cooperation from others to help us survive. To solve complex problems, we seek assistance from relevant others in society. For example, we regularly visit health-care professionals, who help us fight life-threatening diseases. Communication enables us to identify and gain access to health-care organizations, where there are health professionals (doctors, nurses, pharmacists, therapists, counselors, and so on) who might help us. We use communication to explain the nature of our problem to the health-care providers, who, in turn, communicate with us and with one another to diagnose and treat our problem. With effective communication relationships between health-care providers and consumers, health-care services can be delivered to the public (Kreps and Thornton, 1984). We are able to seek help from many others in society, including plumbers, lawyers, accountants, therapists, teachers, carpenters, and bankers, through our ability to communicate and establish effective working relationships with these people.

Just as communication helps individuals survive in society, so it serves as a crucial adaptive mechanism for organization members and for organizations. It helps organization members respond appropriately to the changing constraints of organizational life by enabling them to recognize and adapt to changing tasks and problems. As a student, your ability to receive and interpret different messages through communication from a wide range of information sources enables you to survive academically each of your classes. For example, you interpret messages from the instructor, from class handouts, from course texts, and from class members about different class assignments and tasks. Your ability to communicate effectively by listening carefully, interpreting readings, and asking pertinent questions will determine how well you adapt your behaviors to accomplishing class assignments and, ultimately, how well you do (what grade you receive) in the class.

Similarly, communication enables the organization leaders to direct the organization as a whole and to adapt to changing tasks, conditions, and environmental constraints. The successful operation of a class, an exemplar organization, depends on communication among members to conduct class activities and to accomplish course goals. For example, the instructor uses various communication strategies (lectures, discussions, handouts, media presentations, structured exercises, readings) because different topics may lend themselves to different means of presentation. The instructor's ability to adapt these communication strategies to specific course tasks and to the class members' abilities to interpret and utilize the strategies will help the class achieve its goals. Furthermore, an effective instructor seeks feedback (information) from the class, through questions, exams, or other means, to determine how well course objectives are being met. If students do not seem to be understanding course material, the instructor uses this feedback to attempt to adapt to this constraint by adopting new, perhaps remedial, instructional communication strategies. It is through communication that the instructor can attempt to identify the constraints on effective organizational operation and direct activities toward maintaining the quality of education in the class. It is communication that enables this organization to adapt and accomplish its educational goals, to survive as a class.

A clear understanding of the adaptive-mechanism functions of communication for individuals and organizations serves to reinforce and emphasize the centrality of communication and information in organizing activities. It is through the use of human communication that individuals can adapt to their environments. It is also through the use of human communication that organizational processes can be directed toward continually meeting the changing information constraints facing organization members and the organization they are members of.

INTERNAL AND EXTERNAL DIMENSIONS of ORGANIZATIONAL COMMUNICATION

Many different sources of communication can provide organization members with pertinent information. Two primary communication systems are internal and external organizational communication channels both of which perform important, distinct, yet interrelated functions in the process of organizing. We now will introduce some of the key information functions of internal and external message systems as well as an integrating model of organizational communication, which emphasizes the way the balance between internal and external information channels is accomplished and enables organizational adaptation to occur.

Internal Communication Channels

The most traditional and frequent point of focus of past examinations of organizations and organizational communication has explored the means by which activities are created and maintained within organizations. The focus has been on the subprocesses in which organization members engage to accomplish organizational tasks and on the ways that internal communication channels are used to facilitate the accomplishment of prescribed organizational activities. (Do not let this emphasis of past organizational communication research mislead you into thinking that internal communication is always task related. In Chapter 9, we will discuss the development of informal internal communication systems that often carry message patterns that are not task oriented.) Simply defined, internal communication is the pattern of messages shared among organization members; *internal communication is human interaction that occurs within organizations and among organization members.*

A primary organizational function of internal communication channels is to enable formal task development, coordination, and accomplishment. For example, internal communication channels are used to provide workers with job-instruction and job-evaluation messages, to share messages about the coordination of job activities among organization members, and to carry feedback from workers to people higher in the organization's hierarchy, such as messages registering employee complaints or employee suggestions in business organizations. All these internal communication message systems provide organization members with pertinent task-related information that helps them perform important organizational activities and processes. Formal internal communication channels are extremely important managerial tools for directing, coordinating, and restructuring organizational activities.

Internal channels carry messages between organization members that inform these members about current organizational goals, tasks, activities, and problems. These messages help organization members understand the present state of the organization and the roles they are to perform within the organization. Moreover, internal channels are used to direct organization members to perform organizationally designated activities to accomplish specific tasks, which will eventually help the organization move toward the fulfillment of its goals. Internal communication channels direct the accomplishment of organizational tasks by directing the activities of organization members.

External Communication Channels

Organizational communication does not occur only among individuals who are members of an organization. There must be communication among organizations to bring about interorganizational coordination. Organizations reside within interorganizational fields, in which they are functionally linked to the activities of a wide range of other organizations. For example, a production company probably depends on communication with many related organizations, which might include organizations that supply it with raw materials (lumber, steel, food, plastics, or chemicals), organizations that distribute, market, and sell its products (department-store chains, catalog stores, small retail stores, or mail-distribution companies), government organizations that license and regulate its industry (the Federal Trade Commission, state regulatory boards, or local chambers of commerce), and financial organizations that finance its operations (banks, savings and loan organizations, or mortgage companies). These organizations and individuals with whom organization representatives have direct contact are known as the organization's *relevant environment.* These members of the organization's environment are relevant because they can exert significant influence on the organization. External communication enables members of an organization to coordinate its activities with those of its relevant environment.

External communication channels are used to enable organization members to interact with individuals outside the organization. *External communication channels carry messages between the organization and the organization's relevant environment.*

Messages are both sent to and received from the organization's relevant environment. External messages are sent to attempt to influence the way environmental representatives behave in regard to the organization. For example, marketing and advertising campaigns are external message systems that often are designed to influence the buying patterns of the consumers of an organization's products and services. Messages received from the organization's relevant environment can be used to direct the course that the organization takes and the activities in which organization members are to engage. For example, messages garnered from government sources might inform organization members of new federal regulations for their industry that may be implemented. By learning of these new regulations before they are enforced, the organization members may have time to examine the impact of the regulations on their activities and to design the most effective ways for adapting to these new organizational constraints.

External message systems are used to gather relevant information from the organization's environment, and provide the environment with information from the organization. The messages gathered from the environment will be used to inform internal organizational activities about how well present organizational activities are meeting current environmental conditions. The messages the organization sends to their relevant environment are designed to influence members of the environment to coordinate their activities with the internally directed activities of the organization's members.

Coordinating Internal and External Communication

One of the major themes of this book is the importance of coordinating internal and external communication systems in organizations. The functions of these two primary message systems are related, and the channels are mutually dependent. Internal and external communication systems must be orchestrated. Organizational leaders must promote the development of both message channels and coordinate their interdependent functions.

To summarize the interrelationship between internal and external communication channels, internal channels of communication are used to direct organizational activities to accomplish goals that are based on information gathered from the organization's relevant environment through the use of external channels. For example, if a computer company learns (through the external communication system) that there is a large, untapped market for personal home microcomputers that are used to manage family financial affairs and prepare annual tax forms, it will use this information to direct its members (through the internal communication system) toward designing and producing products to meet this environmental demand. External channels will be employed to present relevant information about these internal processes of the organization to the organization's relevant environment to attempt to influence the public's behavior. More specifically, the computer company will use its external communication system to inform consumers of the availability of its new microcomputer (as well as probably inform them of the high quality and great utility of the product for home use). Internal and external communication channels are used to support each other and must be operated in concert to fully accomplish organizational goals.

Our discussion of the interdependent functioning of internal and external communication in organizations leads us to the introduction of an integrating model of organizing (Figure 1.2), which illustrates the manner in which internal communication channels and external communication channels are interconnected. Internal communication processes are directed toward establishment of organizational structure and stability in conducting organizational activities, while external

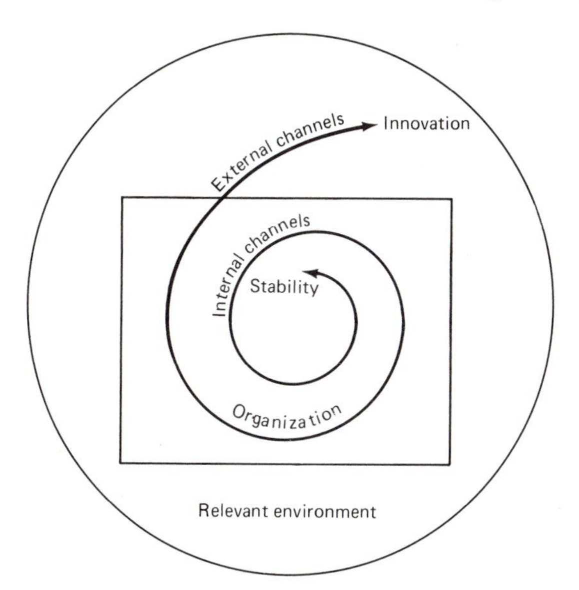

Figure 1.2 The integrating model of organizing.

communication channels are directed toward innovation by facilitating identification of directions for ongoing organizational development. This integrating model of organization will be reintroduced throughout this book and will be explained more fully in Chapter 11, indicating the specific ways that both internal and external communication channels help the organization maintain a productive balance between stability and innovation in organizational activities.

CHAPTER 2

Human Communication Processes

THE NATURE OF HUMAN COMMUNICATION

Perhaps one of the greatest problems with human communication in organizational life is the assumption that many people make that communication is an easy thing to do well. This assumption is only half true. It is easy to communicate, but it is very difficult to communicate well. Even though we have been communicating with others since we were born, we are not always effective communicators. This chapter will examine the intricacies of communication in the organizing process. Many of the complexities, subtleties, and idiosyncracies of human communication processes will be explored. You will come to recognize the truly fragile nature of human communication and the ever-present potential for misunderstanding and misinterpretation between communicators. Moreover, you should become aware of several communication strategies you may adopt as a message sender and receiver to improve the quality and effectiveness of your communication with others.

What is human communication? In this book, a very encompassing definition of human communication will be used to help us recognize its pervasiveness in organizational life. *Human communication occurs when a person responds to a message and assigns meaning to it.* The two key parts to this definition are the message and the meaning. *Messages* are any symbol or thing that people attend to and create meanings for in the communication process. Messages can take many forms: spoken words, written words, facial expressions, environmental cues, thoughts, or feelings. Basically, there are two groups of messages: *internal messages*, those we send to ourselves, and *external messages*, those we react to from our environment (including other people). *Meanings* are mental images that we create to help us interpret phenomena and develop a sense of understanding. People respond to messages (emanating both internally and externally) and create meanings for them when communicating.

Communication as Organizational Process

Human communication is a *dynamic, ongoing process*. It is the process that enables organization members to work together, to continue to evoke cooperation, and to interpret ever-changing organizational needs and activities. *Human communication does not start and stop*. People are constantly involved in communicating with themselves and with others, especially in organizational life. They are immersed in a sea of messages and meanings. Organizational life provides an especially rich and varied message system. Organization members must be able to recognize and interpret the wide variety of messages available to them that enable them to respond appropriately to different people and situations. No one can choose not to communicate. Communication is an inevitable reality of organization membership and of life in general. *Human beings cannot not communicate* (Watzlawick, Beavin, and Jackson, 1967). As long as you are alive, you are involved in some means of communication, even if it is only communicating with yourself.

It is easy to oversimplify the communication process. Many early models of human communication assumed that it is a linear process: one person, the source or sender, sends a message to another person, the receiver. This is an oversimplification. These early linear models of human communication failed to recognize the continually developing nature of communication. No one individual is only a sender or only a receiver. *As communicators, we simultaneously send and receive many messages on many levels*. We are constantly interpreting messages that are available to us and creating messages to communicate our needs, ideas, and feelings.

By regarding communication as an ongoing organizational process, you must recognize that human *communication is irreversible*. It is bound to the context in which it occurs. *Context* refers to the time and space surrounding human communication. When communication takes place and how people feel about the timing of the communication have a major impact on human communication. For example, it is a far different communication situation if a co-worker phones you at 8:00 P.M. or at 3:00 A.M.! Time also refers to the day of the week, the month of the year, and so on. The setting where communication occurs also has great impact on the interaction. You certainly communicate differently with people in a class, at a party, in an office, or in a court of law. Even if you say exactly the same thing to the same people, but in different situations, the changes in context inevitably affect the communication that takes place. Indeed, if one says the "same thing" to the same people in different contexts, it is no longer the same thing.

Once you have communicated something to someone, you cannot retract it. The communication event became permanent the moment it occurred. By restating or changing earlier messages, you do not erase them but merely add to them. For example, if a store owner accuses a clerk of stealing and later learns that the clerk is innocent, no matter how repeatedly the owner explains the mistake, the impact the communication has had on the clerk remains. It is similar to a judge in a murder trial telling the jury to disregard an outburst from a courtroom spectator who has screamed that the defendant is a killer. No matter how the judge implores the members of the jury to be impartial and not allow the outburst to affect their interpretation of the defendant, the communication has had its effect. The irreversible nature of human communication underscores the importance of careful communication in organizations.

Human communication is a deceivingly complex process. Many aspects of communication interrelate in the communication phenomenon. In this book, we will take a *transactional* perspective on human communication. Transaction implies that communication is a process composed of myriad components that interact simultaneously. Some of these key components include the messages to which people react, the meanings that people actively create, the time and place of the communication (context), the relationships established between the communicators, the past experiences of the communicators, the personalities and dispositions of the communicators, the purposes people have for communicating, and the effects of communication on people and situations. Throughout this book, we will be examining communication in organizations from a transactional perspective, identifying the crucial parts of the communication process and determining the influences of communication on organizing activities.

Meaning and Information

Human beings have an insatiable appetite for creating meanings. We strive to know what is going on around us, to understand the people with whom we interact, and to get a handle on the different situations in which we find ourselves. Organizational life is complex, and organizations are often confusing to members. As organization members, we need information to help guide our actions. Communication is our primary tool to help us understand different people and situations. As organization members, we identify and perceive key messages available to us and interpret these messages to create satisfying meanings that help us cope effectively with the many demands of organizational life.

Information is a construct that is very closely related to meaning. Whereas meaning is the process of making "sense" of messages, information is the "sense" that we make in creating meanings. The meanings that we create have information value for us, to the extent that they help us understand, interpret, and predict phenomena. Information allows us to narrow the strategic choices available to us in attempting to accomplish our goals. Some meanings provide us with more information than do others. For example, meanings that you have created about phenomena that you have had a great deal of experience with, such as a job you have held for a long time, are very rich meanings that contain much information: how to do your job quickly and effectively, how your job interrelates with the work done by others, what things to watch out for on the job, how to cope with certain problems that often arise, and so on. In reaction to phenomena with which you are less familiar, you create less intricate meanings that do not provide you with very much information. For example, if you are given a new and complex job, the meanings that you create initially will contain little information about the way to do the job, and you will be less certain about your actions. As you continue to work on the new job, you will interpret more messages about the job and undoubtedly enrich the meanings you create about it, developing more information. The more information you have about the job, the easier it will be for you to accomplish it. *Information is derived from the experiences we have and the meanings we actively create by responding to and interpreting messages.*

The approach to information taken in this book is fairly unique. Typically, people think of information as an external commodity that they gather from others as well as from their environment. The perspective on information we have taken regards information as internally developed interpretations of reality. Each individual derives information out of the meanings that he or she has created. Moreover, information serves an important sense-making function in human endeavors, helping individuals understand complex organizational phenomena and develop effective strategies for coping with these phenomena.

Fisher (1978) differentiates among three conceptualizations of information. The first approach is the external view, which we do not follow in this book. The second and third conceptualizations relate to interpretation and human sense making and are combined in the perspective on information taken in this book.

1. In the most typical approach, "information is conceptualized as a physical quantity that can be transferred from one point to another, from one person to another. It is not an event as such, but a conceptually material entity by virtue of its being extended through time" (Fisher, 1978, p. 309).
2. "A second conceptualization of the term information refers to the meaning of data" (Fisher, 1978, p. 309). This view of information is consistent with Thayer's (1968) differentiation between information and data. According to Thayer, data are stimuli available to communicators within their environment. Once these stimuli are attended to and interpreted, they become information. Hence, information is based on the creation of meanings.
3. The third conceptualization of information refers to the reduction of uncertainty. This approach to information is based on information theory, which describes how information helps limit the number of potential interpretations of and reactions to phenomena, thereby making individuals more certain about their responses to phenomena.

The perspective on information taken in this book recognizes the individuality of communicators and the different meanings and information that people create in response to the same phenomena. Just as meanings are personal and idiosyncratic, so the kinds of information that an individual generates from his or her meanings are specific to that individual. It is because of the individuality of information development that different people have so much to offer one another in interpreting complex organizational phenomena and developing creative strateiges for organizing.

The creation of meaning is a very personal process. *All people are unique, and their perceptions of reality and creations of meaning are unique.* Humans have the cognitive ability to create very rich meanings of great depth at many levels. Because the creation of meaning is a personal process, individuals create meanings in various ways, often interpreting the same situation very differently. The creation of meaning is not a mechanical process; it is part of a learned communicative process.

Meanings are in people, not in words, objects, or things (Korzybski, 1948; Hayakawa, 1972). People actively create meanings in response to the world around them. No object has inherent meaning; no word is imbued with meaning. Human beings create meanings for objects and words in order to understand them. The idiosyncracy of meaning can result in problems or benefits for organizational communicators, depending on the quality of interpersonal and organizational communication. People are bound to disagree on many topics because of their individual creations of meaning, and these interpretive disagreements may lead to mutual suspicion, hostility, and unresolved conflict. But they also may lead to increased insight and creativity. The unique types of information that they derive from their meanings may be extremely useful to organization members, if they can overcome conflict and share some of the information they have developed.

Communication and Perception

Perception is the process by which people become aware of internal and external messages and interpret these messages into meanings. Human beings perceive the world through their senses: sight, hearing, touch, taste, smell, balance, and awareness of heat, cold, pain, pleasure, and pressure. In addition to perceiving *external messages* through the senses, people perceive internally generated messages. *Internal messages* are both physiologically oriented (as in hunger, fatigue, or nervousness) and mentally oriented (as in thinking, daydreaming, and choicemaking).

An important internal channel of mentally oriented messages is something I label "channel Z," or the ability to imagine and create rich fantasies. Channel Z is a mental mechanism that people create to transport themselves from their physical environment to a convivial fantasy land. Humans' ability to enter channel Z can be very therapeutic if they use their imaginations in appropriate situations. Use of channel Z can be a refreshing and rejuvenating experience, helping people cope with stressful situations by providing them with an important repose from reality. However, some people are unable to control their use of channel Z, daydreaming and fantasizing in inappropriate situations, when they should be focusing their attention on externally generated messages.

The ability to control perceptual processes is an important communication skill that is learned and developed over time through experience. A major problem in controlling perception is the overwhelming number of potential messages available to the perceiver. People cannot possibly perceive all the messages in any given situation because even if they are able to block out their internally generated messages, there remains a wide range of external messages. Humans are limited as to the amount of *cognitive space* available to them for processing information. Attempting to perceive all the available messages would lead to *information overload*. There are so many messages available that even with sensory limitations we are subject to overload.

To complicate the perceptual process even more, people do not have the ability to perceive everything around them due to their *sensory limitations*. Humans cannot hear all frequencies of sound or see all wavelengths of light.

Human beings have developed the cognitive process of selective perception to maximize the effectiveness of the messages they do perceive and minimize the perceptual problems caused by cognitive and sensory limitations. *Selective perception* is the process by which people attend to the most important messages out of the total pool of potentially perceivable messages and use those chosen messages to make sense out of their current situation. There are three interrelated parts to the selective-perception process.

1. *Selective attention* focusing on the key messages in any situation
2. *Habituation* blocking out of consciousness extraneous or unimportant messages in any situation
3. *Closure* putting together the messages collected through selective attention and arranging them into a meaningful configuration

People select some messages and not others because of their unique past experiences and predispositions. They not only select those messages that they consider most important, but also rank the messages they attend to. The most important messages are given the most cognitive space (attention), and the less important messages are afforded less cognitive space. Every second, people update and change the priority of the messages that they have selected.

Selective attention and habituation work hand in hand and operate simultaneously. Habituation is crucial. In order to give full attention to any set of messages chosen as being important, individuals must be able to block out both external messages and internal messages that they judge to be unimportant sources of information in any given situation. External messages that compete for attention might be noises or distracting visual cues, while common competing internal messages are fatigue and daydreams. People develop their ability to habituate well through continued practice.

In undertaking closure, individuals must make sense of the current situation using limited information gathered from the messages attended to. This is done by filling in the blanks between messages through educated assumptions based on the perceivers' past experiences and sense of logic. The better individuals are at creating closure, the more likely they are to understand the perceptual situation.

Since each person develops a method of perceiving the world through his or her own version of selective perception, it is likely that different people will select different messages on which to focus. Additionally, it is likely that they will block out different messages and put together the selected messages in different ways. These individual differences in the selective-perception process lead to divergent creations of meaning by different people. Human beings interpret reality idiosyncratically. Reality is not always an objectively agreed on phenomenon. Rather, reality is a subjective interpretation of phenomena that people create for themselves, based on their individual perceptions and their cultural orientations. Shared perceptual frameworks promoted by common cultural affiliations are important moderating factors that decrease the idiosyncracy of perception and increase shared interpretations of reality. The cultures to which people belong influence the way they see the world by influencing the messages they choose, the messages they habituate, and the ways they interpret messages. Tompkins and Cheney (1983) further explain that organizational membership promotes member identification, which often leads to shared perspective taking. However, since people have different combinations of cultural affiliations, cultural influences on perception are unique from person to person. (We will examine cultural influences on perception in Chapter 7.)

A major implication of the perceptual differences among people is the need for interpersonal communication to check and clarify the meanings that people create. Feedback, which we will discuss later in this chapter, has reality-checking functions in organizational endeavors. *People cannot exchange meanings; they can exchange only messages in communication.* The more effective the messages they send to one another, the more likely it is that communicators will be able to create overlapping (similar) meanings, thereby developing communicative understanding of one another.

Content and Relationship Information

Messages provide people with both *content* and *relationship* information. The *content* level of communication refers to the basic factual information being presented in the message. The primary subject, topic, and theme of what is being said is contained within the content level of communication. The *relationship* level of communication refers to the subjective feelings that communicators express for each other through their communication. Expressions of respect or disrespect, like or dislike, powerfulness or powerlessness, love or hate, and comfort or discomfort are parts of the relationship dimension of human communication.

Content and relationship information are expressed simultaneously in every interpersonal-communication message sent and received. Since interpersonal communicators send and receive a multitude of messages all the time, content and relationship information have a major impact on interpersonal and organizational communication, as we will see later in this chapter. It is important to recognize that every time you tell someone something, you are not merely sending your communication partner messages about the specific topic under discussion (content information), but also defining the relationship that you are in the process of establishing with him or her (relationship information).

Even the most common statement—for example, "How's it going stranger?"—contains both content and relationship information. On the content dimension, the statement expresses an inquiry into the status of the receiver's mental, physical, and social condition at that given moment and a greeting from one person to another. On the relationship dimension, the statement might imply concern for the receiver's well-being, interpersonal attraction between the sender and the receiver, empathy for the receiver's current situation, or merely an expression of friendship and solidarity.

The content level of communication provides people with fairly objective data about the organizations with which they interact and the environment in which they live. The world is a complex and confusing place, and information helps people understand it by reducing their uncertainty about other people and things.

Every situation in which people find themselves is, to some extent, uncertain. No one ever knows everything there is to know about any given person, place, or situation. Organizations are often among the most complex and uncertain of social contexts. Every bit of information we gather through content communication provides us with more knowledge about the organization and the world around us. The content level of human communication helps us to understand the world we live in and to cope with uncertainty.

The relationship level of human communication provides people with information about the way others feel about and relate to them. Relationship information is used to assess and influence the nature of the relationships that people develop with one another. Human beings are social creatures who depend on their relationships with others to provide mutual emotional support, to help solve difficult problems, and to coordinate complex activities.

Every time a message is sent between people, at least one aspect of that message communicates something about the nature of the relationship being established between them. Relationships develop out of the communication established between people. Communication can either increase the effectiveness of relationships or decrease the effectiveness of relationships, often depending on the relative degree of per-

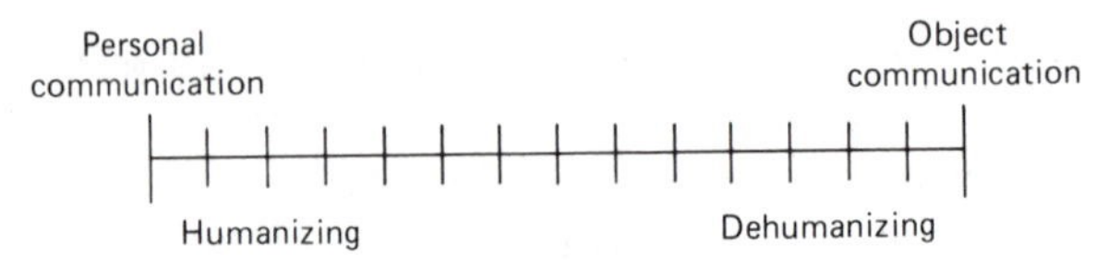

Figure 2.1 Continuum of personal and object communication.

sonal or object communication inherent in the messages being communicated.

The quality of relationship development is closely related to the sensitivity of interpersonal communication, which can be understood clearly when messages are visualized on a continuum from personal messages to object messages (Figure 2.1). This continuum depicts the quality of relational communication in terms of personal and object communication. *Personal communication* shows the communicator's respect for the other person, treating the receiver as an equal, allowing his or her perspective to affect the messages sent, and generally communicating in an honest and trustworthy manner. *Object communication,* on the contrary, is insensitive and demonstrates the communicator's lack of respect for the other person, telling the receiver what to do without seeking his or her input on the matter and treating the receiver as unintelligent and unimportant. Personal and object communication can best be understood from a receiver orientation. Something you say that you think is respecting and caring might be interpreted by the receiver of your message as callous and insensitive (object communication). Although you were attempting to communicate personally, you did not accomplish your goal. To communicate personally, you must take into account the feelings and position of the receiver of your message.

Personal communication tends to be a humanizing form of interaction, while object communication tends to be a dehumanizing form of interaction (Figure 2.1). Personal communication makes us feel good about ourselves. It bolsters our self-image by communicating the relationship message that who we are and what we have to say are useful and important. Conversely, object communication tears down our self-image by making us question our worth, and we often become disenchanted and angry with a communicator who treats us as an object rather than as a person.

Since personal and object communication are parts of the relationship aspect of communication, it is possible to communicate the same general content information in very different ways by using either personal- or object-communication messages. For example, a supervisor may ask a worker to change the way he or she accomplishes an organizational task in a personal or an object manner. On an object level, the supervisor might say, "Do that this way now, stupid, or you'll soon be looking for a new job"; on a personal level, the supervisor might say, "I think this may be a better way to do that job. We've found that it saves time and is easier on the workers. Why don't you try it my way and see if it works any better." The object approach to communication treats the worker as though he or she had to be bullied into complying, while the personal approach treats the worker as a responsible individual who will cooperate with the supervisor if given good reasons. Which manner of communication would you prefer? More than likely, you would want to be communicated with as a person rather than as an object.

Personal communication can be beneficial to the establishment of effective organizational relationships because it facilitates interpersonal cooperation. Object communication, on the contrary, can be detrimental to relationship development because it makes people feel uncomfortable with others. We are less likely to voluntarily cooperate with those who treat us like objects, which undermines coordinated organizational relationships. It often takes no more time or energy to communicate in a personal manner with people than to communicate in an object manner. It does take respect, honesty, and a genuine concern for yourself and for the other person. Additionally, personal communication opens you up to be influenced by what the other person has to say. This opportunity for interpersonal influence often is regarded as a risk, but, as we will discuss in Chapter 8, interpersonal influence can improve interpersonal relationships, help people make better decisions, and also encourage productive outcomes of interpersonal conflict.

Unfortunately, there appears to be quite a lot of object communication in organizational life. People often seem to be too busy to treat one another as human beings. Members of formal organizations, such as businesses, corporations, and universities, often are identified by job titles, by employee or student numbers, or by last names, rather than by preferred names. Bosses often tell workers what to do, rather then explaining why certain activities should be done. Organization members are often resistant to feedback from others, seeking compliance in lieu of cooperation. What is worse, members of many socially based organizations, such as families, clubs, and fraternities or sororities, seem to utilize a great deal of object communication with other members. These forms of object communication seriously undermine the cooperative nature of organizational life and make our organizational involvements less personally satisfying. Object communication is often used because people are unaware of or insensitive to the impact of their messages on others to communicate with others in a respecting manner. Throughout this book, we will advocate the development and use of personal-communication strategies in organizational relationships to increase interpersonal cooperation and satisfaction in organizational life.

Functions of Feedback in Communication Systems

Feedback is a communicated response to the messages that an individual sends. It functions by providing communicators with information about how the people with whom they are communicating are reacting to them and to the communication situation. With feedback, communicators can adjust their message strategies to communicate more effectively. Because feedback guides people in adjusting the messages they send to one another, it helps clarify human communication.

Effective communicators continually seek feedback and thus humanize the interpersonal interaction. It is important for organization members to request feedback from one another not only to clarify information, but also to elicit cooperation. On a relationship level, seeking feedback communicates to the other person that you value his or her perspective and point of view.

A specialized form of feedback is *metacommunication*, or communication about communication. The communicator is given evaluative feedback about the way he or she is communicating. *Metacommunication is a primary tool in socialization because rules of interaction are learned from metacommunicative processes.*

Every human relationship, group, organization, and culture develops rules for the ways in which participants and members are supposed to communicate. In Chapter 7, we will discuss these communication rules in more depth, identifying them as norms. Some of these rules relate to accepted manner of address, dress codes, the use of specialized language (jargon, slang, or foreign languages), and the ways in which people are allowed to touch one another in different situations. The primary function of metacommunication is to teach people the correct rules for communicating.

When you were a child, you probably were given many metacommunicative messages to teach you how to act correctly in different situations. For example, to teach their children to speak politely, parents often use such a metacommunicative message as "Always say thank you when you are given a present, even if you don't like the present." As people grow older, the metacommunicative messages they receive become more subtle. Adults usually teach other adults communication rules by using nonverbal metacommunicative messages. When a person breaks a communication rule, his or her contemporaries may indicate through a frown, a harsh look, or laughter that the rule breaker has said or done something that is not acceptable.

Some people are less perceptive about metacommunicative messages than are others and therefore are slow to learn the correct rules for communication in different organizational situations. These people often are shunned by others within the organization because they do not act in accordance with social rules and norms. Individuals who ignore organizational metacommunication sometimes are described as being politically naïve. Metacommunicative interaction provides individuals with information about the political climate in an organization and lets them know whether their behaviors are in accord with political norms. To be effective in any communication situation, whether it be interpersonal, group, or organizational, participants must be able to recognize metacommunicative messages and learn the rules for appropriate communication behaviors.

Human Communication Message Systems

Messages are the tools people use to communicate with one another. As we have discussed, in communicating, people exchange messages to evoke one another's creation of meaning, serving to provide them with information they can use to interpret reality and direct their actions. We have identified two kinds of messages: internally generated messages (thoughts), and externally generated messages. Human beings use external messages to communicate with one another in organizational life. There are two kinds of external message systems, verbal and nonverbal.

Verbal message systems include the use of words and language, both spoken and written, while *nonverbal message systems* include the use of a wide range of wordless messages, from body movements to environmental cues, that people perceive and to which they assign meaning.

Verbal and nonverbal communication often work closely together. Indeed, there is no way to use verbal communication without using some form of nonverbal communication. Nonverbal messages always surround and influence verbal messages because the medium used for sending verbal messages (words) is nonverbal (vocal or visual cues). It is extremely important for organization members to be able to communicate effectively using both verbal and nonverbal message systems. Later in this chapter, we will discuss in more depth the specific relationship between verbal and nonverbal communication in organizational life.

Verbal communication generally involves the use of digital thinking, since words represent objects or ideas. *Digital thinking* is based on the use of an arbitrary symbol system designed to name a phenomenon. Words are not the things they name. They are symbols that are used to signify an experience. There is nothing about the words *tree* or *house* that directly describes either a tree or a house. Language is a synthetic means of communication because people designate which word will stand for which experience. This is one of the main reasons, as we stated earlier, that meanings are in people, not in the words people use.

Nonverbal communication generally evokes analogic thinking, since nonverbal messages usually describe the actual phenomenon that they are communicating. *Analogic thinking* is based on the use of symbols that have a direct likeness to the objects they are representing. Such nonverbal messages as facial expressions, postures, gestures, or vocal cues directly represent the attitudes and emotions of the communicator who expresses them.

There are some significant differences between analogic and digital modes of thinking. Analogic thinking is primarily used to interpret emotionally oriented messages, while digital thinking is used to communicate data-oriented, technical messages. To take this one step further, nonverbal communication (primarily analogic) is most effective at conveying relationship messages, and verbal communication (primarily digital) is most effective at conveying content messages. It is difficult to convey very technical, complex information nonverbally, and it is equally difficult to express an intense emotional feeling with words (unless the words are surrounded by powerful nonverbal messages such as vocal volume, touch, or eye contact). Watzlawick, Beavin, and Jackson (1967) go as far as to write, "Indeed, wherever relationship is the central issue of communication, we find that digital language is almost meaningless" (p. 57).

The implications of the relationships among verbal messages, digital modes of thinking, and content information indicate that words are most effective at expressing complex technical topics. The relationships among nonverbal messages, analogic modes of thinking, and relationship information imply that nonverbal cues are most effective at expressing emotionally rich messages and have a strong effect on defining and developing interpersonal relationships (see Figure 2.2). An important point that will be reiterated throughout this book is that effective organizational communication involves the coordination of both data and relationships, indicating that effective organizational communicators must competently utilize both verbal and nonverbal message systems. Let us examine verbal and nonverbal message systems in more depth.

Verbal Message Systems

Verbal message systems involve the use of language. Language as a transmitter of complex information has performed an important timebinding function for modern societies (Korzybski, 1948). *Timebinding*

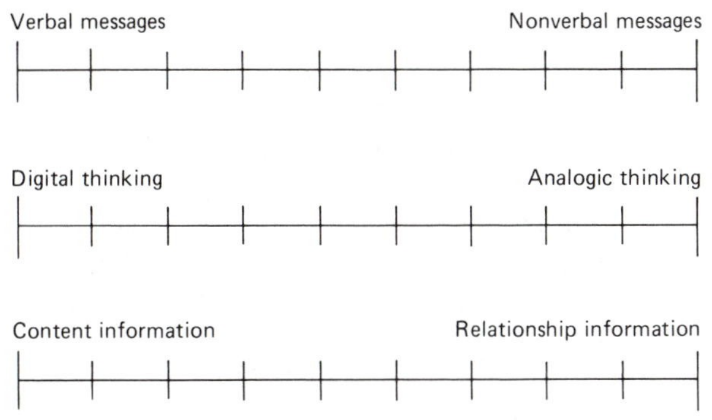

Figure 2.2 Corresponding continua of verbal and nonverbal message systems, analogical and digital modes of thinking, and content and relationship information.

is the storing of human knowledge and experiences and the conveying of this knowledge over time. Written language has provided humankind with relatively permanent, stable, and widespread sources of information. The development of computer languages and advanced technologies will allow present and future generations to timebind information and process complex messages more effectively than ever before. The use of such communication technologies in organizational life guarantees the storage of relevant organizational information for future timebinding.

Verbal communication often is thought of only in the spoken mode, but written language is also an important part of verbal communication, especially in formal organizations. The spoken word and the written word perform important and complementary functions in organizational life. The spoken word allows people to communicate about information in a personal and dynamic manner. Yet it is common for people to forget or to misinterpret information that was spoken. The spoken word is usually very transitory; the words fly past so quickly at times that it may be difficult to understand and recall all the messages being sent. This can cause serious problems in organizing activities when complex directions are given verbally and important points are forgotten or misinterpreted. The transitory nature of spoken communication underscores the importance of actively using feedback when speaking with others.

With written communication, however, people usually can read at their own rate, as well as review carefully the difficult parts of the text. They can reread complex directions to clarify parts of the message about which they may be unsure. Written communication, although less dramatic than spoken interaction, has the advantage of stability, permanence, and formality. Message-recording technologies such as videotape, audiotape, computer graphics, word processing, and mechanical printing have increased our ability to preserve and duplicate both spoken and written verbal messages.

To derive the benefits of both spoken and written verbal communication in organizing activities, it is wise to use both oral and written verbal message channels together. Oral messages can be used to augment written messages when you want to make a personal impact on the individual with whom you are communicating and to keep a formal record of your messages. For example, when applying for a job, it is often wise to speak directly with a representative of the organization about the job, and then follow up the conversation by sending the representative a letter that reviews what you spoke about, as well as enclosing a résumé. In this example, the written messages reinforce the oral messages, but oral messages sometimes reinforce written messages. For example, a salesperson might send a potential customer a letter describing and explaining the benefits of the products that he or she wishes to sell, and follow up the letter with a phone call or a personal visit to attempt to conclude the sale.

There are four interrelated historical approaches to the study of verbal message systems.

1. *Phonemics* examination of the performance of spoken language, focusing on the sounds and pronunciations of words
2. *Syntactics* examination of the structural aspects of language usage, emphasizing the grammar of verbal communication
3. *Semantics* examination of the meanings associated with words, developing such tools as dictionaries and thesauri
4. *Pragmatics* examination of the behavioral functions of language use by people in different situations

Each of these four perspectives on language use clarifies a distinct aspect of verbal communication. We will be most concerned with the semantic and pragmatic aspects of language because we will examine the ways that people use language to evoke meanings in organizational life and the specific functions of language use in different organizational contexts.

As we discussed earlier, meaning is a very rich mental process whereby messages are interpreted and information values are assigned to communication. The study of semantics recognizes the depth of meanings created in response to language use by designating two major types of meanings that people create in response to words, denotations and connotations. *Denotations* are the generally accepted public meanings that have been assigned to words. Definitions that you might find in a dictionary are the denotative meanings that cultures develop for their languages. *Connotations* are more personal, subjective meanings that people create and assign to interpret words.

Whereas there are a limited number of denotative meanings that a culture assigns to a given term, usually fewer than 10, the connotative meanings that an individual might create in response to any given word are limitless. For example, in Chapter 1, we identified several denotative definitions of the word *organization*. There is the structural-system organization, such as IBM; there is the state of organization, in which a person or a system is well organized; there is the process of organization, during which people work at coordinating their activities. On a connotative level, however, there are myriad possible interpretations of the word *organization*. It might intimidate an individual, evoking constraining images of Big Brother (from George Orwell's famous novel *1984*). Another person might react extremely favorably to the word *organization*, envisioning a warm, supportive group of people wishing to provide him or her with food and shelter. In different circumstances, the same person might create different connotative interpretations of the term. These many different (both denotative and connotative) variations on the meanings that people assign to language point up the fact that meanings are very personal and subjective constructs. The likelihood that people will interpret the same message in different ways is very great. It also indicates how important it is to continually seek feedback from others in organizational life, to check others' perceptions of words and creations of meaning, so we can coordinate our activities.

The pragmatic perspective examines the ways in which language is used in different situations by different people. An important type of pragmatic language in organizational life is jargon. *Jargon* is a secretive linguistic code used by a group of people. Jargon sometimes is technical, while at other times, it is used to communicate social information. Jargon serves a variety of functions for its users.

By combining complex concepts and terms into one word or phrase that can be recognized by other group members, jargon *expedites interaction*. An example of this expediting function is the use of abbreviations to communicate lengthy terms, complex concepts, or titles: VCR, for videocassette recorder; DNA, for deoxyribonucleic acid; or ICA, for the International Communication Association. The military system is notorious for its extensive use of abbreviations and acronyms.

Jargon *establishes group membership* by identifying individuals with access to specialized vocabulary and information. If you can use the jargon of a specialized group of people, such as accountants, computer programmers, truck drivers, lawyers, researchers, or neurosurgeons, you are far more likely to evoke cooperation from these individuals when speaking to them about their specialized area because you can identify yourself as being knowledgeable about it. But, if you use jargon incorrectly with specialists, you will immediately identify yourself as a novice!

Jargon *creates status* for users over nonusers of the specialized vocabulary. People sometimes use jargon to impress or intimidate the uninitiated by making those who do not understand the jargon feel confused and foolish. In organizations, information is powerful. Jargon users can attempt to establish power over nonusers by intimating through their word choices that they possess specialized organizational knowledge and information that the other person does not. Wielding power through jargon use, however, may not always be a good strategy in organizational practice because it can undermine the relationship between communicators and interfere with the development of cooperation. Moreover, use of specialized jargon with nonusers will most certainly block the communication of information because the nonusers do not have denotative meanings for the jargon terms and phrases.

Jargon *insulates* users from nonusers. It can be employed to protect a group from infiltration by people who do not understand the specialized language. This function of jargon can be useful, for example, when a corporate lawyer has to communicate proprietary legal information that for reasons of confidentiality should not be known by others. The lawyer can use jargon to explain the situation to a peer without risking loss of confidentiality if nongroup members happen to overhear the communication exchange. But this insulating aspect of jargon can frustrate others who would like to know what the professional is talking about and believe that they have a legitimate right to possess the organizational information.

Human language is a tool that is used in different ways by different groups of people. Languages change as the needs of the people who use them change. Because language continually evolves to fulfill the needs of its speakers, it is an *emergent phenomenon*. An effective user of language must be able to keep up with the changes and developments in language use. Not only are words coined and introduced into the language, but also existing words acquire new meanings. For example, as the computer industry has developed, dictionaries have been updated to include such terms as *floppy disk*, *microprocessor*, and *cursor*. Existing words that have been given new usages include *mouse*, *menu*, and *scroll*.

Because information and knowledge are stored and transmitted through language, it is important for language to be in continual flux to keep up with the growth in knowledge. Nowhere has information expanded more rapidly than in modern society and the technological sciences. It is important for organization members to learn linguistic additions, by reading current literature and talking to other professionals, so that they are up to date on the growth in specialized knowledge.

Nonverbal Message Systems

Nonverbal communication is every possible external message source, other than words, to which people respond. Moreover, as we discussed earlier, nonverbal communication surrounds and influences all verbal communication. It is evident that nonverbal communication is a major source of messages in human communication.

There are many types of nonverbal messages, and to lump them under the extremely general rubric of "nonverbal communication" would be simplistic and confusing. Rather, we will identify seven different, but interrelated, nonverbal systems that work together, usually simultaneously, in organizational communication.

Artifactics. Physical appearance (body shape, size, smell, skin color, body hair), personal appearance (make-up, hair style, perfume, clothing style, jewelry, watch), objects that people carry (briefcase, books, pens, combs), and objects that people use to decorate their environment (clocks, charts, plaques, paintings, furniture, carpets, books) are *artifactics.* These messages have a strong influence on the initial perceptions and first impressions that people have about others. People generally attempt to exert great control over many aspects of their artifactic nonverbal system, carefully choosing their clothing and the objects with which they surround themselves. Homes and offices reflect the interests, cultural affiliations, and social status of their occupiers. It is not a trivial matter to decide which pair of eyeglasses best frames a face, which automobile best proclaims a life style and image, or which briefcase best suits a job and personality. Certainly the clothing you choose to wear and the objects you take to a job interview have a strong influence on the way a potential employer perceives you. You will want to strategically select the artifactic cues you utilize to best represent your skills, talents, experience, and character and to best fit the norms of the organization's dominant culture. In Chapter 7, we will discuss the ways that organizational cultures influence the behaviors and artifactic choices of their members.

Kinesics. The ways people move their bodies and position themselves, including postures, gestures, head nods, and leg movements, are called *kinesics.* There are three basic types of gestures: *emblems,* which have direct verbal translations, such as nodding the head for "yes," shaking the head for "no," or waving the hand for "hello"; *illustrators,* which accompany speech and accentuate what is being said, such as banging the hand on a table when angry; and *adaptors,* which are unconscious nervous movements, such as cracking the knuckles, scratching, or tapping the foot. Emblems are used in place of words. Illustrators are used while speaking to add drama and emphasis to what is being said. Adaptors often can indicate a person's internal nervous state. The more uncomfortable an individual is in a social situation, the more likely he or she is to demonstrate adaptor movements. People who demonstrate many adaptor behaviors often are evaluated as being insecure or deceptive. Thus it is important to avoid the use of adaptors in organizational situations where your character and motivations are being scrutinized. Such situations might include giving a business presentation, perhaps to an organization's board of directors, making a sales pitch to a potential client, or interviewing for a job.

Postures also are an important aspect of kinesic behavior that communicate an individual's reactions to different people and situations. Postures often indicate the level of a person's involvement in a situation as well as his or her reaction—positive or negative—to those around them. For example, when your boss is talking to you, if you lean away from him or her, you will seem to be acting rudely toward your organizational superior—not paying close attention to and generally demonstrating less interest in your boss and what he or she has to say than if you leaned toward the boss.

Occulesics. *Occulesics* consist of facial expressions and eye behaviors. The face is the primary emotional-message-sending center of the human organism. Thus people monitor the facial expressions of others and keep close track of their own facial expressions to determine the emotions that the face is signaling. It is important to mirror others' facial expressions with your own if you want them to believe that you agree with them. When others' facial expressions contrast with ours, we may feel uncomfortable with and suspicious of them. Moreover, it is important to demonstrate the facial emotion that is most appropriate to the specific organizational situation in which you find yourself. For example, it is generally inappropriate to smile at a funeral or frown at a party. Certainly, you might cause yourself difficulties if you frowned at your boss every time he or she spoke with you.

Eye behavior, another part of the occulesic system, includes eye contact (making visual connection with someone and holding it), gaze (direction, intensity, and duration), and blinking. Eye contact can communicate a wide variety of feelings, depending on the facial expressions that accompany it. For example, you might demonstrate hostility with your eyes, when you accompany eye contact with an angry facial expression. You also may demonstrate affection with eye contact, when you accompany it with a loving facial expression. Direction and intensity of gaze provide others with cues about a person's level of interest and involvement in a social situation. For example, if you do not look at your boss when he or she is speaking to you, you are demonstrating a lack of respect. It seems that high-status individuals in organizations are less compelled to direct their gaze at low-status speakers than vice versa. Blinking behaviors, as well as gaze aversion, seem to perform an important perceptual function for communicators. By closing your eyes or looking away from complex visual input (perhaps by looking at the ground or the ceiling), you can physically block out many visual messages (a mechanical form of habituation) and concentrate on internal messages and meanings. For example, when you are put on the spot by your boss, and you do not have a ready answer for his or her questions, you are likely to blink more often or avert your gaze while pondering an appropriate answer. That is why frequent blinking behaviors and averted gaze, like adaptor behaviors, can indicate lack of sincerity and purposeful deception in a person's communication. In summary, occulesic messages can tell us about others' emotional states and levels of interest in social situations or persons.

Paralinguistics. Vocal cues accompanying speech, as well as environmental sounds, are referred to as *paralinguistics*. Vocal cues include the volume, pitch, tone, and expression in a voice and the rate of speech. Environmental sounds include music, wind, heavy machinery, and train whistles. The vocal aspect of paralinguistics is the form of nonverbal communication that is most closely tied to verbal communication. Research has indicated that a person's tone of voice has a significant influence on other persons' willingness to cooperate with the speaker (Milmoe, Rosenthal, Blane, Chafetz, and Wolf, 1967). Paralinguistic cues can add drama to speech, if the speaker is expressive, uses volume to emphasize points, varies pitch to maintain interest, and changes rate to fit the topic. If you have a class with a professor who presents very dull lectures, one of the reasons the lectures seem dull may be the professor's failure to utilize paralinguistic cues effectively. Perhaps the professor speaks in a monotone, speaks too low for the whole class to hear, or speaks too quickly.

The sounds in an environment also affect the disposition and feelings that people have for the situation. One of the main reasons that many organizations pipe music into work environments is to keep their workers alert and cheerful. We seem to adapt our behaviors to the pacing of music. Certainly, we all can attest to the soothing influences of gentle music or the stimulating influences of boisterous music. Some work environments are very noisy, with loud equipment and machinery, and not only may have an irritating effect on workers' dispositions, but also may cause hearing difficulties. The supervisors of work environments, like those of airports, attempt to muffle the volume of sound or provide their workers with earplugs to help them cope with loud noises. Dentists have found that their clients are more relaxed and less fearful when they hear the sounds of music, rather than the sounds of dental drills. Organization leaders can and should adjust the sounds within organizational contexts to help make organization members (and customers) more comfortable. In Chapter 9, we will examine a number of ways that the internal organizational communication systems, such as sounds, affect the development of organizational climates.

Tactilics. Touching behaviors, including self-touching, touching others, and touching objects, are called *tactilics*. Touch is perhaps the most intimate channel of human communication. Skin-to-skin touching (*haptics*) is the most intimate form of touch. Research has indicated that human touch fulfills physiological and sociological needs for people (Montagu, 1971). Sensitive touch can be used to establish interpersonal support, communicate caring, and develop solidarity. Yet in organizations, there are specific social and cultural rules and constraints regarding touching behaviors. Touch can be used to intimidate and bully others. Unwelcome touch is an invasion of privacy. In Chapter 9, we will discuss the use of touching in organizations to establish interpersonal power, especially in organizational politics and sexual harassment.

Those of higher status have more access to initiating interpersonal touch to subordinates, than subordinates have access to their organizational superiors. For example, a boss may more readily pat a worker on the back for a job well done, than a worker will pat a boss on the back. Certain body areas are more accessible to touch than are others, and males and females are differently accessible to touch (Jourard, 1966). A primary channel for interpersonal touching in formal organizations is the use of the handshake as a salutation. This is a severely limited channel for enabling organization members to use interpersonal touch to establish support and solidarity with one another. In Chapter 8, we will examine how sensitive touch can be used to help develop therapeutic relationships in modern organizations.

Proxemics. The study of the distance between people and objects, including the distances established in interpersonal relationships, group meetings, and environmental design, is *proxemics*. Proxemic nonverbal message systems play very important roles in organizational life. Every person maintains an expandable spatial bubble around him- or herself as an interpersonal buffer against others. This is referred to as *personal space*. We desire less personal space in social situations with people with whom we are comfortable and more personal space in social situations in which we are uncomfortable. Personal space is a relational process. In a two-person communication situation, both communicators make personal-space decisions and attempt to maintain "acceptable" boundaries of personal space. The personal-space expectations of organization members may conflict, and the resultant perception of spatial invasion will precipitate discomfort and perhaps lead to a communicative reaction of either fight or flight. Obviously, neither reaction is useful for the maintenance of healthy relationships, so in organizational practice, the personal-space expectations of members must be recognized and respected.

Territoriality, another aspect of proxemics, deals with the objects and space claimed and protected by people. Territoriality differs from personal space in that it usually does not expand and contract in response to different situations and does not have to surround the person. People are territorial about their "possessions," or objects for which they claim ownership. These objects can range from clothing and books to homes and automobiles. People generally protect their territory vigorously and become quite angry if it is limited or their possessions are taken from them. For instance, hospitalized patients sometimes are denied many of their belongings, such as clothing or jewelry, and may become upset and angry. Representatives of the health-care organization should be careful to explain to these patients why they cannot have their possessions and exactly how and where the institution is holding them in safekeeping. In business offices, workers often become very territorial about their work spaces, furniture, equipment, and offices. Interestingly, even in such a temporary organization as a college class, students often become territorial about "their" seating position within the class. Certainly, the instructor is extremely possessive of the desk or podium. Can you imagine the defensive reaction of most college instructors to a student who attempts to sit at the instructor's desk in front of the class? This unlikely scene should illustrate the intense emotions that territoriality often evokes in organization members.

Still another part of the proxemic system of nonverbal communication is *small-group ecology*, or the spatial arrangement of group members at meetings. Different spatial arrangements can have strong impacts on the group communication that occurs at meetings. For example, it is easier to have a participative group discussion if members sit around a table or in a circle than if they sit in rows or are bunched haphazardly. Additionally, different positions around a rectangular table tend to evoke different communication roles. For example, people who sit at the heads of the table are most likely to become group leaders, while those who flank the leaders are likely to form coalitions with and support the leaders. People sitting toward the middle of the table are likely to participate less in the group discussion. People communicate more actively with one another if they are positioned face to face (*sociopetal orientation*) than if they are positioned away from one another (*sociofugal orientation*) (Sommer, 1969).

Architectural design and environmental planning also have a major impact on human communication. Open offices with glass windows are more conducive to active communication than are closed offices with solid walls. Some modern organizations have designed facilities with movable walls and partitions (*semifixed space*) to elicit increased communication among members of project teams who otherwise would be separated from one another by unmovable walls and doors (*fixed space*). Moreover, the amount of space available to workers in their immediate environment can affect their moods and attitudes. Small offices with low ceilings and no windows can cause people to feel boxed in and make them sullen and depressed, while cathedral ceilings and picture windows framing views of gardens and open spaces evoke feelings of peace and contentment.

Bürolandschaft, more commonly known as office landscaping, is a technique, originally developed in Germany, used to physically arrange the space within office buildings to create "nonterritorial" office environments (Rogers and Agarwala-Rogers, 1976, p. 102). In *Bürolandschaft*, organization members were moved from individual offices into an open office environment in which they had more direct contact with the colleagues they had to interact with most often. Permanent office walls were taken down and replaced with movable partitions that could be positioned to fit the interpersonal communication needs of organization members. Desks and other furnishing were arranged and rearranged to facilitate increased proximity and opportunities for communication among the members of different work and project groups that were formed to handle different organizational tasks. In office landscaping, the design of organizational space is matched to the interpersonal- and group-communication needs within the organization.

Case 2.1 presents a seemingly perplexing situation in one department of a large company.

1. How does the case illustrate the influence of proxemics on the meanings that organization members create?
2. What impact does the arrangement of desks have on individual status within the department?
3. How do the status norms in this case relate to territoriality?
4. How do the status norms in this case relate to small-group ecology?
5. Does distance from Williams give some group members a communication advantage over others?
6. How might you attempt to reconcile the communication problems that are brewing within the department?

Chronemics. The effect of time on communication, including communication behaviors patterned over time, appointment keeping, and length of time communicating with others, is referred to as *chronemics*. Time is, perhaps, the form of nonverbal communication of which peo-

Case 2.1

Tyler Industries, Inc.*

Len Williams, manager of Export Parts order section of Tyler's North European division, was puzzled and troubled. Something had obviously gone sour, but what?

Len had always prided himself on the relaxed, friendly atmosphere in the section. Good-natured bantering had been the order of the day and the men would frequently stop by his desk for an informal chat.

Suddenly things were different. Len hadn't had a "visitor" for over a week and everyone seemed "too busy" with his own affairs for intraoffice needling. With the men becoming more taciturn, Len felt himself growing progressively uneasy and unwilling to go out of his way to initiate conversations.

The change had occurred shortly after young Paul Brock had joined the section. But how could there be a connection? Paul seemed eager to learn and gave every indication of wanting to be a good "team player" but the group had clearly not accepted him.

Tyler Industries, Incorporated, was a large multidivision organization headquartered in Cleveland and operating in the Americas, Europe, Africa, the Far East, and Australia. The service functions of the corporation were organized by geographical areas such as the Great Britain Division, the North European Division, and so on. Some of these functions were located in the regions they served. Others, such as Export Parts, were centralized in Cleveland.

The North European Division's Export Parts section consisted of Williams and seven other interpreters. Their eight desks were arranged in a straight line. Williams's desk was at the head of the line and Brock's was second. This desk had been vacated by Lou Dewitt who had just been promoted to chief of another section. Williams assigned the desk to Brock because Paul was new to the corporation as well as to the section and would probably need considerable coaching. Moreover, Len confided to a friend, "I want to avoid that silly desk reshuffling the guys did two years ago when Jack Rosen was promoted out of the section." Coincidentally, Rosen had occupied the second desk.

* *Reprinted from William V. Haney,* Communication and Organizational Behavior: Text and Cases, *3d ed. Homewood, Ill.: Irwin, 1972, pp. 234–235.*

ple are least aware, yet time has a major impact on human behavior and interaction. Human beings develop cyclical behavior patterns based on the day, week, month, and year, depending on schedules and appointments to organize their lives. The more time you spend communicating with others, regardless of the topic of conversation, the more you are telling them that you believe they are important individuals. Conversely, the more time you keep people waiting to interact with you, the more you are implying that they are insignificant to you.

Because time is so invisible a channel of nonverbal communication, it is often taken for granted and its influence ignored. It is interesting to observe the changes in students' nonverbal behaviors five minutes before the end of a class. In preparation for the end of the class, students often check their watches or the clock, pack their books and other artifacts, put on their coats, fidget in their seats, look toward the door, and even lean toward the door awaiting their release. Office workers often psychologically structure their workdays around lunchtime, coffee breaks, and the end of the workday: "If only I can make it until lunch time."

Time, like proxemics, and several other nonverbal systems, is a message system that is strongly culture bound. For example, prompt appointment-keeping behaviors are very important to American business people. If you are 15 minutes late for a sales call or a job interview, you are in big trouble. The person who is waiting for you usually is quite annoyed if you are late and assumes that you are irresponsible and unprofessional. Yet appointment keeping is less strictly adhered to in other countries. In Mexico, for example, if an appointment is kept within an hour of the time set, everything is fine. Indeed, the Mexican businessperson may be surprised when a salesperson shows up at exactly the time set for an appointment and may not be ready to receive the sales call. Chronemics is an important nonverbal message system in organizational communication.

Nonverbal communication is a large and important part of the total human communication process. Each of the seven nonverbal systems includes a wide range of message types that affect innumerable communication situations. Yet none of these nonverbal systems operates in isolation of the others, and nonverbal communication in general operates in concert with verbal communication. Knapp (1978) suggests, "Verbal and nonverbal communication should be treated as a total and inseparable unit" (p. 20). He describes six ways that nonverbal messages affect verbal messages in the total communication process: "Nonverbal behavior can repeat, contradict, substitute for, compliment, accent, or regulate verbal behavior." By developing sensitivity to the verbal and nonverbal messages that we constantly send and receive, we can learn how to develop our abilities both to create the most appropriate messages to send to others and to interpret the wide range of messages available to us in organizational contexts.

LEVELS OF COMMUNICATION IN ORGANIZATIONS

Human communication is an extremely complex and encompassing social process. Communication occurs at various levels in organizational life. We now will examine the differences and similarities among four basic hierarchical levels of human communication in organizations: intrapersonal, interpersonal, small-group, and multigroup communication.

Intrapersonal Communication

The most basic level of human communication is *intrapersonal,* in which we interpret messages and develop messages to send to others. In a sense, it is communication with ourselves. People constantly maintain an internal dialogue of thoughts. For example, a production-line supervisor uses intrapersonal communication to make choices about personnel, to interpret messages from higher-ups in the organization, and to decide how to explain job-related instructions to the workers. The intrapersonal process of creating messages is known as *encoding,* and the intrapersonal process of interpreting messages is known as *decoding.*

Both encoding and decoding are translation processes used to link the two most crucial elements of communication: meanings and messages. In encoding, the organization member translates his or her meanings about a given situation into the most appropriate messages available for use in communicating with others. In decoding, the member translates messages into meanings and thus can identify relevant organizational information. Intrapersonal communication is the most basic form of human communication because the processes of encoding and decoding enable people to send and receive messages, which, in turn, enable them to communicate on interpersonal and small-group levels in organizational life.

Interpersonal Communication

Interpersonal communication is between two people (a dyad), usually face to face, although people can use communication media (such as the telephone) to communicate interpersonally without being in each other's immediate presence. Interpersonal communication builds on intrapersonal communication because each member of the dyad must communicate with him- or herself to communicate effectively with the other. Intrapersonal and interpersonal levels of communication occur simultaneously when one person speaks with another person. The interpersonal communicator uses intrapersonal communication to decode the messages of the other person and to encode the messages that he or she intends to send to the other person.

One of the most important outcomes of interpersonal communication is the development of human relationships. People depend on their interpersonal relationships to elicit cooperation from others. The relationship is the basic social unit of organization. In terms of the definition of organization presented in Chapter 1, the interpersonal relationship is the smallest social system that can demonstrate the development of coordinated activities between individuals in an attempt to accomplish individual and collective goals. In Chapter 8, we will examine in depth the interpersonal process of relationship development, noting the important functions of interpersonal relationships in organizational life. As with intrapersonal communication, interpersonal communication enables people to communicate at the next higher level—the small group.

Small-Group Communication

Small-group communication occurs among three or more people interacting in an attempt to adapt to their environment and achieve commonly recognized goals. As with interpersonal communication, small-group communication usually occurs face to face but may also develop through use of communication media (such as teleconferencing). The total number of group communicators generally is limited to the number of people who can actively participate in a group conversation.

Small-group communication is more complex than interpersonal communication because group interaction is composed of many interpersonal-communication relationships. As the number of communicators within the small group increases, the number of potential message exchanges virtually explodes. Bostrom (1970) has calculated the number of interactions possible in groups ranging from two to eight communicators (Table 2.1). It is evident that the size of the small group can greatly increase the complexity of the group's communication.

Another aspect of small-group communication that differs from interpersonal communication is the dimension of *group dynamics*, the potential for the development of subgroups and opposing coalitions among the group's membership. These coalitions complicate group communication and the relationships among group members. The dif-

Table 2.1

Group Size as Compared with Potential Number of Interactions

Group Size	*Interactions*
2	2
3	9
4	28
5	75
6	186
7	441
8	1,056

Data from R. Bostrom, "Patterns of Communication Interaction in Small Groups," *Communication Monographs* 37, 1970, pp. 257–263.

ferent ways that group dynamics develop within a group have a strong impact on the output of the group.

The small group is an important work unit in organizations. Small-group communication occurs in work groups, staff and management education classes, and decision-making committees within the organization. These groups perform important functions in organizations by providing information, support, and problem-solving expertise that individuals cannot possibly provide independently.

Multigroup Communication

Multigroup communication occurs within a social system composed of interdependent small groups that share the performance of tasks to achieve commonly recognized goals. Multigroup communication encompasses the lower levels of communication: intrapersonal, interpersonal, and small group. Multigroup communication is integral to the functioning of large organizations because it is the means by which organization members (from all divisions of the organization) coordinate their activities to accomplish the goals of the organization. Because of the great size and complexity of many modern organizations, it is virtually impossible to arrange face-to-face communication among all the organization members. To cope with the complexity of multigroup communication, organizations must develop formal channels of communication among different parts and members of the organization. In Chapters 8 and 9, we will discuss in depth some of the formal channels of organizational communication developed to handle internal communication and external communication.

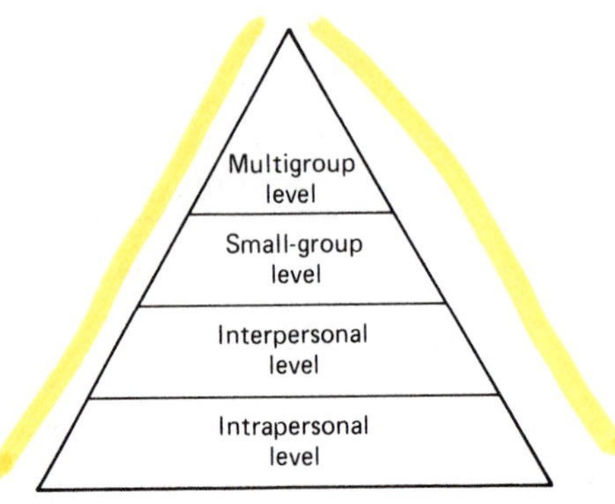

Figure 2.3 Hierarchical levels of organizational communication.

The hierarchical nature of the four basic levels of organizational communication is illustrated in Figure 2.3. As you can see, intrapersonal communication is the most extensive and most basic form of human communication. It is at the intrapersonal level that we think and process information. Interpersonal communication builds on the intrapersonal level, adding another person to the communication situation and introducing the dyadic relationship. Small-group communication, in turn, builds on interpersonal interaction, utilizing several communicators and adding the dimensions of group dynamics and multiple interpersonal relationships to the communication situation. Multigroup communication exists through the combination of the three other levels of communication in coordinating a large number of people in the shared accomplishment of complex goals. It is important to recognize that effective communication at the interpersonal, small-group, and multigroup levels is developed through effective communication at successively lower levels.

Public Communication and Mass Communication

In addition to the four basic levels of organizational communication, there are two special forms of communication that do not fit neatly into our hierarchy but utilize elements from each level. These additional forms of communication are public communication and mass communication. *Public communication* takes place when a small number of people (usually only one person) addresses a larger group of people. Although the speaker assumes the major responsibility for the public communication and sends the preponderance of verbal messages, he or she is not the only person engaging in communication. The audience sends messages to the speaker, primarily through nonverbal channels. Speeches, lectures, oral reports, and dramatic performances are forms of public communication.

Mass communication occurs when a small number of people send messages to a large, anonymous, and usually heterogeneous audience through the use of specialized communication media, including film, television, radio, newspapers, books, and magazines. Mass communication is similar to public communication in that the source of the message assumes primary responsibility for the communication. Mass communication has the potential for reaching larger audiences than does face-to-face public communication, however, and offers less opportunity for audience participation.

Feedback, as we discussed earlier, is people's reactions to communication. It tends to both clarify and humanize human interaction. Intrapersonally, you send yourself feedback about your thoughts or actions when you review your ideas and behaviors. Interpersonally, feedback helps you determine the effects of your communication on your dyadic partner and his or her attitudes and feelings about you. In small groups, feedback is used to elicit the ideas and reactions of group members to problems and their solutions. In organizations, feedback appraises the adequacy of members' information and the effectiveness of organizational policies. In public communication, feedback allows the speaker to gauge the responses of the audience to his or her presentation. Even in mass communication, where feedback works most slowly, it can evaluate the effectiveness of a mass-communicated event or program. For example, television ratings provide feedback to television networks about public response to their shows. To maximize the large-audience advantages and minimize the feedback disadvantages of public and mass communication, they can be used to augment existing intrapersonal, interpersonal, small-group, and multigroup levels of communication. By utilizing all these forms of communication, the organization member can reach a large number of people, in a clear and personal manner.

In Case 2.2, we see a clear demonstration of some key functions of communication in organizational life.

1. How were intrapersonal, interpersonal, small-group, and multigroup levels of communication used by the company?
2. Think about how the case illustrates the integrating model of organizing, presented in Chapter 1. Identify key internal communication channels. How were these channels utilized?
3. Identify key external communication channels. How were these channels utilized?
4. How did the combination of internal and external channels facilitate effective organizational adaptation?

Case 2.2

The New Product*

The Jarman Manufacturing Company has been in business for 40 years. It employs about 1200 people in plants located in Eugene, Oregon, Glendale, Arizona, and Los Angeles, California. Jarman has always been noted for its major product, canvas deck shoes. For many years, Jarman held about 17 percent of the casual footwear market and competed fairly successfully with larger national organizations.

About five years ago, Jarman began to experience severe organizational problems. It had been able to exist fairly well on its 17 percent share of the market, which provided a good return on investment with enough left over for an attractive profit-sharing program for employees. But as the cost of labor and raw materials rose, Jarman began to fall on bad times. The Glendale plant was closed, and 250 employees were laid off. Jarman's share of the market dropped to just over 7 percent, as major companies entered the casual footwear field. At the annual meeting of employees that year, Sam Lyon, Jarman's president, told workers: "Things don't look too good for us, but we are not going to give up. What we need are new ideas, fresh approaches, and innovative plans. We are going to listen to people, and we are going to try to be flexible when people have good ideas."

Dave Murchison was Jarman's Los Angeles area sales representative. Recently, Dave's doctor had told him that he needed to take off 15 pounds. The doctor said that Dave should enter some kind of exercise program. The thought of going to the gym every day depressed Dave, so he decided to jog around his neighborhood each morning. Dave began his jogging program with a half mile course. Soon he had worked up to one mile and was now running about five miles a day. He loved the activity. Each morning a feeling of escape and freedom came over him as he began to hit the pavement. Dave easily lost his 15 pounds, but he enjoyed running so much that he kept up his program religiously. One thing that Dave noticed each morning as he ran was that lots of other people were out doing the same thing. It seemed as if everyone he knew either was running or was involved in some type of exercise program.

In the beginning, Dave had started running in the old pair of tennis shoes he wore when he was cutting the lawn. But, the longer he ran, the less support the shoes gave him. He went to the sporting goods

* *This case is reprinted from Gary T. Hunt,* Communication Skills in the Organization. *Englewood Cliffs, N.J.: Prentice-Hall, 1980, pp. 25–27.*

store to find himself a pair of shoes for running, but all the store carried was a light track shoe popular with high school and college runners, which sold for $45. Dave was both disappointed and excited: disappointed because he couldn't find what he wanted, but excited to share his experiences with his boss, Larry Tuller. Larry was Jarman's vice-president for marketing. It was his responsibility to handle customer research and make recommendations on new products.

The next day Dave and Larry met over lunch. "You wouldn't believe the number of people running, and yet you can't find a good pair of running shoes. We're already geared up to make these shoes. All we need is a little expert advice, some advertising, and a little public relations. We can produce a shoe runners will buy," Dave told Larry.

Larry began to get excited too. Together he and Dave learned all they could about running. They talked with track coaches, podiatrists, orthopedic surgeons, world class runners, and local joggers. In their research, the two spent nearly $5,000 of company money and were under much pressure to justify their expenses. Finally they had an idea solid enough to sell to Sam Lyon and the board of directors.

They developed a written proposal of their plan. It had four parts:

1. the development of an advisory committee of running experts to help with the design of a solid midpriced shoe for runners,
2. the conversion of the Arizona plant to the manufacture of the shoe,
3. the securing of a $300,000 loan to help finance the project, and
4. the mounting of a national sales campaign to promote the Jarman shoe.

After they had presented their written proposal to the board, Sam asked Dave and Larry to make a brief oral summary of the project. They were very persuasive in their appeals, and the board—almost as a last resort to save the company—decided to go along with the proposal.

It took about eight months of lead time to get the shoe designed and into production. Larry was given authority over the running shoe division and Dave was put in charge of marketing and distribution. For eight months both Larry and Dave worked 70- to 80-hour weeks, often commuting between company headquarters in Los Angeles and the production facilities in Glendale. Finally, the Jarman running shoe, under the trade name Street Pounder, was ready.

The advertising campaign consisted of displays in sporting goods stores and advertisements in running magazines. The focus of the campaign was "Now runners, a shoe made just for you." Because this represented such a large investment for the company, Larry had to frequently act as a liaison between the project and the president and board of directors. He met weekly with Sam and twice a month with the board.

Dave used all of his sales and marketing expertise. He attended coaches' conventions, sporting goods dealers' meetings, and track meets. At a marathon in San Diego, a 26-mile race with many runners competing, he set up a booth with the Street Pounder on display. To get people to notice the shoe, he gave complimentary samples to some runners.

The advertising efforts began to pay off. *The Runner,* a magazine written by and for runners, did a story on the Street Pounder that said it was the best running shoe on the market. Sales began to take off. A local Los Angeles runner wore a pair of Street Pounders when he won the 1974 Boston Marathon. Requests for the shoe became so numerous that the Glendale plant could not keep up with the demand. The Eugene plant was converted from deck shoes to running shoes. Athletes formed the habit of wearing their running shoes even when they were not running. After just two years, sales topped $5 million nationally.

Larry and Dave knew they had a hit on their hands. But instead of resting on their success, since they knew their competitors would soon be entering the market, they started thinking up new products. Plans were begun for a Lady Street Pounder and a Little Street Pounder. They used the Street Pounder design to produce other models, such as a long-spiked shoe for outdoor track. They put small spikes on the Street Pounder for cross-country runners. They designed shoes for basketball, racquetball, volleyball, and tennis. Now the Jarman name is associated with high-quality athletic shoes. The athletic shoe division has far outdistanced the deck shoe division in sales and profits. Jarman is now on solid financial ground.

SUMMARY

In this chapter, we have explored the communication process, identifying the major theories and principles of communication that relate to the development of effective organizational communication skills. In an attempt to organize and summarize all the information presented here, the most important propositions about the nature of human communication are listed below.

1. Human communication occurs when a person responds to a message and assigns meaning to it.

2. Human communication is a dynamic, ongoing process.
3. Human beings cannot not communicate.
4. In human communication, we simultaneously send and receive many messages on many different levels.
5. Human communication is bound to context and is irreversible.
6. Human communication is a transactional process.
7. Human communication is the primary tool people use to develop a sense of understanding about people and situations.
8. All people are unique, and their perceptions of reality and creations of meaning are unique.
9. Meanings are in people, not in words, objects, or things.
10. The meanings we create have information value for us, to the extent that they help us understand, interpret, and predict phenomena.
11. Information is derived from the experiences we have and the meanings we actively create by responding to and interpreting messages.
12. Every message that people send one another has both a content and a relationship dimension.
13. Personal communication shows respect for the person and tends to be a humanizing form of interaction.
14. Object communication shows disrespect and tends to be a dehumanizing form of interaction.
15. Feedback helps to clarify communication among people.
16. Rules of interaction are learned through metacommunication.
17. Verbal communication is a digital form of communication and is most effective at communicating content information.
18. Nonverbal communication is an analogic form of communication and is most effective at communicating relationship information.
19. Language is an emergent phenomenon.
20. Verbal and nonverbal communication work together as a total inseparable unit.
21. Organizational communication is composed of succeedingly more complex and encompassing hierarchical levels of intrapersonal, interpersonal, small-group, and multigroup communication.

PART II

PERSPECTIVES ON THE ORGANIZING PROCESS

There are many theories about the nature of organization. In Part II, we identify and describe the key elements of five theoretical perspectives on organizational behavior that provide especially rich, powerful, and useful accounts of human organization. The perspectives are presented chronologically, each in its historical context, from among the earliest theories of organization to some of the most modern theories.

The classical theory of organization was one of the first attempts to explain the nature of organizational behavior. Classical theory became popular in the early 1900s in both Europe and the United States and was largely based on the writings of German sociologist Max Weber (1909; translated into English, 1948), French industrialist Henri Fayol (1916; translated into English, 1949), and American mechanical engineer Frederick Winslow Taylor (1911). Classical theory concentrated on identifying the most efficient and ordered methods for accomplishing organizational tasks.

The human-relations theory of social organization was introduced in the 1930s with the pioneering work of Mayo (1933), Barnard (originally published in 1938), and Roethlisberger and Dickson (1939). (Barnard often is viewed as a bridge figure between the classical and the human-relations schools.) The human-relations perspective grew in popularity with the work of theorists like McGregor (1960) and Likert (1961). It developed largely in reaction to the frustratingly strict regulations and control of classical theory and stresses the importance of the individual and of social relations in organizational life, suggesting strategies for improving organizations by increasing employee satisfaction and for creating organizations that help individuals achieve their human potential.

The social-systems model of organization became popular in the late 1950s and early 1960s with the work of such theorists as March and Simon (1958), Katz and Kahn (1966), and Lawrence and Lorsch (1967), all of whom applied the concepts of general-systems theory to organizational phenomena. The social-systems perspective emphasizes the functional integration and coordination of organizational processes both within organizations and among organizations.

Weick's model of organization was articulated in his book *The Social Psychology of Organizing* (1969). It has not enjoyed the widespread popularity of the three earlier perspectives, perhaps because of its newness or complexity, but it has been adopted recently by a growing number of organizational-communication researchers. The model is included here because of its explanatory strength, its departure from static models of organization, and its clear relevance to organizational communication and information. Weick's model expanded the systems model introduced in the social-systems perspective by clarifying the role of information in organization and providing an in-depth description of how organizational systems coordinate information-processing activities to promote ongoing organizing processes.

The organizational-culture theory is the most modern of the perspectives that we will examine. It was popularized in the early 1980s by such best-selling books as *In Search of Excellence: Lessons from America's Best-Run Companies* (Peters and Waterman, 1982) and *Corporate Cultures: The Rites and Rituals of Corporate Life* (Deal and Kennedy, 1982). The organizational-culture perspective describes the powerful interpretive nature of organizational life and illustrates the influence of shared significant symbols on organizational processes.

These five theories of organization have had mixed influence on directing organizational practice. Logically, the theories that have been around the longest should have had the greatest influence on organizational practice, due to their tenure. And such has been the case. Classical theory and human-relations theory, both of which are very prescriptive approaches to organization, have had great impact on organizational practice. Principles of classical theory and of human-relations theory have been widely translated into specific management strategies and techniques used by many business and professional organizations. Social-systems theory, Weick's model, and organizational-culture theory, all of which are generally descriptive theories of organization, have not been applied as widely to organizational practice as have the two more established perspectives. All five perspectives have great applicability in organizational life, both as diagnostic models for evaluating organizational phenomena and as guidelines for establishing directives for organizational practice. As we discuss them, we will identify their applications to organizational practice by suggesting specific strategies.

The five perspectives have influenced the study of organizational communication. Classical theory emphasizes formal, hierarchical channels of organization to provide members with directions and job instructions. The human-relations perspective emphasizes the development of informal social communication in organization to help satisfy the needs of organization members. The social-systems theory emphasizes the role of communication between the organization and its environment and among different functional components of the organization to promote coordination of efforts. Weick's model emphasizes the role of human communication in interpreting and responding to challenging information inputs as well as in preserving organizational know-how. The organizational-culture perspective emphasizes the ways in which communication binds members together in shared interpretations of reality. In the next five chapters, we will examine the influences of these historical perspectives on the development of organizational-communication research, theory, and practice.

CHAPTER 3

The Classical Theory of Organization

ORGANIZATION AS MECHANISM

One of the most pervasive models of organization is based on an analogy between organizations and machines. It was intuitively appealing for many organizational analysts to view organizations as predictable mechanical tools. The analogy envisions effective organizations as well-built machines, with clearly differentiated functional components working reliably to accomplish predetermined goals. The key organizational activities, according to this analogy, are planning, design, and maintenance of organizational structures and activities. The mechanistic model of organization stresses order, machinelike regularity, and rationality in organizational processes.

The classical theory of organization is largely based on this mechanistic model. In classical theory, the role of the individual is underplayed in favor of a clear emphasis on organizational rules, structure, and control. Organization members are molded to fit the needs of the organization. Administrative statements like "Shape up, or ship out!" are indicative of the importance placed on having organization members fit into clearly planned and specified functional roles. The mechanistic model is useful for clarifying the specific activities that organization members must perform, but, as we will discuss in more depth in Chapter 4, the mechanistic model was often regarded as dehumanizing and insensitive to the individual needs of organization members.

CLASSICAL THEORY OF ORGANIZATION

The classical theory of management developed in the late nineteenth and early twentieth centuries and is generally recognized by organizational scholars as the first standardized attempt to analyze and direct organizational activities. Classical theory emphasizes the importance of organizational structure and administrative control on organizational performance. The impact of the classical theory of organization has been widespread. Just about every large organization that has an administrative hierarchy and formal system of rules relies on principles of classical theory.

Classical theory is based on three different, yet related, areas of study that were developed independently by different theorists: the study of bureaucracy, the study of administrative theory, and the study of scientific management (Hicks and Gullett, 1975). The theory of bureaucracy was primarily an academic area of study undertaken by sociologists, most notably Max Weber. *Bureaucracy* theory provides a descriptive model of the nature and structure of effective hierarchical organizations. Administrative theory and scientific management are parallel approaches to organizational behavior. Both were developed by engineers as specific prescriptive strategies for applying rules (often covered in the laws of bureaucracy) to actual practice by standardizing and structuring organizational activities. The difference between the two approaches is in their scope and focus. *Scientific management* deals with more microscopic issues of management practice and task design, while *administrative theory* deals with more macroscopic issues of organizational design (Hicks and Gullett, 1975). Administrative theory builds on the theory of bureaucracy by prescribing specific strategies for developing structure and order in complex organizations. Scientific management builds on the theory of bureaucracy by identifying specific strategies for designing tasks to increase organizational efficiency.

Bureaucracy and Organization

Bureaucracy refers to the ideally structured human organization. Bureaucracy is achieved through the formalization of rules, structures, and processes within organizations. Classical theorists, such as Fayol (1949), Taylor (1911), and Weber (1948), have for many years advocated bureaucratic models for increasing the effectiveness of organizational administration. Max Weber is generally known as the father of bureaucracy. According to Weber (1948), the ideal bureaucratic organization exhibits eight structural characteristics.

First, *formalized rules, regulations, and procedures* standardize and direct the actions of organization members in the accomplishment of organizational tasks. Weber envisioned the development of an encompassing set of specific rules and guidelines to designate tasks and regiment organizational activities.

Second, *specialization of organization members' roles* provides a division of labor to simplify worker activities in the accomplishment of complex tasks. By breaking down complex tasks into specialized activities, worker productivity could be increased.

Third, *hierarchy* of formal organizational authority and the legitimation of power roles of organization members is based on the office held and the expertise of individual officeholders, helping to direct interpersonal relationships between organization members toward the accomplishment of organizational tasks.

Fourth, *employment of qualified personnel* is based solely on their technical competence and ability to perform the job to which they are assigned. Managers should logically evaluate applicants' job qualifications, and the best qualified individuals should be sought to work for the organization.

Fifth, *interchangeability of personnel* in relatively self-perpetuating organizational roles enables organizational activities to be accomplished by different individuals. This emphasizes the relative importance of organizational tasks in comparison with that of the particular organization members performing the tasks.

Sixth, *impersonality and professionalism* in interpersonal relationships among organization members direct individuals toward the performance of organizational tasks. According to this principle, organization members are to concentrate on organizational goals and stifle their own goals and needs. This emphasizes, once again, the high priority of organizational tasks in comparison with the low priority of individual organization members.

Seventh, *detailed job descriptions* should be provided for all members of the organization to outline their formal duties and job responsibilities. Employees should have a clear understanding of management's expectations of their job performance.

Eighth, *rationality and predictability* in organizational activities and the accomplishment of organizational goals help promote order in organizations. According to this principle, organizations are to be run by clear-cut logical and predictable rules and guidelines.

The bureaucratic model has received a bad public image in recent years because of the extreme formality and inflexibility of bureaucratic organizations. In modern usage, however, "the word bureaucracy has often been used to criticize failure to allocate authority and responsibility clearly, rigid and impersonal rules and routines, blundering officials, slow performance, buck-passing, conflicting procedures and directives, duplication of effort, empire building, too much power in the hands of the wrong person(s), waste of resources, and inertia" (Hicks and Gullett, 1975, p. 128). The word *bureaucracy* has almost become synonymous with organizational inefficiency, red tape, and insensitivity. Bradley and Baird (1980) report that "complaints against bureaucracy have been numerous: it has been accused of stifling individual creativity, encouraging conformity and modifying the personality" (p. 10).

Certainly, large universities have had many of these criticisms leveled at them. Universities are notorious for their red tape. Stories abound about students who were prohibited from graduating because of an error in their records, undergraduates who waited on long lines only to be told that they were closed out of the classes for which they had registered, or library users who received overdue notices for books they had returned to the library. Stories like these attest not only to the red tape and insensitivity of bureaucracies, but also to the ways that the overdevelopment of bureaucratic structures can become self-defeating to the accomplishment of organizational goals.

Bureaucracy, however, offers many advantages to large, complex organizations such as universities. Precision, speed, clarity, continuity, discretion, unity, and strict subordination of personnel are reported as benefits of bureaucratic structure (Tortoriello, Blatt, and DeWine, 1978). Bureaucratic structure adds predictability to organizational behavior by prescribing specific rules, guidelines, and procedures for dealing with tasks. As we will discuss in Chapter 6, rules help organizations cope with low-equivocality (unambiguous, simple) inputs, indicating that bureaucracy is useful for handling routine, predictable organizational tasks. Yet rules are not useful for responding to high-equivocality (very ambiguous, difficult) inputs, suggesting that the bureaucratic model is inappropriate for handling complex organizational problems. Bureaucracy does not lend itself to creativity and flexibility, even though there are many situations where organization members must react creatively to complex and unpredictable problems. In summary, bureaucracy can offer many strong advantages to standardizing organizational practice, yet it can also be very constraining for organization members and the individuals whom organizations serve.

Administrative Theory

Administrative theory is the second part of the three-part theoretical base of the classical theory of organization (Hicks and Gullett, 1975). There is a distinctive bias toward managerial practice in administrative theory. Whereas bureaucracy theory provides a description of the "ideal" structured organization, administrative theory designates specific strategies for implementing bureaucratic structure. Administrative theory translates many of the descriptive principles of the bureaucratic model into prescriptive principles of managerial practice. In fact, administrative theory has been popularly titled the "principles of management" (Hicks and Gullett, 1975).

The earliest and most influential theoretician of administrative theory was the French industrialist Henri Fayol. In 1916, Fayol identified several management principles in his milestone text *General and Industrial Management* (translated into English, 1949) that have become the cornerstone of administrative theory. These principles have been broadly applied to organizational design and practice and are extremely influential in the design and administration of modern industrial organizations. Some of the key principles of management introduced by Fayol may seem like common sense to us today, but that is merely a reflection of their widespread application and use. Many of the principles are very similar to those of bureaucracy defined by Weber. Fayol (1949) defined 20 key principles of management.

Planning directs managers to analyze the tasks and goals of the organization and to design specific strategies, as well as identify personnel and raw materials needed, to accomplish organizational goals. (Note how similar this principle is to Weber's "formalized rules, regulations, and procedures" principle of bureaucracy; see Table 3.1, page 78.)

Organizing directs managers to allocate the personnel, equipment, and resources needed to accomplish the organizational goals identified in planning.

Commanding instructs managers to direct the activities of organization members to accomplish the organizational goals identified in planning.

Coordinating instructs managers to regulate, direct, and integrate the activities of different groups of organization members to accomplish organizational goals.

Controlling instructs managers to use their authority to make sure that the actions of workers comply with the goals and regulations of the organization. (Note how similar this principle is to Weber's "hierarchy" principle of bureaucracy; see Table 3.1.)

Division of work directs the development of specialized work skills by organization members so they might concentrate on specific tasks leading to increased productivity and efficiency. (Note how similar this principle is to Weber's "specialization of organization members' roles" principle of bureaucracy; see Table 3.1.)

Authority empowers managers to wield power and control over subordinates to direct their activities for the good of the organization. Subordinates are required to yield to the authority of their higher-ups

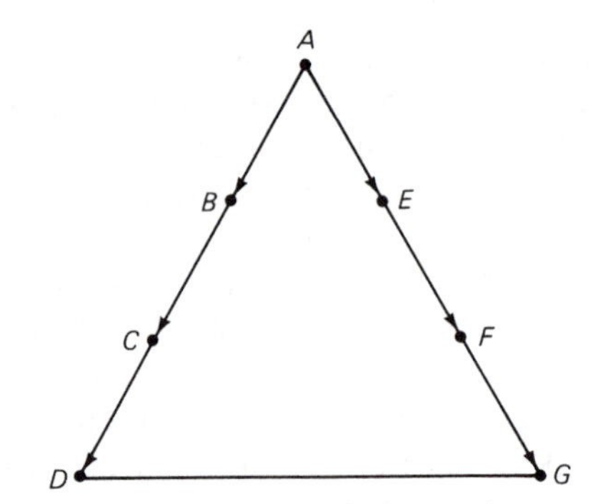

Figure 3.1 Hierarchical chain of command.

within the organization. (Note how similar this principle is to Weber's "hierarchy" principle of bureaucracy; see Table 3.1.)

Discipline directs all organization members to submit to the rules and guidelines of the organization and specifies penalties for organization members who fail to abide by organizational rules. (Note how similar this principle is to Weber's "impersonality and professionalism" principle of bureaucracy; see Table 3.1.)

Unity of command asserts that every organization member should receive directives from only one superior and be responsible to that person. This principle serves to increase the clarity of work roles by identifying who has responsibility for what and who has authority over whom in organizational activities.

Scalar chain asserts that organization members should answer directly to their superiors and directly supervise their subordinates. The scalar chain establishes a clear vertical line of interaction between subordinates and superiors along the organization's hierarchical chain of command (Figure 3.1). It identifies the primary route for directives and rule setting following a downward communication path and can make interaction difficult between organization members who are in positions on parallel chains of command within the organization. To cope with this problem, Fayol asserted that in certain circumstances (emergencies, for example), organization members can communicate horizontally, or across parallel chains of command, with peers to coordinate organizational activities. This principle solves the problem of restricted horizontal communication between organization members on the same hierarchical level within the organization. Fayol termed this horizontal channel, which, in effect, breaks the scalar chain, a "gangplank," but it became popularly known as "Fayol's bridge" (Figure 3.2).

Unity of direction asserts that organization members should be of one mind, working together toward the accomplishment of organiza-

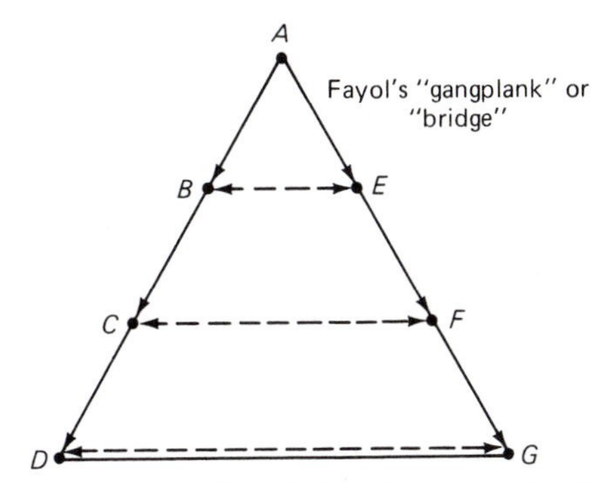

Figure 3.2 Scalar chain of communication.

tional goals. This principle illustrates the emphasis on the good of the organization over the good of the individual organization member. (Note how similar this principle is to Weber's "impersonality and professionalism" principle of bureaucracy; see Table 3.1, page 78).

Subordination of the individual to the larger group directs individual organization members to act in the interest of the organization. (Note, once again, how similar this principle is to Weber's "impersonality and professionalism" principle of bureaucracy, which places importance on the organization as opposed to the individual organization member; see Table 3.1.)

Remuneration asserts that organization members are to be rewarded for their work with salary and other material benefits (bonuses, profit sharing, piecework, shares of stock) that match their job productivity. This principle is based on the notion that organization members are primarily financially motivated and that their work performance is dependent on the amount of monetary remuneration they receive from the organization.

Centralization of power asserts that organizations operate most successfully when there is close control over organization members' activities by central administration and that decentralization of organizational processes should not develop to the point where these processes are not under direct hierarchical supervision. (Note how similar this principle is to Weber's "hierarchy" principle of bureaucracy; see Table 3.1.)

Order directs clear organization, planning, and classification of activities. This principle asserts that nothing should be left to chance in organizations. All organizational activities and processes should be clearly designated and integrated into the formal goals of the organization. (Note how similar this principle is to Weber's "formalized rules, regulations, and procedures" principle of bureaucracy; see Table 3.1.)

Equity establishes that all organization members should be treated fairly and justly. Objectively determined rules and guidelines should be used to govern organizational personnel. (Note, once again, how similar this principle is to Weber's "formalized rules, regulations, and procedures" principle of bureaucracy; see Table 3.1.)

Stability of tenure states that organization members need sufficient time to learn to accomplish their assigned tasks, and as long as they are doing a good job, their continued employment and position within the organization should be secure.

Initiative asserts that organization members should be alert to work in the best interests of the organization. Managers should be aware of jobs that have to be accomplished and direct subordinates' activities toward fulfilling these tasks.

Esprit de corps suggests that organizational goals can best be achieved when members take pride in their organization. Fayol stresses the importance of loyalty and emotional commitment of organization members to their organization.

Line and staff functions identify the need for specialized support personnel (staff) to assist managers who have primary responsibility for making decisions and directing activities to accomplish organizational goals (line). Staff members handle technical, clerical, personnel, and other matters to free line managers from administrative details so that they can focus their attention on directing the accomplishment of organizational tasks and goals.

It is easy to see many of the similarities between Weber's theory of bureaucracy and Fayol's administrative theory (Table 3.1). Both are attempts to promote logic, order, and structure in organizations. Administrative theory was developed as prescriptive guidelines for the management of industrial organizations according to strict use of rules and authority. Herein lies both the strengths and the weaknesses of administrative theory. The prescriptive principles of administrative theory make the theory very pragmatic and highly applicable to business organizations. Yet, since there are no universal principles of management that apply equally well to all organizational situations, the principles of administrative theory can be misleading, contradictory, and inappropriate to use when dealing with idiosyncratic organizational problems. Moreover, as we will discuss in more depth later in this chapter, the principles of administrative theory, like those of bureaucracy, often were regarded as being inflexible and insensitive to the human needs of organization members.

Scientific Management

Scientific-management theory is the third part of the three-part theoretical base of the classical theory of organization (Hicks and Gullett,

1975). Scientific management shares with administrative theory and bureaucracy theory the emphasis on logic, order, and hierarchy in organizations. As in administrative theory, there is a distinct bias toward managerial practice in scientific management. The focus of scientific management is more microscopic than is the focus of administrative theory. While administrative theory describes the way organizations should be structured, scientific management describes the way specific organizational tasks should be structured to increase the efficiency of their accomplishment.

The most influential proponent of scientific-management theory was Frederick Winslow Taylor. Taylor, an American mechanical engineer, was convinced that scientific observation, analysis, and intervention should be used to improve the way that tasks were accomplished in industrial organizations. He was concerned with the sloppy, haphazard, and unsystematic operation of organizations in the first two decades of the twentieth century.

Taylor felt that there was unnecessary waste and inefficiency in the way that organizations went about their business, due to both poor work design in organizations and poor work habits by organization members. He argued that by getting workers to give their best effort in accomplishing well-designed, task-related activities, organizations could save money and increase productivity, while workers could receive higher wages based on their better performance. He suggested paying workers for the amount of work they performed, rather than for the number of hours they worked. Therefore, if workers were more productive at accomplishing their tasks, they would make more money.

By scientifically examining the nature of a specific organizational job, Taylor asserted, that task could be designed so as to promote efficiency and increase productivity. Once the best way of accomplishing a job was set, time and motion studies could be used to determine the optimal rate for its accomplishment. By setting a rate for performance, Taylor argued, monetary incentives could be established for workers whose performance surpassed the rate. He is given credit for having coined the adage "Time is money," which in many ways embodies the spirit of scientific management (Cummings, Long, and Lewis, 1983, p. 74). Taylor attempted to persuade all organization members to accept the tenets of scientific management to promote its implementation. In a sense, Taylor was encouraging a "mental revolution" in the way that organizational activities were conceptualized and practiced.

Taylor wrote about many success stories to document the benefits of scientific-management practices. For example, in *Scientific Management* (1947, originally published in 1911), he reported the use of scientific-management techniques for examining how ball bearings were inspected. After the work methods were scientifically evaluated and the task was redesigned according to the most efficient procedures, 35 workers were able to do a job that had been accomplished by 120 workers, with more than a two-thirds improvement of work quality (Hicks and Gullett, 1975).

Similarly, in a now famous study at a Bethlehelm Steel Corporation machine shop, Taylor again demonstrated the utility of scientific-management techniques in improving worker productivity and increasing efficiency. Through time and motion studies of coal and iron-ore shoveling at the steel company, he determined that the weight of a shovelful of material picked up by workers varied from 16 to 38 pounds (Rogers and Agarwala-Rogers, 1976). Yet maximum efficiency in shoveling occurred when the shovel load was slightly over 20 pounds. Depending on the specific materials that workers had to shovel, different shovels were provided that accommodated approximately 21 pounds of material. Workers received instructions about which shovel they were to use to shovel which material, as well as the shoveling technique that was most effective and least tiring. Additionally, pay incentives were given to workers who shoveled more than the established rate.

The results of Taylor's intervention at Bethlehem Steel were amazing. The amount of material shoveled per day increased from 16 to 59 tons. Even after paying the expenses of Taylor's time and motion studies and the incentive pay the workers earned, the company was able to cut its handling costs in half. Additionally, it was able to reduce the number of workers needed to do the shoveling by more than 65 percent to 75 percent (Koehler, Anatol, and Applbaum, 1981). These results provide dramatic testimony that scientific-management techniques can increase efficiency and productivity in industrial organizations.

Taylor introduced several important management principles and concepts in *Scientific Management* (1911) that are worth examining.

First, *science should be emphasized over rule of thumb* in guiding the design of tasks and organizational activities. The effectiveness of organizational operations should be scientifically and objectively measured.

Second, *harmony should be promoted over discord* within the organization by making the rules, regulations, and formal roles of all organization members scientifically based and clearly assigned.

Third, *cooperation should be stressed over individualism.* Management should cooperate with workers to ensure that tasks are accomplished in the most efficient, scientifically based ways. (Compare this principle with the sentiments about the relative unimportance of the individual in both Weber's bureaucracy and Fayol's administrative theories; see Table 3.1.)

Fourth, achieving the *maximum output,* instead of restricted outputs, should be the primary goal of organizations.

Fifth, *all workers should be developed to their maximum productivity and work potential* so that they might achieve their greatest efficiency and prosperity. This can be accomplished by scientifically selecting and training workers for a specific task. Only first-class workers should be kept on jobs within organizations.

Sixth, *there should be a division of work between managers and workers;* managers should take responsibility for the accomplishment of tasks that they are better equipped to handle than are the workers. Planning and administrative tasks should be performed by managers who were trained to be functional specialists in the task they are in charge of, while workers should be directed to accomplish the tasks designed by managers.

Seventh, care should be taken to *eliminate all shouldering (loafing)* in organizational activities. Organization members should take their work seriously and give their best effort. (Compare this principle with Weber's principle of "impersonality and professionalism" and Fayol's principle of "initiative"; see Table 3.1.)

Eighth, *workers should be paid for the amount of work they perform* through the use of piece rates. Based on rates set through time and motion studies, minimum standards for production should be established, and workers should be remunerated according to their ability to meet the minimum standard. Additional "bonus" pay would be offered to workers who could surpass the minimum production standard.

Taylor's scientific-management concepts stress the importance of structure and design in the accomplishment of organizational tasks. His work contributed mightily to the development of improved management techniques in work standardization, task planning, time and motion studies, piece rates, and cost saving and to the birth of such fields of study as supervision, industrial engineering, industrial management, and personnel management.

Frank and Lillian Gilbreth were contemporaries of Taylor who worked to apply Taylor's scientific-management principles to organizational practice. They refined his time and motion studies to a science, often using motion-picture analysis to evaluate worker performance (Spriegel and Myers, 1953; Gilbreth, 1915). They stressed the importance of human factors in management and the study of individual workers (Hicks and Gullett, 1975). Together with Taylor, they helped popularize scientific-management techniques in a wide range of organizational settings.

Many organizational situations do not seem to benefit from the work of Taylor and his contemporaries, however. Scientific management is particularly well suited to industrial organizations that have "routine, repetitive, standardized jobs, and perhaps such jobs will become increasingly rare in a society where machines do more and more

Table 3.1

Comparison of the Key Principles of Bureaucracy, Administrative Theory, and Scientific Management

Bureaucracy	*Administrative Theory*	*Scientific Management*
Rules	Planning Order Equity	
Specialization	Division of work Organizing Coordinating Line and staff	Division of work
Hierarchy	Authority Commanding Controlling Unity of command Scalar chain Centralization	
Qualified personnel	Stable Tenure	
Interchangeable personnel		
Impersonality	Discipline	Harmony
Job descriptions	Unity of direction Subordination Initiative	No loafing
Rationality	Remuneration	Science Pay for work
	Esprit de corps	Cooperation Maximum output High productivity

such work" (Hicks and Gullett, 1975, p. 184). Many people are intimidated by efficiency experts who seem to care more for the best way to accomplish a task than for the individual performing the task. Just as do bureaucracy theory and administrative theory, scientific management suffers from its insensitivity to the individual. (This attitude helped lead to the development of the human-relations perspective, as we will see in Chapter 4.)

In Case 3.1, studies based on classical theory were done in a very modern organization.

1. Whose position do you agree with, that of Mr. Schwartz or of Mr. Horowitz?
2. Can you think of ways in which the plant can be operated more efficiently?
3. Is the classical theory of organizations appropriate to this organizational situation? Why or why not?

Emphasis on Output, Efficiency, and Order

Classical theory is an important perspective on the study of organizations because it emphasized for the first time the importance of planning and structure in organizational performance. It advocates production of organizational outputs through efficient and orderly organizational activities. Bureaucracy theory identified the primary elements of organizational structure; administrative theory identified specific strategies for establishing order within organizations; and scientific management identified the techniques by which efficient organizational operations could be promoted.

According to classical theory, the organization is a machine, and organization members are merely cogs in the machine. (Recall the mechanistic model of organization introduced at the beginning of the chapter.) The role of the individual is not very important. To make the organizational machine work efficiently, the cogs (workers) have to be molded to fit the goals and tasks of the organization. If a cog does not work well, replace it with another. Organizational effectiveness is measured by what the machine produces—the amount and quality of organizational output. Communication serves the function of establishing managerial control, providing workers with job instructions, and enabling managers to gather information for planning.

Organization membership is not a totally random, value-free activity. People who join organizations and perform organizational roles do so for many reasons. The classical theorists identified rational, economic goals as the primary influence motivating organizational membership and performance. That is, they assumed that people join organizations and perform organizationally designated activities solely for the tangible (usually financial) rewards they receive in return for their performance. Identification and provision of adequate monetary rewards was thought by classical theorists to be a primary personnel responsibility of managers in organizations. That is why classical theo-

Case 3.1

Glenview Nuclear-Power Plant

Glenview Nuclear-Power Plant provides electricity to a 100-square-mile region of a northeastern state. It is a highly automated power plant, using state-of-the-art technology and equipment. Glenview has very high standards for hiring and placing its employees. All plant employees are required to have had at least two years of college. Most employees have a minimum of a bachelor's degree. Many have graduate training. They also must have passed demanding entrance exams assessing their knowledge about nuclear energy and testing their technical aptitude. Moreover, employees are required to successfully complete a rigorous company training program, which educates them about the specific equipment, processes, and safeguards at the plant. Only then are they assigned to a particular department and allowed to operate plant equipment.

Bob Horn operated a typical monitoring and control station in the plant. Bob had an M.S. in electrical technology and had worked at the plant for nine years. The station monitored and evaluated the changing operating conditions at the plant using a computerized control system that automatically received readings from sensors that measured conditions at significant points in the electricity-generating process. The computer was programmed to continuously compare sensor readings with preset "optimal" conditions. Based on the sensor readings at any given time, the computer printed out recommendations for equipment adjustments. Bob monitored the computer-generated readings and recommendations and decided whether to follow the recommended adjustments. Bob also manually monitored equipment values displayed on different electrical panels in the control room and decided whether to make adjustments in the process irrespective of the computer.

Much of the equipment was totally automated and operated on its own unless a problem occurred. Bob was merely on call to react if a problem arose, periodically checking the meters indicating current technical conditions. If there was a problem, Bob was able to make any needed adjustments to the process from the control room. Bob spent most of his time on the job reading the newspaper or working crossword puzzles, but he was always available for an emergency, which would be indicated by an alarm. Emergencies were very infrequent, but they demanded instant and precise corrective action to avoid any possibility of a meltdown and to maintain electrical service and protect property and lives within the region.

Mr. Schwartz was an efficiency expert with the State Office of Personnel and Budget. He was sent by the State Office to evaluate the operations at Glenview Nuclear-Power Plant and see if the plant could be operated more efficiently and less expensively. After making observations and conducting several time and motion studies, Mr. Schwartz submitted to Mr. Horowitz, the plant manager, a report recommending several operational changes at the plant. He also sent a copy of the report to the State Office. Among the changes suggested by Mr. Schwartz were:

1. Eliminate the lengthy entrance exams and lower the hiring standards to admit high-school graduates. This would cut operating costs and enable the power plant to reduce the salaries paid to plant personnel.
2. Eliminate the position held by Bob Horn, since the process was already largely automated. The computer could be programmed to actually make the adjustments that it now recommended to Bob Horn. (Further, Mr. Schwartz noted that "during a half-hour time and motion observation, Mr. Horn hardly looked up from his newspaper once to look at the meters. Obviously, the salary being paid Mr. Horn is a waste of the taxpayers' money.")

Several days later, Mr. Horowitz replied to Mr. Schwartz by sending him a letter (as well as sending a copy of the letter to the State Office), from which the following is excerpted:

"It is our considered opinion that the time and motion studies conducted at Glenview Nuclear-Power Plant were totally inappropriate for our type of plant. Our power plant is not a labor-intensive organization. Most of our costs are technical. The employees at the plant are responsible for operating and maintaining the complex equipment used to provide electrical power for the state. The effect of your time and motion studies on our employees' morale and our plant operations have been extremely detrimental. The findings of your study are misleading, at best. The changes suggested in your report are extremely ill-advised and would pose a significant danger to the people of this state."

Mr. Schwartz, who was trained in classical theories of management, was shocked at this response and wondered how he should reply to Mr. Horowitz.

rists, especially those who subscribed to the scientific-management approach, espoused establishing production rates and paying workers according to their output.

Classical theory is a very logical approach to the study of organizations. Unfortunately, organizations are composed of human beings, who do not always act in rational ways. The notion of rational, economically oriented workers accepted by classical theorists is a gross oversimplification of the nature of organization members. Indeed, classical theory, for all its scientific rigor and in-depth planning, seems to oversimplify organizational life by focusing on only the accomplishment of formal tasks. Each of the other four perspectives on organization that we will discuss identifies aspects of the study of organizations that were overlooked by the classical theorists. The human-relations theory, to which we now turn, added to the classical theory by focusing on an important element of organization that was short-changed in classical theory—the individual organization member.

CHAPTER 4

The Human-Relations Theory of Organization

ORGANIZATION AS CONTEXT FOR INDIVIDUAL ACTUALIZATION

As we saw in Chapter 3, the classical theory of organization is rooted in the analogy between organization and machine, which accords great importance to organizational structure and control, but largely overlooks the importance of the individual organization member to organizations. Classical theory attempted to structure organizational phenomena, on the assumption that they are orderly, precise, and predictable. As we all know, human beings do not always act in orderly, precise, and predictable ways. They make mistakes, act irrationally, forget things, get drunk, flirt, become frustrated, fall asleep, get angry, act mischieviously, fall in love, and do all kinds of unpredictable things. Human beings do not fit neatly into the orderly scientific system of classical theory. Therefore, classical theorists avoided human factors in analyzing organizational behavior.

Avoiding the influence of human beings on organizations is an obvious limitation of classical theory. Human beings, as organization members, are the very essence of social organization. Human beings engage in organizing behaviors. Organization members decide what organizational roles to perform and how to perform them. Obviously, without organization members, there is no organization. Human-relations theorists recognized this limitation of classical theory and focused directly on the role of the individual in organizational phenomena.

The human-relations theory of organization rejected the economic description of organization member motivation used in classical theory and promoted a model of human behavior based on self-actualization. Self-actualization is the process by which a human being develops individual knowledge, skills, and abilities. Working toward self-actualization helps organization members reach their potential as human beings (Maslow, 1954). The human-relations theorists repudiated the mechanistic model of organization in favor of a self-actualization model. They argued that the major long-term motivation of human beings for joining and working for organizations is to facilitate their personal development, growth, and self-actualization and that the self-actualization that occurs in organizations is at least as important to organization members as the tangible financial rewards they earn.

The focus in human-relations theory is on fulfilling the needs of organization members. The more satisfied they are with their organization, the more disposed they are to work on its behalf. Human-relations theorists asserted that increased worker need satisfaction would lead to worker self-actualization and, in turn, to higher levels of worker motivation and increased production. The notion that "a happy worker is a more productive worker" is based on the human-relations approach.

HUMAN-RELATIONS MODEL OF ORGANIZATION

Human-relations theory stresses the importance of the individual and of social relations in organizational life, suggesting strategies for improving organizations by increasing organization member satisfaction and for creating organizations that help individuals achieve their potential. The human-relations theory of organization was introduced in the 1930s with the pioneering work of Barnard (1938), Mayo (1933), and Roethlisberger and Dickson (1939). These early human-relations theorists rejected the structural tenets of classical theory, arguing that the mechanistic view of organizations was insensitive to the individual social needs of organization members. The human-relations perspective developed largely in reaction to the frustratingly strict regulations and control of classical theory. Indeed, some refer to human-relations theory as "neoclassical theory," identifying it as a theoretical alternative to the classical perspective (Hicks and Gullet, 1975, p. 192).

The move from classical theory to human-relations theory was a major paradigmatic shift. The two theories are quite different from each other and emphasize very distinct variables affecting organizational phenomena. Kuhn, in his enlightening book *The Structure of Scientific Revolutions* (1970), identifies the emergent process by which a theoretical paradigm develops, competes with existing prevalent paradigms, and eventually gains credence as a viable perspective. Human-relations theory went through such a revolutionary process, as it developed as an alternative perspective to classical theory. Human-relations proponents competed head to head with classical theorists. Members of the classical-theory camp denigrated proponents of human-relations theory by referring to them as "happy boys," implying that they wanted merely to please the workers and had little concern for the financial welfare of the organization. Classical theorists feared the loss of control of organization leaders in the human-relations approach, envisioning organizations that were run by and for organization members, rather than organizations that directed the members' behavior. Members of the human-relations camp retaliated to attacks by classical theorists by intimating that they were "oppressors of the masses" or "fascists." They implied that proponents of classical theory were not concerned about the welfare of the workers and were interested only in reaping organizational profits, usually at the expense of the workers.

Competition between the two perspectives still exists, although in a less fierce way, since each camp has generally come to recognize the legitimacy of the other. Currently, neither theoretical perspective is able to establish its absolute dominance as a model for organizational practice, although classical theory is probably more influential in modern organizational practice. Large industrial organizations, military organizations (the armed forces, police forces), government agencies, and even educational institutions often are representative of the classical approach to management. Human-relations theory has been accepted more in principle than in practice in most organizations, although it is gaining in influence.

Human-relations theory was able to compete effectively with classical theory and establish its legitimacy largely through the evidence provided by a landmark series of experiments conducted by Mayo, Roethlisberger, and Dickson that came to be known as the Hawthorne Studies and were reported by Roethlisberger and Dickson in their extremely influential book *Management and the Worker* (1939). The Hawthorne Studies, designed to identify the ideal work environment for peak efficiency, were conducted at the Western Electric Hawthorne plant in Cicero, Illinois, between 1925 and 1932. Dickson, an industrial engineer at the plant, combined efforts with two professors from the Harvard University School of Business, Roethlisberger and, later, Mayo.

The initial focus of these studies was very much in line with classical theory. More specifically, the experiments followed a marked Taylorist scientific-management design. (Note how similar the initial goals and design of the Hawthorne Studies were to the studies conducted by Taylor at the Bethlehem Steel plant, discussed in Chapter 3.) Interestingly, the Hawthorne Studies resulted in some very unexpected findings, which ultimately led the researchers to question the validity of the scientific-management premises on which their experiments had been based and to develop some of the basic tenets of human-relations theory.

In the first of the Hawthorne Studies, begun in 1924 and lasting for about three years, the lighting in work areas was manipulated (increased and decreased) to determine the effects of the changes in illumination on worker productivity. The experimenters ultimately hoped to find the ideal light setting for maximum worker productivity. Expectedly, the researchers found that increasing illumination in the work areas resulted in increased productivity. Unexpectedly, however, they also found that decreasing illumination in the work areas resulted in increased productivity. Even in the control work area, where the lighting was maintained at the original illumination level, productivity increased. These results confounded the researchers.

How could all the different lighting conditions affect worker productivity in the same way? Eventually, the researchers hypothesized that the consistent increases in worker production were not related to the changes in the level of illumination, but were due to the fact that the workers being studied were reacting to being watched by the researchers. The attention they were being paid influenced the workers to improve their work performance. (This tendency for research subjects to alter their behaviors in response to being studied has become known as the Hawthorne effect.) People tend to respond in artificial ways when they know they are being observed. The workers under study felt as though they were special because they were chosen to be observed. They reacted to the special treatment by working harder than usual. This was one of the first studies that identified social factors as an important influence on worker productivity.

The illumination experiments led to additional studies of worker productivity at the Hawthorne plant to further explore this phenomenon. For example, in the relay-assembly studies, begun in 1927, work conditions—number and length of coffee breaks, number of work hours per day, amount of pay incentives, and even provision of hot lunches—were varied to identify their influence on the productivity of groups of six workers who were assembling telephone-relay systems. As in the lighting experiments, production increased with each experimental variation. Even with the longest working day and the elimination of all incentives, breaks, and refreshments, worker production increased! The interpretation of this study, similar to that of the previous study, was that the special attention the researchers were paying to the relay-assembly workers, not the variations in work conditions, was the reason for their rise in productivity.

The next set of experiments that were part of the Hawthorne Studies began in 1928 and were designed to explore the effect of workers' feelings about themselves, their jobs, and their work groups on their work performance. Rather than manipulating work conditions, as in the previous studies, the researchers conducted anonymous, nondirective "ventilating" interviews with workers, who were asked to share their feelings about themselves and their jobs. They were encouraged to air their gripes about the organization and to discuss their work-related problems. Workers generally seemed to enjoy these interviews and, in fact, often reported that the interviews helped them feel more positive about the organization, feel better about their jobs, and resolve their problems (Roethlisberger, 1956).

In 1931 began the last of the Hawthorne Studies, in which workers in a bank wiring room were closely observed by researchers. The researchers recorded the activities of the workers to determine the social influences on worker behavior. For example, they recorded several instances of spontaneous cooperation. They also noticed that production rates among the workers were extremely consistent, even though the plant management attempted to establish higher production rates. How did these workers know to cooperate and to comply with the production rate established by the group? How was the production rate established by the group enforced? The researchers deduced that the workers had developed over time a comprehensive set of norms and routines for accomplishing their tasks. Group members exerted social pressure on one another to conform to the informal group norms.

The Hawthorne Studies were important because they identified several significant human issues in organizational performance that had not been stressed previously. Three key implications of the Hawthorne Studies seem to have provided the basis for the development of human-relations theory as an alternative perspective to classical theory for the study of organizations, as well as for the study of organizational communication.

First, the influence that the researchers had on worker production in the illumination and the telephone-relay-assembly studies began to indicate *the powerful influence of human communication on organization member behavior.* This implication that workers are influenced through communication became a very important part of human-relations theory and led to the development of the field of organizational communication. Classical theory regarded communication merely as a necessary evil in which supervisors communicated down the organizational hierarchy to tell workers what to do.

Second, the positive influence of the ventilating interviews on workers led to the identification of *upward communication and feedback from workers to supervisors as a useful organizational activity* (Tompkins, 1984). Until this time, classical theorists had emphasized downward communication as the primary channel of communication in organizations. Recall the emphasis in classical theory on authority, control, and directing worker behavior, all of which are accomplished through downward communication. (In Chapter 9, we will discuss in more depth the functions of upward and downward channels of formal communication in organizations.)

Third, the discovery of social norms for worker performance in the bank wiring room led to the identification of the existence and *influence of informal channels of communication on organization members.* Previously, in classical theory, formal channels of communication that follow the lines of the organizational chart had been emphasized as the primary, legitimate, and most influential form of organizational communication. Human-relations theory began to look at informal, social lines of communication in organizations. (In Chapter 9, we will discuss in more depth the functions of networks of formal and informal communication in organizations.)

These three implications from the Hawthorne Studies caused organizational theorists and practitioners to question the classical theory of organization. Classical theory did not take into account the influence of social factors on organizational performance. Human-relations theory developed in marked contrast to classical theory because it was based on very different assumptions about organizations and organization members.

McGregor's (1960) classic dichotomy between "Theory X" and "Theory Y" styles of management most clearly distinguishes the basic values of human-relations theory from those of classical theory. McGregor set up Theory X and Theory Y as diametrically opposed philosophies of human nature that he believed are indicative of classical theory and human-relations theory. He argued that the way organizations are operated is largely due to these basic assumptions about human nature that managers hold about their workers. Theory X, which is representative of the classical theory view of workers, has three primary assumptions.

First, people generally have an inherent dislike of work and will avoid it if they possibly can (McGregor, 1960, p. 33). This assumption implies that workers are basically lazy and irresponsible and cannot be trusted.

Second, "because of this human characteristic of dislike of work, most people must be coerced, controlled, directed, threatened with punishment to get them to put forth adequate effort toward the achievement of organizational objectives" (McGregor, 1960, p. 34). Based on this assumption, a primary goal of management is to direct, control, and regulate workers because if managers do not do so, little, if anything, will get done.

Third, "the average human being prefers to be directed, wishes to avoid responsibility, has relatively little ambition, wants security above all" (McGregor, 1960, p. 34). This assumption asserts that workers not only are irresponsible and lazy, but also really do not want the opportunity to exercise responsibility and like to be told what to do by their supervisors. It legitimates the rules, directives, and coercive strategies that many organization leaders establish to direct worker performance.

How do you like the assumptions of Theory X? Do you agree with them? How well do these assumptions about human nature describe you? You probably will agree that Theory X does not paint a very pleasant picture of human beings. It asserts that people are irresponsible, cannot be trusted, and must be controlled to perform organizational tasks. This set of assumptions illustrates why hierarchy, authority, control, and rules are such important aspects of classical theory. It also illustrates why classical theory is so restrictive.

Theory Y is representative of the human-relations perspective on workers. Note how the six basic assumptions of Theory Y differ from the three of Theory X.

First, "the expenditure of physical and mental effort in work is as natural as play or rest. The average human being does not inherently dislike work. Depending upon controllable conditions, work may be a source of satisfaction (and will be voluntarily performed) or a source of punishment (and will be avoided if possible)" (McGregor, 1960, p. 47). This assumption implies that human beings have the capacity to work hard if they want to and that the more personally satisfying a job is to an individual, the more likely he or she is to expend significant effort to accomplish the job.

Second, "external control and threat of punishment are not the only means for bringing about effort toward organizational objectives" (McGregor, 1960, p. 47). Human beings can and will exercise self-direction and self-control in accomplishing organizational objectives to which they are committed. This assumption suggests that the key to workers' performance lies in their level of commitment to a job, rather than in managerial control. According to this assumption, the effective manager attempts to foster and build worker commitment, which is developed by increasing workers' opportunities for individual growth through increased responsibility and increased involvement in the activities of the organization.

Third, "commitment to objectives is a function of the rewards associated with their achievement. The most significant of such rewards, e.g., the satisfaction of ego and self-actualization needs, can be direct products of efforts directed towards organizational objectives" (McGregor, 1960, pp. 47–48). This assumption identifies the relationship between self-actualization and worker commitment. McGregor asserts that workers can indeed achieve personal satisfaction and growth from their jobs. Work can be self-actualizing. If workers are to become committed to working hard at their jobs, they must be able to find personal fulfillment in accomplishing their tasks. Jobs must be designed to help individual workers become more fulfilled.

Fourth, "the average human being learns, under proper conditions, not only to accept but to seek responsibility. Avoidance of responsibility, lack of ambition, and emphasis on security are generally consequences of experience, not inherent human characteristics" (McGregor, 1960, p. 47). This implies that workers' willingness to accept work-related responsibility lies largely in the experience that they have had with their organization. If they have been treated as though they were irresponsible, they are likely to act irresponsibly. If they have been shown respect and confidence by management, they are likely to live up to those expectations by acting in the best interests of the organization. The expectations of managers for their workers' performance acts as a self-fulfilling prophecy. Responsibility is a human trait that can be nurtured by the way managers communicate with their workers. (In Chapter 8, we will discuss self-fulfilling prophecies, the implications of relational expectations on individual performance, and leadership styles that nurture worker responsibility.)

Fifth, "the capacity to exercise a relatively high degree of imagination, ingenuity, and creativity in the solution of organizational problems is widely, not narrowly, distributed in the population" (McGregor, 1960, p. 47). Human beings have the ability to make novel choices and devise unique solutions. Given the opportunity, workers might very well make some insightful decisions about how to accomplish their particular tasks. This assumption indicates that the classical theory emphasis on strict management control may limit the opportunities for creativity and ingenuity to be exercised within the organization. It is fallacious to assume that managers are the only organization members who can make creative choices and good decisions. Indeed, it is more likely that workers can do a better job of evaluating their own tasks and solving work-related problems than can their managers because the workers are more intimately involved with and experienced in their particular work. Note how this assumption is in direct contradiction to classical theory, which holds that the only organization members who are directed to make active decisions are organization leaders; all other organization members are directed to follow the decisions made by those on top.

Sixth, "under the conditions of modern industrial life, the intellectual potentialities of the average human being are only partially utilized" (McGregor, 1960, p. 47). This implies that organizations have intellectual resources in their membership that they probably have not fully utilized. A new goal of management, according to this assumption, is to uncover and use these resources. This assumption leads directly to the human-relations notion that effective organizations nurture participative management and decision making among all organization members. (In Chapter 6, we will explore this notion of dormant organization member information when we discuss Weick's notion of organizational intelligence.)

Theory Y is certainly a more uplifting view of human nature than is Theory X. You probably prefer to think of yourself as being more representative of Theory Y assumptions about human nature than of Theory X assumptions. Theory Y assumptions identify human beings as mature, responsible individuals who will participate actively in organizational activities if given proper opportunity and personal reinforcement (self-actualization). Theory Y is an intuitively attractive view of human beings. This appealing perspective on human nature contributed to the growth of the human-relations theory. People generally prefer to be treated with respect and confidence than to be treated as though they were irresponsible. Recall our discussion in Chapter 2 of personal and object levels of communication. Do you see how Theory X assumptions about workers can lead to object managerial communication and Theory Y assumptions can lead to more personal managerial communication with workers? What influences do you think personal and object communication can have on worker commitment, worker responsibility, and worker–management cooperation? Can you think of times when people have made Theory X and Theory Y assumptions about you? How did those different assumptions influence the communication between you and the other person?

Participative-Management Approach

Participative management became an important part of the human-relations theory. It developed as a strategy for improving organizational operations. Human-relations theorists suggested that, as much as possible, organization leaders should try to involve their workers in the operation of their organizations. These theorists hypothesized that the more workers participate in organizational decision making, the more likely they are to develop an understanding of and appreciation for the problems of the organization and the role of management. Participative management was promoted to help increase management–worker cooperation. The work of Follett (1971, originally published in 1925), Argyris (1957, 1964), and Likert (1961) was extremely influential in helping to identify this need for cooperation between managers and workers in the accomplishment of organizational activities. These three theorists also clearly described the failure of many industrial organizations to foster such cooperation.

Mary Parker Follett was one of the organizational theorists who bridged classical theory and human-relations theory. She was interested in helping managers effectively wield authority over workers and effectively give orders in organizations. This is a typical topic of concern of classical theory, but Follet (1971) approached it from a markedly human-relations perspective. She argued that managers' most effective use of authority is to establish personal face-to-face contact with their workers, seek feedback from workers, and elicit cooperation from workers. She stressed the importance of subordinates working *with* their managers, rather than working *under* them (Tompkins, 1984). Follett's emphasis on worker–management cooperation was a precursor to the human-relations movement away from classical theory autocracy and toward participative management.

Argyris (1957) described the lack of congruence between management and workers in many industrial organizations. He explained that the goals of workers and the goals of management often are very different. Due to this lack of goal congruence, psychological distance and competition between management and workers flourished. Many workers resent managers and their organization, developing antiorganizational sentiments. Argyris explained that workers often are alienated from their organization because they are not involved in organizational decision making and are systematically dehumanized by the cold, uncaring ("Take it or leave it," "Shape up, or ship out") manner of organization management.

Argyris (1964) suggested that organization leaders can increase the congruence between workers and management by increasing worker participation in the organizational process. He argued that the more actively involved workers are in determining organizational operations, the more likely they are to identify with the organization and adopt organizational goals as their own. The more workers identify organizational goals as their own, the more likely they are to work in the best interests of the organization. When the organization does well, workers feel that they also are doing well. Accomplishing organizational tasks becomes a means by which workers accomplish their own goals, increasing their opportunities to reach self-actualization. Argyris (1964) further suggested that jobs can be redesigned to get individual workers more involved in the organizational process, give them more responsibility and decision-making opportunities, and help them develop more pride in their work and their organization.

Likert (1961) was also a proponent of participative decision making in organizations. He clearly illustrated the problems that organizations may face when workers are not involved in organizational decision making. He described how different organizational styles either can isolate and alienate workers or can foster workers' involvement in and identification with the organization. He stressed the importance of full worker participation in organizational processes. The key element for initiating such participation, according to Likert, is the development of supportive communication between workers and management. Likert regarded the manager as a linchpin between workers and organization leadership. It is the job of the manager to promote participative management by channeling worker messages up the hierarchy and leader messages down the hierarchy. In this way, the manager acts as a communicative conduit for including workers in organizational activities.

Based on this linchpin notion of management, Likert identified four systems of organizational design, each of which illustrates either more or less enlightened organizational leadership. The first two systems of organizational style seem to be based largely on McGregor's Theory X (classical theory) assumptions about workers, while the other two systems seem to be derived from Theory Y (human-relations theory) assumptions about workers.

The *exploitative authoritative* is the least effective organizational style, yet, paradoxically, it is most often used in formal organizations. This style is characterized by tight control and authority. Workers are motivated by fear of punishment and are given little opportunity to participate in any meaningful way in organizational planning and decision making. (Note how representative this organizational style is of pure classical theory.) This style pits managers and workers against one another, rather than fostering cooperation and creativity.

The *benevolent authoritative* is a softened form of autocracy. Workers still contribute little to organizational decisions, but managers do allow them to voice their complaints and opinions. This can be frustrating for workers because their feedback has minimal impact on organizational operations. In a sense, this is a very manipulative form of management, since workers are given the semblance of involvement in organizational processes without being given any real power and responsibility.

The *consultative* organizational style encourages communication and cooperation between workers and management, yet management has limited confidence in workers' ability to make adequate organizational decisions. Managers seek feedback and ideas from their workers before *they* make major organizational decisions. They realize that workers have valuable hands-on information, just by virtue of their tenure on the job. But the managers do not trust workers' judgment in evaluating and applying the information they possess. Likert characterizes this style as a more enlightened approach than exploitative authoritative and benevolent authoritative, yet since worker involvement is limited to information giving, organizations do not benefit fully from worker involvement and initiative.

The *participative* is the most effective organizational style according to Likert. Workers are encouraged to participate fully in organizational goal setting and decision making. Managers are highly supportive of workers, depending on worker feedback and ideas to direct the organization. Likert asserts that this organizational style leads to highest organizational performance because workers and management alike are able to identify with one another and with the organization.

Case 4.1 describes the management and operation of the ABC Ski Company.

1. Identify which of Likert's four organizational styles is being used in the company.
2. What effect does this organizational style have on workers?
3. How does it influence the organization?
4. Would you suggest changing the organizational style in this company? If so, How?

Emphasis on Individual Need Satisfaction

Human-relations theory regards communication with workers as being extremely important. In contrast, in classical theory, the primary channel for organizational communication is downward through the hierarchy of control. Workers are told what to do by their bosses. Fayol (1949) acknowledged that horizontal communication among hierarchical peers (Fayol's bridge) is useful, but only in times of emergency when the chain of command is too slow. In human-relations theory, upward and downward channels of communication are identified as being important for eliciting management–worker cooperation. Horizontal communication, among peers, helps members of work groups cooperate in activities and make decisions. Moreover, informal social channels of communication are important sources of information about group norms. (In Chapter 8, we will examine in depth the specific functions of both formal and informal channels of organizational communication.)

Chester Barnard, former president of New Jersey Bell Telephone, in his extremely influential book, *The Functions of the Executive* (1968, originally published in 1938), was one of the first human-relations theorists to clearly explain the key role of communication in organizational activities. He noted that the primary role of the executive is to be a communicator. Similar to Likert's notion of the manager as a linchpin, Barnard identified the organization leader as a communicative link among organization members. The executive must use communication

Case 4.1

It's as Easy as ABC

Jack Black is president of ABC Ski Company, a small ski-manufacturing firm located in Boulder, Colorado, and owned by a large California-based sporting-goods corporation, Western Sports. Black began ABC 10 years ago on a small scale and built it up himself until last year, when he sold ABC to Western Sports for $500,000 and a lifetime position as company president, with minimal interference from Western as long as the company continues to make a profit. Black is 28 years old and began designing and building skis at 16 in his parents' garage, forming ABC two years later. When he was 24, he designed a pair of skis that were used by the United States Olympic ski team. Just before selling to Western, he designed and built skis specifically for former president Gerald Ford, which he gave to Ford as a present at Vail, Colorado, bringing a great deal of public acclaim to Jack Black and ABC Ski Company. Black is very involved with the art of ski making, perceives himself as a master craftsman, and spends most of his time thinking about and designing skis. The only sign of his recent wealth is his new Ferrari sports car, which he bought after selling to Western. He is usually very reserved and does not have many close friends. He did not go to college, but is self-educated.

ABC Ski Company employs 24 people, 4 of whom are management (including Jack Black). Ken Green is the general manager at ABC. He is 45 years old, has a B.A. in management, and has worked at ABC for 5 years. He had 11 years' management experience in the sporting-goods field before starting at ABC. He handles employment and personnel, and supervises the ski-finishing process. Len Blue was hired one month ago as line supervisor. He was hired to assume some of Black's supervisory functions so that Black can spend more time on design. Blue is 34 years old, has an M.B.A., and worked in a management capacity in an automotive-parts factory for nine years; he did not have prior experience in the sporting-goods field. Blue supervises the production line. Laura Brown is the comptroller and has worked for ABC for two years. She is 25 years old and has a high-school education. She worked as a secretary and clerical office worker before coming to ABC. In addition to working with Black in keeping the books and accounting records for ABC, she handles quality control. She has been dating Black for the past year and a half. Brown does not mingle with the other employees at ABC.

There are 20 workers at ABC Ski Company. All are males with

high-school educations and range in age from 19 to 53 years. None has worked for ABC for more than two years. The workers are divided into four work groups: the production line (with eight workers), finishing (with seven workers), material handling (with three workers), and warehousing (with two workers). The line cuts the skis. The finishers smooth and polish the skis. The material handlers prepare the materials that are made into skis. The warehousers take care of shipping, handling, and maintenance.

The workers are unhappy at ABC. They often complain of low wages, lack of advancement opportunities, and poor equipment. There is a very high turnover rate of workers at ABC. Management does not seem to care, since there is a large labor pool available in the Boulder area to replace disenchanted workers. ABC has no seniority program, and regardless of how long a worker has been employed by ABC or how much experience he has, he receives the same pay as all other workers and wields the same authority as all other workers. The workers resent Laura Brown, who gives the finishers a hard time about the quality of finished skis. They feel that she rejects good skis for no apparent reason. They believe that Black hired her solely for her good looks. The workers also dislike Len Blue, who they claim "runs the production line like Marines boot camp." They respect Black, but when they have lodged work-related complaints with him, he has failed to make changes. In worker disputes concerning Brown or Blue, Black has always supported management. When workers complain about similar problems to Green, he refers them to Black.

Every month or so, Black posts a sign on a Friday afternoon to announce a company meeting for that evening at 6:30. The workday ends at 6:00 P.M. for the workers. When workers have attended these meetings and made demands, Black always agrees to make changes but has never delivered. Last Friday, at one such meeting, in an effort to increase ski production for the Christman rush, Black announced a prize of a pair of skis for the coming week's best worker. The word of the prize got around the workers quickly, and they worked hard that week to earn the skis. At the end of the week, no announcement about a winner was made. When asked by the workers, Black replied, "None of you worked hard enough."

This was the last straw for a few of the workers, and they decided to send a written complaint to the State Office of Safety and Health accusing ABC of poor ventilation, unsafe equipment, and inadequate medical facilities. The workers really did not care about any of these conditions, but knew that based on the complaint, the State Office would close ABC during the busy Christmas season. They felt that it was their only way to get back at the system.

to facilitate cooperation among organization members representing all levels and divisions of the organization. Barnard regarded communication as the most essential ingredient of organization. In fact, he asserted that "an organization comes into being when (1) there are persons able to communicate with one another (2) who are willing to contribute action (3) to accomplish a common purpose. The elements of an organization are therefore (1) communication; (2) willingness to serve; and (3) common purpose" (1968, p. 82). Barnard identified communication as a management tool for eliciting cooperation from individual organization members.

Consistent with Barnard's focus on communicating with the worker, the human-relations theory of organization identified the individual organization member as the most important variable in organizations. Human-relations theorists asserted that in order for organizations to function effectively, the needs of individual members have to be satisfied. The most important of these needs are self-actualization needs. (In Chapter 8, when we discuss organization member motivation, we will examine Maslow's hierarchy of needs, in which self-actualization is the top human need.)

Human-relations theory suggested the development of humanistic management, which acknowledges that it is important for organization leaders to determine the individual needs of organization members. This can be accomplished only through effective management–worker communication. Once worker needs are identified, the activities that will be most fulfilling (actualizing) for individual organization members should be designed into their tasks. Human-relations theory posited that increased involvement, recognition, responsibility, decision making, and opportunities for creativity make jobs more fulfilling for most people and lead to more effective, satisfying, and humanizing organizations.

CHAPTER 5

The Social-Systems Theory of Organization

ORGANIZATION AS SOCIAL SYSTEM

The social-systems approach to organizational behavior is a comprehensive, multidimensional, descriptive perspective on organization. Systems theorists assert that all organized entities demonstrate similar sets of properties and patterns. Systems theory developed as a means of describing the sets of properties and patterns that enable organization to occur.

Systems theory provides a powerful descriptive model of organizational processes. It has enjoyed many applications and has been used to describe organizational phenomena in a host of contexts. For example, some of the widespread applications of systems theory are in the biological sciences (Bertalanffy, 1951, 1952), describing the way that different chemical components are coordinated to enable living systems to exist; in the social sciences and economics (Boulding, 1952), describing the multivariate social and environmental influences on economic and social structures; in philosophy and semantics (Korzybski, 1948), describing the dynamic ways that human beings use language and other symbols to create reality; and in engineering and physics (Wiener, 1948), describing the way that cybernetic mechanisms could be designed to demonstrate artificial intelligence. Indeed, the model is so encompassing and heuristic and has so many disciplinary versions that the generic title general-systems theory was coined to describe its widespread applications.

A logical application of systems thinking was in describing the development, structure, and maintenance of human organizations. As such, general-systems theory was adopted as a model for describing organizational behavior (Katz and Kahn, 1978; Miller, 1972). Proponents of systems-theory approaches to organizations argued that classical theory and human-relations theory are overly simplistic and prescriptive, failing to fully describe the multivariate emergent properties of organization. Systems theory, they claimed, does capture the complex interrelated nature of human organizations and describe the means by which such organizations develop and grow. In this chapter, we will examine some of the key properties of general-systems theory, describing how they relate to modern organizations. We will also explore some of the implications of systems thinking for directing organizational communication.

GENERAL-SYSTEMS THEORY OF ORGANIZATION

General-systems theory represents the organization as a complex set of *interdependent* parts that interact to adapt to a constantly changing environment in order to achieve its goals. Some of the key components that make up organizations are individual organization members, structural and functional groups (such as departments or work units), and organizational technologies and equipment. All the system parts are dependent on one another in the performance of organizational activities. Any change in or influence on one component inevitably affects other system components.

Organizations are systems. Every system takes in resources, or *inputs*, from its environment, processes these inputs, and exports products, or *outputs*, to its environment. The output of a system is never the same as the input. The organization does something to process the inputs to create an output that will help achieve the organization's goals. The mediating process of interaction among system parts and between the system and its environment allows the organization to create an ouptut that is more than just the materials and information that the organization started out with as inputs. The combined and coordinated activities of all the system components create a synergy, or added energy, to the output of the system, allowing the system to transform raw materials into advantageous finished products.

System processes are *nonsummative*, which implies that the synergistic aspects of system processes are not merely additive but that the processes of all system parts combine to accomplish far more than they could individually. *The whole is equal to more than the sum of its parts.* Or, by working together, members of an organizational system

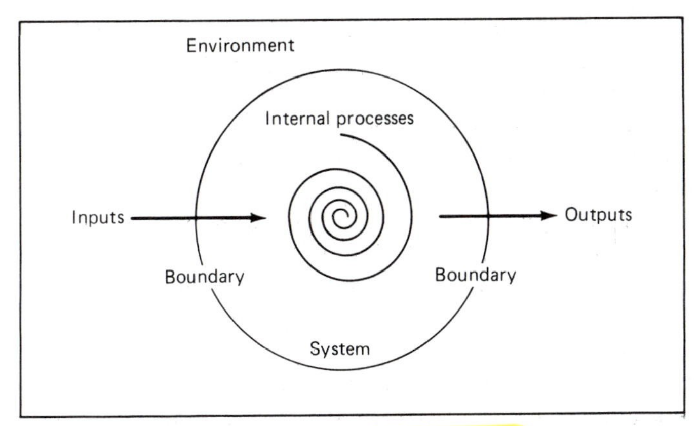

Figure 5.1 The system transformation model.

can do far more to achieve organizational goals than they can by working independently. This nonsummative nature of cooperative activities in organizations indicates, as we pointed out in Chapter 1 and in Chapter 4 (recall the work of Barnard, Likert, and Argyris), the importance of teamwork in organizational practice.

Furthermore, the systems-theory principle of *equifinality* infers that the final state of a system's output is not determined by the initial conditions, or inputs, confronting the system, but the same final conditions can be reached by the system from different initial conditions in many different ways (Bertalanffy, 1968). The interaction among system parts allows the system as a whole to act creatively in the processing of different inputs in different ways to produce appropriate outputs for achieving its goals. This indicates that organizations, through the interdependent efforts of their members, have the ability to perform many different activities to achieve a wide range of goals beginning from a variety of conditions by adapting the activities of its personnel and utilizing its organizational resources flexibly. Communication is the means by which organizations can adapt personnel and processes to the specific situations and problems they face.

As we have indicated, the system (or organization) transforms raw materials (inputs) from its environment into finished products (outputs) that help it achieve its goals. This is known as the *transformation model* (Figure 5.1). Every organization must import resources and raw materials from its environment—customers, money, technologies, materials, foods, or personnel—and export products to its environment—retail goods, entertainment, processed information, or serviced customers. The system imports and exports materials through its *boundaries*. As we will describe in depth in Chapter 6, the boundaries of the system play an important role in selecting, evaluating, and utilizing the inputs and outputs of the system.

Communication occurs at various *levels* within the system. There is communication among the parts of the system; there is communication within each part; there is communication between the system and its *environment*. This communication enables the different parts of the system to coordinate their activities. For example, in a company that produces widgets (a fictitious salable product), we might identify the sales department and the production department as two interrelated organizational subunits. These two departments must coordinate their efforts. If the sales department promises 200 widgets to customers and the production department builds only 100 widgets, there will be organizational problems. Through interdepartmental communications, these two related departments can share relevant information and coordinate their activities. These organizational subunits must maintain a *homeostatic balance* with each other to enable them to adequately perform their organizational functions.

To maintain a productive balance of activities, each department sends feedback loops to the other. These feedback loops are used to adjust and correct the other department's activities to maintain a homeostatic balance. There are two types of feedback loops: positive-feedback loops and negative-feedback loops. *Positive-feedback loops* are deviation amplifying. That is, they encourage the other subunit to move from a steady state and perform a specified new behavior. *Negative-feedback loops* are deviation counteracting. That is, they encourage the subunit to refrain from a certain activity and return to a steady state. In the widget-production-company example, the sales department, after securing contracts for 200 widgets, would contact the production department, sending the production department a positive-feedback loop requesting increased production of widgets. As soon as 200 widgets were built, the sales department would send the production department a negative-feedback loop, asking its representatives to stop building widgets and to return to a steady state. This is a rather simple two-department example of how homeostatic balance is maintained between system components. In actual practice, many feedback loops are sent among organizational components, some of which are complied with and others of which are rejected.

There are several *hierarchical levels* to systems analysis. Any organism or mechanism that processes raw materials into finished products through the combined efforts (processing) of its components is a *system*. Those internal parts of the system that do the active processing of inputs into outputs are known as subsystems. Each subsystem works interdependently with other subsystems in the accomplishment of system goals.

In an educational organization (system), such as a university, the components (subsystems) might be the various functional units of the organization, such as the School of Medicine, the School of Arts and Sciences, the School of Business Administration, the School of Pharmacy, the Graduate School, and the School of Social Work. These organizational subsystems are dependent on one another in the performance of the overall goals of the organizational system (university). Every system is itself a part of a larger system known as a *suprasystem*, perhaps an organization of related institutions (the Ivy League Conference or the Pacific Ten Conference of universities).

Even though we have identified only three successively larger levels of systems analysis—subsystem, system, suprasystem—this does not mean that there always are only three levels to any organization. Any of the system levels can be viewed as either subsystem, system, or suprasystem, building *macroscopically* to larger and larger levels of organization or dissecting *microscopically* to smaller and smaller units of organization. For example, we might have focused initially on the School of Arts and Sciences as a system. This school is composed of a variety of subsystems, for example, the departments of English, biology, sociology, political science, and so on. The suprasystem surrounding the system of the School of Arts and Sciences is the university as a whole. The School of Arts and Sciences interacts with the other schools within the university to accomplish the goals of the university. One of the major attributes of systems thinking is that it allows the organizational analyst the opportunity to examine both the "big-picture" view of an organization and the components view of the organization (Figure 5.2).

Relative Openness of Living Systems

The system's *environment* plays a large role in system functioning both by providing the system with raw materials to process and by creating markets and outlets for system outputs. Furthermore, the environment surrounds the system and affects the goals and operation of the system. Every system strives for survival, even though environmental demands challenge its survival. The *second law of thermodynamics* asserts that every system inevitably moves toward disorganization (Bertalanffy, 1968). The process of organizing and reorganizing is used to resist this natural threat to system survival. This indicates the constant struggle in systems between entropy and negative entropy. *Entropy*, the end product described by the second law of thermodynamics, is total disorganization. *Negative entropy* is the system's ability to resist entropy, develop organization, and grow. Negative entropy allows the organization to survive; whole entropy causes the organization to deteriorate.

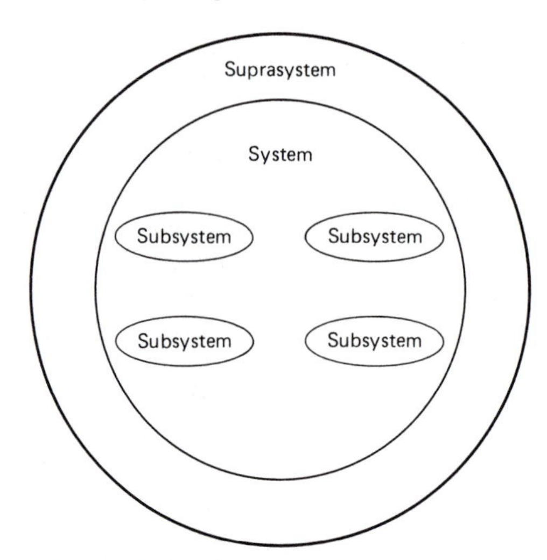

Figure 5.2 Hierarchical system levels.

To maintain negative entropy and survive, every system must generate more energy from its processes than it expends in gathering inputs and transforming them into outputs. In other words, a system must maintain a positive balance between energy expended and energy generated in order to survive. Two examples make this system notion extremely clear, one from biology and the other from business. Biologically, if you exert more energy in breathing, digesting, and doing other key biological processes than you gain from these processes, you will die. That is why individuals who have impairments in these biological processes generally are put on life-support machinery to help them perform the biological functions while expending less effort. Any businessperson knows that if you spend more money on producing a product than you generate by selling it, you probably will not last in business for very long because you will eventually dissipate your capital. By maintaining a positive balance between energy output and energy input, systems can resist entropy and demonstrate negative entropy.

System openness refers to the degree to which organizations are responsive to their environments. No living system is an island. Every system is influenced by and influences its environment. If we stretch the idea of hierarchical system levels we discussed earlier, every system is intimately connected to its environment. From a macroscopic perspective, each system is also a subsystem of a larger system, its suprasystem, and must work with other subsystems to enable the larger system to resist entropy and survive. Therefore, all systems must interact with their environments.

Systems range from being relatively *open* to the environment to being relatively *closed* to the environment. This is known as *relative openness*. No living system is ever totally open or totally closed to its environment. It is impossible for an organization to completely ignore all messages from its environment or to perceive all messages from its environment. Systems are also relatively open or closed to their environments in terms of the amount of information they export. As we discussed in Chapter 2, it is impossible to perceive all the information that is available in any given situation because of both sensory and cognitive space limitations of decoding processes. It is impossible to convey the entirety of meanings into organizational messages because of the limitations of encoding processes. Moreover, as in interpersonal communication, organizations disclose information selectively to their environments. Organizations, like human beings, must selectively attend to key information from their environments, and it is wise for organization members to communicate key organizational information to their environments strategically. (We will discuss some of the issues involved in the selection and dissemination of organizational information more fully in Chapter 10.)

It is not always best to be too open or too closed in giving or receiving information, but it is sensible to adapt the system's level of openness to its environment in response to the situation at hand. For example, in times of great social turmoil and change, it is wise for the organization to keep close tabs on social changes to monitor the influences of these changes on its operations. In this situation, relative openness is an effective communication strategy for the organization to adopt. In times of complex changes within the organization, it is best for the system to expend its energy on coordinating its own processes rather than on monitoring and communicating exclusively with its environment. In this situation, being relatively closed is an effective communication strategy for the organization to adopt. (We will discuss this notion of focusing organizational attention on internal matters in times of internal stress and on external matters in times of external stress in much greater depth in Chapter 11.)

It is, however, important for organization members to be aware of what is going on in the organization's environment to help plan for future demands. Being aware of the kinds of environmental constraints that are most likely to impinge on the functioning of the organization most certainly helps the organization gather appropriate personnel and resources to deal with potential problems and issues. As the environment changes, the organization should make changes in its operations and resources to meet new constraints. It often becomes too late for organizational representatives to merely react to environmental changes and demands in the business world. By the time organization members have gathered new resources and devised new plans for meeting changing constraints, the problem may have overcome the organization.

In the modern world, where environmental change often occurs rapidly and many constraints face the organization, an organization leader must learn to be *proactive*, to gather information from the organization's environment about imminent problems and to plan organizational strategies for meeting them. (In Chapter 8, we will examine the importance of proactive planning by organizational leadership.) For example, members of a health-care organization might act proactively by developing specialized procedures and methods to process and treat flood victims in an area where flooding is a strong possibility. It might be too late to develop and implement these methods when a flood occurs, but having them available makes the health-care organization better able to cope with potential health-care demands brought on by its environment. This need for acting proactively and innovatively is important not only in health-care organizations, but in all organizations. (In Chapter 11, we will discuss the essential nature of organizational adaptation and innovation, relating adaptation to organizational effectiveness.)

As you read Case 5.1, evaluate how proactive Sprint Air Freight was. See if you can perform a systems analysis of Sprint Air Freight.

1. Can you identify some of the hierarchical system levels within Sprint Air Freight? What are some of the primary components of each system level? Do these components maintain a homeostatic balance? Are feedback loops used effectively?
2. Identify the transformation process used at Sprint. What are the inputs? What is the process? What are the outputs? Is the company maintaining an advantageous balance between input and output? Does Sprint demonstrate the principle of equifinality?
3. How open is Sprint to its environment? Is its level of openness appropriate to its environmental situation? What strategies do you suggest for Sprint Air Freight to help it resist entropy?

Emphasis on Functional Integration

Systems theory seems to be more closely aligned to the classical theory of organization than to the human-relations theory. Systems theory is functionally oriented toward system goal accomplishment. The theory is more comprehensive than classical theory and less punitive to organization members. In fact, there is little concern for the individual organization member in systems theory. As in classical theory, individ-

Case 5.1

Sprint Air Freight

Sprint Air Freight is a multimillion-dollar commercial-freight forwarder, acting as an agent for various companies and arranging transportation for these organizations' industrial cargo. Sprint Air Freight is one of the pioneer companies in the air-freight-forwarding business. It handles primarily domestic and international cargo moving by air, but also handles some shipping (ocean) and trucking cartage.

Sprint's air-transport business is separated into domestic and international operations. Domestic air transportation is controlled by the Los Angeles main office, supervising its 17 branch offices in San Francisco, New York, Chicago, Dallas, Philadelphia, Pittsburgh, Boston, Atlanta, Denver, Detroit, Minneapolis, Miami, Tampa, Seattle, Phoenix, Portland, and Honolulu. The company also has a network of 30 independent air-freight agents in smaller American cities where it would be unprofitable for Sprint to set up its own offices. International air freight is controlled by the New York office (New York being the company's primary point of international-cargo departure and arrival). The New York office supervises 35 overseas agents (15 in Europe, 5 in Asia, 5 in South America, and 5 in Africa and the Middle East). Additionally, the New York office handles any international freight originating at any of the Sprint domestic offices.

Sprint is a service organization. It arranges its customers' cargo pick up, storage, delivery to and pick up from carriers, delivery to final destination, preparation of all documents, payment of carriers, and insurance of cargo, and it keeps a written record of all shipped goods and costs. Sprint has stressed personalized service to its customers as one of its chief advantages over its competitors, and Sprint has lived up to its claim of personal service, even though the company's rapid growth sometimes has made this difficult.

In the early 1970s, Sprint Air Freight was at the peak of its organizational growth, making approximately $2 million profit per year. At this high point in Sprint's sales growth, it held a 14 percent share of the air-freight-forwarding market and was ranked as the third largest combined domestic- and international-air-freight forwarder in the world (and was rapidly threatening to overtake the number 1 and 2 freight forwarders). Since the early 1970s, however, Sprint's sales growth and profits have steadily eroded and decreased. At the end of fiscal year 1979, it was running in the red by approximately $1 million and was considering either declaring Chapter 11 or bankruptcy, merging with another forwarder, or revamping its organizational structure and marketing approach.

Before taking any of these courses of action, Sprint's board of directors hired an external consultant to evaluate its organizational situation. The consultant provided the board of directors with a report that identified four major problems the company had faced since the early 1970s that may have been causing its financial problems:

1. Steady decrease in sales and loss of many large customers.
2. Increases in operating costs due to unionization of truck drivers, warehouse workers, and office personnel, who demanded pay raises with the threat of a strike in many of Sprint's larger offices (New York, Los Angeles, Chicago, San Francisco, and Miami). Additional higher operating costs due to inflation, causing increases in the price of fuel, loading equipment, and other supplies.
3. The long time-lag between Sprint's appeals to the Civil Aeronautics Board to raise its rates (in accordance with airline rate hikes that the CAB had approved). Sprint had to absorb the additional costs of paying the airlines higher rates while their freight-forwarding rates were frozen.
4. High international inflationary trend, upsetting the balance of international monetary values, made it difficult for many foreign markets to purchase American goods, which had been forwarded by air. This resulted in a decreased demand for international freight-forwarding services.

The consultant also noted that Sprint's chief competitor, Johnson Air Freight, the largest air-freight forwarder for the past two decades, had steadily increased its market share and profits since the early 1970s. For example, Johnson Air Freight's market share in 1970 was 21 percent, and by fiscal year 1979, its market share had increased to 27 percent of the domestic- and international-air-cargo business. Sprint Air Freight and Johnson Air Freight had faced many of the same increases in operating costs and foreign-market problems, yet Johnson had been able to enhance its sales in the private sector, selling air-freight services to many small customers and not depending so much on a few very large customers.

The Sprint board of directors evaluated the information available to them and pondered the best action to take.

ual organization members are subordinated to the accomplishment of organizational goals. The central unit of analysis in the systems approach is not the individual organization member, as in the human-relations theory, but the interdependent activities of functional organizational units. The key element of the systems-theory approach to organizations is the emphasis on the functional integration of system units in the accomplishment of organizational activities.

There are four important implications of systems theory for organizational analysis and organizational communication.

First, *interdependence* implies that all parts of the organization are interrelated. For the organization to operate effectively, all functional units within the organization have to be coordinated. This coordination can be elicited only through communication, which is used both to inform interdependent components of changes and to persuade components to cooperate by coordinating activities. This interdependence also refers to the interrelationships between the system and its surrounding environment.

Second, *openness* implies that the organization must be aware of changes in its environment. Because the environment can constrain organizational activities, organization members must actively communicate with representatives of relevant organizations within the system's environment both to determine the nature of environmental constraints and to influence the activities of those organizations. (In Chapter 10, we discuss the ways that external communication channels are used in organizations to establish coordination among organizations.)

Third, *microscopic and macroscopic analytic framework* implies that there are many levels of organization within any organization. To understand an organization, we have to microscopically interpret the inner workings of the system as well as macroscopically examine the interrelationships between the organization and its environment. Classical theory and human-relations theory emphasized primarily microscopic internal concerns of organizations. Systems theory identifies the external influences on organizations. This also introduces the importance of both internal channels of organizational communication and external channels of organizational communication, suggesting how these channels work together. (In Chapter 11, we will examine how internal and external organizational communication channels can be coordinated to promote organizational effectiveness.)

Fourth, *organizational adaptation and innovation* implies that organizations are not static entities, as classical theory sometimes seems to suggest. Organizations must be flexible and adaptive, continually innovating to meet the changing constraints of the system environment.

External channels of communication are utilized to gather relevant information from the environment to inform organization members about needs for innovation. These external channels of communication also are used to inform and influence relevant organizations in the system environment.

CHAPTER 6

Weick's Model of Organizing

ORGANIZATION AS RESPONSE TO INFORMATION EQUIVOCALITY

In this chapter, we will examine a theory of organizing proposed by Karl Weick that describes the organizing process in terms of resolving the ambiguities (equivocality) inherent in the problems that human beings confront. These ambiguities are resolved organizationally through collective information processing. Weick (1979) argues that human beings organize primarily to help them reduce the information uncertainty they face in their lives. He explains that people are confronted by many complex, difficult, unpredictable, and equivocal problems and issues in life. (Not the least of which is the most basic of problems: how to survive and prosper.) Each of the issues confronting an individual presents him or her with an information-processing problem: "What does this situation mean?" "How can I respond appropriately to this situation?" Many of the issues are so challenging that they are virtually impossible for any one person to interpret and resolve individually. We need help from other people, so we organize. Weick explains that we join with others to cooperatively interpret complex problems and develop meaningful strategies for accomplishing our individual and group goals.

Weick asserts that the more equivocal the information-based problems, the more we need help from others in coping with them. Organizations have developed as social systems for resolving equivocality and increasing the certainty of life. Organizations are established to undertake many of the more difficult tasks that human beings face. As we discussed in Chapter 1, organizations perform many functions for human beings, providing shelter, sustenance, social support, and a sense of identity (as we will see in Chapter 7). Organizations exist because life is complex.

WEICK'S MODEL OF ORGANIZING

In 1969, Karl Weick published his influential book, *The Social Psychology of Organizing*, in which he presented a process-oriented model of organizing, stressing human interaction as the central phenomenon of organization. Weick contends that organizations do not exist but are in the process of existing through continual streams of organized human activities. Communication is the crucial process performed by organization members to enable this ongoing organization to occur. In the theory, Weick traces the specific communicative activities in which individuals engage to demonstrate organization and describes the information-processing functions of organizing.

Theoretical Underpinnings

Weick's theory and its corresponding model are built on three primary theoretical foundations: sociocultural evolutionary theory, information theory, and systems theory. Weick adopts different pieces of each perspective and adapts them to organizational analysis. By combining aspects of these three theories, Weick derives the major themes of his model.

Sociocultural evolutionary theory describes the processes by which people adapt to changes in their social and cultural environments. The theory is derived from the biologically based organic-evolution theory suggested by Charles Darwin in his famous treatise *The Origin of Species* (1948, originally published in 1859). Organic evolution describes the biological adaptation of organisms through the natural selection of advantageous genetic mutations. For example, certain mammals were able to adapt to cold climates through the natural selection of such useful mutations as hairy coats and warm-bloodedness (Nason, 1968). Although organic evolution is an effective survival tool, it is extremely slow and haphazard. A species might have to wait thousands of years for a single advantageous mutation to appear—not very comforting when there is a problem to deal with right now. In response to myriad imminent social and environmental threats, human beings developed more rapid, behaviorally based evolutionary strategies. Building on this perspective, Campbell (1965) explained the manner in which people change their behaviors in response to social pressures by

Figure 6.1

The Sociocultural Evolutionary Process

Variation of random behavioral deviations	*Selection* of potentially advantageous deviations	*Retention* of most adaptive behavioral deviations

devising strategies and social innovations that help them survive. For example, in response to cold climates, different groups of people created behavioral innovations to help them survive, such as making warm clothing from animal skins, building shelters out of stone and wood, and using fire for heat.

The sociocultural evolutionary process involves the interrelated processes of variation, selection, and retention of socially advantageous behavioral innovations (Figure 6.1). The innovations that occur during the variation stage become the pool of potential adaptive responses from which the organism or social group can choose when confronted with environmental changes. In organic-evolution theory, variations are in terms of biological mutations. In sociocultural evolutionary theory, the variation process is manifested by the development of adaptive behaviors and norms for behavior by people in response to their social pressures. The most advantageous variations are selected by the cultural group for use and retained as functional attributes of the cultural group. Weick borrows this three-stage model of adaptation, modifying it to the three phases of organizing: enactment, selection, and retention. (We will describe these three phases in depth later in the chapter.)

Information theory is concerned with the efficiency of message transmission. Shannon and Weaver (1949), the major proponents of information theory, attempted to discover how to send telegraphic messages as efficiently as possible without loss of information between sender and receiver. Information theory is concerned neither with individual interpretations of messages nor with the behavioral effects of messages. Instead, it deals with the structural relationships between message codes and channel capacities (Broadhurst and Darnell, 1965). By identifying these relationships, information theorists attempt to discover "how to send a message through a communication system having a source with certain characteristics and a channel with certain characteristics, doing this with maximum efficiency and a tolerable level of error or equivocation in the presence of noise" (Darnell, 1972, p. 158). In other words, how to eliminate message distortion between source and receiver, increasing the fidelity of message transmission.

The concept of information in information theory does not refer to meanings that people create in response to messages. Information refers to "what you don't know about what is going to happen next" (Darnell, 1972, p. 159). Something has information value if it reduces a receiver's uncertainty and increases the predictability of future messages. Information helps to reduce the number of decisions an individual has to make, increasing the certainty with which an individual can direct his or her behaviors. Information theory posits that different channels have differing capacities for handling ambiguity. In order to reduce the receiver's uncertainty in communication, appropriate message codes must be matched with specific channel capacities to provide the receiver with information.

Weick integrates the concept of uncertainty from information theory into his theory of organizing. In information theory, information is used to reduce uncertainty. In Weick's theory of organizing, organization members attempt to reduce uncertainty by generating information through the use of rules and cycles. Weick's concept of equivocality is virtually identical to Shannon and Weaver's (1949) concept of uncertainty. In information theory, specific message codes are adapted to specific channel capacities to reduce uncertainty and increase information. In Weick's theory of organizing, specific rules and cycles are adapted to informational inputs to bring the information to an optimal level of equivocality (certainty) for the organization members. In essence, organization members attempt to transform equivocal information inputs into more predictable, less equivocal messages. Different organizations, just like different individuals or different channels, have differing capacities for handling the equivocality inherent in different information inputs and must make use of appropriate rules and cycles in response to its capacities and message inputs. The relationship that Weick proposes between organizational inputs and information-processing strategies is very similar to the relationship posited in information theory between message codes and channel capacities. (Later in this chapter, we will clarify the specific nature of organizational rules and cycles and describe how they are used in organizational information processing.)

General-systems theory, which we examined in Chapter 5, attempts to explain complex organizational processes with a highly flexible analytical structure. As we noted earlier, systems theory identifies different hierarchical levels of complexity: the system, the subsystem, and the suprasystem. The concept of interdependent parts is crucial to the systems approach. Each level of organization is composed of interconnected and mutually influenced components, each of which performs a functional process for the system level of which it is a part. It is the combination of all the functional processes of these system components that allows the system to exist and adapt to its environment. If the performance of any component or group of components is impeded within a system, the performance of all other components will be influenced. This interdependence of system components indicates a need to view the system as a whole because it is the joint efforts of all the system components that transforms system inputs into system outputs. This transformation is the central focus of systems analysis. The concept of equifinality indicates that the output of the system is never equivalent to the input; the mediating process of functional interaction among system components creates system outputs (Bertalanffy, 1968).

Feedback between system components is a major part of general-systems theory. The cybernetic concepts of positive- and negative-feedback loops provide a homeostatic mechanism for monitoring system activities. Positive-feedback loops between system components send deviation-amplifying instructions, while negative-feedback loops between system components send deviation-counteracting instructions. Through the use of these feedback loops, certain system processes can be either facilitated or inhibited according to the needs of the system as a whole.

Weick adopts a great deal of systems theory in developing his theory of organizing. Like the systems model of organizations, Weick's organizing model can be applied to a multitude of organizing contexts and hierarchical organizational levels. It is a model of the organizing process, not of a particular organization. The basic organizing processes that occur at one level of Weick's model occur at both higher and lower hierarchical levels. All the phases and subprocesses within Weick's model of organizing are mutually dependent. The whole process of organizing is more than the sum of the processes used in organizing. It is by creatively adapting organizational activities to specific information inputs that organization members can transform these inputs into appropriate functional outputs. Moreover, Weick identifies feedback loops that allow organization members to maintain a homeostatic balance of organizing processes. Weick's theory of organizing conforms neatly with the systems concepts of hierarchy, interdependent parts, nonsummativity, equifinality, the transformation model, homeostatic balance, and cybernetic feedback loops.

Information Environment

An important part of Weick's model is the organizational environment. Environment, according to Weick, is not the physical surroundings (buildings, offices, equipment, people) that organization members encounter, but the information to which they react. Thus the focus on organizational environment shifts from a traditional structural, static view of physical surroundings to an action, process view of the messages that organization members perceive and the meanings that they create in response to these messages.

The concept of organizational environment, according to Weick, can be conceptualized as a communication construct. Human interactions and the messages that link communicators become the crucial units of analysis in studying organizations. Instead of focusing on the physical structures and technologies of organizations, organizational analysts are directed by Weick to focus on the human communication processes used in organizing.

Organizations rely on a variety of sources of information in organizing, including interviews, sales calls, letters, documents, telephone conversations, or group discussions. In a medical organization, health-care personnel rely heavily on medical records, patient charts, lab reports, nursing reports, and practitioner–patient interviews as sources of information in performing their organizational tasks. Recall Case 1.2, which discussed the hospital as an information system. How well did the members of the Veterans Administration hospital use information sources to perform their tasks? Not very well. It was because they did not maintain information about Erwin Pawelski that he was "lost" within the hospital complex for such a long period of time. Automobile shops utilize information derived from customer–mechanic interactions, from discussions among mechanics or between mechanics and parts suppliers, and from diagnostic examinations of injured automobiles to aid them in the process of organizing. These are some examples of the primary sources of information used in two types of organizations, hospitals and automobile shops. Many more potential information sources make up an organization's information environment. The wide variety of messages interpreted by organization members in the performance of their tasks is the information environment in which the organization resides.

Weick takes a phenomenological tack when arguing the primacy of information environments over structural environments. He asserts that since human beings actively create the world around them through perception, organization members do not merely *react* to an objectively accepted physical environment but *enact* their environment through information and the creation of meaning. The organization's environment is derived from the exchange of messages and creation of meaning by organization members. Organizing occurs within the context of human interaction. Weick explains, "Rather than talking about adapting to an external environment, it may be more correct to argue that organizing consists of adapting to an enacted environment, an environment which is constituted by the actions of interdependent human actors" (1969, p. 27). Weick's model is thus a representation of how organization members react to the information that surrounds their organization. The processes used by organization members to respond to the organization's information environment are communication processes.

Information Equivocality

A crucial part of Weick's model of organizing is the concept of information equivocality. *Equivocality* is the level of understandability of messages to which organization members respond. Some aspects of equivocality are the level of ambiguity, complexity, and obscurity of messages. The equivocality of a message relates to the certainty with which an organization member can decode that message. Weick uses equivocality much as information theorists use the concept of uncertainty. Recall that according to information theory, a message has information value if it helps the receiver figure out what comes next in a string of messages. Weick asserts that organization members attempt to process equivocal information so they can predict future information and respond to information inputs with appropriate organizational actions.

Organizations are necessary because they help people deal with complex phenomena. Organization members perform communication processes designed to cope with information equivocality. It is this ability to cope with equivocal information that Weick refers to as the process of organizing: "Organizing consists of the resolving of equivocality in an enacted environment by means of interlocked behaviors embedded in conditionally related processes" (1969, p. 91).

Organizations strive to manage equivocality, to maintain a balance between highly equivocal and highly unequivocal messages. Each organization processes the messages it has to deal with in an attempt to transform these information inputs into understandable and predictable messages. Highly equivocal (very complicated) message inputs must be processed by the organization. The ambiguity of the information must be worked out in order for the organization to create appropriate reactions to the information input. For example, in an uncertain product market, leaders of a production company must gather information to determine what types of products will sell and how their company can produce and sell these products at a profit. The uncertain market conditions are high-equivocality message inputs. If the production company is to survive, it must reduce the equivocality of the situation to predict the best possible business strategies to take.

"The activities of organizing are directed toward the establishment of a workable level of certainty. An organization attempts to transform equivocal information into a degree of unequivocality with which it can work and to which it is accustomed" (Weick, 1969, p. 40). Each organization develops its own communication processes to transform information inputs (messages) into their own optimal level of certainty. In the process of organizing, organization members develop communication processes that enable the organization to cope with information equivocality.

Organizations must react to message inputs with the same amount of equivocality that is present in the messages themselves. This is known as the principle of *requisite variety.* To cope with a very complex situation (high-equivocality information input), organizational representatives should perform a highly complex communication process to adequately handle the input. Conversely, to deal with easily understandable information (low-equivocality inputs), an organization should react with very clear, simple behaviors. Weick explains that "it takes equivocality to remove equivocality. This means that processes must have the same degree of order or chaos as there is in the input of these processes" (1969, p. 40).

Weick identifies two related communication processes used by organizations to cope with the level of equivocality of information inputs. These two processes are rules and communication-behavior cycles. *Rules* prescribe the two related activities that organization members perform in response to information inputs. First, rules are used to ascertain the level of familiarity, or equivocality, in any message input into the organization. Second, rules are used to search the pool of standardized message responses available to the organization that are compatible (appropriate) with the specific message input.

The organization usually can respond to simple (unequivocal) message inputs with preset rules. For example, form letters, catalogs, rate sheets, and printed directions are rules that are often used in formal organizations in response to common organizational inputs. If you write to a local university asking about admissions requirements, you probably will be sent a form letter or a catalog with the relevant organizational information. Assembly rules are very similar to human decoding and encoding processes (Chapter 2). Organization members decipher information inputs, interpreting the level of ambiguity of messages, just as an individual decodes messages in creating meanings for them. Organization members create their appropriate responses to information inputs just as an individual encodes message responses. Assembly rules allow the organization to determine the equivocality of message inputs and choose appropriate behavioral responses to these inputs.

Communication-behavior *cycles* are a series of interlocked communication behaviors among organization representatives that allow the organization to process highly equivocal information. Cycles are communication tools that the organization uses to reduce the equivocality of complex inputs. Weick describes a cycle as a double interact, a three-part exchange of conditionally related messages: act, response, and adjustment. For example, a factory worker might ask a co-worker, "How can I reset this machine?" (an act). The co-worker might answer, "Push this button and realign the guide" (a response). The first worker might react by saying, "Thanks, I'll try it" (an adjustment). The communication cycle is a double interact of communication behaviors that introduce an idea, respond to that idea, and adjust to the response. It is a means of gathering information and feedback. "Thus, the double interact specifies a behavioral unit of cybernetic form, casting the adjustment as a response to the response (feedback)" (Bantz, 1975, p. 3).

The more equivocal information inputs are for the organization, the more organization members must depend on performing communication cycles to cope with the input. Each cycle processes some equivocality out of the input, making it more understandable to the organization and enabling organization members to apply rules for responding to it. Not every cycle reduces the same amount of equivocality from an information input, but each cycle reduces some of the initial equivocality. For example, a highly irregular question from a customer cannot be answered adequately by a form letter; instead, the organization must perform a variety of new behaviors to competently handle the situation. If you sent a local university admissions office a letter with your transcript from a German university you attended, asking which course credits you received are transferable, the admissions officers probably would not be able to react adequately to your input with a form letter or other rule. Your request is rather equivocal, and the admissions office would have to perform a number of communication cycles to remove some of the equivocality before it could respond to your request. The officers might have to call the university library, asking the reference librarian to find out whether the German university you attended is accredited; they might have to ask a member of the German language faculty to translate your transcript into English; they also might confer with different departments to determine which courses are comparable to their courses and acceptable to them. Each of these cycles will help the admissions office demystify the information input you have introduced until an appropriate course of action (rules) can be applied to the problem. Each communication cycle removes some equivocality from the information input.

There are three major relationships among information equivocality, rules, and communication cycles posited in Weick's theory of organizing.

First, there is a direct relationship between the equivocality of information input into an organization and the organization's dependence on the performance of communication cycles to respond to the input. As equivocality increases, the organization will attempt to cope with these complex messages by acting out a series of communication cycles designed to process out enough equivocality from the messages to make them manageable for the organization. As equivocality decreases, there is less need for cycling out equivocality. The more equivocality, the greater the need for communication cycles, while the less the equivocality, the less the need for cycles.

Second, there is an inverse relationship between the equivocality of information input into an organization and the organization's dependence on rules for registering and composing organizational responses to the input. The less equivocal the input, the more the organization can depend on rules to guide organizational behaviors. There is no need for communication cycles to reduce the equivocality of an already easily understandable information input. The more equivocal the input, fewer rules are available to guide action, so communication cycles are needed.

Third, there is an inverse relationship between the organization's use of rules and the organization's need for performing communication cycles. When rules for dealing with an input are available to the organization, communication cycles become superfluous. When there are few rules to guide the organization, communication cycles are needed to resolve equivocality and create rules.

In summary of our discussion of equivocality, rules, and cycles, if the information input into an organization is highly equivocal the organization must rely on performing cycles to cope with the input; if the information input into the organization is unequivocal the organization can apply rules to the input for guiding organizational response to the input. The more equivocal messages input into the organization are, the more the communication cycles are needed to reduce the information equivocality to a manageable level. The less equivocal information inputs are, the more the organization can rely on communication rules to cope with the information situation. If information is very clear it becomes easy for the organization to register the amount of equivocality in the input and assign standardized behaviors to respond to the input. The more rules the organization has available to interpret and develop responses to message inputs, the fewer actual communication cycles have to be performed by organization members.

In Case 6.1, the mechanics at an auto-repair shop deal with some problems that are all in a day's work.

1. Identify the different information inputs into the Ace Auto-Repair Shop. How equivocal are these inputs?
2. Identify the different rules and cycles used by the organization. Are they used appropriately?

Case 6.1

Ace Auto-Repair Shop

At the Ace Auto-Repair Shop, customers tell the head mechanic, Harry, what they want him to have done to their automobiles. The mechanical problems and automotive services that these customers describe to Harry vary in their difficulty. Some of the problems are difficult because of the strange ways customers describe them. "My car is making a strange sound. Bop-pop-blam, bop-pop-blam, bop-pop-blam. Can you fix it quick?" It generally takes a lot of time and energy to determine the nature of these problems. Some of the problems are difficult because the customers ask the mechanics to perform strange and involved tasks. "Can you exchange the transmissions in my two cars?" Some of the problems can never be solved because the shop does not always have the equipment or expertise to get these jobs done. However, it is Harry's job as head mechanic to interpret the different problems customers bring him, determine what has to be done, figure out if the job can be done at the shop, estimate the cost and time required to do the repairs, and assign the task to one of his mechanics.

On Tuesday morning, Mrs. Blanchard, a regular customer at the shop, brought in her 1977 Chevy Impala and asked Harry to have a six-month tune-up performed on the car. Harry was able to easily interpret the job that Mrs. Blanchard wanted performed. She had been bringing her Chevy in for tune-ups every six months for the past five years, and the shop did a lot of tune-ups on Chevys. Harry knew that her tune-up would take about three hours to complete. He knew that Bob, who was working that morning in bay number 4, was the mechanic who always worked on Chevys. He knew, from experience, that the tune-up would cost Mrs. Blanchard about $45. He also knew that all the parts needed for the tune-up were available at the parts desk. Harry smiled at Mrs. Blanchard and said, "No problem, Ma'am; we will have the car ready for you by noon. I'll have Bob work on it right away. If there are no special problems, it will cost you approximately $45." Harry thought to himself, "I hope all of our customers have such easy requests today."

Right after Mrs. Blanchard left, however, a customer approached Harry with a humdinger of a problem. A gray-haired man asked Harry in an anxious, high-pitched voice, "Is the differential on my 1953 Studebaker Hawk compatible with the series C Nash Rambler autoglide transmission with manual overdrive, or do I have to modify the transaxle to handle the problem?" Harry sputtered, "Wait a second, Mister. Slow down. What is the problem?" The man explained his request further, "I'm certain the differential is slipping on my Studebaker. Its the original differential installed in the car. The repair shop down the street told me it needs to be adjusted or replaced, but they can't do the job. They suggested that I buy a new transaxle or junk my car. I refuse to give up!" "O.K., O.K.," said Harry, "calm down. I see what you're saying. But what is it that we can do for you, and what does it have to do with a Rambler transmission?" The man explained that he hoped the shop could fix the differential on his Studebaker, and if the mechanics needed any spare parts, he had a Rambler transmission that they could use. "Now it's getting clearer," said Harry.

Before Harry could determine what exactly to do and how to react to this request, he had to gather some information. He had to check with his mechanics, look at the car, look at the Rambler transmission, talk to his parts manager, and consult several repair manuals. After checking with these information sources, Harry knew a lot more about fixing Studebaker differentials. As it turned out, one of his mechanics knew quite a bit about Studebakers and was able to work on this man's car. The Rambler transmission was incompatible with the Studebaker, but the shop's parts department had some universal differentials that just might work on this Studebaker. "I think we may be able to help you, Sir," Harry told the customer.

3. How does this case demonstrate the principle of requisite variety?
4. How does this case demonstrate the three relationships among equivocality, rules, and communication cycles?

Enactment, Selection, and Retention

In the process of organizing, the organization goes through three major phases: enactment, selection, and retention. Rules and cycles are used in each of these phases, in which the level of equivocality of the input is ascertained, appropriate rules are selected (if available to the organization), or communication cycles are performed (if the input is too complex to be handled by rules). In each phase of organizing, information is processed through subprocesses of assembly rules and communication cycles (Figure 6.2).

In the *enactment* phase of organizing, the organization attends to the information environment that surrounds it. The organization recreates (or enacts) its environment in the sense that organization members assign meaning to information events through their decoding pro-

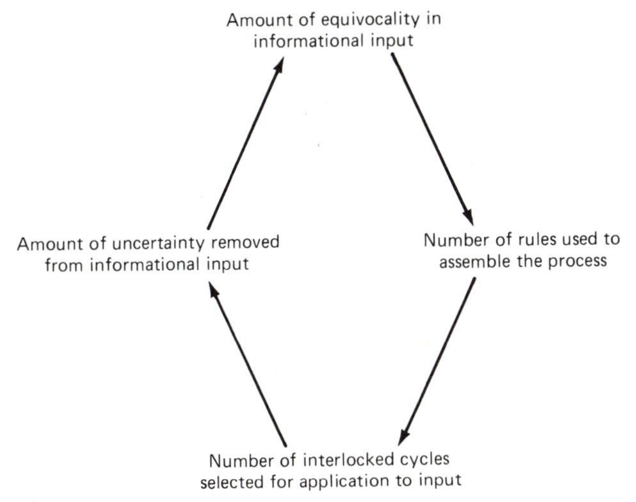

Figure 6.2 Sequence of a subprocess. Reprinted from Karl E. Weick, *The Social Psychology of Organizing*. Reading, Mass.: Addison-Wesley, 1969, p. 77.

cesses. During the enactment phase, the organization is made aware of changes in its information environment, the level of equivocality of information inputs is determined, and appropriate rules and cycles are called on to process the information inputs.

In the *selection* phase of organizing, decisions are made about how the rules and cycles used by the organization have affected the equivocality of the information inputs and which cycles should be repeated by the organization to further process the inputs. On the basis of decisions made in the selection phase, additional rules and cycles are chosen and repeated to continue reducing the level of equivocality of the messages imported into the organization, enabling the organization to better understand and react to the inputs.

In the *retention* phase of organizing, information about the ways the organization has responded to different inputs is gathered and stored. The various communication cycles developed and used by the organization to process equivocal information are evaluated for their usefulness to the organization, and if they are deemed to be successful strategies for coping with equivocal situations, they are made into rules for how the organization can respond to similar inputs in the future. A *repertoire of rules* is developed in the retention phase to be used as a form of *organizational intelligence* to guide organizational actions.

The enactment, selection, and retention phases of organizing work together in the process of organization, and feedback loops among the phases are used to coordinate their activities. *Feedback loops* are mes-

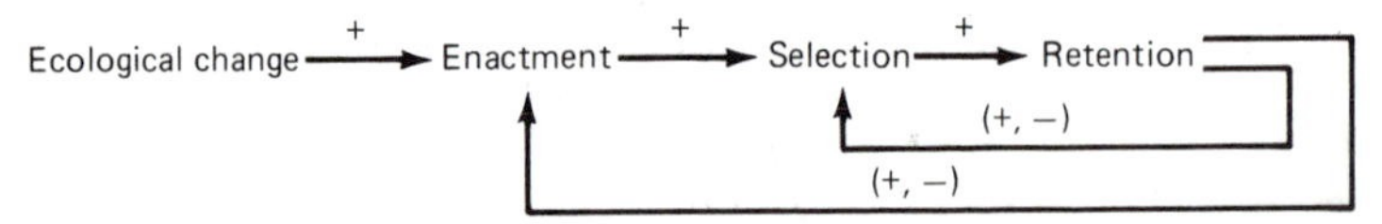

Figure 6.3 Organizing phases and feedback loops. Reprinted from Karl E. Weick, *The Social Psychology of Organizing*. Reading, Mass.: Addison-Wesley, 1969, p. 87.

sage systems connecting the phases, allowing coordinating communication among them. In his model of organizing, Weick identifies two feedback loops: one connects retention to enactment, and the other connects retention to selection. In this way, the retention phase, which contains the organization's intelligence, can be used to guide the enactment and selection activities. In Weick's model, positive-feedback messages are used to elicit information from the retention phase for use in selection and enactment and to seek information from enactment and selection for storage in retention. Negative-feedback messages are used to stop the flow of information from retention to enactment and selection, halting the performance of new behaviors, and to check the flow of information about enactment and selection activities to the retention phase (Figure 6.3).

In the enactment phase of organizing, message inputs are perceived and evaluated for their level of equivocality by the organization. Feedback loops between enactment and retention allow the organization both to utilize the information from retention to guide the evaluation of messages and to store the information about the messages enacted for future reference. In the selection phase, during which rules and cycles are chosen and created in response to information inputs, feedback loops from retention are used to guide the organization in deciding how to process message inputs by drawing on organizational intelligence and the repertoire of rules stored in the retention phase. The retention phase constantly draws information from enactment and selection through feedback loops to update its information about message inputs and organizational response strategies.

To use the example of an auto-repair shop, as we did in Case 6.1, mechanics search their past experiences in deciding how to diagnose problems that customers are having with their automobiles. Hopefully, the mechanics will find some precedents in their past experiences (repertoire of rules) for the automotive ailments at hand and use this stored information for trying to treat them. The past experiences that are relevant to the automotive problems are accepted through positive-feedback loops. Of course, some past experiences will be inappropriate to or will not relate directly to the specific problems at hand, and the mechanics will reject them because the information they offer is of little value. These past experiences are rejected through negative-feed-

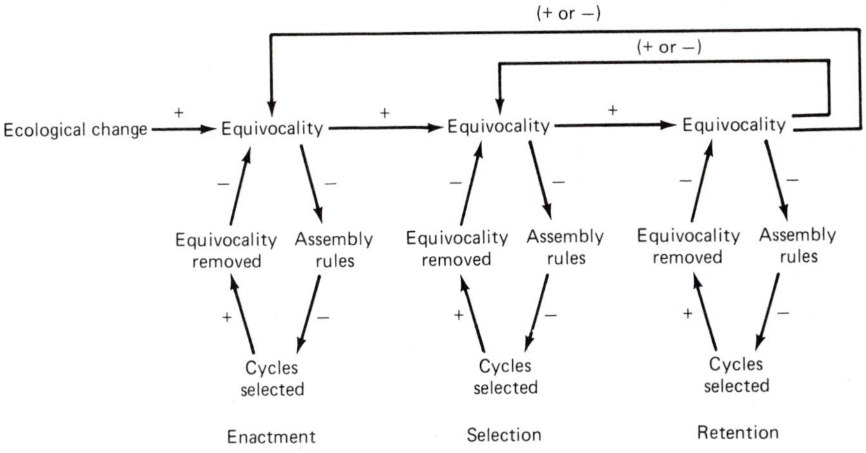

Figure 6.4 Weick's model of organizing. Reprinted from Karl E. Weick, *The Social Psychology of Organizing*. Reading, Mass.: Addison-Wesley, 1969, p. 93.

back loops. In this way, effective auto repair, and effective organizing in general, depends on the coordination of enactment and retention phases of organizing.

During the course of organizational practice, organization members must monitor the results of different organizational strategies and activities to determine their effectiveness in accomplishing organizational goals. If a strategy does not accomplish its objectives or if it results in unpopular side effects, the organization members must search for alternative strategies. These alternative strategies will be identified in the repertoire of rules of the organization members themselves or of the organizational intelligence. If there are no rules to cover the problems that the organization is encountering, the members will have to develop new behavior cycles to address the problems. Advantageous cycles (those that adequately treat organizational demands) will become part of the organization's repertoire of rules to be used in future organizing situations. Effective organizational activities depend on the coordination of selection and retention phases of organizing. (Figure 6.4 illustrates the organizing model.)

Organizational intelligence often is distributed throughout the organization, and in order to make a knowledgeable decision about organizational practice, organization members must rely on obtaining information from other organization members. Moreover, in highly equivocal organizational situations, organization members may have to interact with knowledgeable others outside the organization—lawyers, accountants, consultants, and such—to process the equivocal information down to an understandable level through the performance of communication-behavior cycles. For example, lawyers might engage in litigation and court trials to help the organization cycle equivocal information. Accountants might perform financial audits to cycle equivocal information. Consultants might conduct surveys or interview organization members to reduce information equivocality.

The organizing model stresses the importance of the organization's response to the information in its environment. In Chapter 5, the organization's boundary was identified as the point where the organization exchanges information with its environment. It is at the boundary where enactment processes occur. The proactive organization must keep on top of changes in its information environment by paying particular attention to its boundary-spanning mechanisms and personnel. In business organizations the boundary-spanning personnel are often concentrated at the top and the bottom of the organizational hierarchy (Rogers and Agarwala-Rogers, 1976). For example, at the bottom of the hierarchy, boundary spanners (often called cosmopolites) include the receptionists, secretaries, complaint-department members, security staff, and sales staff. Conversely, at the top of the organizational hierarchy, chief executives often have extensive contact with representatives from the environment. These organization members must be trained to evaluate information from the environment and be given the organization resources to respond to information inputs intelligently and effectively. (We will discuss boundary-spanning communication in more depth in Chapter 10.)

Weick's theory of organizing describes the way that human beings coordinate efforts (organize) to process equivocal information and direct organizational activities. How might members of business organizations best benefit from knowledge of Weick's theory? Kreps (1980) suggests six basic recommendations for organizational practitioners based on Weick's theory of organizing.

First, supervisors should allow adequate communication contact among organization members when processing equivocal information inputs.

Second, to remain viable and efficient, organizations must process information with the same degree of equivocality as is present in the input itself. If organizations handle equivocal inputs as though they were unequivocal (without constructing appropriate communication-behavior cycles), fatal mistakes are likely to occur because the organization will be unable to process the equivocal information into understandable information and probably will react inappropriately to the inputs. If organizations handle unequivocal inputs as though they were equivocal (by performing a variety of double interacts), they probably will waste organizational energy and will atrophy.

Third, organizations can exist only to the degree that they can accurately register the level of equivocality in information inputs, construct appropriate communication-behavior cycles in response to the inputs, and process the equivocal inputs into desired organizational outputs. Care must be taken to accurately evaluate information inputs.

Fourth, management can facilitate organizational adaptation to informational equivocality by fostering interaction among organization members on difficult organizational tasks. Workers should be encouraged to ask questions when processing difficult information inputs, and groups of workers should be used to deal with tasks that are too complex for individuals to easily comprehend and perform.

Fifth, management should concentrate less on individual organization members' behaviors and more on the interlocked communication behaviors of groups of organizational members because the process of control within organizations is accomplished through relationships among individuals, rather than by individuals.

Sixth, training programs can be developed in organizations stressing teamwork; daily and weekly meetings among organization members can be arranged; problem-solving organizational groups can be formed to provide the interlocked communication behaviors necessary for organizational adaptation.

Weick's theory of organizing identifies the communication among organizational members as crucial to organizational survival. Communication must be recognized as an indispensable organizational activity. This recognition can aid organizational adaptation by encouraging concern for the adequacy and accuracy of interaction in organizations. From this perspective, it becomes the formal responsibility of all organization members to communicate actively on the job, giving and receiving messages in response to informational inputs.

As you read Case 6.2, analyze it from the perspective of Weick's theory of organizing.

1. Identify some of the relevant information inputs. What is the most equivocal input? How effectively are the information inputs being dealt with by the hospital administrators?
2. Are the administrators using rules or cycles? How is the consultant used as communication-behavior cycle for the organization?
3. How does the consultant's retention research program demonstrate the principle of requisite variety?
4. Can you identify enactment, selection, and retention phases of the consultant's proposed retention research-and-development program?
5. How are feedback loops employed in the retention program?
6. Compare the retention program with the recruitment program as an

Case 6.2

Nurse Retention at Memorial Hospital*

Memorial Hospital is a large public hospital in a major midwestern city. Like many other urban public hospitals in the United States, Memorial Hospital has been experiencing significant turnover of its nursing staff during the past several years. Excessive employee turnover has been linked to many organizational problems, including increased costs, disruption of social and communication structures, productivity reduction, loss of high performers, decreased satisfaction among stayers, negative P.R. from leavers, and deterioration of communication climate. These problems served to frustrate members of the hospital staff at Memorial, leading to increased work load of nursing staff, decreased cohesion, and reduction of employee commitment to the hospital.

There were many theories about why nurses were leaving Memorial Hospital and why turnover among nurses was so high throughout the country. Many people believed that the cause was employee burnout. They argued that nursing is such a stressful occupation that people can remain in the profession for only a limited time before they become burned out. Others argued that high turnover among nurses was due to poor working conditions at many hospitals. Still others claimed that turnover was due to insufficient financial remuneration and benefits. Additional theories include inconvenient work shifts, ongoing conflicts between doctors and nurses, poor security in urban hospitals, unpleasant hospital environments, unappetizing hospital food, too much paperwork, lack of opportunities for job advancement within clinical areas, lack of respect for the nursing profession, role conflicts among nurses, and even parking difficulties.

The Memorial Hospital administrators did not subscribe to any of these theories. They attempted to cope with the high rate of turnover by increasing their efforts to recruit nurses. The hospital administrators developed a comprehensive recruitment strategy. They began actively advertising for nurses in local newspapers and regional nursing periodicals. They hired recruiters, whom they sent to nursing schools and nursing conferences to publicize the hospital and persuade nurses to join the Memorial nursing staff. The hospital even began offering bonuses to nurses who would come to work at the hospital and guarantee that they would stay there for at least one year. As nurses left the

* *Suggested by Kreps (1985b) research.*

hospital, nurses were recruited to take over their jobs at Memorial. These recruitment efforts were successful, but were also very expensive for the hospital to maintain.

The overall influence of the recruitment strategy on the hospital was less than satisfying to hospital administrators, however. Turnover rates continued to rise, necessitating increased recruitment efforts and resulting in higher costs. The more the recruitment efforts seemed to work, the more nurses had to be recruited. Moreover, the higher the turnover rate at the hospital climbed, the unhappier the nurses at the hospital became.

In desperation, the hospital administrators hired an external consultant to evaluate the turnover situation and determine what problems existed in the recruitment program. The consultant, after an initial investigation of the problems at Memorial Hospital, submitted a preliminary report, which stated that the recruitment strategy was ineffective because it was reactive and mechanistic. It did not address the issues behind nurse turnover, and rather than reducing the problem, it exacerbated it. In the report, the consultant suggested that the recruitment program be refocused with the implementation of a retention research-and-development program at the hospital.

The consultant stressed that the administrative philosophy behind a retention program would be a radical departure from the recruitment perspective. He claimed that the recruitment philosophy views nurses as cogs in the hospital machine. If a cog proves to be ineffective, it is replaced. As turnover increased at the hospital, the logical recruitment reaction was to find new nurses to replace the old ones. The retention philosophy suggests that the more a hospital replaces nurses, the more problems are created for the organization. Every nurse who leaves the hospital takes away valuable information resources from the organization.

The consultant presented the hospital administrators with a retention research-and-development proposal. He explained that the program was designed to identify the specific recurring problems facing nurses that lead to turnover and that it would preserve and utilize this relevant information. The retention program, he explained, rejects the recruitment philosophy and recognizes each nurse as an individual with valuable talents and information about accomplishing hospital activities and goals. The retention program suggests that the health-care organization should spend more energy on keeping nurses at the hospital than it spends on replacing nurses.

A three-part research program was designed to gather information from the nursing staff about the specific problems they were facing. Questionnaires would be used to identify general issues that the nurses were concerned about. In-depth interviews then would be conducted to gather more information about the nature of the problems identified through the questionnaires and to ask nurses to suggest strategies for relieving these problems. Finally, focus group discussions with nursing staff would be held to evaluate which of these problems were most pressing and which potential solution strategies could be most effectively implemented at the hospital. The information generated through the three-part research program would be used to develop strategies and implementation plans to resolve the problems facing the nursing staff.

The consultant suggested that the research program be followed up by an ongoing retention committee composed of members of the nursing staff, whose job it would be to evaluate the issues and solutions generated through the research, continue to gather information about nurses' dissatisfactions and suggestions, and develop strategies for initiating and implementing solutions to the problems. He claimed that the retention committee would serve as an important two-way communication link between nursing staff and hospital administration. It would provide the nurses at the hospital with a powerful communication channel through which they could air their gripes and suggest new directions for hospital policy, and it would provide the hospital administration with valuable information about hospital problems and solutions of which only nurses might be aware.

The administrators listened carefully to the consultant's report presentation. They promised the consultant that they would take the proposal under advisement and get in touch with him with a decision about whether they would support the retention research-and-development program.

organizing strategy. How effective do you think the retention program will be? Why?

Emphasis on Information Processing

Weick's theory of organizing takes an action perspective on organizations, depicting and assessing the actual behaviors performed in the process of organizing. In fact, the emphasis in Weick's theory of organizing is on the dynamic process of organizing, as opposed to the more static structural approach to organizations taken in the classical approach. Weick's action perspective of organizations is highly amenable to process approaches to human communication. In taking this operational approach to organizations, Weick echoes the research emphasis on communication process introduced by Berlo (1960) and argued by Smith (1972).

According to Weick, organizations do not merely exist, but are actively in the process of existing. It is only through the interlocked communication-behavior processes performed by organizations through their organizational members that they develop the ability to exist. Weick explains, "An organization can be understood only in terms of the processes that are underway, or its organizing activities, yet it is possible to see regularities in these activities. Organizing and the consequences of organizing are actually inseparable—they are interchangeable notions. The same things are involved, and we can call them either organizing or organization depending on how broad a portion of time we observe" (1969, pp. 16–17).

Weick's theory of organizing stresses human interactions and information processing as the central activities of organizing. Weick's theory of organizing is, in fact, a communication theory, representing communication interactions and collective information processing as the primary elements of organization. Interpretation and strategic reactions to environmental information inputs enable organizational adaptation and survival. Information is the major input and output of organization. The primary activity of organizations is to process this information through communication so that organization members can adequately react to inputs, creating the primary output of organizations—processed information.

CHAPTER 7

The Organizational-Culture Theory of Organization

ORGANIZATION AS CULTURE

In the 1970s and early 1980s, several scholars—including Cohen, March, and Olson (1972), Geertz (1973), Weick (1974, 1979), March and Olson (1976), Pondy and Mitroff (1979), Pettigrew (1979), and Dandridge, Mitroff, and Joyce (1980)—began to question the popular rational, goal-directed, systemic descriptions of organizations in prevailing classical and systems theories of organization, discussed in Chapters 3 and 5. These scholars claimed that the rationally based organizational theories do not take into account the symbolic influences on the ways that organization members collectively interpret organizational life. A new perspective was needed to explain the development and use of such elements as organizational symbolism, underlying logics, metaphors, and values. The new perspective that developed to interpret the symbolic aspects of organizational life was organizational-culture theory.

Critics of the rational approach to organization argued that organizational behavior is rarely rational and that under close observation, organizational activities often can be seen to be absurd, self-defeating, disjointed, and anomalous. People make sense out of organizational life retrospectively, with the guidance of interpretive frameworks developed in organizational cultures. For example, Cohen, March, and Olson (1972) likened organizational decision making to a "garbage can" in which problems, people, alternative choices, and solutions sift about until enough of these elements make contact for a decision to be made.

Whether the decision is effective is more a matter of chance than of plan. With hindsight, however, organizational practitioners usually make sense of haphazard decision-making processes in terms of culturally approved organizational logics, legends, and visions. Weick (1976, 1979) described many organizing activities as being "loosely coupled" or random and as having limited mutual impact. He argued that these activities only seem to organization members to be logically connected because these individuals interpret the phenomena as parts of coherent cultural explanatory schemes. The many anomalies of organizational life only appear to be ordered and rational. Organizational activities are rendered purposeful and meaningful to organizational representatives through their membership in organizational cultures. Cultures provide their members with collective sense-making logics for interpreting organizational life.

Organizational-culture theory explains the way that collective sense-making processes are accomplished in organizations. Cultures develop as interpretive frameworks that organization members use to help them attach significance to organizational activities. Organization members interpret organizational phenomena through sense-making guidelines provided to them by communicating with other members of organizational cultures and behave in accordance with "shared symbolic logics" gained though their own membership in different organizational cultures. In this chapter, we will examine the nature of organizational culture, identify the relationships between culture and communication, and explore the functions of the symbolic logics and explanatory frameworks promoted by organizational cultures.

ORGANIZATIONAL-CULTURE MODEL

The organizational-culture model has its roots in anthropologically and sociologically based theories of culture as a societal phenomenon. Organizational cultures have virtually the same characteristics as societal cultures. Culture, according to social theory, is developed through human interaction and is an outcome of social experience. "It refers to the sum and organization of human invention and discovery, to the accumulated results of human effort" (Reuter, 1955, p. 141). Culture "refers to all the accepted and patterned ways of behavior of a given people. It is a body of common understandings. It is the sum total and the organization or arrangement of all the group's ways of thinking, feeling, and acting. It also includes the physical manifestations of the group as exhibited in the objects they make—the clothing, shelter, tools, weapons, implements, utensils, and so on" (Brown, 1963, pp. 3–4). Additional artifacts of culture include member attitudes and values, languages and writing systems, religious practices and social rituals, mythology and scientific knowledge, art, social systems and groupings, government, property, norms, laws, philosophy, prejudices, and material traits (such as food habits, transportation, dress, equipment, and technologies) (Reuter, 1955). Obviously, culture is a very pervasive social phenomenon. It influences everything we do. Spradley and McCurdy (1972) effectively narrow the broad scope of culture by focusing on "the knowledge people use to interpret and generate social behavior," rather than on the artifacts of culture (p. 8). This approach to culture stresses the information that people have about social activities. Accordingly, culture serves to inform its membership about how to interpret and respond to social life.

Culture has traditionally been viewed as macroscopic societywide characteristics. Researchers have examined large cultural units, such as national, regional, and ethnic cultures. This "big-picture" approach to culture clearly identifies large societally based cultural groupings. However, it misses the many smaller cultural groupings (sometimes known as subcultures) that exist within large cultures. Countries, or national cultures, are host to many smaller cultural groups. "Within the United States, for example, women have a somewhat separate culture from men, blacks from Indians, and children from the elderly. In the area of health care, physicians have a culture difference from that of other health care providers. Language, friendship, eating habits, communication practices, music, social acts, economic and political activities, and technology dictate culture and its different groupings" (Kreps and Thornton, 1984, p. 192). In comparison with societal groups, organizations are small cultural groupings.

Several ethnographic researchers (ethnography involves the description of cultures) began to study the cultural attributes of smaller social groupings, which set the stage for cultural analysis of organizational life. For example, Whyte, in his classic study *Street Corner Society* (1955), analyzed the cultural norms of inner-city street gangs; Cicourel (1968) studied the culture of a juvenile-justice system; Garfinkel (1967) examined the cultural norms and logics of an urban suicide-prevention center; Goffman (1961) investigated the cultural activities and expectations of patients in a mental hospital; Roy (1960) studied the organizing logics and rituals of factory workers. These studies demonstrate that small cultural groups have the same characteristics as large cultural groups and that culture is as influential a variable in organizational life as it is in society.

The organizational-culture model has developed in two separate, yet related, schools of thought (Smircich, 1983). The first approach to organizational culture regards culture as an influential element of organizational life, the "cultural-variable approach." According to the variable approach, key cultural attributes of organizations influence organizational outcomes, similar to the way that climate, conflict, or leadership influences organizational performance. The second school of thought envisions culture as the essence of organization, the "culture as sense-making approach." Rather than culture being merely an attribute of organizations, culture provides members with shared interpretations of reality that facilitate their abilities to organize. That is, culture promotes a sense of order and logic that symbolically constitutes organization. Much of the popular functionally oriented work about culture (Peters and Waterman, 1982; Deal and Kennedy, 1982) view it from the variable approach, while the more anthropologically oriented interpretive work on culture (Putnam and Pacanowsky, 1983; Pacanowsky and O'Donnell-Trujillo, 1982) view it from the sense-making orientation. In this chapter, we will integrate key elements of both approaches to culture.

There are organizationwide cultures in organizations, and there are subcultures composed of groups of individuals within the organization. The different subcultures within an organization combine to comprise the overall culture of that organization. For example, in a large manufacturing company, the organizationwide culture is composed of all individuals who define themselves as part of the company. In addition, factory workers might have their own subculture; office workers, another; and computer technologists, still another. There are probably many types of subcultural groups in the organization, such as those based on department (sales, purchasing, production, marketing), on organizational position (secretaries' culture, executives' culture, truck drivers' culture, accountants' culture), or on age, education, or social affiliation and habits (old guards' culture, young Turks' culture, M.B.A. culture, church-group culture, bowling-team culture, swingers' culture).

Every organization has its own cultural identity, made up of the history and unique combination of individuals who are part of the organization. The same characteristics that anthropologists and sociologists identified as being artifacts of societal cultures are elements of organizational cultures. However, the primary ingredient of organizational culture is the collective interpretations that organization members make about organizational activities and the outcomes of these activities. Some examples of such interpretive schemes are the meanings that members assign to the organization's products; technologies and tools; identities and character traits of well-known organization members; uniforms and dress codes; designation of company property, buildings, and architectural design; and the organizational rules that govern formal activities. For example, Bonnie Johnson, a communication specialist with Intel Corporation, tells a story about how organization members identify "old-timers" and "newcomers" by the type of employee badge they wear. These badges serve as a symbol for an interpretive framework that describes employees by their affiliations with specific organizational subcultures.

The interpretive frameworks provided in organizational cultures combine to form idiosyncratic organizational themes that direct organization members' actions. These themes influence the attitudes and values of members; the specialized jargons and languages they use; the social and professional rituals they engage in; the company history that is passed on; the company philosophies that are held; legends, stories, and jokes that are told; informal norms and logics used to guide actions; the visions that organization members have of the organization's future; and the identification of organizational friends and foes. The stronger a cultural theme, the larger the percentage of organization members who abide by it.

Strong cultural themes can be either productive or destructive. For example, a strong theme that exerts a productive influence on an organization is IBM's self-image: "IBM means service." Just about all IBMers know of this theme and act accordingly. The theme encourages IBM employees to give their customers extra service that makes a lasting impression and validates customers' decisions to spend their money on IBM products. An example of a strong but destructive cultural theme is the "R.U. Screw" theme at Rutgers University. The R.U. Screw is an underlying logic that explains away all organizational problems and mishaps that occur to students as an inescapable evil property of the university. The R.U. Screw is like an organizational Murphy's Law: "If anything can go wrong at Rutgers, it will." What's more, students believe that university administrators purposely perpetuate the R.U. Screw. If a student's registration is mishandled, grades do not show up on transcripts, or duplicate bills are sent, these mistakes are explained by the R.U. Screw. This theme has become a destructive self-fulfilling prophecy; students are sure that mishaps will occur and act defensively before a problem even exists. The strength of a cultural theme and the effect of that theme are separate cultural properties (Figure 7.1)

Although the theoretical underpinnings of organizational-culture theory are in the ethnographic studies of anthropology and sociology and in the interpretive criticisms of rational approaches to organizational behavior, the organizational-culture model was popularized by three nonscholarly, but very influential, publications in the early 1980s. First, in 1980, *Business Week* published a cover-story article entitled "Corporate Culture: The Hard to Change Values that Spell Success or Failure," which identified organizational culture as a primary influence on employees' motivation and commitment and en-

	Productive theme	Destructive theme
Strong theme	Strong productive	Strong destructive
Weak theme	Weak productive	Weak destructive

Figure 7.1 Cultural theme strength/cultural theme impact grid.

couraged executives to become more aware of the cultures of their organizations. Then, in 1982 appeared two popular books about organizational culture: *Corporate Cultures: The Rites and Rituals of Corporate Life* by Deal and Kennedy, and *In Search of Excellence: Lessons from America's Best-Run Companies* by Peters and Waterman. Both books were best sellers that presented a wide range of convincing organizational examples and anecdotes about how "strong" organizational culture led to high profits and effectiveness for several large business and industrial corporations. Although these two books may have oversimplified the nature of organizational culture and the ways to influence culture, they did bring popular attention to the organizational-culture construct and identify some important aspects of the organizational-culture model.

Deal and Kennedy (1982) described four key attributes of organizational cultures.

First, *values* are the shared beliefs and philosophies of organization members. They set the direction for organizational activities and help organization members interpret organizational life. For example, corporate slogans like Du Pont's "Better things for better living through chemistry," Ford's "Quality is goal one," and Vidal Sassoon's "If you don't look good, we don't look good" illustrate cultural values and set the agenda and direction for activities and interpretations of organization members.

Second, *heroes* are the organization members who best personify and illustrate the strong values of an organization's culture. They are successful visionaries who other organization members look up to and emulate. For example, Lee Iacocca exhibits Chrysler's new vision for an innovative and successful future, Colonel Sanders epitomized the pride and tradition of Kentucky Fried Chicken, and Mary Kay Ash embodies the successful effects of positive-thinking and hard-work values at Mary Kay Cosmetics.

Third, *rites and rituals* are symbolic ceremonies that organization members perform to celebrate and reinforce interpretations about the values and heroes of organizational life. Ceremonies are expressive events that help add drama, excitement, and pageantry to organizational activities. For example, in higher education, several rituals are used to reinforce and celebrate the values of university life: graduation ceremonies with academic regalia and processions glorify the accomplishments of graduates; homecoming games with cheering alumni in school colors rekindle loyalties to dear old alma mater; posting of the names of those students whose grades earned them election to the dean's list celebrates successful academic achievement.

Fourth, *cultural-communication networks* are the informal channels of interaction that are used for indoctrinating members into organizational cultures, recounting stories and legends that illustrate cultural values, and informing members of recent experiences and developments of organizational life. For example, by being a fraternity member, a student might learn about course exams and assignments from fraternity brothers who have taken the class; through informal contacts, organization leaders might learn of new government regulations before they go into effect; through an "old-boy" network, an organization member might identify opportunities for advancement within the organization before they are posted. (We will discuss informal communication networks in more depth in Chapter 9.)

Deal and Kennedy naïvely asserted that by developing these four key cultural attributes, organizations can create strong cultures, which inevitably lead to business success. They also described how weak organizational cultures can be transformed into strong cultures. Their perspective on organizational cultures, although extremely popular, may be somewhat misleading and simplistic. Their promise of a quick fix for ailing organizations with a cultural face-lift has attracted a great deal of attention and activity. In fact, in a cover story by Uttal (1983) in *Fortune*, entitled "The Corporate Culture Vultures: Can They Help Your Company," the difficulties inherent in directed cultural change and development are examined. It is an exceedingly complex matter to change and develop entrenched cultural themes. Additionally, culture is a more complex concept than many quick-fix consultants and/or practitioners may realize. Strong cultural themes do not always lead to organizational successes. Some strong themes can lead to disaster. For example, Ford Motor Company's unshakable belief in the Edsel (an automobile they built in the late 1950s) did not lead to success and great profits. Cultural themes that are effective at one point in organizational life may be totally inappropriate at another point. Chrysler's cultural belief in continued American demand for large luxury cars almost brought the company to bankruptcy in the 1970s. As we discussed earlier, cultural strength refers more to how widely a cultural theme is held within an organization than to how the theme will influence the success of the organization.

Peters and Waterman (1982) reported the results of their analysis of the cultural traits of 62 excellent business organizations representing high-technology companies, consumer-goods companies, general-industrial-goods companies, service companies, project-management companies, and resource-based companies. They identified eight primary cultural themes in their sample of excellent business organizations:

First, excellent organizations have a *bias toward action* rather than toward spending time on excessive planning and analyzing, which has been emphasized in the applications of classical theory and systems theory to organizational practice. The action bias leads organization members to try different tactics to solve organizational problems. Peters and Waterman explain that too often, organization members overanalyze problems rather than work to rectify difficult situations. Both systems theory and Weick's model of organizing emphasize the emergent adaptive nature of organizational life and organizational innovation, which would seem to support this action bias.

Second, excellent organizations are *close to the customer.* They gather relevant information from key representatives of their environment (their customers) about organizational operations. This theme is consistent with open systems theory, which suggests that organizations must coordinate with their environments to adapt to environmental constraints. It is also supported by Weick's model of organizing, which posits that customers provide potentially rich communication cycles for resolving equivocality because they are knowledgeable about key business-organization issues like product demand, product quality, influences of marketing strategies, and adequacy of pricing.

Third, excellent organizations emphasize *autonomy and entrepreneurship.* They encourage organization members to assume responsibility for organizational activities, make organizational decisions, and take the risk of initiating innovations. This theme seems to be representative of the human-relations theory edicts of the value of participative management, the Theory Y emphasis on individual worker responsibility, and the attempt to enhance worker self-actualization.

Fourth, excellent organizations emphasize *productivity through people.* These organizations have a people orientation, treating their employees supportively, with respect and positive regard. They stress intimacy and caring. Members often feel like the organization is their extended family. This theme is most representative of human-relations theory, which takes into account the individual needs of workers and integrates organization goals with member goals. This theme can be clearly seen in the Japanese approach to organizational life. When asked where they work, Japanese workers have been known to reply, "I belong to Nissan" or "I belong to Sony." When they say they belong to their company, it is not in the sense of servitude, but as membership in a social club or a family.

Fifth, excellent organizations emphasize *hands-on, value-driven organizational activities*. The hands-on notion suggests that the best leaders are those who are most in touch and involved with organizational activities. Hewlett-Packard's philosophy of "management by wandering around," where managers are highly visible and in contact with organization members, illustrates this hands-on aspect of organization (Peters and Waterman, 1982, p. 51). The value-driven theme suggests that leaders should point organizational activities in directions that are consistent with the key philosophies and values of the organization. In this way, organizational activities reinforce the central values of the organizationwide culture. This theme does not seem to be part of earlier organizational theories but is particularly representative of the organizational-culture theory.

Sixth, excellent organizations *stick to their knitting*. In these organizations, leaders determine what the organization does best and what activities are consistent with its cultural values, and they focus on accomplishing these activities. For example, a theme at Kentucky Fried Chicken is "We do chicken right," which emphasizes the company's concentration on one primary product it makes well, rather than on 30 products that it makes poorly. General Motors is in the automotive business; it does not try to market soft drinks or computer components. It knows what its primary product emphasis is and sticks to it. This theme seems to be representative of the scientific-management concept of order and efficiency. (Remember Taylor's famous design of the "correct" way to shovel coal.) Once organization members identify the best ways to accomplish a task, they should utilize these effective methods.

Seventh, excellent organizations emphasize *simple form and lean staff*. Rather than develop many layers of management, these organizations keep things small so that leaders can communicate more directly with workers and vice versa. (This is reminiscent of Barnard's [1938] principle of keeping communication channels as short and direct as possible.) The "KISS" principle of management ("Keep it simple, stupid") is enforced. Without simple form and lean staff, hands-on management would be impossible. Excellent organizations attempt to get the most out of the fewest individuals. Quality is a more important and valued outcome of organizational activities than is mere quantity. This theme is somewhat representative of the parsimony (a rule to handle every possible alternative) of Weber's theory of bureaucracy and the efficiency of Taylor's theory of scientific management. It also emulates the simplicity of organizational rule use in situations of low equivocality according to Weick's theory of organizing.

Eighth, excellent organizations demonstrate *simultaneous loose and tight properties*. Loose qualities include ability to innovate in response to different constraints, while tight properties indicate unanimity in spirit and action among organization members. Loose and tight properties are similar to the contrasting needs for innovation and stability in organizations that we discussed in Chapter 1. This organizational theme is most representative of the use of rules and cycles in response to differing levels of equivocality during organizing activities according to Weick's theory of organizing. Cycles are creative, innovative, "loose" organizational activities, while rules are structured, rational, "tight" organizational activities.

These eight attributes of excellent organizations may be based on data gathered from business and industrial organizations, yet they seem to be applicable to other organizations as well. For example, a family can benefit from a "bias toward action." Rather than continually talking about and planning for a vacation that never occurs, it may be more effective for the family to seize the moment and try to accomplish its members' goals. A family should be "close to the customer," its members. By staying aware of the needs of individual members, a family can work to fulfill these needs. Parents can help children mature and develop responsibility by stressing "autonomy and entrepreneurship," in allowing children to make decisions and accomplish individual tasks. Certainly, a family's product of mutual support is based on "productivity through people," since it is the family members themselves who provide mutual support. The "hands-on, value-driven" theme suggests that family members should keep communication channels open and act in accord with family goals. When a family "sticks to its knitting," the primary goal of mutual support and preservation of members is promoted. "Simple form and lean staff" suggests that family communication networks optimally should be tight and well integrated. Finally, the "simultaneous loose and tight properties" of a family would indicate the dual needs of family stability and order, along with the need for individual growth and change.

Every organization has a culture. The cultural themes that an organization develops have powerful influences on both the interpretations that organization members make about reality and the activities in which they engage. Some cultural themes can help promote organizational growth and development, and other themes can work to the detriment of the organization. Communication is the primary channel used to promote the development and maintenance of organizational culture. There is a very close relationship between organizational communication and organizational culture.

Organizational Culture and Organizational Communication

Culture is defined by the renowned anthropologist Edward T. Hall (1959) as patterned communication. Morton Deutsch (1966), a well-known social psychologist, concurs. He explains that culture is based on the community of communication that consists of socially stereotyped patterns. These stereotypes include habits of language and thought that are carried on through various forms of social learning, particularly through methods of child rearing. Organizational communication is an undeniably powerful influence on culture, just as culture influences the way that organization members communicate. Organizational culture is created through organization members' development of collectively held, underlying logics and legends about their organization and its identity. These logics and legends are imbedded in and transmitted through formal and informal channels of organizational communication.

Two primary cultural functions of organizational communication are to provide organization members with information about their organization's culture and to socialize members into their organization's culture (Pacanowsky and O'Donnell-Trujillo, 1982; Kreps, 1983a). Organizational culture is communicated to organization members and relevant others informally through interpersonal storytelling and gossiping, using the organization's grapevine as a primary medium, and formally through advertising, slogans, organizational documents (such as newsletters, annual reports, handbooks, and other company publications), group meetings, and public presentations.

As an organization's identity emerges, members interpret the organization's past and present, making sense of the phenomena of organizational life and creating stories and legends about organizational activities. These stories and legends provide a thematic base for the development of collective visions about the future development of the organization. Culturally derived explanations about what the organization is, what it does, how it goes about accomplishing its goals, where it has been, where it is going, and what role organization members play in these activities comprise organizational folklore. They are essential elements in the development of an organizational identity (Kreps, 1983a).

Funny stories and "inside" jokes (which culture members frequently tell and can fully appreciate) often are used by organization members to illustrate cultural themes. For example, at a large county hospital whose name had been changed from County General to Wishard Memorial, there was an interpretive theme held by hospital employees that the general public was uninformed about the hospital and unrealistically held the hospital in low esteem. A joke was told among the hospital staff that illustrated this theme. It concerned an emergency patient brought to the hospital while unconscious. When the patient awakened, he worriedly asked a nurse, "Where am I?" The nurse replied, "You are at Wishard Memorial Hospital." The patient gave a sigh of relief and responded, "Thank goodness I'm not at County General." To fully appreciate this joke, you have to understand the theme about the public image of the hospital. This story reinforces the accepted cultural image about an ignorant public, while demonstrating to hospital employees how unrealistic the public image is.

At Rutgers University, there is a popular organizational myth held by undergraduate students about the high level of student promiscuity and partying on campus (although there probably is no more partying or promiscuity at Rutgers than at any other large university). A joke that illustrates this theme is told about a prominent statue built in a well-traveled spot on campus. The statue is of a university benefactor who donated some of the land on which the university was built in the 1760s. However, the joke describes the statue differently. It begins with an insider to the organizational culture telling a culturally naïve person that the statue is called *Willie the Silent.* The naïve individual invariably responds by asking, "Why is it called *Willie the Silent?*" The insider replies, "Because he whistles every time a virgin walks by."

Jokes often are used to establish and reinforce themes of competition to the organizational culture. External competition often increases internal cultural unity. Members of the organizational culture join to resist a common foe. For example, the U.C.L.A. Bruins, who compete with their crosstown Los Angeles rivals, the U.S.C. Trojans, denigrate U.S.C. by chanting, "Trojans burst under pressure." This joke parodies the U.S.C. cultural metaphor of the invincible Trojan warrior by likening a Trojan to an ineffective prophylactic.

Another joke that illustrates cultural competition is told at M.I.T. about rivalry between M.I.T. and Harvard University. In the joke, a male Harvard professor and a male M.I.T. professor were using a men's rest room at Harvard. The M.I.T. professor had just finished and was about to leave when the Harvard professor addressed him in a sharp tone of voice, "Sir, at Harvard, we always wash our hands before leaving a rest room." The M.I.T. professor looked back at the Harvard professor, paused, and calmly replied, "Sir, at M.I.T., we do not drip on our hands." Who is the hero and who is the villain in this joke? What does this joke say to you about the way members of the M.I.T. culture perceive the faculty at M.I.T. and at Harvard? Can you see how the joke supports the theme of competition at the universities?

Organizational communication is an important channel for socializing new organization members into the cultures within the organization. Current members of organizational cultures initiate new members into their culture through formal and informal interpersonal communication—formally through job instruction and orientation sessions and informally through the telling of culturally approved stories and legends (Kreps, 1983a). Such interpersonal communication is used as an important organizational tool for socializing new members into organizational cultures by helping members learn about cultural history, values, themes, and expectations. Louis (1980) distinguishes between two types of content conveyed in organizational socialization. The first is role-related content, largely learned through job instruction and counseling (often in terms of "this is the way things are done around here"), and the second is a general appreciation of the culture of the organization, largely learned through storytelling. "Whether through formal or informal channels, organizational communication is the primary means used to socialize members into an organization's culture" (Kreps, 1983a, p. 244).

Interpretation of Organizational Culture

The organizational-culture model suggests that traditional product-oriented approaches to studying organizations by focusing on organizational outputs, such as production, profit, and technology, will not provide the cultural analyst with information about the sense-making interpretive frameworks promoted by and used in cultures. An interpretive approach to studying organizations by examining the sense-making strategies used by organization members was proposed by Berger and Luckmann (1967), Geertz (1973), Giddens (1976), Burrell and Morgan (1979), Frost (1980), Morgan and Smirchich (1980), Evered and Louis (1981), Deetz (1982), and Putnam (1983). Deetz (1982) and Putnam (1983) explain that this interpretive method of inquiry is not new, but is based on a large body of earlier work in philosophy, sociology, communication, organizational sciences, and other disciplines. The key to interpretive organizational research is to study the ways that organization members collectively create meanings for organizational reality through communicative processes.

Interpretive organizational research examines transcripts of organizational communication to identify sense-making patterns in the messages exchanged by organization members (Deetz, 1982). The theoretical rationale for this emphasis on studying messages is that, as we discussed in Chapter 1, meaning is a very personal and idiosyncratic creation. Meaning can never be fully shared among people; only messages can be exchanged. To increase the reliability and commonality of organization members' interpretations of organizational reality, culture members attempt to share similar aspects of meaning by creating common interpretive frameworks for assessing organizational phenomena. The messages that organization members exchange inform these individuals of the interpretive frameworks that are promoted by cultures to increase intersubjective reliability (the amount of sharing among organization members) of meaning creations. By studying transcripts of organizational messages, interpretive researchers can discover the logics that are used to create culturally approved interpretive frameworks.

For example, in an applied study of organizational culture at RCA reported by Kreps (1983a), a wide range of transcripts of organizational messages were analyzed to identify the primary themes of RCA culture. Kreps and his associates analyzed the content of organizational documents and artifacts (such as annual reports, transcripts of speeches by influential organization members, employee handbooks, marketing and promotional materials, recruitment pamphlets, and in-house reports) to identify relevant constructs, symbols, vocabulary, metaphors, and stories that were part of the RCA organizational culture. They interviewed a broadly based sample of organization members, asking them to define and explain key characteristics of the organization, describe interesting experiences they had had as organization members, and recount stories they knew about the organization. Additionally, members of the research team engaged in nonparticipant observation of employee behavior within the organization to identify communication patterns in naturalistic interaction among organization members. Each of these points of communication analysis provided the research team with interpretive data from which they could reconstruct key elements of RCA's organizational culture. These elements of culture were organized to produce a media program used to help socialize new members into the company's culture.

Emphasis on Shared Underlying Logics

The central element of organizational culture is the underlying logics the culture develops that are used to create interpretive frameworks that members of the culture use to assign meanings to organizational phenomena. Underlying logics, sometimes referred to as "logics in use," explain why unexplainable things happen in organizational life, identify specific causes for phenomena that are too complex to pin down to an actual cause, and generally help organization members make sense out of insensate phenomena (Hawes, 1971, 1974; Pacanowsky and O'Donnell-Trujillo, 1982). They are similar to Weick's notion of assembly rules, which organization members use to interpret equivocal information inputs.

Underlying logics do not have to be either true or logical; they only have to help organization members interpret phenomena that are difficult to interpret. For example, Pettegrew (1982) describes the underlying logic used by organization members to explain management behavior in nonprofit health and human-service organizations—the "S.O.B. theory of management." This logic describes the activities of organization decision makers, regardless of their actual management style, as being generally negative, uncaring, and ineffective. The S.O.B. logic describes managers as villains. It is used by organization members to interpret different management activities. If special-interest groups within the organization do not get what they want from management, the logic is employed to explain that it is because the manager is an S.O.B.; if these groups do get what they want from management, the logic explains that it is because they were able to overcome the S.O.B.

Two interpretive functions of underlying logics develop in organizational cultures: to create retrospective meanings and to create prospective meanings. Retrospective meanings interpret what has happened in the organization. Underlying logics are used retrospectively to develop stories, legends, and myths about the organization. (The distinction among stories, legends, and myths is based on how pervasive and symbolically rich the tale becomes. Over time, minor stories about organizational experiences may become legends if they are enriched and popularized in their telling by organization members. Legends may become myths if they take on supernatural significance for organization members. For example, a story about the successes of a specific salesperson in a company may become a legend if the salesperson's successes grow larger and larger as the story is recounted and if the tale becomes famous within the organization. The legend can take on mythic proportions if it is used to embody the heroic characteristics that salespeople within the company are socialized to aspire to.) Prospective meanings develop visions of where the organization will go and what organization members should do. Underlying logics are used by organization members to decipher organizational activities and to describe future goals and directions of the organization.

Case 7.1 shows how a large and excellent organization can suffer as a result of its image among both members and outsiders. Analyze this case from an organizational-culture perspective.

1. Identify several prominent cultural themes that exist in this organization. (Hint: What are some of the underlying logics that organization members use to direct their behaviors; what are some of the

Case 7.1

I.U.P.U.I.

Indiana University–Purdue University at Indianapolis (I.U.P.U.I.) is a comprehensive urban state university located in the capital of and largest metropolitan area in Indiana. I.U.P.U.I. is primarily a nonresidential commuter university, with students living in Indianapolis or its suburbs. The university enrolls approximately 24,000 students and is the third largest university in the state, behind two residential campuses, Indiana University (I.U.), located in rural Bloomington, and Purdue University (Purdue), located in semi-industrial West Lafayette. Both I.U. and Purdue are approximately 60 miles from Indianapolis, which has about 1 million people.

I.U.P.U.I. has many outstanding attributes. It is the only major public higher-educational institution in Indianapolis. It is one of the fastest growing educational institutions in the state. Because of the university's location in a metropolitan area, it is able to serve many workingpeople with a wide range of specialized programs. I.U.P.U.I. students, who generally are older than students at I.U. and Purdue, tend to be very serious about their education. The university hosts many cooperative education and research programs with local industry and government, offering more than 100 degree programs. It has one of the largest and most comprehensive health-care complexes in the nation. The School of Medicine and the School of Nursing at I.U.P.U.I. are among the largest in the United States. The I.U.P.U.I. main campus hosts a major medical center composed of five large hospitals. The Indiana University School of Dentistry, famous for state-of-the art dental research, is on the I.U.P.U.I. campus, as is the School of Social Work. It is also the home of the Indiana University Natatorium, one of the finest indoor swimming complexes in the world.

In the late 1960s, I.U.P.U.I. was formed by merging several educational institutions in Indianapolis. The Indiana University Medical Campus, including the Schools of Medicine (plus allied health programs), Nursing, and Dentistry, was joined with the Indiana University School of Law at Indianapolis, the Herron School of Art (a private art school), and two regional colleges, Indiana University at Indianapolis and Purdue University at Indianapolis. The State Commission on Higher Education recognized that there was a great deal of duplication of effort among all these independent institutions, both academically and administratively. Its answer to this inefficient overlap of efforts was to merge these institutions to form one major comprehensive urban state university. The university was made part of the I.U. system, which is composed of two core campuses—I.U. and I.U.P.U.I.—and several smaller regional campuses throughout the state. Organizationally, the different schools at I.U.P.U.I. are affiliated to either the I.U. system or the Purdue system, although university funding is channeled through the I.U. system, located in Bloomington. The vast preponderance of schools are connected to I.U., including Law, Public and Environmental Affairs, Liberal Arts, Social Work, Business, Medicine, Dentistry, the Herron School of Art, Education, Nursing, Physical Education, and the Graduate School. The two schools connected to Purdue at I.U.P.U.I. are Engineering and Technology, and Science.

The merger ran into some problems when no one name could be found that was acceptable to each of the founding divisions of the university. The I.U. divisions wanted to maintain their identification with dear old I.U., and the Purdue divisions fought to keep the proud Purdue name in the new institution's title. The only acceptable choice became the rather unwieldy Indiana University–Purdue University at Indianapolis, probably one of the longest names of any institution of higher learning in the country. The name was too long for most people to comfortably fit into normal conversation, so it was shortened to I.U.P.U.I., reminiscent of such institutions as U.C.L.A., U.S.C., and L.S.U. Unfortunately, the I.U.P.U.I. name was broken down phonetically by someone to the strange-sounding "Ooey-Pooey." This odd name caught on. Thus this major institution of learning became widely known throughout Indianapolis and much of Indiana as Ooey-Pooey.

I.U.P.U.I. faculty and students were often frustrated by and jealous of the differences between I.U.P.U.I. and the other two large public institutions in the state, I.U. and Purdue. They felt that there was a marked disproportionate distribution of resources among I.U., Purdue, and I.U.P.U.I. For example, the ratio of library holdings per student at I.U. and Purdue was much higher than at I.U.P.U.I. Faculty salaries were perceived to be higher at I.U. and Purdue, even though the cost of living at their campuses was lower than in Indianapolis. Campus facilities, such as laboratories, classroom buildings, student centers, recreational equipment, dormitories, and restaurants, were seen as being superior at I.U. and Purdue to those at I.U.P.U.I. Students noted that student activities and night life was richer and more exciting at the two rural campuses. Faculty teaching loads were generally lower at I.U. and Purdue than at I.U.P.U.I.

These perceived inequities were thought to be structurally based. I.U.P.U.I. ran into trouble negotiating within the I.U. system. Structurally, I.U.P.U.I. had the status of a core campus, along with I.U. at

Bloomington, in the I.U. system. I.U.P.U.I. often was given funds for building on the campus, but when it came time to allocate money for academic programs, faculty and administrative salaries, and library holdings, the lion's share of the state appropriations went to I.U. at Bloomington. The library holdings in Indianapolis were not even one-quarter the library holdings at Bloomington, even though I.U.P.U.I. enrolled approximately two-thirds the number of students enrolled at Bloomington. Additionally, much of the laboratory and educational equipment at I.U.P.U.I. was old and in extremely poor condition, especially in comparison with the equipment available in Bloomington. Perhaps this had something to do with the fact that the heardquarters for the administrators of the I.U. system were located in Bloomington.

When academic departments in the undergraduate School of Liberal Arts began asking for graduate programs, there was great resistance in the system. The Graduate School, which was located in Bloomington, was slow to elect I.U.P.U.I. faculty members to the graduate faculty. Even many of the most respected senior I.U.P.U.I. faculty were denied graduate-faculty status. This was rather humiliating, since many of the new assistant professors at Bloomington, some without even completing their terminal degrees, were allowed to teach graduate courses in their programs. I.U.P.U.I. upper administration did not seem to recognize, or at least publicly acknowledge, the second-class treatment that the university, its faculty, and its students were getting. Several faculty members grumbled that much of the university administration were "good old boys" from the I.U. or Purdue systems who were "rewarded for not rocking the boat."

I.U.P.U.I. suffered a marked lack of national recognition, although it had many accomplished faculty members and some excellent academic programs. Many people assumed that these excellent I.U.P.U.I. faculty and programs were at the I.U. or Purdue campuses in Bloomington or West Lafayette. People were confused by I.U.P.U.I.'s long name. Compounding this recognition problem, professors and students at I.U.P.U.I., depending on their field of expertise, often claimed allegiance to I.U., Purdue, or their professional school. At a national conference, four I.U.P.U.I. faculty members from the same department were observed wearing name badges with four institutional affiliations noted, not one of which was I.U.P.U.I. One name badge had Indiana University; one, Indiana–Purdue; one, Purdue at Indianapolis; and one, University of Indianapolis (a name proposed for the university that had not been implemented). Faculty members also noted a wide range of institutional affiliations in their publications and résumés.

Although the enrollment at I.U.P.U.I. steadily increased from semester to semester, as other state institutions' enrollments waned, students and faculty seemed to feel a lack of pride in the institution. When students were interviewed about how they felt about attending I.U.P.U.I., many replied that they were going here while they saved enough money to transfer to Bloomington or West Lafayette. Other students, especially those enrolled in the Schools of Law, Medicine, or Dentistry, denied that they were students at I.U.P.U.I. They claimed allegiance to the professional school at which they were enrolled, rather than to the I.U.P.U.I. institution as a whole. Many of these students acted as though I.U.P.U.I. referred only to the undergraduate programs in Liberal Arts and Sciences at the university, and not to the graduate professional schools. Faculty also claimed allegiance to their own individual academic programs, such as law or medicine, and not to the university as a whole. Some faculty members regarded I.U.P.U.I. as a stopping point in their careers where they could build their academic records to get jobs at more reputable institutions. Other faculty members saw I.U.P.U.I. as a relatively easy place to get by with minimal work, with lower demands for performance than at other large institutions, allowing them more time for their outside interests. These perceptions about the university severely limited the school's potential for growth and excellence. As one faculty member explained, "This school suffers from a branch campus mentality."

significant symbols in this organization's culture; who are some of the heroes or villains in this culture; how does the history of the organization influence the organizational culture?) Are these themes primarily productive or destructive to the organization? Explain why.

2. Evaluate this organization in terms of the criteria for organizational excellence identified by Peters and Waterman (1982). Which of these criteria, if any, does the organization meet?
3. Can you think of specific strategies that this organization might employ to further develop its organizational culture? Explain your ideas.

ORGANIZATIONAL CULTURE AND EQUIVOCALITY

The organizational-culture model and Weick's model of organizing have a great deal in common (Kreps 1982a, 1983b). Organizational culture is an instrumental equivocality-reducing mechanism for organization members, providing them with a sense of order when interpreting the many organizational processes, goals, and predicaments they encounter. Deal and Kennedy (1982) address this state of uncertainty in modern organizational life and describe the beneficial sense-making role of organizational culture in corporations: "Uncertainty is at the core of it all. Yet strong culture companies remove a great degree of that uncertainty because they provide structure and standards and a value system in which to operate" (p. 16). The development of an organization's culture helps to reduce the equivocality of being an organization member by providing its constituents with information about the organization and their role within it.

Recall that Weick (1979), in his model of organizing, describes the organizing process as organizational adaptation to equivocal information inputs. According to Weick, people become members of an organization only through their ability to organize their activities with one another in the process of interpreting and responding to information equivocality. That is, they are involved in an ongoing collective process of developing organization by establishing structure, predictability, and direction for their conjoint actions. The more organization members can resolve equivocality in informational inputs and develop strategies for organizational action, the more they are able to exhibit organization (Weick, 1979; Kreps, 1980). The development of organizational culture provides organization members with an interactive means of interpreting reality, which facilitates organized behavior. Organizational culture helps organization members resolve the equivocality of being an organization member and helps organizational actors cope with equivocal informational inputs.

Organizational culture constrains the activities of organization members by presenting them with a social reality that invokes social order within the organization. The organization's culture encourages organization members to accept culturally approved beliefs, values, and attitudes as their own (Bormann, 1983). In strong organizational cultures, these culturally approved beliefs, values, and attitudes are clearly defined and widely accepted (Deal and Kennedy, 1982). Members of the organization are socialized to accept these notions about social reality and must behave in accord with the social order presented to them if they are to be accepted as members of the culture. Continual, often unanimous, support for adherence to the norms of the organizational culture are reinforced by members of the organization through metacommunicative interaction that punishes cultural deviance and rewards adherence to cultural norms.

The constraining influences of social reality and of organizational activity makes organizational life predictable for members. Organizational culture helps organization members interpret complex organizational phenomena in terms of the logics and legends that are part of the culture. Members' reactions to new phenomena are guided by culturally derived logics about organizational activities. Organizational culture enables its members to behave in accordance with the particular organization's philosophy and goals by providing them with guidelines for their interpretations and reactions to organizational inputs.

Organizational cultures encourage the development of collaborative activities among organization members. In strong organizational cultures, members share a frame of reference on organizational activities and organizational life. This common frame of reference is based on the underlying logics and legends of the culture that members of the culture share. These organizational members recognize their interdependence and feel a bond with one another due to their common cultural affiliation. The culture provides its membership with a common language, value system, and vision about the organization's future, which enhances communication and cooperation among members and facilitates their ability to coordinate their activities and creations of meaning.

Symbolic-interactionist philosophy has long posited that "human beings act toward things on the basis of the meanings that the things have for them" and that the meanings created develop through "the social interaction one has with one's fellows" (Blumer, 1969, p. 2; Mead, 1934; Fisher, 1978). Since organizational culture prescribes the ways in which members react symbolically to organizational phenomena by presenting them with culturally approved explanations for those phenomena, it provides its members with shared perceptions of social reality and a common sense of social order. This sense of social order enables constituents of the organizational culture to coordinate their behaviors and act interdependently. Ultimately, the development of organizational culture facilitates the cultural constituents' abilities to exhibit collaborative activities and organization.

Organizational Culture and Organizational Intelligence

Organizational culture provides organization members with information about how they are to react to situations that the organization has encountered in the past. Weick (1979) describes the development of "organizational intelligence" (during the retention phase of organizing) as a means of preserving information about how the organization can deal with different inputs. Every time an organization copes with a new input, it learns something about how to organize. Rather than reacting to each successive input as though it were totally new, in effect "reinventing the wheel," an organization member can utilize information that the organization has gained from past experiences and has stored in its organizational intelligence.

Recall that in Chapter 6, we explained that organizational intelligence benefits organizations by providing its membership with guidelines for behavior. Organizational intelligence acts as the memory of the organization; organizational culture is used as a primary repository for organizational intelligence. Stories about how the organization has dealt with difficult situations in the past are recounted through the organization's communications systems and become part of the organization's culture. These stories give organization members insight into how the organization has solved problems or erred in the past, providing them with information about how they can react to present informational inputs to achieve culturally approved organizational goals (Kreps, 1983b).

Organizational culture provides structure and predictability to organizational phenomena by linking organizational members in a common social reality (Mehan and Wood, 1975). Culture enables organization members to interpret phenomena in the framework of organizational history. Culture facilitates interlocked organizational activities by joining organization members in a common frame of reference. Culture provides the organization with a repository for organizational intelligence, fostering the performance of rule-governed organizational activities. In these ways, organizational culture is an important equivocality-reducing communication mechanism for organizations.

The potential benefits of organizational culture in helping organization members both interpret and respond appropriately to complex organizational phenomena can be of great utility to modern organizations. When knowledge of the benefits of organizational culture is coupled with recognition of the role of organizational communication as a pervasive channel for cultural information, several directions for enlightened organizational practice become apparent. Organizations can utilize formal and informal communication channels to educate their members about the organizational culture, socialize them into the culture, and eventually develop a strong organizational culture.

Formal organizational communication channels, such as advertising, slogans, annual reports, newsletters, written correspondence, internal memorandums, group meetings, and speeches, should be designed to promote the development of organizational culture. Cultural values, company history, organizational heroes, significant cultural symbols, and cultural visions for the organization's future can be presented to the organization's relevant publics through formal communication. Orientation programs and in-house training and development programs can be designed to help organization members learn about their organization's culture, identify more fully with the organization and their co-workers, and direct their organizational activities in accordance with cultural norms (Kreps, 1983a).

Informal communication also can be used to promote organizational culture, although the grapevine can be more difficult to direct than can formal communication channels. Management often concentrates solely on formal communication channels, either avoiding informal communication or allowing it to develop on its own. Informal communication channels, however, can be integrated with formal communication channels in organizations, developing a complementary overlap between the formal and informal information carried throughout the organization (Davis, 1953; Rogers and Agarwala-Rogers, 1976). Management can help direct the grapevine by supplying its informal leaders with culturally relevant information. (We will examine informal organizational communication in more depth in Chapter 9.)

Organizational stories and storytelling should be recognized as a potentially important informal communication channel for disseminating cultural information throughout the organization. Storytelling is generally an enjoyable social form of organizational interaction that enables members to get to know one another and develop cooperative interpersonal relationships. It can be utilized by organizations to help members learn about their organization by providing them with information about the history and heritage of their organization. Additionally, stories serve to educate members about how the organization utilizes organizational intelligence to accomplish its goals. Knowledge of organizational intelligence helps to guide members' future organizational activities.

Organizations can promote the development of their culture by utilizing their formal and informal communication systems to disseminate cultural information. Well-developed organizational cultures can help organization members cope with the equivocality of complex organizational phenomena. Although strong cultures do not always promote effective organization, they can promote organization in many ways. Strong cultures can facilitate increased member solidarity by enabling cultural constituents to identify with one another and with their organization. Increased member identification and knowledge often leads to improved cooperation and coordination among organization members. Awareness of cultural information can also help organization members develop enhanced abilities to utilize organizational intelligence in guiding their organizational activities.

THEORETICAL CONVERGENCE

Organizational-culture theory is concerned with the meanings held by organization members. In some ways, the perspective (especially the culture as variable approach) is reminiscent of the human-relations theory, which is concerned with satisfying the needs of individual organization members. Both theories emphasize the importance of organization members, informal communication patterns, the development of group norms, and the emotional tone of organizational life. Note how different these two perspectives are from classical theory and systems theory. Classical theory, systems theory, and, to a certain extent, Weick's model of organizing emphasize rational planning, functional organization, and control in human organizations. The classical, systems, and Weickian theories we will call the "rational perspective," and the organizational-culture and human-relations theories we will call the "human-intuitive perspective."

The rational and the human-intuitive perspectives on organization mirror a basic dichotomy in human consciousness, based on two distinct modes of consciousness indigenous to the left and right hemispheres of the brain. The left hemisphere is involved primarily with analytic, logical thinking, especially in verbal and mathematical functions; the right hemisphere is involved primarily with artistic endeavor, relational information, and emotion (Ornstein, 1972). In effective information processing, human beings coordinate the two hemispheres of the brain, identifying logical and linear elements of reality through the left brain and recognizing interesting patterns of events and interpreting nonverbal cues through the right brain.

The different functions of the two hemispheres of the brain mirror a historical conflict concerning the acquisition of knowledge between the behaviorist and the humanist traditions as described by C. P. Snow in his classic text, *The Two Cultures* (1963). Behaviorists search for logical, objective, and scientifically derived explanations of phenomena, while humanists seek intuitive, subjective, and experiential accounts of phenomena. Snow argued that these two approaches lead to unnecessary fragmentation of knowledge and called for meaningful communication and coordination between behaviorists and humanists in the search for knowledge. Similarly, to effectively understand the nature of human organization, we must combine both the rational and the human-intuitive perspectives.

The chronological development of organizational theory that we have discussed has moved toward this convergence of perspectives. While classical theory is firmly rooted in the rational perspective, and human-relations theory is firmly rooted in the human-intuitive perspective, systems theory, Weick's model, and organizational-culture theory begin to deviate from their respective perspectives. Systems theory and Weick's model begin to diverge from the rational perspective because they emphasize not only functional integration of components, but also the use of creative adaptation and innovation in organiz-

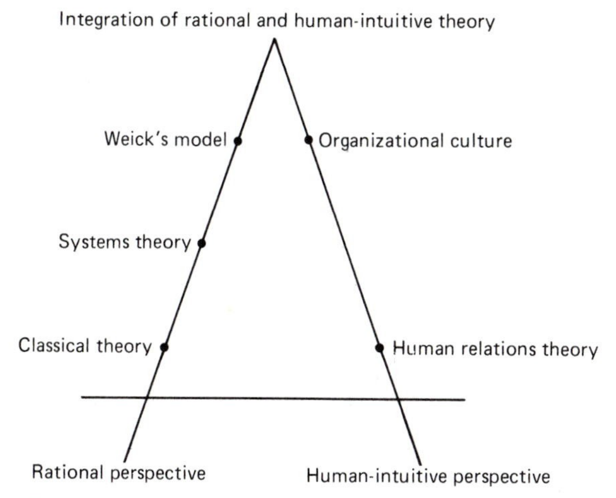

Figure 7.2 Convergence in organizational theory.

ing activities. Organizational-culture theory begins to deviate from the human-intuitive perspective because it not only emphasizes human values and emotion, but also examines the use of strategic logics in organizing activities. The development of organizational theory is moving toward convergence of the rational and the human-intuitive perspectives (Figure 7.2). In this book, we will strive for theoretical convergence by emphasizing both the rational and the human-intuitive aspects of organizational behavior.

PART III

COMMUNICATION AND ORGANIZING

In Part III, we describe and explain the functions of communication in organizing. Chapter 8 explores the development and use of interpersonal relationships in organizations. Interpersonal relationships are presented as the primary functional unit of analysis of all social coordination, the level on which all organizations are built. Key aspects of interpersonal communication in organizations are examined, including relationship development, communication reciprocity, leadership and relational influence, conflict management, power politics, and therapeutic-communication development.

Chapter 9 examines internal communication systems in organizations. The administrative functions of internal message systems are explained. Formal and informal channels of internal organizational communication are described. The reciprocal impact of organizational structure and communication patterns is explored. Motivation, control, and communication climate are examined as crucial aspects of the internal information system of organizations.

Chapter 10 describes the external organizational communication system. Open systems theory is presented as an explanatory model for describing the interdependent relationships between organizations and their relevant environments. Organizations are represented as existing within a suprasystem interorganizational field, where they must be able to coordinate their activities and outputs with organizations with which they are interdependent. The development of functions of external message systems, such as public relations, marketing, advertising, lobbying, recruitment, management information networks, market research, and long-range planning, are examined as message strategies used to elicit interorganizational coordination. Ethical constraints on external message systems are examined and external communication abuses are discussed in light of organizational responsibility for external accountability.

CHAPTER 8

Interpersonal Communication and Organizing

RELATIONSHIP DEVELOPMENT AND ORGANIZING

In Chapter 2, we presented a summary of key aspects of human communication. Recall that we described organizational communication as based on four hierarchically related levels of human communication.

1. Intrapersonal communication, which enables the individual to process information
2. Interpersonal communication, which enables individuals to establish and maintain relationships
3. Small-group communication, which enables members of organizational work units to coordinate activities
4. Multigroup communication, which enables different functional units of organizations to coordinate efforts

In this chapter, we will reintroduce and explore interpersonal communication, which is an extremely important level of human communication because it is at this level that relationships are established. Moreover, interpersonal communication is a crucial element of social organization, since the ability to communicate interpersonally enables human beings to coorient their behaviors. *Coorientation* involves the elicitation of behavioral coordination among communicators for the accomplishment of commonly recognized goals. Coorientation is the essence of human organization. If we cannot influence other people to coorient their behaviors with our own, we will not be able to organize with one another.

Relationship Development as the Basic Level of Organization

Relationships develop among individuals who agree to coorient behaviors with one another. The better developed the relationship, the more cooperation and coorientation is elicited among relational partners. Since interpersonal cooperation is necessary for social organization to occur, relationship development is crucial to human organization. In fact, relationship development is the most basic level of social organization.

Weick (1969) argues that no one person can do very much individually within an organization. It is only through interlocked coordinated activities that anything of consequence is accomplished in organizational life. This notion can be rather disconcerting to individuals who see themselves as powerful organization members. What they may fail to realize, though, is that power is not a trait that is exercised alone. Someone has to recognize them as being powerful and agree to comply with their requests. Power is based on a person's ability to influence the behaviors of others. The more influential an organization member, the more power that person will have over organizational activities. Relationships help individuals influence the behaviors of others. (Later in this chapter, we will discuss interpersonal influence as a crucial element in organizational leadership, as well as the use of power in interpersonal conflict.)

Developing and Maintaining Human Relationships

Strong interpersonal relationships are based on the mutual fulfillment of needs by relational partners. Each partner in a dyadic relationship expects the other to act toward him or her in specified ways. The key to establishing effective relationships is to make these expectations clear to interpersonal communicators so that they can direct their actions in accordance with the needs and expectations of relational partners.

Marital partners, for example, have many mutual expectations about appropriate interpersonal behaviors. The husband might expect the wife to vacuum the carpet, and the wife might expect the husband to wash the dishes. Often, however, these expectations remain unspoken, until they are violated. Each relational partner might think that the other knows what is expected of him or her without being told. This can be dangerous because if one partner is unaware or unsure of the expectations of the other, there is a high probability he or she will not act in accordance with the other's wishes. To complicate this situation one step further, the expectations of relational partners continually change, making the potential for the fulfillment of these expectations less likely.

This same relational pattern holds true for business and professional relationships. Co-workers have certain expectations about one another's behavior. For example, two secretaries working in a small office probably depend on each other to share organizational tasks. Secretary A might expect secretary B to handle certain jobs, and B probably expects A to handle other jobs. These secretaries can work cooperatively and fulfill each other's expectations only to the extent that they are aware of and willing to go along with these mutual expectations. If a rush typing job is sent to the office and secretary A is not available, secretary B is expected to complete the job. If, while secretary B is working on this typing, a large filing job is sent to the office, B will expect secretary A to handle the filing. As the office work load changes, the cooperative working relationship between these secretaries must change also. If the secretaries rely on old expectations to guide their behaviors, they will not be able to cope with new office demands. As the work load changes, relational expectations must be updated and revised through interpersonal communication. (This is similar to the notion of requisite variety suggested by Weick [1979]. Routine organizational inputs can be handled by existing rules, but new and equivocal inputs demand new rules be generated through communication cycles.)

Obviously, learning about the expectations of others is essential in enhancing interpersonal relationships. Every time you communicate with another person, you are affecting the relationship you have with that person in some way. To the extent that your behaviors match the expectations that the other person has about you, you can strengthen the relationship. When your behaviors do not match the other's expectations, you frustrate that person and weaken the relationship.

When people fail to meet the expectations that relational others set for their behavior, they disappoint those persons and jeopardize their relationships. The interpretations most often assigned to behaviors that fail to meet relational expectations are very negative. It is often assumed that the noncompliant person is either *mad* (crazy or stupid) or *bad* (purposefully uncooperative). Mad or bad interpretations are generally stereotypes that serve to weaken the credibility of the communicators and foster suspicion and mistrust within the relationship. The more communicators fail to meet the expectations of those they are in a relationship with, the more the relationship is weakened. Communicators are frustrated by the negative responses they receive and often are unaware that they are violating each other's expectations. The failure to meet another's expectations can instigate inappropriate, often angry and retaliatory, responses. These behaviors, in turn, instigate additional inappropriate behaviors, all of which fail to meet relational expectations, causing a vicious cycle of escalating relational deterioration.

To a certain extent, effective relationships are very much like contractual agreements. They are not usually explicit written contracts, such as those used by lawyers to govern legal arrangements, although in some organizations, like the military, many bureaucratic rules govern interpersonal relations among organization members. Relationships usually are less formal than are legal contracts, generally taking the form of implicit contracts, in which relational partners learn from experience what each wants from the other. Subtle metacommunicative messages (messages that provide feedback about communication) are used to establish most implicit relational contracts. There are two parts to the development of implicit contracts.

1. Relational partners must recognize the expectations each has about the other.
2. Relational partners must agree to try to fulfill each other's expectations.

For example, in a relationship between two construction workers who work together framing the top floor of a high-rise building project, the implicit contract they have established might evoke informal and playful interaction in nonrisky situations (during coffee breaks, at lunch, or after work) but calls for serious helpful interaction in risky situations (when one is carrying a heavy load on a narrow steel girder on the top of a building). Since the nature of their high-rise construction work may lead to dangerous job situations, this implicit contract is designed to make sure that the two workers help each other. If worker A violates this implicit contract by teasing worker B in a potentially dangerous situation, worker A runs the risk of jeopardizing their relationship, as well as endangering worker B's life. The workers' recognition of their mutual expectations and unspoken agreement to act toward each other in ways that fulfill these expectations is an illustration of their effective use of an implicit contract.

In effective interpersonal relationships, partners establish clearly understood and agreed-on implicit contracts. Communicators not only are aware of their expectations about each other, but also work at seeking new information and continually updating their perceptions of these expectations. By being sensitive to the changing needs of their relational partners, they can update their relational expectations and renegotiate their implicit contracts. These communicators try to update their awareness of the implicit contract by continually giving and seeking interpersonal feedback, which enables them to continue to act appropriately as their relationship grows. The more they are able to effectively update their implicit contracts, the better relational partners are at mutually fulfilling needs and strengthening their growing relationship.

Reciprocity in Human Relationships

Relationships are built on an extremely powerful rule of human behavior, the *norm of reciprocity*, which suggests that in interpersonal relationships, the behaviors of each participant are contingent on the behaviors of the other. Each person patterns his or her actions in response to the way the other person behaves. (This does not mean that the two interactants behave in exactly the same way, mirroring each other. It means that they react to each other based on their perceptions of the other's behaviors.) When person A accepts and fulfills the expectations of person B, it encourages person B to accept and fulfill the expectations of person A.

Based on the norm of reciprocity, people communicate with others in accord with the way they perceive these others communicating with them. We alluded to the norm of reciprocity in Chapter 2 when we discussed the interpersonal influences of personal and object communication. The more you treat someone as an object, the more likely that person is to treat you with disrespect; conversely, the more you communicate with another person as a person, the more likely he or she is to treat you with respect.

The norm of reciprocity suggests that interpersonal relationships develop incrementally over time (Wilmot, 1980). The more you demonstrate your willingness to fulfill certain expectations of the other person, the more likely that person is to fulfill your expectations. For example, if you say hello to a co-worker, your behavior demonstrates that you acknowledge the other person's existence and that you probably would like him or her to acknowledge you. The person to whom you say hello generally feels compelled by the norm of reciprocity to greet you in return. If you both agree to greet each other, you have established an implicit contract—a simple one, but an implicit contract nonetheless. Based on this initial implicit contract, you may begin to develop additional implicit contracts with this person. If you try to help your co-worker accomplish a difficult task, it is likely that when you need help, he or she will be willing to help you. In this example, the norm of reciprocity is helping you to develop a cooperative relationship step by step (incrementally) with your co-worker.

The norm of reciprocity helps to govern equity of effort between relational partners. If person A in a relationship does more for person B than B does for A, they will violate the norm of reciprocity, and the relationship will deteriorate. For example, when a salesperson offers us a deal that is too good to be true, we are inclined to feel uneasy with the offer and wonder what "catches" there might be to the deal. The updating of implicit contracts generally involves interpersonal negotiation to maintain equity within the relationship. If a relational partner wants you to update your implicit contract by doing something to help him or her, you have the right, due to the norm of reciprocity, to ask for a favor in return. In the movie *The Godfather,* when Vito Corleone, the godfather, tells someone who asks him for a favor that he will grant that person's request but that someday he will ask for a favor in return, he is exhibiting the principle of equity inherent in the norm of reciprocity.

The expectations we have about other people's behavior often act as interpersonal self-fulfilling prophecies (Wilmot, 1980; Watzlawick, Beavin, and Jackson, 1967). An interpersonal self-fulfilling prophecy occurs when one person's expectations about another leads the second person to respond in accordance with those expectations. For example, if manager A believes that subordinate B is dishonest and untrustworthy, the manager is likely to communicate these suspicions to the subordinate through verbal and nonverbal behaviors, such as unwarranted questioning, staring, and unfriendly facial expressions. The more the subordinate detects these untrusting behaviors, the more he or she will feel uncomfortable with the manager. Subordinate B may be hesitant to disclose full and honest information to manager A because the subordinate does not trust the manager. Since the subordinate is not providing full and honest information to the manager, the manager's expectations about the subordinate are fulfilled.

Self-fulfilling prophecies need not be destructive; they can also be used advantageously in organizational life. If you want a person to act thoughtfully, the more you treat that person as being thoughtful (perhaps by asking his or her opinion on difficult problems), the more likely the person is to develop the ability to think through problems. (Recall our discussion in Chapter 4 of Theory X and Theory Y assumptions about human nature. How do you think self-fulfilling prophecies influence workers' reactions to these assumptions?)

By reciprocally fulfilling one another's expectations, we develop and maintain interpersonal relationships and elicit interpersonal cooperation. Fulfilling others' relational expectations leads us to structure and pattern our behaviors in accordance with the needs of others. These behavior patterns develop into interpersonal roles that we perform in the process of organizing. *Roles* define and constrain individual behavior by dictating how relational partners are to act in different situations. For example, if you have accepted the role of student, you have also accepted certain behavior patterns that go along with being a student, such as attending classes, taking notes, listening to lectures, doing assignments, answering questions, and taking exams. The role does not totally constrain your behaviors because you can make personal choices about how you fulfill the relational expectations established by your role, but the role does have a large influence on the types of behaviors in which you engage.

Part of becoming an organization member is developing working relationships with other organization members. These working relationships necessitate the fulfillment of others' expectations and the development of organizational roles. People perform many common organizational roles. Leaders engage in authority-wielding and decision-making activities as part of their roles, while subordinates follow leaders' orders, engaging in compliant behaviors as part of their roles. The formal position that a person accepts within an organization exerts pressure on that individual to behave in accordance with role expectations. If you accept a job as a receptionist, you are expected to answer the phone and forward messages to appropriate organization members. If you accept a job as a salesperson, you are expected to represent the organization with the public by acting and dressing appropriately.

The roles that organization members develop enable them to accomplish a wide range of functions in organizational life. Two important types of functionally oriented organizational roles are task roles and maintenance roles (Benne and Sheats, 1948). Task and maintenance roles are designed to perform very different, yet mutually dependent, organizational activities.

Task roles are primarily concerned with job accomplishment. They involve such individual activities as initiating ideas, seeking information, coordinating efforts, evaluating activities, clarifying procedures, and energizing activities in accomplishing organizational objectives (Benne and Sheats, 1948). Typically, formal organizations like businesses and industries stress the performance of task-oriented roles to accomplish specified organizational activities.

Maintenance roles are primarily concerned with preserving and maintaining interpersonal relationships within organizations. They involve such activities as providing others with support, expressing feelings, releasing tension, keeping channels of communication open, encouraging others, and promoting harmony among organization members. Maintenance roles help organization members develop effective relationships and cooperate with one another.

Organization leaders often incorrectly stress task roles as being more important to the organization than maintenance roles. For example, management orders that direct workers to concentrate on accomplishing their jobs without conversing with one another fail to recognize the importance of maintenance factors in accomplishing organizational activities. Task and maintenance roles work together in performing equally important and mutually dependent functions in organizing. Emphasis on the development of task roles in organizations often occurs at the expense of the development of maintenance roles. To accomplish the organizational tasks that are emphasized by task roles, organization members must be able to work cooperatively, which is emphasized by maintenance roles. Certainly, emphasis on maintenance roles at the expense of task roles is also problematic, since organization members probably get along well with one another but are not directed to accomplish organizational goals. In effective organizations, task and maintenance roles are well integrated.

Organization members sometimes perform roles that are nonfunctional to the organization. These role activities are neither task nor maintenance oriented. Benne and Sheats (1948) refer to these nonfunctional behavior patterns as *self-centered roles* because they are directed toward individual goals rather than cooperative organizational goals. Self-centered roles are characterized by activities that are overly aggressive, seek personal recognition at the expense of other organization members, trivialize organizational activities, and fail to exert appropriate effort in accomplishing organizational tasks. Self-centered roles must be discouraged because they inhibit the accomplishment of task and maintenance organizational functions and ultimately limit the effectiveness of organizational activities. (Figure 8.1 lists examples of task-oriented, maintenance-oriented, and self-centered organizational roles.)

LEADERSHIP AS INTERPERSONAL COMMUNICATION

Perhaps the most important and complex roles performed in organizational life are the roles of leaders. Leaders influence the activities of other organization members through their interpersonal communication. They depend on the development of effective interpersonal relationships with other organization members to help gather information and elicit cooperation. Information and feedback help them make organizational decisions and influence the behaviors of others. The strength of leadership depends on interpersonal influence (Pelz, 1952). Interpersonal communication is the means by which the primary activities of organizational leadership are accomplished. Indeed, Pace (1983) asserts, "Communication is therefore the only process by which a leader can exert influence" (p. 71).

Figure 8.1

Roles

Task roles help accomplish organizational jobs; maintenance roles help promote comfortable socioemotional relations among organization members. Self-centered roles impede the accomplishment of both task and maintenance organizational goals.

Task Roles

1. *Initiator-contributor* contributes ideas and suggestions; proposes solutions, decisions, and new ideas; restates old ideas in novel ways
2. *Information seeker* asks for clarification in terms of the accuracy of comments; asks for information or facts relevant to accomplishing group tasks; suggests information if needed for decisions
3. *Information giver* offers facts or generalizations that may relate to personal experiences and are pertinent to the task
4. *Opinion seeker* asks for clarification of members' opinions; asks how members feel
5. *Opinion giver* states beliefs and opinions about suggestions made; indicates what members' attitudes should be
6. *Elaborator-clarifier* elaborates ideas and other contributions; offers rationales for suggestions; tries to deduce how an idea or a suggestion would work if adopted by the organization
7. *Coordinator* clarifies relationships among information, opinions, and ideas; suggests an integration of ideas
8. *Diagnostician* indicates what the task-oriented problems are
9. *Orienter-summarizer* summarizes interaction; points out departures from agreed-on goals; brings members back to the central issues; raises questions about the direction in which the organization is headed
10. *Energizer* prods organization members to action
11. *Procedure developer* handles routine tasks, such as seating arrangements, obtaining equipment, and handing out pertinent papers
12. *Secretary* keeps notes on the member progress
13. *Evaluator-critic* analyzes accomplishments; checks to see that consensus has been reached

Maintenance Roles

1. *Supporter-encourager* praises, agrees with, and accepts the contributions of others; offers warmth, solidarity, and recognition

Figure 8.1 *(continued)*

2. *Harmonizer* reconciles and mediates differences; reduces tension by giving members a chance to explore their disagreements
3. *Tension reliever* jokes or in some other way reduces formality of interaction; relaxes members
4. *Compromiser* offers to compromise when own ideas are in conflict with those of others; admits errors so as to maintain cohesion among members
5. *Gatekeeper* keeps communication channels open; facilitates interaction among some members and blocks interaction among others
6. *Feeling expresser* makes explicit the feelings, moods, and other relationships in the organization; shares own feelings with others
7. *Standard setter* expresses standards in evaluating organizational processes and standards for the members to achieve
8. *Follower* goes along with the movement of other members passively, accepting the ideas of others and sometimes serving as an audience for interaction

Self-Centered Roles

1. *Blocker* interferes with progress by rejecting ideas or taking a negative stand on all issues; refuses to cooperate
2. *Aggressor* struggles for status by defining the status of others; boasts; criticizes
3. *Deserter* withdraws; remains indifferent, aloof; sometimes formal; daydreams; wanders from the subject; engages in irrelevant side conversations
4. *Dominator* interrupts and embarks on long monologues; authoritative; tries to monopolize others' time
5. *Recognition seeker* attempts to gain attention in an exaggerated manner; usually boasts about past accomplishments; relates irrelevant personal experiences, usually in an attempt to gain sympathy
6. *Confessor* engages in irrelevant personal catharsis; uses the organization to work out own mistakes and feelings
7. *Playboy* displays a lack of involvement in the organization through inappropriate humor, horseplay, or cynicism
8. *Special-interest pleader* acts as the representative for another organization or specialized group; engages in irrelevant behavior

Adapted from K. Benne and P. Sheats, "Functional Roles of Group Members," *Journal of Social Issues* 4 (1948): 41–49, with permission from the Society for the Psychological Study of Social Issues.

Leaders and Managers

Leadership is a crucial aspect of organizational life because leaders provide organization members with direction. Leaders identify organizational goals and designate the activities in which organization members should engage to accomplish these goals. Yet several organizational theorists have decried the absence of effective leadership in modern organizations (Bennis, 1976a, 1976b; Zaleznik, 1977; Peters and Waterman, 1982). Without effective leadership, organizational activities are not directed toward the accomplishment of organizational goals.

Bennis (1976a, 1976b) has argued, based on his experience as president of the University of Cincinnati, that the growing complexities of organizational life have made it increasingly difficult for a leader to actually make and enforce leadership decisions. He explains that both the external and the internal organizational environments constrain leaders' choices. The external environment provides the organization with a multitude of organizational dependencies to which the leader must answer. The internal environment has become increasingly politicized, with many advocates urging the leader to support specialized, and often contradictory, activities. Furthermore, Bennis argues that society has become so litigious that organization leaders have become more concerned with avoiding problems with internal and external agents and resulting legal suits than with directing the accomplishment of organizational activities.

These constraints on leadership have led to a dichotomy between leadership and management behaviors described by Bennis (1976a, 1976b) and Zaleznik (1977). Bennis (1976a) explains that the goals of leadership are to set the direction for organizations, while the goals of management are to accomplish set organizational tasks. Similarly, Zaleznik suggests that there are distinct personality differences between leaders and managers. Managers rationally assess organizational tasks and develop strategies to accomplish these tasks, while leaders must be visionaries who are able to intuitively interpret environmental conditions, predict future conditions, and creatively chart the course for organizational activities. The leader is interested in direction and innovation, while the manager is interested in order and efficiency. An analogy that might enlighten the distinction between leaders and managers is that a leader can be likened to a chef who artfully creates a soup to fit an occasion by selecting and combining available ingredients, while the manager stirs the soup, making sure that the pot does not boil over.

There is need for both leaders and managers in organizational life. Yet both Bennis and Zaleznik assert that there is an imbalance between leadership and management in modern organizations, with many more managers than leaders. Peters and Waterman (1982) also point out this overemphasis on task accomplishment to the detriment of direction in modern organizations, in which activities often are accomplished blindly and which suffer from a lack of imagination, ingenuity, and innovation. (In Chapter 11, we will examine the need for balance between stability and innovation, indicating the important role of organization leaders in coordinating internal and external communication systems.)

Bennis (1976a) suggests the development of specific leadership characteristics to transform managers into leaders. He asserts that leaders should

1. develop vision and assertiveness to make effective and decisive organizational decisions;
2. look at the larger organizational picture rather than at the nuts and bolts of organizational life;
3. see things in context, interpreting organizational situations in terms of the organization's unique history and goals;
4. have the strength and courage to make difficult decisions and take calculated risks;
5. gather relevant organizational information and be able to interpret the multitude of organizational messages;
6. recognize the importance of organizational culture and shape that culture to enhance interpersonal cooperation within the organization and loyalty to the organization;
7. feel comfortable with themselves so that they can handle the stress of leadership.

Zaleznik (1977) suggests that leadership must be developed. He argues that the organizational structure of modern society does not nurture leadership skills and, in fact, may discourage the development of leadership. Family, work, and educational organizational experiences encourage people to comply with authority more often than they encourage people to take risks and act creatively. For example, in college classes, where students should be encouraged to think independently, how often are you asked for "your own" ideas in comparison with the number of times you are asked to recall the ideas of your instructors or textbook authors? In most classes, the emphasis probably is on accurate recall and not on creativity. To develop effective leadership skills, individual self-esteem, self-reliance, and creativity must be encouraged.

Mentorship is suggested by Zaleznik as a valuable process by which potential leaders can be nurtured, guided, and taught. *Mentors* are senior organization members who develop helping relationships with promising junior organization members, or *mentees*. Mentors provide the junior members with successful leadership role models, inside information and organizational advice based on their extensive experience, protection from other organization members, and opportunities to handle responsibility, make decisions, and take risks. Zaleznik suggests that organizations should encourage the development of mentor–mentee relationships because mentors can help mentees learn how to become effective leaders.

The differentiation made by Bennis and Zaleznik between the roles of leaders and the roles of managers in organizations is not a trivial distinction, although the use of the words *leaders* and *managers* may be misleading. This distinction identifies the ongoing struggle in organizational life between innovation and stability that we identified in Chapter 1 and will discuss again in Chapter 11. The leadership role these two theorists describe aptly illustrates organizational need for innovation and change, while the management role they describe illustrates the organizational need for stability and structure. Since organizations need both innovation and stability simultaneously, the roles of both leaders and managers are important for the survival of organizations. Leaders help direct the course organizations will take, while managers oversee and preserve the processes organization members engage in to accomplish organizational goals. The best executives are able to accomplish both goals. They are able to see the larger picture of organizational life and direct the organization accordingly, and they are able to see the smaller picture of organizational life and coordinate organizational processes.

Models of Leadership

Trait Model of Leadership Early organizational theorists oversimplistically described leadership as inherited sets of traits (White and Vroman, 1982). The trait approach to leadership followed the historical precedent of civilizations that believed in the natural succession of royalty, that certain royal individuals were born to be leaders and rule countries. Popularly, many people still talk about someone who is "naturally born to be a leader." Yet people are not born to be leaders. Given basic intelligence and ability to learn and communicate, anyone can be a leader in some situations. People learn to perform leadership behaviors in specific social contexts. We will discuss leadership as a multidimensional set of communication behaviors exhibited by individuals to exert interpersonal influence in an extensive array of organizational situations.

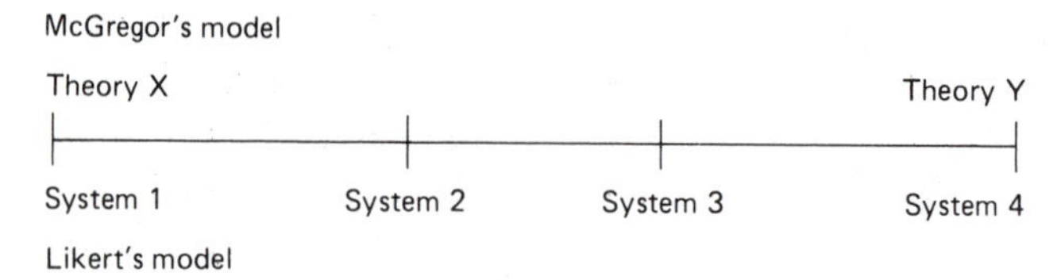

Figure 8.2 Comparison of McGregor's and Likert's models of leadership.

McGregor's and Likert's Models of Leadership There are many models that describe leadership. Recall that, in Chapter 4, we discussed two models of organizational leadership: McGregor's Theory X and Theory Y, and Likert's four systems of management (Figure 8.2).

McGregor's (1960) Theory X and Theory Y posit two sets of managerial assumptions about workers that illustrate different approaches to leadership. The Theory X leader does not trust subordinates to be self-directed and responsible and leads through explicit threats and punishments. The Theory Y leader expects subordinates to seek responsibility and leads by providing workers with challenging tasks.

Likert's (1961) model of four systems of management is similar to McGregor's Theory X and Theory Y, distinguishing between trusting and distrusting management perspectives about workers. Likert added two middle levels of leadership approaches between the polar extremes of Theories X and Y. Likert's four systems of management range on a continuum.

1. Exploitative authoritative, in which workers must be strictly directed by leaders (very similar to Theory X)
2. Benevolent authoritative, in which leaders allow workers to voice their complaints and opinions but maintain strict decision-making authority
3. Consultative, in which leaders actively seek feedback from workers and use this feedback to direct organizational activities
4. Participative, in which workers are encouraged to participate fully in decision making and in organizational goal setting (very similar to Theory Y)

As we pointed out in Chapter 4, Likert argued that participative management was the most effective management style, similar to McGregor's position that Theory Y was superior to Theory X as a leadership perspective. Likert's and McGregor's support of participative management as the preferred form of leadership underscores the importance of effective communication between leaders and subordinates for sharing relevant information and eliciting internal cooperation.

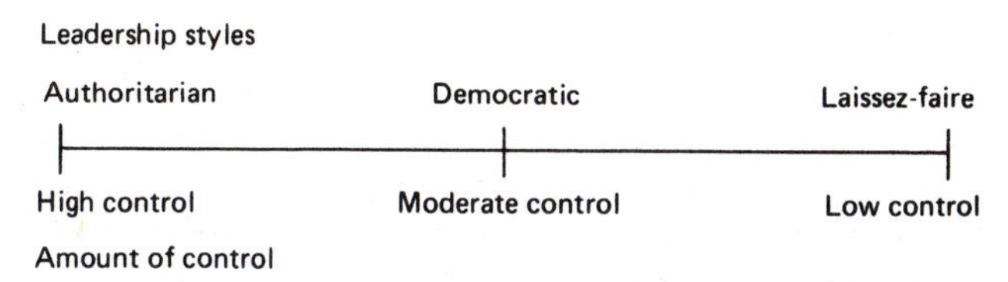

Figure 8.3 Leadership styles and organizational control.

Leadership-Styles Model Lippitt and White (1952) and White and Lippitt (1960, 1968) present another model of leadership, known as the leadership-style model, based on the amount of control that leaders exert over their followers. They identify three major leadership styles: authoritarian (high control), democratic (moderate control), and laissez faire (low control). (Figure 8.3 illustrates the relationship among these three leadership styles and organizational control.) Each leadership style has marked advantages and disadvantages in different organizational situations.

Authoritarian leaders are very dominant and wield strong authority over subordinates. They tell workers what to do and how to do it and sometimes even watch the workers work to make sure that they follow orders correctly. Authoritarian leadership is probably the most common form of leadership in modern organizations. Formal organizations, such as businesses and schools, and informal organizations, such as families and social groups, often are led by authoritarians.

The major benefits of authoritarian leadership are clear lines of authority, strong control, rapid decision making, quick response time of group, and ability of an expert leader to direct novice workers in complex or emergency tasks. The detriments of authoritarian leadership, however, often may outweigh the advantages. Some disadvantages include hindrance of creativity by subordinates, failure to utilize the knowledge and expertise of workers, dehumanization of workers, and resultant lack of motivation by subordinates to abide by decisions. Autocratic leadership should be used in emergency situations or when subordinates lack adequate knowledge about organizational tasks. Can you imagine soldiers questioning an infantry sergeant's direct order in the midst of battle, or an unskilled worker being allowed to operate a nuclear reactor without supervision? These are obvious situations that warrant autocratic leadership.

Democratic leaders attempt to share authority equally with all organization or group members. The democratic leader elicits information from subordinates and asks for their participation in decision making. The democratic leader often seeks consensus among workers for decision making, or if consensus is unreachable, he or she seeks a majority.

Some of the advantages of democratic leadership include active participation by all organization or group members, shared member expertise, generation of much information, and involvement and support of membership. Disadvantages of the democratic style include generation of conflict by airing different (often contradictory) perspectives, length of time required to hear all members' opinions, frustration of slow, labored decision making, and potential for majority cliques outvoting and manipulating smaller cliques. Democratic leadership is best used in complex problem-solving situations where a great deal of information and expertise is needed to make nonemergency decisions. For example, long-range planning for organizational development and innovation might utilize democratic group processes, with group members representing several relevant groups within the organization and its environment.

Laissez-faire leaders delegate authority to organization members. Of all the leadership styles, laissez faire is the most misunderstood and most maligned. It often is regarded as a "weak" form of leadership. In practice, however, laissez-faire leadership often requires the greatest strength of a leader, who must be confident enough in his or her subordinates to allow them to make decisions on their own. The leader provides organization members with information and is available for problem solving but generally gives authority to subordinates for taking care of business.

Advantages of laissez-faire leadership include encouragement of the growth and development of organization members and fostering of creative decision making. (These are similar to the functions of mentors in helping workers develop leadership skills.) The disadvantages of laissez-faire leadership become evident when the leader does not adequately prepare subordinates to work on their own or when workers are unable to handle the demands of the job and either take advantage of the situation or flounder in the performance of the job. Laissez-faire leadership is best suited to well-trained, sophisticated, professional groups of people who can handle the demands of their jobs. For example, laissez-faire leadership might be used effectively in a research-and-development department of a large industrial organization. Since the department is staffed by highly trained, well-educated professional researchers, the department head assigns the researchers specific projects and allows them the freedom to decide the best means of completing the projects, but is available to help with problem solving, if needed.

Situational Model of Leadership No one leadership style is correct for all organizational situations. The most competent leaders are able to adapt their leadership style to the particular group of people they are working with and the specific situations they are confronting through "situational leadership" (Mockler, 1971; Drucker, 1954). The situational leader matches the strengths of each leadership style to the specific constraints of the people, place, time, and problem facing the organization. "The manager's first step is to identify the major characteristics of the situation confronting him" (Mockler, 1971, p. 146). Situational leaders are analytic and flexible.

Lawrence and Lorsch (1969) present a contingency theory of organization that underlies the situational approach to leadership. According to the contingency theory, there is no "right" way to organize. Effective organization is developed to accurately reflect the specific organizational goals, members, technologies, and environmental constraints with which the organization as a whole has to deal. Similarly, the situational leader attempts to accurately identify the organizational constraints affecting his or her decisions, and then adopts the leadership style that best suits the constraints identified.

Task and Relationship Models of Leadership Several models of leadership have been developed concerning task and maintenance functions in organizational life. For example, Likert (1961) reported the work of the Institute for Social Research, the "ISR model," which identified two styles of leadership—job centered (task orientation) and employee centered (maintenance orientation)—as different ends of a leadership continuum. Stodgill and Coons (1957) developed a model that also examined leadership based on the combination of two similar behavioral variables—initiating structure (task orientation) and consideration (maintenance orientation)—although, contrary to the ISR model, these two characteristics are not on a continuum. A leader who is high in initiating structure is concerned with getting the job done, while a leader who is high in consideration is concerned with the needs of organization members. They identified four leadership styles based on different combinations of these two variables.

1. *High initiating structure, high consideration* the leader is very concerned both with getting the job done and with the needs of followers
2. *High initiating structure, low consideration* the leader is very concerned with getting the job done, but is less concerned with the needs of followers
3. *Low initiating structure, high consideration* the leader is unconcerned with getting the job done, but is very concerned with the needs of followers

4. *Low initiating structure, low consideration* the leader is largely unconcerned both with getting the job done and with the needs of followers

Blake and Mouton's (1964) organizational grid model of leadership combines task and maintenance functions. Their model is very similar to the Stodgill and Coons model, although it is visually more appealing. Blake and Mouton's organizational grid model of leadership compares leadership concern for production and concern for people. Their visual illustration of the organizational grid model is a two-axis grid with the horizontal axis representing concern for production (task orientation) and the vertical axis representing concern for people (maintenance orientation). After determining a person's scores on two 1 to 9 scales on concern for production and concern for people, a visual representation of that person's leadership style can be plotted on the organizational grid (Figure 8.4). The two axes of the grid combine to illustrate the many ways the leader's concern for task and for people interrelate in different leadership styles. Five leadership styles are identified based on extreme leadership scores on the organizational grid (Blake and Mouton, 1964; Klos, 1974). These five styles are basically the four styles identified in the Stodgill and Coons leadership model, with an additional middle-range style.

First, 9.9 score is a Team Style, also known as an Executive. This style is virtually the same as Stodgill and Coons's style of high initiating structure, high consideration. Blake, Mouton, Barnes, and Greiner (1964) suggest that this combination of concern for task and concern for people is representative of the most effective managers. This leader is interested in making effective decisions that will help the organization accomplish goals and reflect the ideas and goals of organization members, wants to integrate organization members' goals with the organization's goals, and stresses the establishment of good working relationships through use of open lines of communication with organization members to gather information and feedback. The 9.9 leader is very concerned with communication to establish effective member relations and to get organizational tasks accomplished.

Second, 9.1 score is a Task Style, also known as an Autocrat. This style is very similar to Stodgill and Coons's style of high initiating structure, low consideration. This leader is very concerned with authority, rules, and order in the accomplishment of organizational goals. The individual worker is not as important as the preservation of the organization. Leader communication is primarily downward and often is punitive. This style is consistent with the mechanistic model of organizations promoted by classical theory, discussed in Chapter 3.

Statements like "Shape up, or ship out" or "If you can't do the job, I can find someone else to do it" are representative of this kind of leader.

Third, 1.9 score is a Country-Club Style, also known as a Missionary. This style is virtually the same as Stodgill and Coons's style of low initiating structure, high consideration. This leader is most concerned with keeping followers satisfied and attempts to avoid conflict as much as possible. He or she generally relies on others to accomplish organizational objectives and often is viewed by other organization members as being a nice but disorganized individual. Leadership communication is light and social.

Fourth, 1.1 score is an Impoverished Style, also known as a Deserter. This style is largely the same as Stodgill and Coons's style of low initiating structure, low consideration. This leader is isolated from others within the organization and abdicates authority to other organization members. Leadership communication is all but nonexistent. This leadership style is the least effective, since it fails to accomplish either task or maintenance organizational goals.

Fifth, 5.5 score is a Middle-of-the-Road Style, also known as a Compromiser. This leader attempts to balance moderate concern for task accomplishment and for organization member relations. The mid-

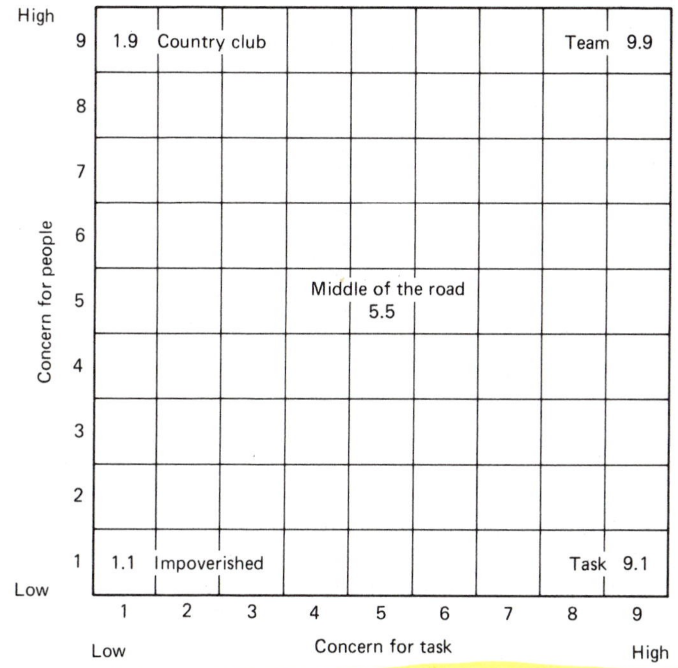

Figure 8.4 Blake and Mouton's managerial grid leadership model.

dle-of-the-road leader compromises between opposing needs in organizational life. A primary concern is keeping the organization going—maintaining a tolerable level of relations among organization members and a moderate level of successful accomplishments of organizational goals. This leader generally does not initiate a high level of communication with other organization members, engaging in enough interaction to keep things going.

The organizational grid model of leadership provides a useful tool for evaluating leaders' concern for accomplishing organizational tasks and for maintaining organization member relations. However, the grid is not an absolute measure of leader effectiveness. As we asserted when examining the situational approach to leadership, every leadership situation is unique and multifaceted. The most effective leaders are those who can influence organization members' actions to best fit the particular constraints of idiosyncratic organizational situations.

Certainly, there are many organizational situations where a leader who has high concerns for both task and maintenance (9.9) might be very appropriate. But there are also organizational situations where the leader should delegate full authority for goal accomplishment to other organization members, perhaps indicating that a 1.9 or even a 1.1 leadership style might work most effectively. Moreover, a leader must be concerned with more than task accomplishment and member relations to be effective. A good leader must be knowledgeable about and influential with the organization's relevant environment (Chapter 10) and knowledgeable about the goals, methods, structures, processes, and technologies of the organization (Chapter 9). Perhaps the most insightful approach to leadership effectiveness is alluded to by Bennis (1976a) and Zaleznik (1977), both of whom differentiated between the leadership functions of innovation and stability in organizations. Effective leaders attempt to coordinate organizational innovation and organizational stability by influencing organization members. We will again address this important balance between innovation and stability in organizations in Chapter 11.

Leadership and Information Management

Likert's (1961) linchpin theory of organizational structure, discussed in Chapter 4, epitomizes the information-management functions that leaders perform in organizations. According to the theory, each leader (manager) should be a link among organizational units. The leader ties together organizational units by communicating information back and forth to members of different groups. For example, middle-level managers perform key information-management functions in organizations by connecting upper levels of the organization with lower levels of the organization. These managers provide upper management with information about the concerns of workers and provide workers with information about the expectations of upper management. The primary function of the leader is to gather and disseminate relevant information among different groups within the organization.

Another key function of leaders is to elicit internal organizational cooperation and coordination. Leaders must be able to gather relevant information to diagnose sources of interpersonal conflict, identify strategies for preventing such conflict from disrupting organizational activities, and provide conflicting individuals with information that will allow them to manage conflict effectively. An effective leader gathers and provides information to organization members to transform potentially destructive organizational conflicts into opportunities to improve relations among organization members and to achieve the goals of the organization.

Case 8.1 shows what may happen when a leader fails to handle conflict effectively.

1. Evaluate Walker's leadership style. Which primary style does he use? How much control does he try to exert over the crew members? Is his leadership style appropriate to this type of organization and these workers? Identify some of the situational constraints that Walker might use to guide his leadership strategies and communication.
2. How high is his concern for accomplishing the task? How high is his concern for maintaining good work relations? Are these concerns balanced? What do you think Walker's score would be on the organizational grid? What kind of leadership style is indicated by his grid score?
3. According to Bennis's and Zaleznik's distinction between manager and leader, is Walker more of a leader or more of a manager? Explain your answer.
4. Evaluate the quality of Walker's interpersonal communication with Otto. How would you characterize their relationship? Identify implicit contracts they have established. Are they fulfilling each other's expectations? How does the norm of reciprocity influence their relationship? How does it affect Walker's influence over Otto and the other crew members?
5. If you could talk to Walker about this problem, what would you suggest he do to improve his leadership style and increase the effectiveness of the construction company?

Case 8.1

The Case of the Phantom Crew

Finster Attic and Basement Company was a small, family-owned, East Coast remodeling and home-construction company. Bob Finster had formed, owned, and operated the company for more than two decades until his death five years ago. After his death, the Finster family hired Mike Walker to manage the company. Walker was a friend of the family who had received a B.S. in mechanical engineering at about the time of Finster's death and had worked as a part-time laborer for the company for two previous summers. Walker made the difficult transition from being a member of the construction work crew to becoming the crew boss by trying to emulate Finster's "tough but fair" approach to running the company. Unfortunately, Walker tended to be better at acting tough than at being fair. The company had a good reputation as high-quality builders and was holding its own in a competitive home-construction market.

Frank Otto worked for Finster Attic and Basement Company for 10 years and had a great deal of pride in his job. Otto was a 45-year-old black man who performed general labor tasks along with the other three members of the work crew. Otto was the most experienced member of the work crew and was a hard worker who rarely complained about the difficult work. He was well liked by the other crew members, who were younger black men, and was respected by them for his hard work and practical, hands-on knowledge of home construction.

One Monday morning, when the crew was to pour concrete for a wooden deck they were constructing, Otto came in with a migraine headache. That was the same morning that he was scheduled to use the wheelbarrow for moving and pouring concrete to finish the foundation for the deck, a rather difficult task. The heavy concrete had to be wheeled along a narrow path around the perimeter of the deck so the concrete could be placed in strategic spots to firmly anchor the deck. The ground around the deck was rocky and uneven, making a bumpy path across which to wheel the heavy and unwieldy wheelbarrow. Otto had to be extremely careful with the wheelbarrow to keep it from tipping over. His headache made the job even more difficult.

The crew members resented Walker, who supervised them with a heavy hand and criticized their performance vocally. Walker had little tolerance for mistakes and always was after the crew to work rapidly and move on to the next construction job. He often stated, "Time is money, so pick up your pace!" The work-crew members considered Walker, who was a young white man, to be a redneck and called him "Cracker" behind his back. Walker seemed to get particularly agitated when the crew was working with concrete. The Monday morning that Otto was pouring the concrete around the deck was no exception, and Walker was closely directing the work-crew members. On one fateful trip with a wheelbarrow full of wet concrete, Otto was distracted by Walker's directions, caught the front wheel of the wheelbarrow on a rock, and dumped the fresh concrete onto a pile of redwood deck lumber. Walker lost his temper and began to berate Otto in front of the work crew, "What is the matter with you! Are you a fool! You've ruined that lumber. Clean that up, and then get off the wheelbarrow. Don't touch it again for the rest of the day!"

Walker told one of the less experienced men, Steve Herbert, who had been placing the concrete, to replace Otto on the wheelbarrow, while Otto was assigned to place the concrete, a rather simple job. Otto did as told, but sulked. Herbert, who had never transported concrete, a job reserved for more senior workers, was frightened by Walker's display of anger and was nervous about accidentally dumping the wheelbarrow and spilling the concrete. He was extremely cautious and worked very slowly. The work slowed down, making Walker even more angry. It was a long, hot, and miserable afternoon, with Walker screaming at the work crew and getting increasingly angry as less work got done.

On Tuesday morning, Otto did not show up for work. He was very upset about the concrete incident and was trying to cool off before talking to Walker. He had talked the problem over with two other crew members on Monday evening, and they had counseled Otto to apologize to Walker for having dumped the concrete. Otto did not want to apologize and claimed that the problem was that Walker was aggravating him. The crew members suggested that Otto try to talk with Walker about the issue and promised that they would come with him to provide moral support. At the end of the workday on Tuesday, Otto went to the construction office with the two other crew members to discuss the problem with Walker. Walker, who was upset with Otto for not having been at work that day, did not want to talk with Otto. He felt threatened by the three men. Instead of discussing the problem, he gave them an ultimatum: "Either be at work tomorrow morning, ready to *earn* your wages, or you are all fired." On Wednesday morning, Walker was the only person who showed up at the work site.

CONFLICT AND ORGANIZATION

Conflict is a natural and inescapable element of human existence and organization. Since all people are unique and perceive reality idiosyncratically, they are bound to disagree on a wide variety of topics and goals. Conflict is the process by which individuals express and negotiate their differences. More specifically, conflict is an expressed struggle between two or more competing positions held by one or more individuals, usually based on incompatible beliefs, ideas, or goals. Conflict can occur at several communication levels and in a wide variety of communication settings. There are at least four distinct communication levels at which organizational conflict occurs.

1. An executive might experience *intrapersonal conflict* when trying to make a difficult decision about directing the growth of an organization.
2. Co-workers might conflict *interpersonally* when arguing over different strategies for accomplishing a specific task.
3. Departments within an organization competing for a share of a limited payroll budget engage in *intergroup* conflict.
4. Rival businesses struggling for increased shares in a competitive market demonstrate *interorganizational conflict.*

Conflict cannot be avoided in organizational life. There are innumerable contexts for organizational conflict, with different people striving for different goals using different communication strategies. This suggests that every conflict is a unique social situation. Human conflict is situation specific.

Conflict often arises in organizations as a struggle over power. The struggle for power in organizational life frequently is referred to as "organizational politics" (Kanter, 1977). Power is a social construct; it is gained through interaction. No person is endowed with power. People are given power by others based on the messages they exchange and the relationships they develop. Conflict is a common communication strategy that is used to gain and challenge power. French and Raven (1960) identify five interactive bases of social power.

1. *Reward power* an individual is seen as controlling the rewards that other people can receive
2. *Coercive power* an individual is seen as controlling the punishments that can be leveled at others
3. *Legitimate power* an individual is seen as holding a position of authority that is accepted by others
4. *Expert power* an individual is seen as possessing special knowledge or information that others need

5. *Referent power* an individual is seen as being personally attractive to others so that others identify with this individual

The unrestrained exercise of organizational politics can create disharmony in organizations and lead members to feel threatened and act defensively (Dunn, 1981).

Conflict is regarded by many people as an unrewarding experience, but as we will argue, conflict can be a very rewarding interpersonal activity in organizational life. The lack of appreciation that people have for conflict usually is based on their unpleasant conflict experiences. Conflict is often unpleasant because few individuals feel comfortable communicating in conflict situations. Most people do not possess effective conflict communicative skills. The most common reactions to interpersonal-conflict situations are attempts to escape the situation or attempts at overt aggression; neither reaction is particularly effective in most conflict situations. Since conflict is inevitable in organizational life, people should learn how to communicate effectively in conflict situations. Conflict is important and can be a potentially useful means of interpersonal communication in organizational life because it can help organization members resolve problems, learn about one another, and develop coorientation.

The Role of Conflict in Organizing

Interpersonal conflict provides organization members with important feedback about potentially problematic situations. Conflict arises out of perceived constraints on the accomplishment of individual and organizational needs and goals. By expressing these needs and goals, organization members are able to recognize differences in individual perception and adjust to these differences. Conflict facilitates interpersonal negotiating and updating of implicit interpersonal contracts. Effective communication in conflict situations can help people improve their interpersonal relationships by becoming more sensitive and responsive to one another's needs and goals and by developing more mutually fulfilling interpersonal contracts.

Since organizing is dependent on interpersonal cooperation and coordination, conflict may initially seem to pit organization members against one another and be a threat to coorientation. Yet effective interpersonal conflict actually enhances interpersonal coorientation in organizations. Organizational life is a continually changing process. Effective organizing strategies at one time are no longer effective at another time. Conflict enables organization members to recognize problematic organizing strategies and to adjust these strategies together. This mutual adjustment process is at the heart of effective interpersonal cooperation and enables coorientation and organization to occur.

Conflict Strategies and Tactics

Frost and Wilmot (1978) identify four primary conflict strategies that people employ based on the intensity of their responses to conflict.

First, *avoidance* excludes active struggles. Those practicing this strategy sometimes refuse to talk, or they leave the conflict setting. The avoidance of conflict in initial stages is common in organizations in which the benefits of conflict are not recognized. Changing the subject is a common avoidance tactic.

Second, *escalation* can include such tactics as labeling, increasing the intensity of the struggle, and yelling or violence. It can also include a purposeful expansion of the issue beyond its legitimate limits. Coalition formation can cause escalation.

Third, *reduction* is a conflict strategy designed to lessen the intensity of conflict. Again, if one's perspective is that conflict can be healthy and creative for a group, reduction is not always an effective technique because issues and needs have to surface before the problem can be understood and resolved.

Fourth, *maintenance* keeps the tension generated by conflict at a level that is manageable to each of the combatants. Maintenance tactics are designed to equalize the power of the participants or to gain symmetry.

Each of the four conflict strategies is appropriate in some situations and inappropriate in others. People who handle conflict effectively ascertain the unique characteristics of the conflict situation they are in and choose the most appropriate strategies to use. Often, however, individuals grow accustomed to using one primary conflict strategy and they develop entrenched, hard-to-change propensities toward conflict.

All people develop their own individual conflict profile based on their personal orientation toward the conflict, toward themselves, and toward the person or persons with whom they are conflicting. Kilmann and Thomas (1975) provide a grid model of personal-conflict profiles comparing concern for self and concern for others. Concern for self is characterized by a scale ranging from low assertiveness to high assertiveness, or "aggressiveness" (Frost and Wilmot, 1978, p. 29), while concern for others is characterized by a scale ranging from low cooperation to high cooperation (Figure 8.5). Their grid model is structurally similar to Blake and Mouton's (1964) organizational grid. Like Blake and Mouton's five leadership types, Kilmann and Thomas identify five conflict profiles from different extreme scores on their grid.

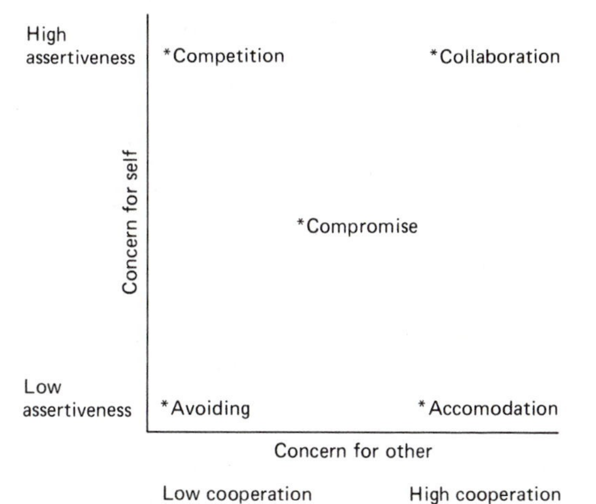

Figure 8.5 Conflict profile. What is your personal conflict style? From Ralph Kilmann and Kenneth Thomas, "Interpersonal Conflict-Handling Behavior as Reflection of Jungian Personality Dimensions," *Psychological Reports* 37 (1975):971–980.

1. Competition profile, which is characterized by high assertiveness and low cooperation
2. Collaboration profile, which is characterized by high assertiveness and high cooperation
3. Avoiding profile, which is characterized by low assertiveness and low cooperation
4. Accommodation profile, which is characterized by low assertiveness and high cooperation
5. Compromising profile, which is characterized by moderate assertiveness and moderate cooperation.

Making the Most of Human Conflict

Conflict can be both productive and destructive (Deutsch, 1969; Frost and Wilmot, 1978; Folger and Poole, 1984). Destructive outcomes of interpersonal conflict include defensiveness, anger, hostility, hurt feelings, alienation, and weakened relationships (Dunn, 1981). As mentioned earlier, these destructive outcomes of conflict usually are emphasized more than are positive outcomes. People often fail to recognize the opportunities afforded by conflict. Kreps and Thornton (1984) identify potential benefits of conflict that people normally do not consider.

First, conflict can act as a smoke detector or a warning light for relational partners, groups, or organizations, helping identify larger underlying problems that should be addressed. Wherever there is smoke (conflict), there is fire (larger underlying problems that have to be handled).

Second, conflict can act as a safety valve, releasing tension and anger in individuals in dyads, groups, and organizations, rather than allowing these tensions to build up and eventually be expressed in destructive, volatile, and dangerous ways.

Third, conflict can encourage interaction and involvement among organization members in discussing issues of concern to the dyad, group, or organization. Conflict is a provoking, exciting, involving form of interaction that can serve to draw people out of their shells and encourage communication. Such communication enables effective organizing to occur.

Fourth, conflict can promote creativity and creative behavior by organization members. In the heat of conflict, individuals often are spurred to think of alternative ideas and create innovative messages that they may not have created without the stimulation of conflict.

Fifth, conflict can facilitate problem solving. Since conflicts are intense, pressure-filled communication situations, people are motivated to seek solutions to the problems causing conflict to reduce the conflict and relieve pressure. Conflict can provide an incentive to address problematic issues that otherwise might not attract attention until they grew to calamity proportions.

Sixth, conflict can promote the sharing of relevant information among organization members by encouraging these individuals to voice their disparate ideas and by increasing the amount of relevant information that is available. Indeed, in succumbing to "groupthink" (Janis, 1967, 1971), organization members go along with what they think is the will of the group. In groupthink, organization members resist ideational conflict, which is needed if the organization is to make a good decision. Conflict over a solution to a problem allows organization members to see different aspects of the solution from the perspectives of different individuals, encouraging organization members to search for alternatives, strategies, and solutions to problems. Hawes and Smith (1973) contend that maintaining organizational conflict ensures development of a pool of ideas for solving emergent problems. Janis (1967) describes how John F. Kennedy and a group of top-level advisors gave their approval for one of the worst government fiascoes of all time, the Bay of Pigs incident. This group approved an ill-advised, CIA-backed invasion of Cuba. The incident was an utter failure and an embarrassment for the Kennedy administration and the nation. Members of the decision-making group later admitted that they did not voice their disapproval for the plan. Failure to engage in ideational conflict led to groupthink in the Bay of Pigs incident.

Finally, conflict can test under fire the strength of organization members' ideas and their potential solutions to problems, by arguing the relative strengths and weaknesses of proposed ideas and solutions. If an idea survives the test of conflict, it achieves a level of intersubjective reliability (amount of agreement generated among individuals) and is likely to be a good idea.

To encourage achieving the productive outcomes of conflict while minimizing destructive outcomes, organization members must engage in *ethical conflict behaviors* (Kreps and Thornton, 1984), which include

1. arguing the specific issue at hand rather than relying on hidden agendas or continually avoiding communicating about conflict issues;
2. refuting a position without resorting to violence, character attacks, slander, or other overly aggressive tactics (try to avoid dirty fighting [Bach and Goldberg, 1974]);
3. constructing a "reasonable" argument against your opponent's position and for your own position, rather than basing your position on rumors, unsubstantiated claims, and overemotionalism (conflict as much as possible by using *substantive* [logical issue-oriented] arguments rather than *affective* [illogical emotion-oriented] arguments [Fisher, 1974; Bell, 1974]);
4. avoiding a win-at-all-costs mentality by keeping an open mind toward the ideas of others (try to maintain a *mutual-win* orientation toward the conflict situation as opposed to a win–lose orientation; conflict is rarely a *zero-sum game*, in which one person must win at the expense of others); and
5. keeping an open mind to new ideas and opportunities for compromise (try to listen and fairly evaluate the ideas of your opponents, as well as seek new strategies for ameliorating conflict).

Since conflict is an inevitable outcome of human interaction, organization members should be taught how to communicate effectively in conflict situations. Effective conflict communication will help organization members benefit from the productive aspects of conflict. The norm of reciprocity suggests that organization members who demonstrate ethical conflict behaviors can encourage others to conflict ethically as well. The introduction of ethical conflict behaviors can help organization members develop effective conflict relationships. When people are able to achieve mutually satisfying outcomes from conflict, they feel good about themselves, the relationship, and the situation. Effective maintenance of conflict can enhance the communication climate within organizations.

THERAPEUTIC COMMUNICATION AND ORGANIZING

Therapeutic communication is a form of human interaction that is largely misunderstood. It sounds like something that happens only in clinical settings, administered by trained health-care professionals to troubled patients in dire need of psychological help. The clinical connotations of therapeutic communication limit its applications in everyday life, obscuring the fact that therapeutic communication is an important, frequently used form of interaction that occurs in all manner of human relationships. Interpersonal relationships have many functions. They can provide communicators with excitement, support, friendship, love, financial gains, and intellectual stimulation, as well as serve to increase or decrease their overall state of health. The more therapeutic interpersonal communication is, the more the communication helps individuals increase their satisfaction with interpersonal relationships (Kreps and Thornton, 1984).

Therapeutic communication has been defined in many ways. Barnlund (1968) explains that interpersonal relationships are therapeutic when they help bring about personal insight or reorientation and when they help individuals to communicate in more satisfying ways in the future. Barnlund's approach to therapeutic communication implies that any individual has the potential for communicating therapeutically if he or she can help another person achieve better self-understanding, thereby aiding that individual in deciding how to direct behaviors to best satisfy personal needs and accomplish personal goals. Furthermore, according to this perspective on therapeutic communication, interpersonal feedback is therapeutic if it informs people about others' perceptions of them, offering them a clearer image about the reactions that people have to their communication.

Therapeutic communication encourages the development of interpersonal relationships by providing communicators with information both about the expectations that others have of them and about their level of success at meeting others' expectations. Therapeutic communication facilitates the development of effective implicit contracts between communicators. Ultimately, therapeutic communication enables individuals to communicate more effectively to achieve their goals.

Therapeutic communication is especially useful in business and professional organizations, where it largely goes unappreciated. Very few managers recognize that therapeutic communication is a primary tool they can use in their organizations, and few business courses stress the importance of therapeutic communication in motivation, problem solving, orientation, performance review, or personnel development. Yet therapeutic communication plays an important role in accomplishing a wide range of organizational goals. The use of therapeutic communication in formal organizations helps organization members cope with the many stresses and ambiguities of organizational life, achieve, reorient themselves, adapt, and grow.

The Therapeutic Communicator

Certainly, all interpersonal communication is not therapeutic. Interpersonal communication often can have nontherapeutic effects by confusing and frustrating communicators rather than helping them achieve personal insight and reorientation. The growth of object communication, dehumanization, job stress, burnout, and other problems in organizations suggests that much organizational communication is nontherapeutic. Nontherapeutic communication is counterproductive to the goals of organizations because it fosters dissatisfaction among communicators and undermines the spirit of cooperation that is essential to effective relationships and organization.

Watzlawick, Beavin, and Jackson (1967) have identified several situations in which interpersonal relationships can become "pathological" as a result of nontherapeutic communication. Pathologies are disturbances that make human communication problematic and dissatisfying, and therapeutic communication functions to ameliorate pathologies. Similarly, Ruesch (1957, 1961) has differentiated between therapeutic communication and disturbed communication, suggesting that human communication can range on a continuum from highly therapeutic to highly disturbed (nontherapeutic). Therapeutic communication can be used in many organizational situations to help individuals grow and adapt, increasing their sense of satisfaction with themselves and with their interpersonal relationships.

Rossiter and Pearce (1975) have described honesty and validation as two key characteristics of therapeutic communication; they contend "that honesty accompanied by validation results in psychological growth for persons and that the lack of honesty and validation is likely to retard psychological growth and possibly bring about psychological deterioration" (pp. 193–194). Truax and Carkhuff (1967) have identified three key characteristics demonstrated by therapeutic communicators that are similar to those offered by Rossiter and Pearce: (1) accurate empathy and understanding, (2) nonpossessive warmth and respect, and (3) genuineness and authenticity. Rogers (1957) has described therapeutic communication characteristics similarly, identifying such attributes as genuineness, congruence, unconditional positive regard, and empathic understanding. Kreps and Thornton (1984) provide a combination and synthesis of the communication characteristics of therapeutic communicators, identifying empathy, trust, honesty, validation, and caring as key aspects of communicating therapeutically.

Empathy refers to the ability to develop a full understanding of another person's condition and feelings and to relate that understanding to the person. Organizational communicators can demonstrate mutual empathy by accurately communicating one another's feelings in interpersonal interaction. Empathy often can be shown nonverbally, as well as verbally, by nodding your head when a person tells you something about him or her and is wondering if you have understood or by maintaining eye contact with the individual with whom you are speaking and mirroring the person's facial expressions in a genuine manner.

Trust is the belief that another person will respect your needs and desires and will behave toward you in a responsible and predictable manner. Trusting behaviors are those that "deliberately increase a person's vulnerability to another person" (Rossiter and Pearce, 1975, p. 123). It is risky to exhibit trusting behaviors to another because the person may not respond to you in a responsible way. In establishing a trusting relationship, it may be necessary for one person to take a chance by disclosing personal information to another that might make him or her more vulnerable to that person. If the other person responds responsibly and perhaps discloses some risky information of his or her own in response, the chances that trust will develop are good. If, however, an individual reacts irresponsibly or inappropriately to another's self-disclosure, trust will not develop. Because of the risk involved in establishing trusting relationships, trust is most often established little by little over long periods of time.

Honesty refers to the ability to communicate truthfully, frankly, and sincerely. There is never total honesty in any situation, because there is never total truth. People perceive the world according to their own interpretations of reality and often perceive the world very differently from one another. Honest communication, however, does not imply objective truth, but subjective truth. It is not purposely deceptive, but is intended to be a truthful representation of information as the individual knows it. People communicate honestly to the extent that their messages accurately express their awareness of their experience and invite listeners to share in that experience (Rossiter and Pearce, 1975, p. 55). Honest self-disclosure in organizational relationships implicitly invites reciprocal honesty by relational partners.

Validation occurs when a communicator feels as though other communicators accept and respect what he or she has to say. Validating communication affirms the worth of the person and of his or her experiences. (Validation is similar to personal communication, discussed in Chapter 2.) To validate other people does not mean that you have to agree totally with everything they are saying but that you respect their right to express their opinions, take what they have to say seriously, and are willing to be influenced by their views. Validating communication tends to humanize interaction. Organizational communicators can validate one another in interpersonal communication by listening carefully to what is being said and responding to one another's messages congruently.

Caring refers to the level of emotional involvement that communicators express for one another. It is what Rogers (1957) calls "unconditional positive regard," the demonstration of interest in and concern for the other person's well-being. To be useful, caring communication must be sincere and appropriate. Communicators can express caring for one another nonverbally by paying attention to what other people are saying (maintaining eye contact and nodding when appropriate), exhibiting emotionally congruent facial expressions, and using their vocal and tactile behaviors to show support. Organization members can demonstrate caring for one another by expressing genuine concern about others' problems and communicating a willingness to help the others work through their hardships.

Each of the five characteristics of therapeutic communication (empathy, trust, honesty, validation, and caring) is an important skill for effective organizational communication. In many situations, the five overlap and merge with one another. For example, empathy and caring can be expressed with the same nonverbal messages of eye contact and head nods; validation, honesty, and trust can be expressed through mutual self-disclosure. Empathy, trust, honesty, validation, and caring are also reciprocally occurring communication behaviors. That is, their expression generally induces a reciprocal expression by those communicated with. Due to the norm of reciprocity, the use of therapeutic communication in organizations can encourage other organization members to communicate similarly, evoking a spiraling or building effect in therapeutic communication. Development of these five communication skills will help organization members communicate more therapeutically, develop more effective work relationships, and increase the quality of organizational communication.

CHAPTER 9

Internal Organizational Communication Systems

FORMAL AND INFORMAL ORGANIZATIONAL COMMUNICATION

In this chapter, we will examine the internal functions of organizational communication. Recall in Chapter 1 that we differentiated between *internal organizational communication*, which occurs within the boundaries of the organization among organization members, and *external organizational communication*, which occurs across the boundaries of the organization between organization members and representatives of the organization's environment. Internal and external communication channels are used to perform important but distinct functions in organizational life.

Internal organizational communication consists of both formal and informal communication channels. Formal communication channels are dictated by the planned structure established for the organization, which includes the arrangement of organizational levels, divisions, and departments, as well as the specific responsibilities, job positions, and job descriptions that are assigned to different organization members. Informal communication channels are not planned and do not generally follow the formal structure of the organization, but emerge out of natural social interaction among organization members (Davis, 1953).

There is an interesting relationship between formal and informal communication systems. Formal communication systems rarely fully satisfy the information needs of organization members, who therefore develop informal information contacts with the grapevine to gather the kinds of interesting information they cannot get from formal channels. The less the formal communication system is used to provide relevant information to organization members, the more they depend on the grapevine for information, and the more powerful the grapevine becomes. Conversely, the more the formal communication channels provide members with relevant organizational information, the less these members depend on the grapevine for information. (The grapevine will be examined in greater depth later in the chapter.)

Vertical and Horizontal Message Systems

Message flow in organizations has traditionally been described in terms of *formal organizational structure*. We will begin our examination of message flow by first describing formal message systems and then describing informal message systems. The formal structure of an organization follows the *organizational chart*, which maps the prescribed hierarchy of power relationships within an organization (Figure 9.1). Depending on the job titles and job descriptions within the organization, certain formal relationships are prescribed among officeholders in the performance of their job responsibilities. For example, the people to whom a specific organization member must report, the people who must report to that organization member, those whom that member supervises, those with whom that member works directly—all have formal communication relationships that show up on an accurate organizational chart. An organizational chart illustrates the planned formal structure of the organization, which indicates the formal lines of organizational communication.

There are three major forms of formal communication message flow that follow three prescribed lines of communication on the organizational chart.

1. Downward communication
2. Upward communication
3. Horizontal communication

Upward and downward channels of communication are commonly referred to as "vertical message systems," while horizontal channels of communication are, understandably, referred to as "horizontal message systems." All three message systems follow relationships among organization members prescribed by the organizational chart and all three perform distinct and important functions for the organization.

Downward communication flows from upper management to lower

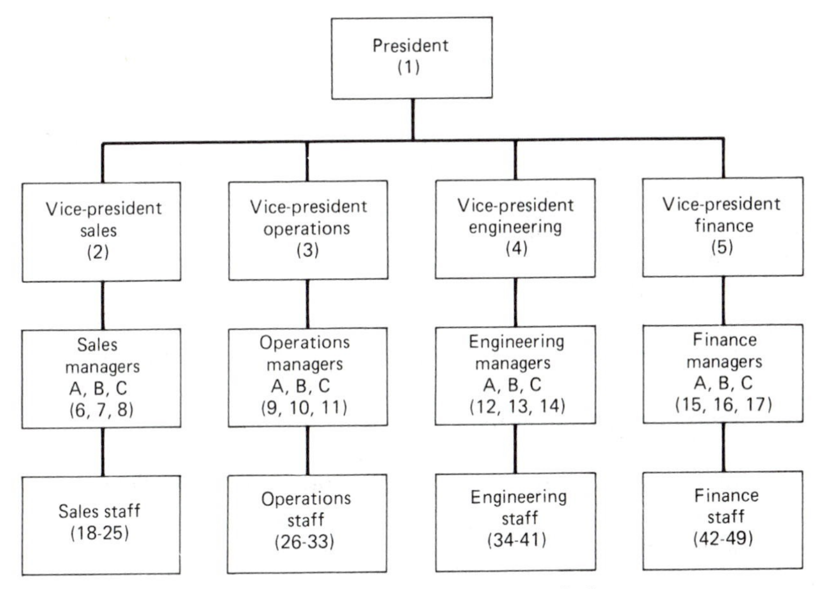

Figure 9.1 A typical organizational chart.

levels in the organizational hierarchy. Downward communication is the most basic type of formal message system. It is difficult to think of an organization that could exist without use of downward communication, which performs several key organizational functions.

1. It sends orders down the hierarchy.
2. It gives organization members job-related information.
3. It provides organization members with job-performance review.
4. It indoctrinates organization members to recognize and internalize organizational goals.

Downward communication is an extremely important management tool for directing the performance of workers in accomplishing their organizational tasks. Recall the emphasis in classical theory on providing directives and job descriptions through downward communication (Weber, 1948; Fayol, 1949) and on clear and sensitive downward communication (Barnard, 1938). There is usually a great abundance of downward communication in business organizations. However, as we will discuss in more depth later in the chapter, the prevalence of downward communication messages does not necessarily indicate the effective use of downward communication in organizational life.

Upward communication flows from lower level employees within the organization to higher level (often managerial) personnel. Upward communication serves several important functions in organizational life.

1. It provides management with feedback about current organizational issues and problems, providing managers with information about day-to-day operations of the organization that they need for making decisions about directing the organization.
2. It is the primary source of feedback that management has for determining the effectiveness of its downward communication.
3. It relieves employees' tensions by allowing lower level organization members to share relevant information with their superiors.
4. It encourages employees' participation in and involvement with the organization, thereby enhancing organizational cohesiveness.

Channels for upward communication often are underdeveloped in business organizations, causing a variety of organizational communication problems. Barnard (1938) was among the first theorists to stress the importance of upward communication in organizations; he explained that the individuals at the lowest levels of the organizational hierarchy are often the most knowledgeable contributors to organizational decision making. We will discuss the problems of insufficient and ineffective upward communication later in this chapter.

Horizontal communication flows among members of the organization who are at the same hierarchical level; it is basically peer communication. Horizontal communication serves several important organizational functions (Lee and Zwerman, 1975).

1. It facilitates task coordination by enabling organization members to establish effective interpersonal relationships through the development of implicit contracts (Chapter 8).
2. It provides a means for sharing relevant organizational information among co-workers.
3. It is a formal communication channel for problem solving and conflict management among co-workers.
4. It enables organization co-workers to give one another mutual support.

Although horizontal communication is an important formal channel of organizational communication, it is often overlooked and underutilized in organizational practice. The specific problems associated with horizontal communication channels will be examined later in this chapter.

Even though downward, upward, and horizontal channels of organizational communication perform important communication functions, in organizational practice, formal message flow is often poorly utilized (McMurry, 1965). Downward communication, although generally recognized by organization management as being an important communication channel, frequently suffers from several problems (Chase, 1970).

First, many organizations overutilize downward communication channels, which often are overburdened with messages, resulting in a plethora of orders, directives, and guidelines for lower level organization members. The sheer number of downward communication messages can confuse and frustrate workers.

Second, organizational superiors often give their subordinates contradictory, mutually exclusive directives, causing confusion and anxiety among these subordinates. Contradictory downward communication messages in organizations lead to "role conflict" for many organization members, who are caught in a "double bind"; they are not sure which directive to follow. Regardless of which directive they choose, they are bound to fail to fulfill one of the directives. Contradictory downward communication messages can frustrate workers and thereby damage organizational morale.

Third, downward communication is often unclear. Many directives are hurriedly communicated and vaguely stated, leaving workers unsure about what it is they are being directed to do. Superiors may use technical or jargon-laden terms that are foreign to workers, making communication less precise. Since workers often do not feel comfortable asking their superiors to explain or restate downward messages, unclear downward communications rarely are clarified. This results in serial communication, which routinely travels down the formal organizational hierarchy. *Serial communication* is a one-way chain of messages that travels from one individual to another without the benefit of feedback (Davis and O'Connor, 1977). Serial communication almost always suffers from loss of accuracy. To understand the concept of serial communication, think about the party game Telephone, in which one person whispers a story to another person, who then whispers the story to the next person in line, on and on until the last person in line relates the story aloud to the group. Invariably, the story that is told by the person at the end of the line is significantly different from the initial story. This distortion of information from one communicator to the next is typical of the distortion that occurs during serial organizational communication. Serial communication is a serious problem in organizations, in which directives from the top of the organization can be dramatically misinterpreted by the time they reach the lower levels of the organization (Figure 9.2).

Fourth, downward communication often communicates superiors' lack of regard for their subordinates. In Chapter 2, we differentiated

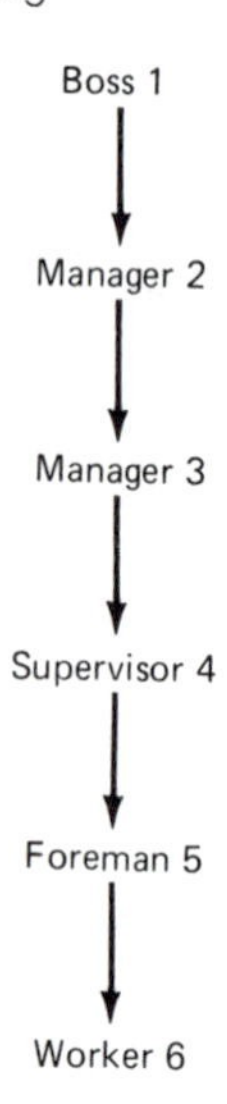

Figure 9.2 Serial organizational communication.

between content and relationship aspects of messages. In downward communication, the content information of explaining procedures and goals can be overshadowed by the relationship information of establishing power and control. Managers' overdependence on repeated downward communication messages to provide their subordinates with orders and instructions can alienate workers from management. Workers may assume that repeated downward messages imply that their superiors do not trust them or do not respect their intelligence and competence. These interpretations of downward communication can result in employee resentment of management and of the organization.

Upward communication channels also suffer from several problems in organizational practice (Roberts and O'Reilly, 1974; Read, 1962; Athanassiades, 1973).

First, it is often very risky for workers to tell their bosses about problems that exist in the organization or gripes that they have with management's downward communication. Since higher-ups in the organizational hierarchy wield power over those below them within the organization, lower-level employees fear retribution from superiors when providing unpleasant messages. If workers' upward communication evokes the wrath of a boss, the workers might jeopardize their jobs. Because of the risks of upward disclosure of unpopular information, workers often communicate only favorable messages to their bosses, a syndrome known as the "mum effect," which results in executive isolation (Krivonos, 1976; Vogel, 1967; Read, 1962).

Second, managers are often unreceptive to honest employee feedback and react angrily and defensively to unpleasant subordinate feedback, evaluation, and upward communication. The story about the ancient Greek monarch who slew the messengers who brought him unfavorable news about military campaigns is similar to the more current stories about workers who inform management about questionable organizational procedures and practices and are reprimanded, harassed, and even fired for their troubles (Stewart, 1980a, 1980b; Peters and Branch, 1972; Walters, 1975). Certainly, situations such as these strongly discourage other workers from presenting management with unfavorable information.

Third, there are often insufficient formal channels of communication devoted to upward communication. Employees at the bottom of a large corporation, for example, usually find it difficult to make communication contact with upper level organization members.

There are also problems concerning the use of horizontal communication in many organizations. Recall Fayol's bridge, discussed in Chapter 3, which suggests the use of horizontal communication in emergency situations to speed communication among organization members on the same level. Yet, Fayol failed to recognize some of the difficulties inherent in horizontal communication.

First, management may fail to recognize horizontal communication as a useful and necessary form of organizational communication. In many organizations, peer communication is discouraged and sometimes is punished. Horizontal communication is often thought of by organization leaders as being merely small talk and fraternizing among workers.

Second, at many levels, organization members often become so busy working within their own area of the organization they have little time for communicating with other personnel at the same hierarchical level in other areas of the organization. Yet, as we discussed earlier, horizontal communication provides organization members with useful information, allowing them to solve problems and coordinate activities.

Third, there are often insufficient formal organizational communication channels devoted to horizontal communication.

To effectively utilize downward, upward, and horizontal message flows in organizations, management must become aware of the importance of these formal communication channels. Downward messages must be clear, informative, and sensitive to adequately prepare organization members for performing organizational tasks without alienating these workers.

Managers must demonstrate genuine receptiveness to open and honest upward communication to encourage workers to provide them with feedback necessary to help them direct organizational activities

(Redding, 1970, 1984). Upward communication often must start from the top of the organizational hierarchy, with organization leaders encouraging workers to share their ideas with managers (McMurry, 1965). After all, those workers who are directly involved with the performance of organizational tasks know firsthand how to get the jobs done, what works, and what does not work in organizational practice. Management can utilize workers' knowledge by eliciting feedback from them.

Horizontal communication among organization members should be encouraged by management, especially in complex organizational situations where task coordination and problem-solving skills are most necessary. Recall Weick's suggestion that in equivocal organizational situations, a variety of communication cycles be available for organization members to help them reduce equivocality and develop specific strategies for reacting effectively to the organizational situation. Horizontal communication is an important source of communication cycles for organization members.

Some communication strategies for improving formal message flow in organizations include the use of group meetings to facilitate interaction among organization members, regular performance review and problem-solving interviews between management and workers, formal communication-training procedures and orientation programs for workers, suggestion boxes, rewards for workers who come up with ideas, and briefing sessions during shift changes. Organizational media such as interactive computers, newsletters, memos, taped messages, training films, and bulletin boards can be used to augment formal message flow. The key, however, to effective formal message flow in organizations, whether it be downward, upward, or horizontal, is the development of meaningful interpersonal relationships among organization members. (Recall our discussion in Chapter 8 of the importance of relationships in organizing.) Only through the development of effective relationships can organization members develop trust in one another, communicate meaningfully with one another, and elicit cooperation.

The Grapevine and Informal Communication

In addition to formal message-flow systems, which are prescribed by the formal hierarchy of the organization, an informal message-flow system emerges naturally through human interaction within the organization. Informal message flow refers to the communication that develops among organization members and that is not necessarily prescribed by the formal structure and hierarchy of the organization but grows out of organization members' curiosity, interpersonal attraction, and social interaction. As we mentioned earlier, informal message flow does not necessarily follow the organizational hierarchy but develops its own social structure. This informal channel of communication in organizations often is referred to as the *grapevine* and is composed of social groups, cliques, club members, family relations, and other informal relationships that develop among organization members (Davis, 1953; Bach, 1983).

One of the primary reasons for the development of informal communication systems within organizations is the members' need for information about the organization and about how changes in the organization will affect their lives. Organizations are often large, complex, and multifaceted systems. To behave effectively within their organization, members rely on information about what is going on behind the scenes and what is being planned by other organization members. As we discussed in Chapter 2, human beings have an insatiable appetite for meaning. To create effective meanings about organization life, organization members need relevant, reliable, and in-depth information. Generally, the formal channels of organizational communication fail to provide organization members with enough information to satisfy their curiosity about organizational life, so they must seek information from other sources. The grapevine provides organization members with interesting information about who is doing what and what changes are occurring within the organization. Informal communication channels provide organization members with information about organizational functioning that can help them understand organizational life and strategically direct their own activities (Kreps and Thornton, 1984; Bach, 1983).

In organizations, information is powerful; whoever possesses relevant organizational information and is willing to barter that information can gain and exercise power within the organization. People who seek organizational power and influence, especially those who do not have powerful formal hierarchical positions within the organization, often attempt to gain power by gathering key information about the organization and organization members and disseminating it through the grapevine. Those organization members who use informal channels to gather a great deal of organizational information and utilize that information to direct the grapevine are typically known as *informal leaders.*

Informal leaders wield a great deal of power within organizations, yet, strangely enough, they are seldom recognized by the formal power structure of the organization as being either legitimate or powerful. Organization members usually become informal leaders because of their extreme desire for power and recognition within the organization. People who have high needs for power and are not often concerned about the means they use to achieve power are referred to as highly

"Machiavellian" personality types. Machiavellian-type individuals who do not have formal positions of power within organizations, as do executives or managers, often seek power informally by gathering information of high interest to other organization members. By developing a stockpile of relevant organizational information and bartering this information for favors rendered by other organization members, Machiavellian individuals develop the ability to influence the behaviors of others within the organization.

The grapevine is generally regarded as an evil or a deviant aspect of an organization's communication system (Bach, 1983). Many people believe that the grapevine serves few useful functions and is primarily concerned with gossip, promoting false and nasty rumors and resulting in tainted reputations and hurt feelings (Davis and O'Connor, 1977). Because of these negative interpretations of informal communication systems, organizational practitioners and theorists have been plotting to do away with the grapevine for many years. Interestingly, most efforts at abolishing the grapevine have further entrenched it within organizational communication systems (Davis, 1973). Restricting informal information flow serves to increase organization members' ambiguities and need for relevant information. The more they need information, the more they seek to develop informal communication networks. There is a direct relationship between the need for information and the growth of the grapevine. The grapevine flourishes in climates of high uncertainty. Informal communication systems serve very important information-dissemination functions in organizations.

Contrary to popular belief, the grapevine is a very powerful and potentially useful channel of communication in organizational life (Davis, 1973; Bach, 1983; Taylor and Farace, 1976). Information disseminated along the grapevine travels extremely rapidly through the organization (Davis and O'Connor, 1977). Informal communication channels are relatively distortion free, losing very little accuracy in comparison with formal organizational message systems (Davis and O'Connor, 1977; Rudolph, 1973; Walton, 1961). (This is not to say that the information initiated in informal networks is always accurate but that the information generally suffers less distortion than information carried on formal communication channels.)

Informal message channels disseminate information rapidly because they carry "juicy" (interesting, timely, and salient) information. Organization members are motivated by their curiosity when communicating on the grapevine. If the information communicated to organization members is interesting, they are likely to pass it along to others (Davis and O'Connor, 1977). The grapevine communication network is characterized as a "cluster chain" of communication along which messages are distributed to a group of organization members, rather than to just one other person, speeding information dissemination by maximizing the size of informal message audiences (Davis and O'Connor, 1977). Additionally, the vast majority of organizational communication is informal, indicating that there are many available informal channels of communication in organizations for disseminating information (Downs, 1967; Rogers and Agarwala-Rogers, 1976).

Informal communication channels are less likely than formal communication channels to distort information because there are far more opportunities for feedback in informal communication networks, reducing the distorting influence of one-way serial communication; there are fewer status discrepancies among informal communicators, making it less risky for feedback to be sought; and there are more opportunities for message redundancies in informal networks, allowing organization members to hear the same information from several sources. Due to redundancy and feedback opportunities associated with many informal communication channels, informal communication does not suffer from the problems of serial communication as often as does formal organizational communication (Davis and O'Connor, 1977).

Managerial lack of appreciation for the grapevine often has resulted in unnecessary competition between formal and informal communication systems within organizations. Yet since both formal and informal communication channels perform important and interdependent functions in organizational life, it is wiser for organization leaders to coordinate these channels than to pit one against the other. Davis (1953) suggests that management not only be aware of the grapevine, but also feed and cultivate it.

Management can benefit from the Machiavellian tendencies of informal organization leaders by keeping these leaders informed about important happenings within the organization and developing good working relationships with them. By providing informal leaders with relevant and accurate organizational information, formal leaders can enlist the grapevine for disseminating formal organizational information, thereby supplementing formal communication channels (Kreps and Thronton, 1984; Rogers and Agarwala-Rogers, 1976). What is more, by providing informal leaders with important and accurate organizational information, management can help eliminate the spread of dangerous and/or untrue rumors. Rarely do informal leaders want to be caught in a lie. They want and need accurate organizational information to maintain their informal power over other organization members. Vicious, untrue rumors are just as dangerous for the informal leader as for their victim because untruths can undermine the informal leader's position and power. Just like the child who cried wolf once too often, an informal leader with consistently false information will quickly lose information appeal to other members of the organization. Furthermore, management can elicit relevant upward communication and feedback from informal leaders, who usually know a great deal about the day-to-day happenings of organizational life.

After reading Case 9.1, describe the role of the informal channels of communication in the hospital.

1. What is the relationship between the formal and the informal communication channels in this organization?
2. Why are problems in morale within the hospital occurring?
3. Who is really at fault for this drop in morale? Why do you think so?
4. If you were hired as an external consultant by this organization, would you evaluate the situation differently from the professor? What would you do to determine the cause of the problems?
5. How effective do you think the professor's recommendations for improving the situation are? Why? What suggestions would you make to improve the situation?

THE MANAGEMENT FUNCTION

Internal channels of organizational communication are extremely important in the accomplishment of tasks and goals within the organization. Organization management has the primary responsibility for directing internal communication channels and accomplishing organizational tasks. Townsend (1965) asserts, "Internal communication must be recognized as an essential tool of good management" (p. 208). Internal organizational communication is instrumental in achieving the "managerial" functions of organization, which include

1. informing organization members of organizational goals, purposes, and directives, as well as identifying members' mutual interests in the success of the organization (Fest, 1975; Townsend, 1965);
2. describing specific organizational tasks that are to be accomplished by organization members (Fest, 1975);
3. identifying specific job responsibilities of organization members and training them to accomplish these responsibilities;
4. developing and maintaining a good organizational climate in which internal channels of communication are optimally used (Townsend, 1965) (we will later describe the development of organizational climates);
5. enforcing members' adherence to organizational rules, regulations, and guidelines;
6. evaluating organization members' work performance and reestablishing optimal work performance when necessary;

Case 9.1

Pain in the Hospital

There was trouble brewing at Glenview County Hospital. The morale of hospital employees was at an all-time low. Several key members of the hospital staff had tendered their resignations, and there was a rumor circulating among the hospital staff that widespread administrative changes and restructuring were in the offing. Low morale was affecting the quality of health care, due to poor staff attitudes and internal squabbles. Bob Wilson, the chief administrator of the hospital, was worried. He did not know what was going on at the hospital or what he should do about it.

Bob Wilson had been hired three months ago by the last hospital administrator, Frank Hyatt, who had retired after 14 years with the hospital. Before coming to Glenview, Bob had been the assistant administrator at a nearby hospital for a little less than two years. Prior to that, he had received an M.A. in health administration from the State University. Neither his past employment nor his education had prepared him for the low morale at Glenview.

Bob decided to bring in his two assistant administrators to discuss the morale situation and find out what was at the root of the problem. They corroborated the fact that there was a problem and, in fact, told Bob that they had heard from several "reliable sources" about the upcoming administrative layoffs. The more Bob denied the layoffs, the more suspicious the assistant administrators became. They wanted to know why he could not confide in them and tell them what was "really" going on. Eventually, they began to assume that they were both potential victims of the administrative restructuring that they were certain was being planned.

Bob was even more concerned about the morale situation after talking to his assistants. It seemed that no matter what he did, the people working for him were becoming more and more paranoid. He gave Frank Hyatt (the previous hospital administrator) a call and asked Frank if he had any idea what was going on at the hospital. Frank answered that he had never encountered a serious morale problem in all his years as an administrator at Glenview; in fact, he always had felt that morale at the hospital was excellent, like a big happy family. This conversation did not make Bob feel any better about the situation.

In desperation, Bob decided to call in one of his former professors from the State University, who was an expert in organizational behavior. Bob hired the professor as an external consultant to solve the morale problem. The professor began work by interviewing members of the hospital staff. Again and again, the professor heard the same story; organization members believed that the new hospital administrator, Bob Wilson, was planning a major administrative reorganization, including massive layoffs. When asked from whom they had heard of this reorganization, staff members mentioned several names. One name, however, was identified as a source of information by almost everyone the consultant spoke to—Horace Jackson, a hospital janitor.

Horace was 64 years old and had been with the hospital for more than 30 years. He was well liked within the organization and, in fact, spent a good deal of his time each day wheeling a large plastic trash container around the hospital and visiting with members of each hospital department. When the professor interviewed Horace, Horace claimed that he had not heard of any layoffs. The professor recognized the contradictions between the report received from Horace and those received from other members of the hospital staff, and realized that Horace was probably the initial source of the rumor about layoffs.

When the professor informed Bob Wilson of what had been found, Bob reacted angrily and wanted to fire Horace. The professor warned against such a hasty action and told Bob that firing Horace would only serve to confirm the false rumor about layoffs. If Horace, who had been with the hospital for 30 years, was expendable, then the hospital staff would really be convinced that the rumor was true. Instead, the professor suggested that Bob recognize that Horace was an informal leader in the organization and could be nurtured as an organizational ally rather than treated as an enemy.

Bob called Frank Hyatt again, and asked him what he knew about Horace Jackson. Frank replied that Horace had been one of his most trusted employees. In fact, Frank told Bob that he had taken special care of Horace. He had invited him into his office every once in a while and asked him how things were going. Horace had provided Frank with information about what was happening behind the scenes at the hospital. Frank said that he usually had sought advice from Horace about problems at the hospital and administrative decisions, and generally had been given good advice. Every Christmas, Frank had made sure to give Horace a bottle of Scotch as a present.

Bob began to realize how important an individual Horace was in the hospital. He recalled how curt he had been when Horace dropped by his office, during his first week at Glenview, and asked if he needed any help. Bob had been busy with some details and had off-handedly dismissed Horace's offer of help. Bob realized that Horace probably had been insulted by the brusque manner in which the new administrator had reacted to him, and had retaliated, perhaps unconsciously, by starting the rumor about hospital layoffs.

Bob followed the professor's advice and began to nurture his relationship with Horace. He invited Horace to have lunch with him in the hospital cafeteria and asked for the janitor's advice about improving hospital morale. He shared with Horace some of his ideas about improving the quality of health care at the hospital. Over the next month, Bob encouraged Horace to drop by his office to discuss any problems or ideas he had. Over this same month, the nasty rumor about layoffs began to subside and morale began to improve. Horace was now sending new information through the organization about how he had intervened with the new administrator on behalf of the hospital employees. He spread the word that he had convinced the new administrator to keep the existing staff. Furthermore, Horace began indicating that Bob Wilson was a wise man and an excellent administrator.

7. coordinating organization members' and work groups' activities in the accomplishment of specific tasks;
8. seeking feedback from organization members to solve internal problems and promote ethical conflict (Chapter 8); and
9. maintaining high-quality organizational output and performance.

These managerial functions are accomplished through use of the internal communication systems and indicate that the manager's role is really a communication role. The manager must communicate effectively with other organization members using internal communication channels to provide and gather relevant information and to accomplish the managerial functions of organization.

Likert's (1961) linchpin model of management clearly illustrates the internal communication role that management must perform. According to the model, managers connect upper and lower levels of the organization's hierarchy through their communication contacts with both levels (Chapter 4). Managers' abilities to perform linking roles and coordinate internal communication flows are extremely useful to the organization and can increase the quality of work life (Wager, 1972; Albrecht, 1984).

Using Information for Evaluation and Adaptation

Internal communication channels provide organization members with key information that enables them to evaluate the quality of organizational processes. Organization leaders and managers must seek information from organization members to identify and diagnose operational problems. Once they have diagnosed the problems, they must be able to use internal communication channels to improve the situations that are causing operational difficulties.

Managers can use several communication strategies and techniques to identify, diagnose, and rectify organizational problems. Perhaps the most common communication technique used to evaluate organization member performance is the appraisal interview (Perrill and Bueschel, 1980). To evaluate organizationwide performance, survey-feedback methods are often employed (Williams, Seybolt, and Pinder, 1975; Gieselman, 1968).

The performance-appraisal interview is formal, one-on-one interpersonal communication between managers and their employees, providing their employees with feedback about the quality of their work, seeking feedback from workers about problems they may be experiencing, and establishing guidelines and goals for future worker performance (Meyer, Kay, and French, 1965; Perrill and Stopek, 1981). The appraisal interview provides organization members with an excellent opportunity for vertical communication. The interview can be used to air employee grievances and encourage upward communication, serving to relieve worker tensions (Gordon and Miller, 1984; Schultz, 1966); to provide workers with downward communication about such important topics as job information, promotions, or organizational changes; and to reinforce effective organization member performance by praising member behaviors (Fournies, 1978; Alexander and Camden, 1980). Additionally, the appraisal interview is an appropriate communication situation for managers to communicate therapeutically with their workers, providing workers with clear feedback and helping them redirect their work behaviors (Kreps, 1981b). The feedback provided to workers and managers through effective appraisal interviews can improve the accuracy of vertical communication and enhance organization member confidence and interpersonal relations (Leavitt and Mueller, 1951).

Managers need information not only about the performance of individual workers, but also about overall organizational performance. Survey-feedback methods are commonly used by managers and organization-development specialists to gather relevant information about organizational performance and organizational needs (Nadler, 1977; Pace, 1983). Survey data are extremely useful in ascertaining problems in organizational performance and directing the development of organizational innovations (Rogers and Agarwala-Rogers, 1976).

Greenbaum (1974) argues convincingly of the importance of management's gathering information about communication performance within the organization through the audit of organizational communication. Sincoff, Williams, and Rohm (1976) describe organizational communication audits as management tools that should be administered repeatedly to keep management posted on the status of the organization's health and alerted to emergent organizational communication problems. Communication audits enable management to gather relevant information about the quality of their organization's internal communication systems and to identify directions for improving internal organizational communication (Brooks, Callicoat, and Siegerdt, 1979).

The International Communication Association's Organizational Communication Division developed and field-tested a standardized Communication Audit Tool and Procedure for evaluating the quality of communication in organizations (Goldhaber, 1976; Goldhaber, Yates, Porter, and Lesniak, 1978). The ICA audit surveys organization members' attitudes and perceptions about topics such as "information accessibility, information adequacy, communication satisfaction and importance, communication content—clarity, accuracy, utility, appropriateness, timeliness, communication relationships, and communication outcomes" (Goldhaber, Yates, Porter, and Lesniak, 1978, p. 81). In a summary of the data from the first 16 ICA audits, Goldhaber, Yates, Porter and Lesniak (1978) report the following 10 preliminary findings.

1. Most organization members want to receive more than send organizational information. They report neither sending nor receiving very much information in their organizations and needing more information about personal, job-related matters and about organizational decision making. They also desire greater opportunities to voice grievances and evaluate their bosses.
2. The higher messages are sent up the organizational hierarchy, the less likely there is to be any follow-up, especially when information is sent to top management.
3. "The best sources of information are those closest to employees, and the worst are farthest away" (Goldhaber, Yates, Porter, and Lesniak, 1978, p. 82). Members report needing more job-related information from immediate supervisors and more organizationwide information from upper management.
4. Top management provides less timely and lower quality information than do many other key information sources.
5. Members prefer getting more information from formal organiza-

tional communication channels than from the grapevine. They perceive the grapevine as being fast and frequently used, but not providing them with as accurate or as high-quality information as they would like.

6. Although generally satisfied with interpersonal communication channels, organization members would like to receive more face-to-face communication, especially from upper management.
7. Organization members are generally satisfied with their immediate departmental communication climates, which demonstrate trust, but are less satisfied with organizationwide communication climates, which limit openness, input, rewards, and advancement opportunities.
8. Members report being generally satisfied with their jobs, but not satisfied with their opportunities for advancement within their organizations.
9. There were no general patterns of relationships between demographic characteristics (age, sex, race, and so on) and communication variables.
10. "The greater the distance between communication sources and receivers in organizations, the less the information received, the less the opportunity to request more information, the less the follow-up, the poorer the information quality, the greater the use of the grapevine, and the poorer the interpersonal relations. In contrast, when distance is decreased, employees receive and want more information, want to send less, receive more follow-up, receive higher quality information, use the grapevine less, and have better interpersonal relations" (Goldhaber, Yates, Porter, and Lesniak, 1978, p. 83).

These findings demonstrate the importance of communication in organizations to organization members and the need for improved organizational communication.

Management Information Systems

The explosion of information in modern organizations has necessitated the development of specialized organizational structures and technologies for storing, processing, and retrieving relevant organizational information (Patterson, 1984; Murdick and Ross, 1975; Offor, 1978). Management Information Systems (MIS) are specially planned computer-based organizational tools that enable managers to gather, store, process, and retrieve relevant organizational data and use these data to make informed organizational decisions (Lynch, 1984). For example, Makris (1983) describes the use of MIS in health-care organizations as "health informatics" (p. 206). Makris explains that hospital information systems have been used to keep track of and organize a wide variety of administrative functions (including accounting, billing, inventory, payroll, and employee scheduling), patient-care functions (including admitting, patient scheduling, laboratory-test results, dietary plans, and pharmacy inventory and prescription records), and managerial control functions (including financial budgeting, productivity evaluation, and service-utilization analysis). It is obvious that MIS systems help managers perform their internal communication functions in modern organizations.

Modern office computer systems are extremely powerful. They are able to store and process large quantities of data. MIS technologies also can process different types of data. For example, modern computer systems often combine data-processing and word-processing technologies (Calise and Locke, 1984), which enables organization members to integrate quantitative analyses of organizational performance with qualitative descriptions of organizational performance, used in reports, memos, newsletters, and other forms of organizational correspondence.

With all the information-related power offered by MIS technologies, access to more data may provide organization members with more useful organizational information or merely with more voluminous and complex data than they can meaningfully interpret (Patterson, 1984; Lederman, 1984; Lynch, 1984). The growth in information technologies has necessitated the development of advanced human information-processing capabilities (Ruben, 1983; Hall, 1982), which has been matched by the development of specialized organizational personnel (information specialists) who can operate MIS technologies, interpret data generated from MIS technologies, and apply these data to relevant organizational concerns.

Information specialists help modern organizations cope with the "information explosion" and prevent organizational information overload (Brod, 1984; Offer, 1978). "Successful managers view information as a corporate resource and provide the means for managing this resource. Information management . . . is a process. The goal of the process is getting the right information to the right people at the right time and in the right form" (Drake, 1984, p. 266). Information specialists are charged with the responsibility for making relevant organizational information available to management. For example, information specialists hold positions in areas of the organization such as records management, special libraries and information centers, personnel administration, accounting, word processing, research and development, training, and corporate communications (Koenig and Kochoff, 1984; Ivantcho, 1983; Mount, 1983). As management increasingly depends on MIS technologies to help in the accomplishment of internal organizational communication functions, the role of the information specialist will grow in modern organizations.

STRUCTURE AND COMMUNICATION

As we discussed earlier in the chapter, structure is the formal designation of the prescribed hierarchy of power relationships within an organization. Structural attributes of organizations include the degree of formalization of organizational rules and procedures, the extent to which organization leaders delegate authority to organization members, the number of subordinates for whom managers are responsible (span of control), the member to whom each other organization member answers (chain of command), the levels of organizational hierarchy, the designation of specialized organizational subunits, and the description of formal organization job positions and responsibilities. Many of the structural aspects of organizations can be identified through examination of organizational charts, which are like blueprints of organizations' planned formal structures (Figure 9.1).

There is an interesting inverse relationship between organizational structure and formal and informal communication channels.

1. Organizational structure directs the development of formal organizational communication channels. The planned structure of an organization dictates the formal channels of communication that are to be used by designating who organization members are to communicate with and what they are to communicate about.
2. Informal organizational communication adds to the planned organizational structure by introducing informal communication structure. Communication relationships that develop informally among organization members often deviate from the formal organizational structure and expand that structure by creating informal communication networks.

This relationship between structure and communication can be illustrated in many large business organizations. According to the formal structure of a typical large business organization, only senior executives are supposed to have direct formal lines of communication with the corporation's chief executive officer (CEO). Informally, however, middle-level manager A may have a personal relationship with the CEO; perhaps manager A is the niece or nephew of the CEO. The personal relationship between A and the CEO accords A the opportunity to communicate with the CEO and allows A to be privy to information to which he or she should not have access according to the formal structure of the organization. Other middle- and low-level organization members who are friendly with manager A may also have indirect access to information from the CEO by talking to manager A. These informal networks of relationships establish informal communication channels within the organization that, as we described earlier, are quite different from the formal communication channels.

Centralized and Decentralized Organizational Communication

Centralization is a structural attribute of organizations in which a relatively small number of leaders control the activities of many followers. Conversely, *decentralization* is a structural attribute of organizations in which many leaders control smaller groups of followers. Narrow span of control is a characteristic of decentralization, while broad span of control is a characteristic of centralization. Decentralized organizations often have many divisions, each with management personnel who have formal organizational responsibility. Centralized organizations have relatively few power and decision points, while decentralized organizations have many points where formal power is wielded and decisions are made.

Decentralization is often advantageous for complex organizations because it relieves the extreme internal organizational communication responsibilities of top management, spreading communication and decision-making responsibility among middle managers, who are directly involved in the operation of the organization. Certainly, decentralization is beneficial in most complex organizations where executives are often quite distant from actual organizational operations. For example, in universities, decentralization puts the responsibility for specialized educational decision making on the educators, who are most knowledgeable about and involved with specific courses, programs, disciplines, students, and educational situations.

On the other side of the coin, decentralization has the disadvantage of giving middle managers decision-making responsibilities when they often do not see the larger organizational picture and the implications of their decisions for organizational divisions or personnel other than those they manage. These decision makers are often so involved with their immediate organizational activities they may not recognize the repercussions of their decisions for the rest of the organization. Moreover, there is great opportunity for contradictory decisions and directives from different sources of authority in decentralized organizations. As we mentioned earlier, multiple authority can lead to role conflict, which, in turn, can lead to frustration and confusion among organization members and to inefficient organizing activities.

Decentralization, multiple authority, and role conflict have become an inevitable part of life in many complex organizations. To minimize the problems of role conflict in organizations, management personnel can serve as communication integrators and liaisons in complex organizations (Kreps and Thornton, 1984; Likert, 1961). These managerial integrators can help coordinate internal communication systems by connecting the different divisions of the organization and allowing organization executives to direct the larger organizational picture.

The problems and benefits we have identified for organizational centralization and decentralization, as well as our discussion in Chapter 3 of the strengths and limitations of bureaucracy for organizational functioning, underscore the ongoing tension in organizations between differentiation and integration. In *differentiated* organizations, authority and control are delegated by central management to a number of organizational subunits that are largely self-governed. In *integrated* organizations, centralized management generally exerts tight control to closely coordinate the activities of different organization members and organizational units. Differentiation helps to accomplish the needs that organizations have for specialized personnel and processes. For example, organizations that empower academic departments and schools to direct specialized professionals, technologies, and procedures in the delivery of disciplinary-specific educational services exhibit differentiation. Integration helps to accomplish the needs that organizations have for coordinating the many activities and processes of organizing to achieve their goals. The concept of interdependence, presented in Chapter 5, where different components of a system share responsibility for accomplishing system goals and mutually influence one another's performance, underlies the need for integration in organizational life. University administrations, for example, strive to coordinate the activities of different academic departments, faculty members, and undergraduate majors by establishing curricular requirements, degree prerequisites, and academic guidelines to provide students with meaningful and comprehensive educations.

Differentiation and integration are often mutually competing processes in organizations, although they need not be. The more differentiated (specialized and departmentalized) an organization, the more difficult it is for the organization to demonstrate integration (interdepartmental coordination and cooperation). Conversely, the more integrated (tightly orchestrated) an organization, the more difficult it is for the organization to differentiate. In a similar manner, bureaucracy (highly structured organizational design) helps organization members respond in regulated, ordered, predictable ways but often makes it difficult for them to develop innovative patterns and processes.

Organizations must develop a workable balance between differentiation and integration to remain viable and must maintain a healthy balance between bureaucracy (structure) and adaptability (flexibility and creativity). These balances are achieved through the maintenance, ongoing evaluation, and continual development of organizational processes by management. The formal organization leaders should continually seek feedback from organization members and customers to evaluate the function and relational effectiveness of organizational processes and structures, utilizing the information gathered to update and develop the organization so it may operate more effectively in the future.

On an individual level, organization members can best cope with the rigidity and impersonality of highly formalized bureaucratic organizations by becoming familiar with the regulations and hierarchical power relationships that make up the bureaucratic structure of the system. By learning the "ropes" of the system, individual members can utilize organizational structure to their best advantage. Knowing who has the authority and power to get things done in an organization and finding out the procedures and mechanisms for initiating changes and facilitating organizational action can help individual organization members achieve personal, professional, and task-related goals within the organization (Kreps and Thornton, 1984).

As we mentioned earlier in this chapter, information is extremely powerful in organizations, and knowing who to speak with and what channels to utilize in an organization can be very influential information for an individual to possess. Additionally, the development of good working relationships with fellow organization members at all levels of the hierarchy can help individuals achieve their goals. It is especially useful to establish communication relationships with formal and informal organization leaders who can provide other members with important information about the operation, present condition, and future actions of the organization. By learning the rules and structures of the organization and establishing effective interpersonal relationships with organization members, individuals can help direct activities within bureaucratic organizations, rather than be manipulated by bureaucratic structure.

Communication Network Structure

The informal patterns of organizational communication that organization members engage in create communication networks. A *network* is a grouping of organization members who engage in patterned interaction. The central unit of analysis in a network is the communication relationship between any two organization members. Networks differ in size and structure. Rogers and Agarwala-Rogers (1976) identify three types of communication networks.

1. "Total system networks" map the patterns of communication throughout the entire organization.
2. "Clique networks" identify groups of individuals within the organization who communicate more exclusively with one another than with other organization members.
3. "Personal networks" are the individuals who often interact with a given organization member.

Personal networks can be of two types: radial and interlocking. In radial personal networks, an individual interacts with other organization members who do not generally interact with one another, while in interlocking personal networks, all members interact. Because all members of an interlocking personal network are connected by patterned communication, they are said to have a high level of communication "integration."

Interlocking personal networks are highly integrated because there are "strong ties" among network members. These members have a great deal of communication contact with one another and often are very similar to one another. Interactions among individuals who rarely have communication contact are indicative of "weak ties." The "theory of weak ties" (Liu and Duff, 1972; Granovetter, 1973; Rogers and Agarwala-Rogers, 1976) suggests that the information strength of weak network ties is greater than the information strength of strong ties. That is, people who do not generally interact have more new information to relate to one another than do individuals who communicate with one another quite often.

Paradoxically, it is easier to communicate with those who are most like yourself than it is to establish effective relationships with those who are very different. Note the many difficulties experienced in interpersonal communication between people from different countries and backgrounds. (Examples of intercultural difficulties abound in tense race relations, competition among religious sects, and active conflict between entire nations.) The main implication of the theory of weak ties for organization members, though, is that it is worth the effort to establish new and different communication relationships in organizations because weak ties can provide organization members with insightful perspectives on organizational life. This suggestion of nurturing weak ties is especially important for organization leaders, who need relevant information about organizational activities, problems, and changes.

Monge and colleagues (1976) list three primary structural properties of communication networks.

1. "Parametrics," or the size of the network
2. "Completeness," or the degree to which all members are connected within a network (generally referred to as network connectedness or network integration)
3. "Dispersion," or the variances that occur within networks, such as network dominance by an organization member (perhaps an informal leader) or by a clique within a total system network

Rogers and Agarwala-Rogers (1976) also introduce the property of "network openness," or the amount of contact between the network and its environment. We will discuss the notion of openness further in Chapters 10 and 11.

Research methods to analyze networks have been developed to identify communication networks in organizations (Richards, 1975, 1981; MacDonald, 1976; Larkin, 1980; Rice, Richards, and Cavalcanti, 1980). "Network analysis" is a research technique in which organization members are asked to identify with whom they have communication contact in the organization and how often they have contact with them. With this information, the informal communication networks within the organization are mapped, usually with the help of a computer, which processes all the sociometric data gathered from organization members (Figure 9.3).

Specific communication networks can be identified from an examination of a network analysis of an organization. The network analysis also can be used to identify several network roles, of which the following six are common.

First, "isolates" are organization members who have minimal contact with others within the organization. These individuals either are "hiding out" within the organization or are being avoided. Some members may be isolates in some organizational networks and central members of other networks.

Second, "opinion leaders" are informal leaders. They do not necessarily hold formal authority within the organization, but do guide organization members' behaviors and influence organization members' decisions. As we saw in Case 9.1, opinion leaders, such as Horace Jackson, can have powerful influences on organizational life.

Third, "gatekeepers" are individuals who control information flow between organization members. They are in the middle of a network and convey messages from one person to another or withhold information. Gatekeepers can help key organization members, such as leaders, avoid information overload by channeling only important messages to

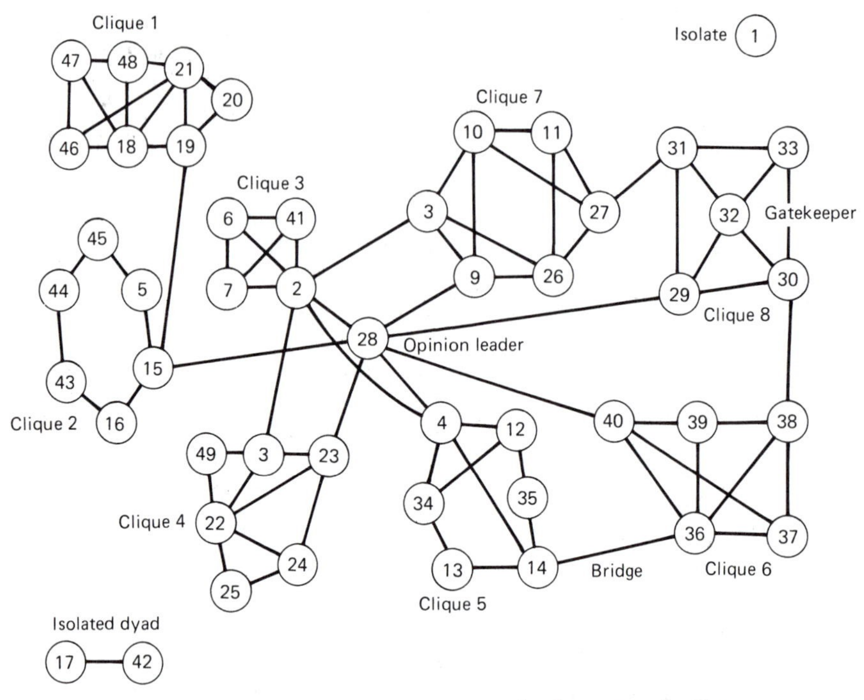

Figure 9.3 Communication network of an organization.

them. Of course, it is the gatekeeper who has the power to decide what information is and is not important. If the gatekeeper decides that certain important information is unimportant, then someone who should get that information may remain uninformed. Obviously, the gatekeeper role is a very important one and should be held by a responsible and informed individual.

Fourth, "cosmopolites" are individuals who connect the organization to its environment. They gather information from environmental sources and provide organizational information to representatives of the environment. (In Chapter 10, we will examine the important external communication functions performed by cosmopolites for the organization.)

Fifth, "bridges" are organization members who connect a clique to which they belong with members of another clique. These individuals help share information between cliques and facilitate intergroup coordination.

Sixth, "liaisons" are very similar to bridges. They are organization members who connect two cliques without themselves belonging to either one. These individuals also help share relevant information between cliques.

See if you can identify any of these six network roles in Figure 9.3. Can you think of network roles that you have performed in your classes, work groups, social groups, or other organizations? Compare Figure 9.3 with Figure 9.1. These two diagrams illustrate the differences between the formal and the informal communication structures in a typical organization. How much overlap is there between these two communication structures?

MOTIVATION AND CONTROL IN ORGANIZATIONS

Much of organizational structure is designed to control the activities of organization members. Job descriptions identify the specific tasks that organization members are supposed to accomplish and the specific activities that they must perform for task accomplishment. Bureaucratic rules are designed to limit the choices that organization members make and the activities in which they engage. Yet human beings do not necessarily comply with structural constraints on their behavior. Human beings must be given reasons and incentives to influence their behaviors. People have free will, which enables them to decide when they want to cooperate with authority and when they want to resist authority. They also decide how committed they will be to organizationally designated activities, tasks, and goals. Since human beings cannot be easily controlled, as can many inanimate tools, technologies, and objects, effective organization management must be concerned with the motivation of organization members to ensure their concerted efforts. A primary function of internal managerial communication is to promote organization member motivation.

Internal and External Dimensions of Motivation

Motivation is the degree to which an individual is personally committed to expending effort in the accomplishment of a specified activity or goal. Many factors are involved in motivating an individual. Two central factors are internal and external incentives, more commonly known as "intrinsic rewards" and "extrinsic rewards." Intrinsic motivators are rather illusory. They are based on the fulfillment of individual beliefs and values. Extrinsic motivators are much more obvious. They are based on providing individuals with valuable economic returns, goods, or services. Katz and Kahn (1978, p. 288) identify four ways that organization members can achieve intrinsic rewards.

1. Development of personally satisfying and meaningful organizational roles

2. Social reinforcement of collective goals through participation in satisfying organizational groups
3. Active involvement, participation, and personal identification with organizational goal setting and goal accomplishment
4. Sharing of social rewards from collective efforts and activities

Recall our discussion in Chapters 3 and 4 of classical theory and the human-relations theory of organizational behavior. Extrinsic incentives are consistent with the classical theory of management and its model of rational, economically motivated human beings. Intrinsic incentives are consistent with the human-relations theory and its goal of individual self-actualization.

Several organizational theorists have condemned organizational emphasis on extrinsic motivators at the expense of intrinsic motivators as being short sighted, manipulative, and ineffective (Hertzberg, 1968; Levinson, 1973; Sherwin, 1972). These authors suggest the combination of extrinsic and intrinsic incentives, with the primary emphasis being given to intrinsic incentives, to increase organization members' motivation. In modern organizational practice, however, the use of extrinsic incentives often seems to overshadow the use of intrinsic incentives. For example, think about the use of sales commissions, bonuses, pay raises, and other monetary reward systems in business organizations to motivate employee performance. Extrinsic incentives are also a common part of educational institutions. Are not grades used as an external threat or reward to motivate student performance? Intrinsic motivators are more difficult to develop than are extrinsic motivators. Individuals are motivated by different intrinsic incentives, since people have different beliefs and values. To facilitate intrinsic motivation, leaders must establish effective interpersonal relationships and implicit contracts with organization members to identify and promote the specific factors leading to individual intrinsic motivation. (See Chapter 8 for a discussion of relationship development, communication, and implicit contracts.)

To further complicate the use of intrinsic and extrinsic incentives in organizational life, Deci (1975) suggests that the two kinds of incentives are not independent and additive, but are interrelated and often counteracting aspects of human motivation. The presentation of extrinsic rewards communicates certain relational messages to organization members that can influence their intrinsic motivation (Deci, 1975; Cussella, 1980; McClellan, Heald, and Edney, 1980). Deci suggests that extrinsic rewards can decrease intrinsic motivation in two ways.

First, extrinsic rewards change the locus of causality from the individual being rewarded to the person providing the rewards, thereby reducing intrinsic motivation. For example, manager A can exert power over employee B by deciding to give rewards to or withhold rewards from employee B, which denies employee B power over rewards.

Second, extrinsic rewards can weaken the rewarded individual's feelings of competence and self-determination, thereby reducing intrinsic motivation. For example, because manager A has the power to determine whether employee B will receive rewards, employee B may begin to feel a loss of self-determination and importance.

To avoid these constraints of extrinsic incentives on intrinsic motivation, leaders must carefully combine the use of internal and external incentives. Internal and external rewards have to be carefully timed and balanced in organizational practice.

Needs Theories of Motivation

We now turn to three well-known theories of human motivation based on the fulfillment of individuals' needs: Maslow's (1943, 1954) hierarchy of needs, Hertzberg's (1966, 1968) two-factor theory of motivation, and Shutz's (1958) interpersonal-needs theory. Interestingly, Maslow's and Hertzberg's theories are very similar and complementary. They are based on the fulfillment and coordination of intrinsic and extrinsic incentives in human motivation. Although these two theories have been criticized, they remain as useful models of human motivation. Shutz's theory differs from the first two theories in that it is not based on coordinating intrinsic and extrinsic needs, but identifies the rewards that people have to give and to get in their interpersonal relationships to increase motivation.

Maslow's Hierarchy of Needs Maslow (1943, 1954) developed his famous theory of the hierarchy of needs based on the notion that human beings have to satisfy a series of five kinds of needs. The most basic of these needs are called lower order needs and the least basic are called higher order needs. He represented these needs as a hierarchy because people have to satisfy their lower order needs before they can concern themselves with higher order needs.

The most basic of all needs is self-preservation, or *survival needs*. These include the need for food, oxygen, and other basic physiological nurtures. Survival needs also might include making enough money to feed yourself and your family or working in an environment that is not life threatening.

Once survival needs are satisfied, human beings become interested in providing for their safety and security, or *safety needs*. Safety needs might include making enough money to afford secure housing, job security, or protection against economic, social, political, or physical attack or threats.

Once survival and safety needs are at least minimally fulfilled, people become interested in developing meaningful and satisfying relationships with others, or *affiliation needs.* Affiliation needs might include establishing good working relationships, having friends to eat with, or feeling a part of a group or clique within the organization.

Once survival, safety, and affiliation needs are met, people become interested in feeling as though they have achieved public recognition and success, or *esteem needs*. Esteem needs might include feeling that others treat you with respect, being known for the quality of your workmanship, having others seek your advice, or moving up within the formal hierarchy of the organization.

Once survival, safety, affiliation, and esteem needs are at least minimally met, people become interested in developing their potential as human beings, or *self-actualization needs*. Self-actualization includes learning more about yourself and the world around you, becoming more satisfied with yourself, becoming more competent at activities you perform, and generally feeling as though you are growing as an individual. No person ever reaches a final state of self-actualization, but becomes either more or less actualized.

Maslow suggests that human beings can be motivated by ascertaining the level of need fulfillment that they have achieved and providing them with opportunities to fulfill their next highest need level. Interestingly, the first two need levels identified by Maslow, survival and safety needs, seem to be fulfilled through extrinsic rewards, while the higher order needs, affiliation, esteem, and self-actualization, seem to be better fulfilled through intrinsic incentives. The higher people move on the hierarchy of needs, the more they attempt to satisfy their own beliefs and values through intrinsic motivation.

Hertzberg's Two-Factor Theory of Motivation Hertzberg (1966, 1968) introduced a theory of human motivation based on the fulfillment of two kinds of needs.

1. Basic hygiene needs, including salary, security, work conditions, status, and company policies and administration
2. Higher order motivational needs, including personal growth, achievement, recognition, advancement, responsibility, and enjoyment of the work

The hygiene factors are extrinsic to the job, and the motivational factors are intrinsic to the job. Hertzberg contends that the basic hygiene needs stem from human beings' animal nature, drive to avoid pain, and drive for biological survival and that the motivational needs derive from human beings' unique abilities to achieve, learn, and grow, and, in turn, to experience psychological growth and satisfaction. Hertzberg's hygiene factors are consistent with Maslow's survival and safety needs, while Hertzberg's motivation factors are consistent with Maslow's affiliation, esteem, and self-actualization needs.

Hertzberg describes an intricate set of relationships among hygiene factors, motivation factors, satisfaction, dissatisfaction, and human motivation in organizational life. If hygiene factors are not provided in organizational life, organization members will become dissatisfied. Dissatisfied organization members cannot be motivated because of their concern with satisfying their hygiene needs. If hygiene factors are provided, they will prevent organization members from being dissatisfied, but they still are not enough to satisfy organization members or lead to their motivation. Motivation factors, however, can lead to worker satisfaction and member motivation if hygiene needs have already been met. Motivation factors cannot satisfy organization members if hygiene needs have not been met because the members will be dissatisfied. Thus to motivate organization members, there are two factors involved. First, basic hygiene needs must be at least minimally met to keep the members from being dissatisfied. Once the hygiene needs are met, organization members' intrinsic motivation needs must be achieved for the members to be satisfied and motivated.

Once minimal hygiene factors are provided to organization members, Hertzberg (1968) recommends "job enrichment" as a strategy for providing intrinsic incentives in organizational life. Job enrichment is concerned with making organization members' formal roles more interesting, meaningful, fulfilling, and challenging. Hertzberg (1968) suggests seven principles to consider in enriching organization members' jobs.

1. Relieve members' administrative controls, while maintaining their accountability for performance, so they have more freedom for individual creativity
2. Increase members' personal accountability for the quality of their work, so they have more responsibility and recognition
3. Allow members to complete an entire project or work unit to increase their feelings of pride in accomplishment
4. Give members more job freedom and authority to increase their responsibility
5. Furnish members with direct periodic feedback, rather than communicating through a supervisor, to increase internal recognition
6. Provide members with new and challenging tasks to increase their opportunities to learn and grow

7. Help members to become experts in their specific job responsibilities to increase their recognition, responsibility, and growth

Schutz's Interpersonal-Needs Theory Schutz (1958) introduced a theory of motivation by identifying three human needs that can be satisfied only through the development and maintenance of effective interpersonal relationships.

People need opportunities to exert *control* over others, as well as to be controlled by others in certain situations. Organization members want opportunities to be leaders as well as followers in their organizations.

People need opportunities to show *affection* to others, as well as to have others show them affection. Organization members need to develop meaningful and therapeutic relationships with other members of the organization. At times, organization members have to be shown that others care about them, and they have to show others that they care.

People need opportunities to *include* others with them in social groupings, as well as to have others include them in social groupings. Organization members need to have others invite them to participate in group activities in such formal situations as task groups or decision-making committees, and they need to be invited to participate in such informal activities as lunches or parties. Additionally, they want the authority to include others with them in different formal and informal organizational activities.

Schutz's interpersonal-needs theory suggests that people are motivated to fulfill these three give-and-take needs. Leaders can identify specific interpersonal needs and give organization members the opportunities to fulfill them. Jobs can be designed to maximize members' opportunities to express or receive control, affection, or inclusion. Providing organization members with opportunities to develop interpersonal relationships within the organization that enable them to express and receive control, affection, and inclusion will encourage them to give their best efforts on behalf of the organization.

Goal Theories of Motivation

In addition to the needs theories of motivation, there are two similar goal-oriented models of human motivation: expectancy theory and path-goal theory. These goal theories of motivation assert that by identifying specific organizational tasks for organization members to accomplish, specifying the activities needed to accomplish these tasks, and matching individual goal attainment with the organizational tasks, leaders and managers will motivate organization members to work toward goal accomplishment.

Expectancy Theory Vroom (1964) introduced expectancy theory to explain the choices that organization members make in the accomplishment of organizational goals. He defines motivation as the process that governs how individuals choose among different voluntary activities. According to expectancy theory, the effort that organization members expend in accomplishing specific goals depends on their perceptions both of rewards for the goals and of the probability that the reward will follow goal accomplishment. The rewards for goal attainment can be either intrinsic or extrinsic. There are three basic assumptions in expectancy theory (Pace, 1983).

1. Organization members have "outcome expectancies," or assessments of the probabilities that certain outcomes will follow specific activities they engage in.
2. Organization members perceive "valences," or specific values or worths, for outcomes of specified activities.
3. Organization members perceive "effort expectancies," or assessments of the amount of effort they have to expend to achieve specified outcomes.

These three assumptions of expectancy theory explain how organization members become motivated. Organization members are motivated when they believe that certain activities will lead to valued outcomes that can be achieved by acceptable levels of effort. Leaders can use expectancy theory to motivate organization members by presenting them with messages that inform them about clearly attainable goals. Leaders' communications should demonstrate how workers can match these goals with rewards that they value.

Path-Goal Theory The path-goal theory asserts that it is the responsibility of effective leadership to motivate organization members by increasing the personal rewards available to these members for accomplishing specified organizational tasks and goals (Georgopoulos, Mahoney, and Jones, 1957; House, 1971). By clearly identifying relevant rewards for accomplishing a specified task, the leader identifies the path for goal attainment. Effective leaders let workers know that the attainment of satisfying rewards is contingent on performance and remove obstacles in the path of workers' goal achievement. Leaders provide workers with coaching, guidance, and support, as well as identify salient rewards necessary to motivate organization members' effective goal attainment (House and Dessler, 1974).

Path-goal theory is very similar to expectancy theory. Both theories match rewards to the achievement of specific organizational goals. While expectancy theory emphasizes organization members' interpretations of the values attached to rewards, path-goal theory emphasizes leaders' actions to motivate members to accomplish specific goals. Management by Objectives (MBO) is a leadership tool based on path-goal theory. In MBO, meetings between superiors and subordinates are used to set goals for workers to accomplish and map specific strategies for goal attainment (French and Hollmann, 1973). Goals are tied to agreed-on rewards and are written so that future performance can be measured against the set goals (White and Vroman, 1982).

COMMUNICATION CLIMATE AND INTERNAL COMMUNICATION

The *organizational climate* is the internal emotional tone of the organization based on how comfortable organization members feel with one another and with the organization. The concept of organizational climate is based on an analogy between the current condition of internal organizational communication and the current condition of the weather. Just as there can be pleasant, warm, and sunny weather conditions, there can be supportive, open, and friendly organizational communication climates (Tompkins, 1984). Just as there can be nasty, cold, and rainy weather conditions, there can be defensive, closed, and unfriendly organizational communication climates.

Internal organizational communication influences and is influenced by the climate within organizations. Organizational climates develop out of the behaviors and policies of organization administrators, as well as the specific communication behaviors of organization members (Pritchard and Karasick, 1973; Hunt and Lee, 1976). Leadership communication has a strong influence on the development of specific organizational climates (Hunt and Lee, 1976). If management's policies and communication demonstrate concern and respect for organization members, the climate will reflect that concern; but if leaders' policies and communication show lack of concern and disrespect for members, the climate will reflect that lack of concern. Recall our discussion of the norm of reciprocity in interpersonal relationships of organization members. Friendly and unfriendly behaviors are generally reciprocated by like behaviors from others, generating a friendly or an unfriendly communication climate. Think about the implications of McGregor's (1961) Theory X and Theory Y management assumptions about human nature for the development of friendly and unfriendly communication climates. Obviously, Theory Y assumptions demonstrate more respect for workers and probably result in more positive organizational climates than do Theory X assumptions.

There is an interesting circular relationship between organizational climate and organizational communication. As just explained, communication behaviors lead to the development of climates. But organizational climates have been found to be a major influence on the ways that organization members behave and communicate (Hellriegal and Slocum, 1974; Hunt and Lee, 1976). Friendly communication climates encourage organization members to communicate in an open, relaxed, and convivial manner with fellow members, while negative climates discourage open and friendly communication. Several researchers have linked communication climate with job satisfaction (DeWine and Barone, 1984; Pritchard and Karasick, 1973; Johanesson, 1971). Redding (1972) asserts that climates develop in response to internal communication. He identifies five managerial strategies leading to the "ideal managerial climate":

1. Support
2. Participative decision making
3. Trust, confidence, and credibility
4. Openness and candor
5. Emphasis on high performance goals

Supportive and Defensive Communication Climates

Every organizational climate is as unique as the individuals who comprise organizations and the different communication behaviors that helped to create the climates. Different climates are not simple bipolar, good or bad phenomena. Organizational climates can vary on a continuum from one polar extreme to the other. Climates often have been described as being more or less positive or negative, open or closed, or effective or ineffective (Adler, 1983; Timm, 1980; Schneider, Donaghy, and Newman, 1975). Gibb (1961) created a model of communication climate that describes each polar end of the organizational-climate continuum as being "supportive" or "defensive" (Table 9.1).

Gibb asserts that certain communication behaviors of organization members lead to supportive climates and that certain communication behaviors lead to defensive climates. Characteristics of supportive communication behaviors include

1. *Description* organization members focus their messages on observable events rather than on subjective or emotional evaluations. This is similar to the distinction made in Chapter 8 between substantive and affective conflict.
2. *Problem orientation* organization members focus their communication on cooperatively solving difficulties.
3. *Spontaneity* organization members communicate honestly in response to current situations.

Table 9.1

Supportive and Defensive Communication Climates

Supportive Climates	*Defensive Climates*
1. Description	1. Evaluation
2. Problem orientation	2. Control
3. Spontaneity	3. Strategy
4. Empathy	4. Neutrality
5. Equality	5. Superiority
6. Provisionalism	6. Certainty

Source: Gibb, J. R. "Defensive Communication." *Journal of Communication* 11 (1961): 147.

4. *Empathy* organization members show genuine concern and understanding for other members.
5. *Equality* organization members treat one another as peers without stressing rank or superiority.
6. *Provisionalism* organization members are flexible and adapt to the constraints of different communication situations.

Characteristics of defensive communication behaviors include

1. *Evaluation* organization members focus their messages on personal assessments of other members.
2. *Control* organization members attempt to direct the behaviors of others through their communication.
3. *Strategy* organization members communicate on the basis of preconceived notions and plans rather than of the specific social situation.
4. *Neutrality* organization members do not communicate concern for other organization members or their problems.
5. *Superiority* organization members demonstrate status, rank, and authority through their communication.
6. *Certainty* organization members are dogmatic and communicate a lack of openness to others' ideas.

It is unlikely that any organization member can communicate supportively in every organizational situation. Compare the communication behaviors leading to defensive organizational climates with the communication behaviors of most formal leaders in organizations. You will realize that it is very difficult for many leaders to avoid evaluative, controlling, strategic communication in performing their jobs. These leaders should try to balance defensive communication behaviors with supportive messages. For example, when appraising the work of subordinates, it is difficult for a leader to avoid being evaluative, but the leader should try to be as descriptive as possible in providing workers with job-related feedback. Additionally, leaders should provide their workers with praise for work that is well done, rather than focusing only on deficient worker behaviors (Alexander and Camden, 1980; Peters and Waterman, 1982). Supportive organizational communication can lead to supportive organizational climate and can increase worker satisfaction (DeWine and Barone, 1984). The quality of organization member communication, especially the communication of organization leaders, can have a major impact on the effectiveness of the organization (Redding, 1972b).

Communication Climate and Organizational Culture

Communication climates and organizational cultures have a great deal in common. Organizational culture, as we explained in Chapter 7, is based on organization members' shared perceptions of organizational reality. Climate is subsumed within culture. It is a part of organizational culture. Climate is based on the shared perceptions of organization members about the emotional tone of the organization. Climate refers specifically to the current feelings that organization members have about how comfortable it is to communicate with others within the organization.

Communication climates are influenced by and influence organizational cultures. Powerful cultural themes and interpretive frameworks influence organization members' judgments about how comfortable it is to communicate with others within the organization. Culture reflects perceptions about the organization's past, present, and future that influence the development of organizational climates.

> Organizational climate reflects also the history of internal and external struggles, the types of people the organization attracts, its work processes and physical layout, the modes of communication, and the exercise of authority within the system. Just as a society has a cultural heritage, so social organizations possess distinctive patterns of collective feeling and beliefs passed along to new group members. (Katz and Kahn, 1978, p. 50)

What is more, consistent communication climates (whether supportive or defensive) eventually become expectations (logics) that organization members hold within an organization's culture.

ETHICAL DIMENSIONS OF INTERNAL COMMUNICATION

Organization members have a moral responsibility to communicate within their organizations in accordance with the ethics and standards of the larger society within which their organization resides (Jones, 1982). In recent years, there has been mounting evidence of serious ethical improprieties in organizational life; people have been lied to, unfairly treated, denied employment, sexually harassed, and given unfair advantages in many organizations, including business, professional, human-service, and educational institutions (Kreps and Thornton, 1984; Bok, 1978; Kanter, 1977; Brownmiller, 1975). Ethical issues in organizations concern such moral principles as promoting truth telling, promise keeping, respect, justice, nonmaleficence (refraining from doing harm), beneficence (doing good), gratitude, and reparation (Rion, 1982). Growing interest in eliminating unethical business practices and promoting the adoption of ethical standards in organizational life has spawned the development of many educational and training programs dealing with business and professional ethics (Jones, 1982; Kreps, 1983c).

Perhaps the most central ethical issue in organizational communication is honesty. Batchelder (1982) describes the influence of honesty on internal managerial communication:

> The commitment to honesty as understood by supervisors and managers is multifaceted. It involves not only truthful reporting of facts and numbers, but also such dimensions of good communication as openly giving employees information about higher management decisions that affect their work; being open to hear the concerns of employees; letting employees know where they stand by being explicit about the standards and expectations by which their performance is judged; giving frequent feedback to employees on both the strengths and weaknesses of their performance; encouraging the development of a relationship of credibility and trust with one's superior as well as with subordinates; and finally, the obligation of each manager to make explicit the expectation that employees are to report accurately on problems as they emerge, rather than tell the manager what they think he or she wants to hear. (p. 53)

Honest managerial communication can help establish trusting organizational climates, develop meaningful interpersonal relationships, and elicit interpersonal coorientation.

Organizational Politics

Every member of a large organization probably has been influenced in some way by internal organizational politics (Velasquez, 1982). Recall from our discussion in Chapter 8 of communication and conflict that organizational politics occurs when organization members struggle for power and interpersonal influence in organizational life. People engage in organizational politics as a way to jockey for power, influence, position, and profit in organizations.

Organizational politics can be an ethical communication activity that organization members engage in to promote valid concerns and issues, but organizational politics is often unethical and manipulative (Browning and Gilchrest, 1980; Deetz, 1979). Organization members embroiled in politics frequently use a variety of manipulative and unethical communication tactics such as dishonesty, coercion, trickery, intrigue, domination, bribery, and violence. Unethical internal organizational politics is often manifested in worker oppression, misappropriation of funds, offering of unwarranted services and/or sexual favors, establishment of feuding coalitions, wrongful employment, conflict of interest, unprofessional behavior, job discrimination, sexual harassment, unfair business practices, and prejudice against certain organization members. As you might assume from this partial list of some of the communication strategies and organizational consequences associated with unethical organizational politics, these situations can be very nasty and stressful for organization members.

What characteristics of internal organizational politics distinguish legitimate ethical political communication in organization from illegitimate unethical political maneuvering? Ethics are judgments people make about what is right and what is wrong. Ethics are based on the specific moral constraints of a given society or culture. What is judged as ethical in one cultural context may be judged as unethical in another cultural context. Moreover, within cultures, there are many disputes over the relative ethics of different activities. Thus there are courts of law, arbitration boards, and ethics committees to help interpret the ethical constraints affecting the moral dilemmas of organizational life.

More specifically, there seem to be three principles governing the ethics of internal organizational communication: honesty, avoiding harm, and justice.

Organization members should not purposefully deceive one another. Yet this principle is imperfect. Some organizational information is proprietary and should not be for general dissemination, for example, patented materials, reports of disciplinary actions, and health or credit records. There is also confusion about depth of information; does honesty mean telling only what you believe to be true, or does it mean telling everything you believe to be true? What is more, what people believe to be true is often only their point of view and may be based on false or incomplete information.

Organization members' communication should not unfairly harm any other organization member. Yet judgment has to be used to determine when organization members are fairly or unfairly reprimanded or punished. Often the behavior of one organization member accidentally injures another member.

Organization members should be treated justly. Judgments must be made about which behaviors are justified and which behaviors are unjust. Since each organization member and organizational context is unique, the old maxim about "equal treatment for all" may not fit every situation. For example, high performers might merit greater rewards than low performers in organizations.

Power and Prejudice in Organizational Life

A common ethical issue in organizational life is the prejudicial use of power by organization members. Certain groups of organization members have been denied the opportunities afforded other organization members (Glueck, 1978). For example, sexism has worked to suppress the advancement of women in many organizations (Loy and Stewart, 1984; Blaxall and Reagan, 1976; Acker and Van Houten, 1974). It is only recently that significant numbers of women have achieved positions of authority in business, industry, academia, and government. Similarly, different racial, religious, and ethnic groups have experienced prejudicial treatment in organizational life (Silberman, 1964; Kanter, 1977; Rosen and Jerdee, 1977; Shire, 1975). Quite often, majority-group members within organizations block the advancement of minority-group members (Kanter, 1977; Loy and Stewart, 1984; Kreps, 1985a; Hagen and Kahn, 1975).

The communication of prejudice in organizational life undermines the organization by creating defensive communication climates and weakening interpersonal trust and cooperation. The theory of weak ties, discussed earlier in this chapter, suggests that communication between minority and majority organization members is likely to lead to the exchange of novel and pertinent organizational information. If organization leaders recognize the benefits of intercultural relationships in organizations, they should promote greater interpersonal equity, integration, and interaction of organization members with different cultural or ethnic backgrounds.

Rocking the Boat

There seems to be little tolerance for deviance in organizational life. The need for organizational stability and order often outruns the equally important need for organizational innovation and change. Organization members are continually pressured through internal organizational communication to conform to the will of the mainstream (Kreps, 1983b). Yet as Janis's (1967) theory of groupthink suggests, blind conformity inevitably leads to poor group decisions and ineffective organizational activities. Obviously, not all deviance is productive. But like evolutionary mutations, deviant organization member behaviors can lead to organizational growth and improvement.

There must be room made in organizations for gadflies and devil's advocates who disagree with the majority, criticize the organization, and deviate from the mainstream. As Weick (1979) so aptly points out in discussing the principle of requisite variety, unique organizational situations beget unique organizational responses. The systems concept of equifinality suggests that as the problems confronting organizations continually change, the organizing processes used must also change. Organizational deviance should be seen as an opportunity to meet the changing constraints of organizational life. (We will address this issue again in Chapter 10.)

Coping with Stress in Organizational Life

Our discussion of organizational politics and organizational conflict should help you recognize how stressful organizational life can be. Many members of modern organizations complain of escalating levels of stress. Stress has been identified by many authors as a serious organizational problem, leading to worker burnout, high organization member turnover, and even employee health problems (Kreps and Thornton, 1984; Kreps, 1985b; McLean, 1979; Schuler, 1980; Mobley, 1982; Weiman, 1977).

Organization members commonly identify a variety of external constraints, such as deadlines, work loads, social pressures, tense environments, and interpersonal conflicts, as causes of stress. They assume an "external locus of control" for organizational stress. Stress is caused by the environment. According to this assumption, stress can be reduced only by removing the environmental conditions leading to it.

Stress is caused as much or more by organization members themselves as by environmental conditions. People feel stress internally in response to the way they define and interpret external conditions. Since stress is largely a perceptual phenomenon, different people develop different levels of stress in response to the same organizational situations. Certainly, different situations have the potential for causing more or less stress, but people's evaluation of these situations influence their responses. Some organization members seem to be able to handle a great deal of work pressure and, indeed, thrive on the pressure, while other members go to pieces when deadlines approach. These organization members are interpreting the organizational situation differently.

This perceptual approach to stress can be understood clearly if we conceptualize stress as an information-processing problem for organization members. People feel stress when they cannot clearly understand and interpret information from different organizational situations. Just as Festinger (1957) described dissonance as an uncomfortable mental state in which people have difficulty making decisions, stress is a form of dissonance in which people are perceptually confused and frustrated. Recall our discussions in Chapters 2 and 6 of information load. Different people have different capacities for interpreting information. If the information they receive is above their threshold for processing it, they suffer from information overload. From the perceptual approach to understanding stress, when people suffer from information overload, they experience stress.

According to the perceptual approach, organization members have an "internal locus of control" for handling stress. When they recognize their internal locus of control, they realize that their own attitudes and perceptual frameworks can be used to moderate work pressures. Every organizational situation poses potential benefits and problems for organization members. People can feel stress from both rewarding and punishing situations. When individuals can identify benefits in organizational situations, these situations become less stressful for them (Selye, 1974). A wise person once said, "Look for the good in people and situations and leave the bad behind." This seems to be very good advice for coping with stress.

In Chapter 8, we discussed the influence of self-fulfilling prophecies on interpersonal relationships. Self-fulfilling prophecies also influence organization members' development of stress. When people feel trapped and are afraid that they cannot handle organizational demands, they are likely to experience stress. Their own fears and lack of confidence make them more vulnerable to stress, leading to negative self-fulfilling prophecies. People who are confident of their abilities to cope with different organizational situations are likely to resist dangerously high stress, creating positive self-fulfilling prophecies for themselves.

Stress does not always cause problems for organization members. A manageable level of stress can be a benefit. Just as organization members can suffer from a lack of information stimulation, or information underload, they can suffer from a lack of stress. People need an optimal level of stress to keep them interested, challenged, and motivated in organizations. "Hyperstress" is the point where stress expands beyond the individual's capacity to cope (information overload), while "hypostress" is the point where the individual does not have enough stress to operate optimally (information underload) (White and Vroman, 1982).

There are several strategies for coping with excessive organization stress.

Effective leaders can help organization members cope with stress by providing them with tasks that are challenging enough for them to develop optimal levels of stress (avoiding hypostress), but are also manageable, clear, and predictable enough to avoid hyperstress. In this way, effective leaders can maintain a productive information load within their organizations. (We will discuss this balance between certainty and uncertainty in Chapter 11, relating this information balance to organizational effectiveness.)

Organization members should develop social-support networks within their organizations or within their personal lives to help them cope with excessive stress. As Weick (1979) has suggested, in situations of high equivocality (information overload), communication cycles should be performed to reduce equivocality. Since hyperstress is an indication that a person is trying to cope with highly equivocal information, organization members can reduce their stress levels by establishing meaningful communication relationships with others. Research on social-support networks has consistently demonstrated the efficacy of supportive relationships in helping organization members cope with occupational stress (Albrecht, 1982; Albrecht and Adelman, 1984; Cobb, 1976). (Recall our discussion in Chapter 8 of how therapeutic communication can be used to help organization members solve problems. Therapeutic interpersonal relationships provide organization members with social support that can help them cope with high organizational stress.)

Organization members can cope with stress by redefining the stressful situations in which they find themselves into nonstressful situations. Watzlawick, Beavin, and Jackson (1967) explain that human beings have the ability to "punctuate" their perceptions of reality, or organize their interpretations of phenomena, in different ways. Redefining stressful situations as being nonstressful can become a positive self-fulfilling prophecy for organization members. A popular adage describes this perceptual strategy: "An optimist sees an opportunity in every calamity, while a pessimist sees a calamity in every opportunity." Accordingly, pessimists probably suffer more stress than do optimists.

Organization members can try to design their schedules and task activities more efficiently through time management and task organization to avoid stressful situations. (The development of strategies of efficient task design and time management is one of the major benefits of Taylor's [1911] scientific-management theory, discussed in Chapter 3.) A "proactive" individual plans ahead to avoid problems before they arise, thereby avoiding stress.

Organizational leaders who find themselves in stressful situations of information overload often can relieve stress through delegation of authority and use of gatekeepers. By having other members of the organization help process information, a leader can avoid information overload.

Organization members can relieve stress through mental relaxation. Meditation, imagination, and humor have been effectively used to achieve mental relaxation. Wallace and Benson (1972) describe the relaxing physiological and psychological effects of meditation. In his well-known book, *Anatomy of an Illness as Perceived by the Patient* (1979), Cousins describes his use of humor to relieve the stress (and even combat the symptoms) of a debilitating disease. Being able to see the humor in organizational life can make difficult situations easier to accept and live with. In Chapter 2, we described the therapeutic benefits of channel Z (personal imagery and fantasy) for gaining mental repose and renewal. Mental-relaxation techniques can help individuals recover from stress and develop strength for processing equivocal information.

Physical rejuvenation through exercise, sleep, or diet can help organization members cope with stress (White and Vroman, 1982).

Development of ethical conflict behaviors and relationships can also help organization members relieve many of the stresses of political activities in organizational life.

As a last resort, organization members can change jobs or leave the organization if stress cannot be controlled in any other way.

CHAPTER 10

External Organizational Communication Systems

OPEN SYSTEMS THEORY AND ORGANIZATIONAL ENVIRONMENT

One of the major strengths of the systems approach to studying organizations (Chapter 5) is the "open systems" theme, which emphasizes the importance of interaction between organizations and their environments. "Openness" became such an influential theme of the systems model that systems theory became popularly known as "open systems theory." Open systems theory suggests that organizations and environments are interdependent. Environmental changes undoubtedly influence organizational life, and organizational changes certainly influence the organization's environment. For example, the health of the economy of the United States (environment) has a powerful influence on consumer behavior and the volume of company sales (organization). In a tight economy, sales of products are likely to drop because consumers have less money available for purchases. Similarly, the principle of supply and demand demonstrates how organizations can influence their environments. In 1983 and 1984, Coleco Corporation experienced extremely high consumer demand for their Cabbage Patch dolls, encouraged by a combination of advertising and limited market availability of dolls at local stores.

Open systems theory stresses the importance of external organizational communication. Proponents of the classical and the human-relations perspectives on organization were not interested in external communication and were primarily concerned with the functions of internal organizational communication. In classical theory, internal organizational communication was used to promote order, structure, and efficiency, while in human-relations theory, internal communication was used to promote organization members' growth, motivation, and satisfaction (Wren, 1972). Systems theorists stressed the need for system openness and expanded the traditional emphasis on internal organizational activities to include external organizational information flow and communication.

The Relevant Environment

The environment consists of all the factors external to the organization. This definition suggests that environment is a very broad set of phenomena. Environmental factors have different degrees of influence on organizations. To specify the elements of environment that are most critical to the organization, the concept of "relevant environment" has been introduced (Rogers and Agarwala-Rogers, 1976). The relevant environment includes all the factors external to the organization's boundary that have direct influence on the organization and its members. Communication contact is a key attribute of relevant environment. Individual representatives of organizations that have communicative contact with organization members are the primary elements of the relevant environment.

As Weick (1979) indicates, relevant organizational environments are really information environments. The relevant environment provides organization members with important information to process. Organization members interpret environmental messages to derive information about environmental conditions. Environmental information helps organization members identify new constraints on organizing activities. The environment is also a primary outlet for messages provided by organization members. Organizational messages provide representatives of organizations' environments with information about organizational activities and products. Organizations and their environments are connected by message flows that provide each with relevant information.

The Interorganizational Field

The interdependent relationships of organizations sharing a similar environment is illustrated by the concept of system hierarchy, according to which every system is composed of subsystems and surrounded by a suprasystem, which it shares with other systems. Translated into organizational terms, organizations are composed of groups of organization members (subsystems) and reside within an environment (suprasystem) that they share with other organizations. Groups of organizations sharing the same suprasystem often are referred to as "interorganizational fields" (Warren, 1967). Members of a typical business interorganizational field might include product organizations, distribution and sales organizations, supply organizations, government regulatory organizations, and consumer organizations. These organizations have myriad competitive and cooperative influences on one another (Turk, 1973; Litwak and Hylton, 1962; Wigand, 1976).

Each level of the system hierarchy abides by the same basic system properties. The systems theory concept of "homeostatic balance" suggests that different system components (subsystems) must coordinate their activities through active lines of feedback. At the suprasystem level, organizations within an interorganizational field are similar to subsystem components and must develop and maintain effective lines of feedback to elicit homeostatic coordination. For example, production organizations must coordinate activities with organizations that supply their raw materials and with organizations that purchase their finished products. Tompkins (1977) describes the management policy of "penetration" used by the National Aeronautics and Space Administration's (NASA) Marshall Space Flight Center in Huntsville, Alabama, to aggressively promote information sharing between the organization and other NASA field centers and aerospace contractors. The penetration policy of interorganizational communication served to reduce uncertainty in interorganizational environments and promote homeostatic balance between the organization and key members of its relevant environment.

Litwak and Hylton (1962) explain that there are many specialized "coordinating agencies" designed to promote homeostatic balance among organizations within an interorganizational field. They identify four types.

1. Organizations that connect interdependent organizations by communicating pertinent information among them, such as social-service exchanges, employment agencies, referral services, and travel agents
2. Organizations that negotiate differences and conflicts between interdependent organizations, such as courts of law and arbitration boards
3. Organizations that promote standards of correct behavior for interdependent organizations, such as hospital- or school-accreditation boards, better business bureaus, and the Federal Trade Commission
4. Organizations that promote areas of common interest among inter-

dependent organizations, such as business and professional associations and chambers of commerce

In addition to the use of coordinating agencies, organizations within an interorganizational field initiate cooperation through direct communication contacts. Interorganizational networks, such as the "old-boy network," are used to influence coorientation. Turk (1973) has identified the use of strategic appointments to organizations' boards of directors as a means to promote interorganizational cooperation. He suggests that members of boards of directors often are chosen to link organizations by acting as an information conduit that provides relevant information and encourages cooperation.

SENDING AND SEEKING ENVIRONMENTAL INFORMATION

External organizational communication involves the giving and taking of information between organizations and their relevant environments. This give-and-take results in two important and interrelated communicative activities in external organizational communication:

1. Sending organizational information to representatives of the relevant environment
2. Seeking pertinent information from the relevant environment for the organization

Those organization members who have the most communicative contact with representatives of the relevant environment are known as "cosmopolites," or boundary spanners (Thompson, 1967). Cosmopolites perform the two important external communication functions of sending information from the organization to the environment and channeling information from the environment back to the organization (Tushman and Scanlan, 1981). They represent the organization to outsiders and represent the outside world to organization members. To a certain extent, all organization members perform boundary-spanning functions, but cosmopolites are the specific organization members who perform most of the boundary-spanning activities.

Boundary spanners often work in such areas of the organization as public relations, media relations, sales, advertising, personnel, and research. Rogers and Agarwala-Rogers (1976) point out a common paradox confronting organizations: cosmopolites often are concentrated at the top and the bottom of organizational hierarchies. Executives, because of their high visibility and mobility, are often afforded opportunities to interact with the relevant environment in situations like fund raising, media interviews, lobbying, and social gatherings. Organization members at the bottom of the hierarchy, such as sales clerks, parking attendants, receptionists, food servers, and customer-service representatives, often interact with nonmembers in the performance of their jobs. The paradox of this situation is that upper and lower level employees are not always the best organizational representatives to communicate with the relevant environment. Top executives often are far removed from the daily activities of organizing and may not represent the organization accurately or sensitively to the environment, and lower level employees often are uninformed about the inner workings of the organization and have little authority to commit resources or make decisions of concern to nonmembers.

Organization leaders can improve external organizational communication by designating specific organization structures and representatives to handle boundary-spanning activities. Middle-level organizational representatives in departments like public relations, marketing, lobbying, and research can often represent the organization meaningfully to the environment. Tushman and Scanlan (1981) suggest that "management could encourage more extensive external networks through: selective travel allowances (professional-technical meetings, university symposia), more liberal telephone budgets, easing access to scientific and/or technical information (books, reports, journals), or support for special education (seminars, short courses). Management, then, can select potential boundary spanning individuals and facilitate the development of their internal and external communication networks" (p. 96).

Public Relations

The term *public relations* will be used broadly here to describe all the communicative activities of sending and seeking information between organization and environment performed by boundary-spanning organization members. Grunig and Hunt (1984) define public relations similarly as the "management of communication between an organization and its publics" (p. 6). In common usage, the term *public relations* often is used narrowly to describe the information-giving activities of corporate image making and press relations, stressing sending messages to the environment over seeking messages from the environment. Public relations is not merely designing and sending organizational messages to the environment, but also involves gathering relevant environmental information for organization members. Moreover, public-relations efforts often involve internal communication in seeking information from (employee surveys) and providing information to (company newsletters) internal organizational publics. In this chapter, however, we will focus on the external, boundary-spanning aspects of public-relations communication.

Public relations serves an extremely important service for organizations. It is the formal means by which external communication activities are used to help organization members effectively coordinate actions with representatives of the relevant environment. As discussed in Chapter 1, internal communication channels are used primarily to accomplish management and administrative objectives, and external communication channels are used primarily to accomplish public-relations objectives.

Popularly, however, the term *public relations* is often used derogatively to stand for the ways that organizations use publicity and advertising to misinform consumers or to avoid disclosing potentially embarrassing information to the public. Undoubtedly, these unethical and obfuscating public-relations communication tactics do occur in organizational life, but public relations involves much more than most people realize. Measell (1980) suggests that these negative views of public relations may be changing: "The persistent stereotype of the slick public relations man who buys favorable publicity over three martini lunches is on the way out, as is the notion that public relations is essentially a defensive job, reacting only to crises or near-crises and then only to smooth things over with vacuous rhetoric" (p. 2). Public relations is the ongoing management of communication relations among organizations that share an interorganizational field. Stereotypes about public relations can mask important public-relations functions in organizations.

Velmans (1984) identified the many important external organizational communication activities encompassed by public relations, including "corporate publicity, . . . shareholder relations, financial relations, environmental and consumer affairs, internal communications, labor relations, broadcasting, community affairs, government relations at all levels, issue advertising, corporate identification, corporate graphics, issue response management" (p. 3). This is only a partial list of public-relations activities. We will review many of these activities as well as describe the public-relations aspects of marketing and advertising, lobbying, recruiting, public-opinion and market-research polling, and long-range planning.

Velmans (1984) summarizes three primary functions of public-relations activities for organizations. Public relations is used to

1. create and maintain organizational identity and reputation by disseminating organizational information to the public;
2. help ensure organizational survival by identifying potential threats to the organization, identifying strategies for resisting these threats,

and enlisting cooperation from agents external to the organization; and

3. increase organizations' effectiveness and enhance organizations' abilities to operate profitably and productively within the limits of the local, national, and international economy by identifying and creating markets for organizational products and services.

Nager and Allen (1984) argue that providing public-relations messages to the environment is a complex and multifaceted activity. To be effective, the provision of public-relations information must be well thought out, designed, organized, and implemented. They present a Public Relations/Management by Objectives model for organizing and managing public-relations efforts (Figure 10.1). (Recall the discussion in Chapter 9 of Management by Objectives as an application of path-goal theory for motivating organization members.) Hager and Allen's model incorporates 10 analytical steps that organization members must consider when planning public-relations efforts. Public-relations practitioners should move sequentially from the first step to the next until they can answer all 10 questions when designing external communication messages.

1. *Client/employer objectives* What information does the organition need communicated to the public? Why does the organization have to communicate this information?
2. *Audience/public and why* To whom does the organization have to communicate this information? Why does it want to communicate with this specific public audience?
3. *Audience characteristics* By identifying the specific characteristics of the audience, organization members can design messages that are meaningful and appropriate to these individuals.
4. *Audience objectives* What issues are most likely to influence the audience? What are the audience's specific goals, needs, and objectives?
5. *Media/channels and why* What media or channels of communication are most appropriate for organization members to use to reach the targeted audience with their message? Why are these communication channels most appropriate?
6. *Media/channels objectives* What are the specific characteristics, biases, and hidden agendas associated with the particular communication channels chosen? What are the strengths and weaknesses of these kinds of media? How can these media be most effectively utilized?
7. *Sources and questions* From whom or where is the public-relations information to be gathered? Are these different sources of

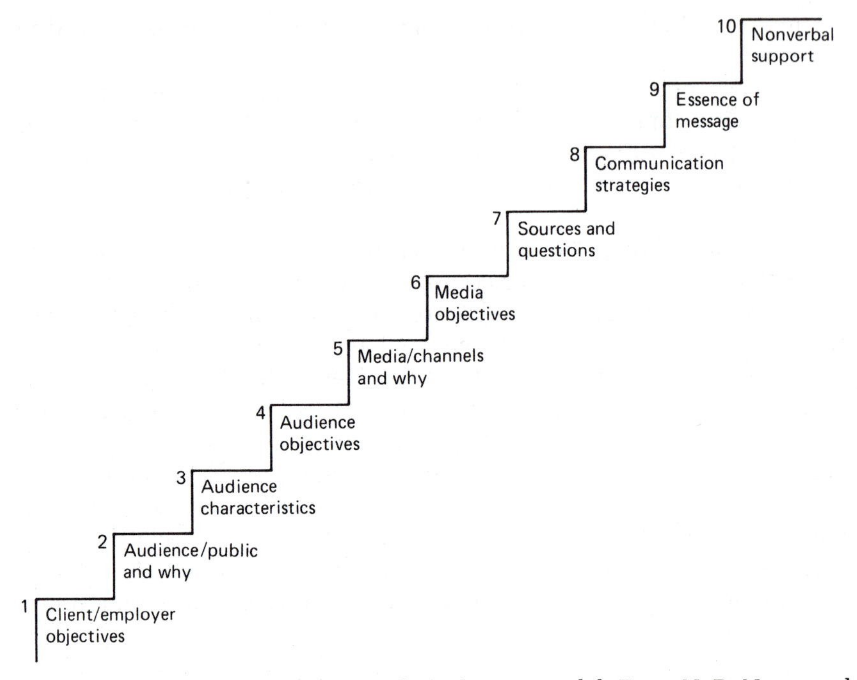

Figure 10.1 Nager and Allen's analytical steps model. From N. R. Nager and T. H. Allen, *Public Relations: Management by Objectives*. White Plains, N.Y.: Longman, 1984, p. 102.

relevant information? How accurate are these information sources? Can their information be verified? What questions and question strategies should be used to effectively gather information?

8. *Communication strategies* How can public-relations messages be designed to best accomplish the organizational objectives for the public-relations effort? What persuasive strategies can be employed?

9. *Essence of message* What is the key message that the public-relations effort should impress on the targeted audience? What are the main points of this message?

10. *Nonverbal support* How can such nonverbal elements as color, sound, music, and packaging be utilized to best complement the message presented in the public-relations effort? How can nonverbal cues be used to attract the audience's attention and help make it feel positively inclined toward the message?

Nowhere in organizational life is the careful analysis of strategies of public-relations messages more important than in crisis management.

Crisis management is the use of public relations to minimize harm to the organization in emergency situations that could cause the organization irreparable damage (Tabris, 1984; Nager and Allen, 1984). Tabris (1984) identifies eight potential results of mismanagement of public-relations efforts in emergencies and crises.

1. Damage to the organization's reputation and loss of confidence in the organization and its management by investors, customers, and employees
2. Deterioration of employee morale, which can lead to problems with labor relations and employee recruitment
3. Declines in stock prices and strained relations with investors
4. Preoccupation of management time with crises issues rather than with important organizational activities
5. Increased scrutiny of organizational affairs by external political agencies, leading to excessive government regulation and punitive measures
6. Costly and time-consuming litigation procedures
7. Threats to organizational autonomy, such as involuntary reorganization or bankruptcy
8. Strained community relations

To avoid these problems, organizational crises should be responded to with careful, sensitive, and timely public-relations efforts.

For example, Johnson & Johnson faced a crisis in late September 1982, when an unknown murderer laced Extra-Strength Tylenol capsules with cyanide, which caused the deaths of seven people in Chicago. The incident caused great fear among the public and had Johnson & Johnson not reacted quickly and decisively, its sales and reputation might have suffered mightily. Leon (1983) reported that Johnson & Johnson, with the counsel of Burson-Marsteller (a public-relations firm), responded to the crisis in a most effective and expeditious manner by championing the consumer. The company began a massive marketing and promotions plan that communicated its concern with the welfare of the public and full cooperation with the media in resolving the crisis. The company recalled all Tylenol capsules, at great expense, and by teleconference linking 30 major United States markets by satellite, it communicated to consumers its new triple-safeguard packaging of Tylenol to deter future tampering with the product and protect the welfare of product users (Nager and Allen, 1984). Johnson & Johnson's crisis-management, public-relations program was so successful that not only did its Tylenol products make a successful market comeback, but its public image as a socially responsible business organization was enhanced (Leon, 1983). So effective was Johnson & Johnson's crisis-management campaign that the organization received a special Silver Anvil Award from the Public Relations Society of America.

Although we have stressed the public-relations activities of presenting information to the public, public relations also involves gathering relevant environmental information. Nager and Allen's 10-step model illustrates that to provide effective public-relations messages to the environment, organization members first must be able to gather relevant information about the messages to be sent, the potential audiences for the messages, and the media to be used in communicating the messages. Giving and gathering relevant information often are interdependent public-relations activities.

The interdependent relationship between information-giving and information-gathering activities is clearly evident in public-relations efforts at fund raising. Fund raising is a crucial preservative activity for many modern organizations. In fund raising, organization representatives encourage members of the environment to contribute money to the organization (Hunt and Grunig, 1984; Rusk, 1984). The information output to the environment is designed to motivate input of information (money) to the organization.

In government relations, organization representatives keep tabs on the activities of national, state, and local governments (Cox, 1984). By consulting relevant publications and communicating with legislators and legislative aides, organization members can relay information about pertinent governmental activities back to the organization. This information can be used to help the organization respond proactively to potentially constraining government actions, rather than waiting and reacting to the legislation when "push comes to shove." Public-relations efforts help organizations become more proactive and less reactive.

Berrien (1968) identifies two types of system inputs: signal inputs and maintenance inputs. *Signal inputs* provide the organization with information that can be used to direct organizational adaptation, while *maintenance inputs* provide the organization with information to sustain the organization. Organizations need both signal and maintenance inputs to survive. Information about a new product being introduced by a competitor is an example of a signal input, while generation of funds through sales is an example of a maintenance input. Government-relations efforts are conducted to primarily gather signal inputs for the organization, while fund-raising public-relations efforts are designed to provide the organization with maintenance inputs. Information-gathering public-relations efforts provide organizations with important signal and maintenance information inputs.

Case 10.1 discusses the public-relations problems faced by organizations whose products and practices are of nationwide significance.

Case 10.1

The Love Canal Crisis*

When I joined Occidental Chemical Corporation (then known as Hooker Chemical) in 1979, my primary assignment was to create a strong public relations capability at corporate headquarters in Houston, Texas. Until then the company had conducted its public relations activities on a decentralized basis with public relations professionals located primarily at divisional or plant community levels.

I had previously heard of Love Canal and was aware that dealing with the issue of chemical waste disposal was to be one of my responsibilities. It was not yet apparent that this issue was becoming a prolonged crisis of national proportions and would be among my first and most pressing projects.

A brief discussion of the Love Canal case will illustrate some of the key concepts of crisis management. The following is a capsule summary of the facts that led to the crisis.

Love Canal, located near Niagara Falls, New York, was originally conceived as a power generation project at the turn of the century. Only about 1,800 feet of the proposed five-mile canal was completed. This portion was not used until 1941, when Hooker Chemical acquired the site as a secure landfill for chemical waste materials. The unfinished canal was ideal as a disposal site for a number of reasons: it was in a remote location; the surrounding area was sparsely settled; the walls of the canal were of impermeable clay that assured the buried chemicals would remain in place indefinitely as long as the site remained undisturbed.

Hooker Chemical used the site from 1942 until 1953. As wastes were placed in the canal, they were covered with a layer of impermeable clay. It is important to note that an environmental protection agency (EPA) official stated that the disposal methods employed by Hooker at the time would meet today's EPA standards for chemical waste disposal.

In 1952 the growing city of Niagara Falls expressed interest in acquiring the Love Canal site for a neighborhood school. The company was reluctant to agree that the property be used for any type of construction, but the school board officials said that they were pre-

* *Excerpted from Michael D. Tabris, "Crisis Management." In* Experts in Action: Inside Public Relations, *edited by Bill Cantor and Chester Burger. White Plains, N.Y.: Longman, 1984, pp. 64–67. Reprinted by permission of the publisher.*

pared, if necessary, to resort to condemnation proceedings to acquire the site.

Faced with the threat of condemnation, the company agreed to donate the property to the school board—but with an understanding that the area containing the wastes be used only as a park, to prevent construction that might penetrate the clay cover over the waste material. The company also insisted on a detailed restriction in the deed to put the school board on notice as to the nature of the buried wastes. Additionally, the company conducted tests that assured that the buried chemicals had remained in place and were essentially unchanged.

On at least two occasions Hooker Chemical officials appeared at public meetings to repeat warnings that the site was unsuitable for development and to oppose plans to build on the site or sell off portions of the property.

Despite warnings by the company, local, state, and federal government agencies later put roads, sewers, and utilities through the site after Hooker Chemical no longer owned or had any control over the property. Those and other invasions of the site allowed water to seep into the canal and it gradually filled up, like a bath tub, and overflowed. This finding was subsequently confirmed by a task force of the American Institute of Chemical Engineers.

By 1976 there had been confirmed instances of chemical waste seepage into basements of some houses that had been built on the periphery of the Love Canal property. In 1978 the EPA issued a report of chemical waste contamination triggering several other studies by state and federal agencies—reports that were later branded as inconclusive.

In August of 1978 the New York State Health Commissioner ordered temporary closure of a school adjacent to the site and recommended that families with pregnant women and children under two years of age living in the first two rings of homes around the canal property be temporarily relocated during remedial work on the site. His recommendations would have affected approximately twenty families.

One week later New York State Governor Carey visited the site and announced that 236 families would be relocated and their homes would be purchased.

Governor Carey's announcement lit the fire that set Hooker Chemical's switchboards ablaze and led to the issue of chemical waste disposal becoming a subject of national recognition and debate. The full extent of the problem—the fact that the company was faced with a genuine, full-fledged crisis as distinguished from an emergency—was not totally clear by the time I joined the company in 1979.

The first problem encountered by the company's public relations staff was one of merely coping with an unprecedented volume and range of inquiries. Faced with imminent press or broadcast deadlines, media representatives were often demanding in their search for information.

Here are a few of the inquiries that typify the thousands received at Niagara Falls, New York, at headquarters in Houston, Texas, and at other Hooker facilities around the nation:

- What chemicals were disposed of at Love Canal?
- What was the volume of each type of material?
- How much of the waste was liquid and how much was solid?
- How much was in drums and how much was in loose form?
- How were wastes transported to the site?
- How were the workers that handled the materials protected?
- How do the various chemicals interact with one another?
- What is the cumulative effect of all the materials there?
- How often were waste deposits made?
- What are the soil conditions at the site?
- What was the use of each chemical?
- How long has each chemical been there?
- What did you know about toxicity at time of disposal?
- How many homes were there in the area when the canal was in use as a disposal site?
- How close were the homes?
- Did the company suspect there were dangers at the time?
- Did the company warn people?

In addition to inquiries regarding factual information, there were countless requests for interviews with company officials and for comments on various company policies.

It should be kept in mind that the disposal site had been closed for 25 years when the controversy erupted. Many of those who might have been able to provide firsthand information were not available. Some had retired or had moved to other companies and could not be located. Much of the information necessary to provide accurate responses simply had to be gathered from stored company files and could not be obtained on short notice.

The company's inability to respond immediately and thoroughly to highly technical complex questions led to charges of "stonewalling." On the other hand, the company was not about to make statements that could not be firmly supported and that might require later retraction, eroding company credibility. Every effort was made to uncover the facts and to release confirmed information to the media.

1. How should the public-relations personnel at Occidental Chemical (formerly Hooker Chemical) respond to public inquiries about chemical contamination at Love Canal?
2. What do you think the possible repercussions for the company are if public-relations communication efforts are not effective in this situation?
3. What is the best that the company can expect if its public-relations communication strategies are effective?
4. Can public-relations efforts really "solve" the external communication problems faced by the company?

Look at the case from the perspective of different involved parties: the Occidental Chemical Company, local-government representatives, area residents, and so on. Apply Nager and Allen's 10-step analytic model to evaluate the various constraints on this crisis-management, public-relations effort.

External communication channels are broadly utilized in organizational life. There are many types of public-relations activities in modern organizations. We next examine how external channels of organizational communication are used to accomplish the important public-relations functions of marketing and advertising, lobbying, recruiting, public-opinion and market-research, polling and long-range planning. Then we will discuss some ethical concerns in external organizational communication.

Marketing and Advertising

Marketing, advertising, and public relations are closely related forms of external communication that often are considered to be separate organizational activities. The distinctions made among these external communication activities are more often based on the precedent of organizational design and interdivisional competition than on major differences in their organizational communication functions. Public-relations, marketing, and advertising professionals frequently have felt as though they were competing with one another for organizational resources and influence. This perception of competition is not always productive, since public-relations, marketing, and advertising efforts perform complementary and interdependent organizational functions.

Lightcap (1984) reports that in recent years, the artificial barriers that have historically separated public-relations, marketing, and advertising functions have worn thin and that cooperation and collaboration in these activities is becoming more common. We have broadly described public relations as the management of external channels of organizational communication. Marketing and advertising are integral parts of external organizational communication and, as such, are key elements of public-relations communication.

Marketing is the process by which organizational strategies for identifying, developing, and positioning products and services to match external market demands are created. Marketing efforts are used to design and implement communication strategies and programs (Webster, 1971), which are used to increase the acceptability of organizational outputs through the decisions that are made about product or service development, pricing, distribution, and promotion (Kotler and McDougal, 1982). Marketing also includes the use of market research to target new markets, identify new products or services, and direct organizational adaptation to changing market conditions. (The use of market research as a form of external communication will be examined later in the chapter.)

Marketing efforts are used to develop general promotional strategies for bringing organizational products or services to the attention of consumers. Promotional strategies include the use of advertising, publicity, and personal sales visits. Advertising is the presentation of persuasive messages to the public by means of paid space or broadcast time to promote organizational products and services, while publicity is the presentation of information about organization members, activities, products, or services by means of public news media to attract attention and influence public opinion (Cantor, 1984).

Advertising involves the implementation of creative communication strategies and techniques for specific products and services, often in media communication campaigns, to bring organizational products and/or services to the attention of potential consumers. Advertising, marketing, and public-relations efforts are interdependent organizational activities. Advertising communication campaigns should be designed to complement the general marketing strategies developed for the organization (Emery, Ault, and Agee, 1968). Moreover, advertising communication should be consistent with the image established for the organization through overall public-relations efforts (Selame and Selame, 1975).

Fay (1984) describes the use of corporate-advertising efforts to help establish and maintain effective corporate images. Corporate advertising brings attention to the organization, separates it from its competitors, or helps ward off problems by presenting the organization's view on a given issue. As forms of corporate advertising, many corporations support activities of public interest, such as the Olympics; public-education media, such as the television programs "Sesame Street" and "Nova"; and public-service events, such as telethons.

Lobbying

Lobbying is becoming an increasingly important form of external communication in modern organizations as local, state, and federal regulation of business and industry expands. Lobbying is essentially the establishment of influential relationships between representatives of organizations and representatives of professional and government accrediting and regulating agencies. Lobbies are "pressure groups which practice the art of making useful friends and influencing people—usually legislators and government regulatory agencies" (Cantor, 1984, p. 440).

Lobbyists serve important functions for both organizations and organizational governing agencies (Grunig and Hunt, 1984). For organizations, lobbyists gather relevant information about upcoming legislation and influence the introduction and passage of legislation that is supportive of organization interests. For governing agencies, both public and private, lobbyists provide useful technical information, evidence, and examples that legislators can use to support arguments and make informed decisions.

Grunig and Hunt (1984, p. 529) identify five primary activities of lobbyists that are of service to modern organizations.

1. Establish coalitions with other organizations sharing interests and goals to combine efforts in influencing legislative representatives
2. Gather information and prepare reports for legislators that represent the organizations' positions on key issues
3. Make contacts with influential individuals and representatives of governing agencies
4. Prepare expert witnesses and speakers to represent the positions of the organizations to legislators
5. Focus debate on key issues, facts, and evidence that will support the positions of the organizations

Perhaps the most important aspect of lobbying activities is preparing cases in support of organizational goals and presenting these cases to legislators. For preparing such a case, Gray (1984) suggests the following six steps.

1. Rehearse your arguments in support of the organization's position
2. Learn about the arguments in opposition to the organization's position
3. Know the political orientations of the legislators you are attempting to influence
4. Leave as soon as the legislators accept the organization's position;

do not oversell a legislator who already agrees with the organization's position

5. Give the legislator a written statement in support of the organization's position
6. Provide follow-up communication contact with the legislators to reinforce the position you are supporting

Lobbyists can use many strategies to persuade legislators to act on behalf of organizational interests. They can provide legislators with compelling information, facts, and examples to move them to action. They can exert pressure on legislators by mobilizing constituents' political support (Cox, 1984). Lobbyists also have used unethical strategies, such as bribery, to influence legislators. (Later in this chapter, we will discuss some of the ethical issues concerning lobbying and other forms of external organizational communication.) Grunig and Hunt (1984) contend that although unethical lobbyist activities receive a great deal of public attention, the majority of lobbying activities are aboveboard and are of great utility to organizations and public interests. They quote an article by John F. Kennedy (1956), written when he was a senator from Massachusetts, in support of their contention:

> . . . lobbyists are in many cases expert technicians and capable of explaining complex and difficult subjects in a clear, understandable fashion. They engage in personal discussions with members of Congress in which they can explain in detail the reason for positions they advocate.
>
> Lobbyists prepare briefs, memoranda, legislative analyses, and draft legislation for use by committees and members of Congress; they are necessarily masters of their subject, and, in fact, they frequently can provide useful statistics and information not otherwise available.
>
> Concededly, each is biased; but such a procedure is not unlike the advocacy of lawyers in court which has proven so successful in resolving judicial controversies. Because our congressional representation is based on geographical boundaries, the lobbyist who speaks for the various economic, commercial, and other functional interests of this country serve a very useful purpose and have assumed an important role in the legislative process. (p. 42)

Ethical or not, lobbying is an important and prevalent facet of external communication activities in modern organizations and, as such, must be utilized effectively in organizational life.

Recruitment

The recruitment of personnel for organizations is not generally viewed as a major facet of external organizational communication. Yet recruitment is an important organizational activity that involves communicating across organizational boundaries in identifying, contacting, evaluating, and selecting personnel for specific organizational needs (Filoromo and Ziff, 1980).

Recruitment of qualified personnel provides organizations with important maintenance and signal inputs. Recall that maintenance inputs provide organizations with sustenance and energy, while signal inputs provide organizations with information to direct activities. Personnel are organizational representatives who perform and accomplish important organizational activities, thereby energizing the organization and providing maintenance inputs. New organization members also bring the organization novel ideas and unique ways for interpreting and solving organizational difficulties, providing signal inputs.

Recruiters are charged with the responsibility of identifying, contacting, and influencing qualified personnel to join the organization. Recruitment and selection of the highest quality personnel provide organizations with the best possible inputs. The quality of personnel selection is of utmost importance because it determines the quality of maintenance and signal inputs provided to the organization. For example, if highly competent, intelligent, and motivated people are hired, they are far more likely to contribute to the accomplishment of organizational activities than are those who are incompetent, unintelligent, and unmotivated. Certainly, inexperienced personnel can be counseled and trained to accomplish specific tasks, but training these individuals will take considerable organizational time and effort. The more qualified new recruits are for specific organizational needs, the easier it is for the organization to utilize their talents and integrate them into the organization.

Recruitment and selection of personnel have long-term implications for the quality of organizational life. In addition to educational and experiential requirements, recruitment involves matching the temperament of recruits to the temperament of the organization. Care must be taken to select recruits who complement current organization members. There are several questions, apart from assessment of the technical competence of recruits, that must be posed and answered in effective recruitment:

1. How well will new organization members fit into the culture of the organization?
2. Are new members likely to cooperate with others in the organization?
3. Are there potential personality conflicts between recruits and existing members?
4. Will new members accept direction?

5. Are new members likely to be committed to the organization and take organizational activities seriously?
6. Are new members likely to act ethically within the organization and represent the best interests of the organization?
7. Will new members represent the organization well to the public?

Effective recruitment involves satisfying the demands of several internal and external agencies. Recruiters must be aware of both the specific internal organizational needs for personnel and the external societal conditions influencing recruitment. Internally, the recruiter must recognize the specific employment demands of the areas within the organization with which the recruit will be working, as well as management interests and requirements for the position. Externally, the recruiter must know if there are union requirements for the position; if there are government requirements, such as affirmative action and equal employment opportunities; and how current economic conditions, such as the nature of competition and of the labor market, affect recruitment (Glueck, 1978). Moreover, recruiters must communicate externally with the public through recruitment interviewing, job posting, and advertising.

Public-Opinion and Market Research

External organizational communication involves gathering pertinent environmental information as well as providing information to the environment. Public-opinion and market research are the formal avenues by which many modern organizations gather and interpret relevant environmental information to be used in making organizational decisions and directing organizational activities. Public-opinion and market research inform many of the other avenues of external communication, such as marketing and advertising efforts, crisis management, corporate image making, and lobbying.

Public relations involves "the evaluation of public attitudes and opinions; counseling management on policies and actions to ensure they're socially responsible and in the public interest; and executing an action and communication program to secure public understanding and acceptance" (Simon, 1980, p. 164). Simon (1980) explains that research provides the following benefits for public-relations efforts.

1. Information about public opinions and attitudes
2. Information about the standing of the organization within the interorganizational field
3. Information about potential environmental constraints on organizational activities

4. Internal organizational support for public-relations activities
5. Information about the effectiveness of external communication channels, methods, and programs
6. Clear activities, goals, and strategies for public-relations activities

Many strategies and techniques are used to conduct public-opinion and market research. Public-relations-research activities can be as informal as reading newspapers and watching television news programs or as formal as administering and statistically evaluating questionnaire surveys of large, national samples of respondents. Finn and Harrity (1984) suggest that audits are probably the most common form of public-relations research: "An audit is a survey of a company's key audiences. . . . An audit will accurately identify problems and suggest possible solutions because it draws conclusions directly from interviews with the audiences of special concern to the corporation" (p. 274). Those interviewed might include knowledgeable organizational representatives from the interorganizational field, expert analysts and consultants, and key members of the organization. Additional external research efforts include formal and informal observations, public-opinion polling, public-issue studies, readership surveys, and content analyses of documents and media (Robinson, 1969; Finn and Harrity, 1984; Nager and Allen, 1984; Grunig and Hunt, 1984).

Market research generally involves gathering information from consumers about their perceptions of product or service needs and their evaluations of organizational products and services (Kassarjian and Robertson, 1973). Market research is used to identify imminent market opportunities for the organization and to evaluate the marketability of current organizational products or services and the effectiveness of the current product or service market strategies utilized. Market researchers gather data that will help them make predictions about market responses to the organization, the organization's external communications efforts, and the organization's products and services (Webster, 1971). The more accurate the market research, the better the researchers' abilities to predict market responses, and the more likely that effective external organizational communication strategies can be planned.

Long-Range Planning

Strategic planning is an essential activity of effective organizational leadership (Rosen, 1973; Hussey, 1982). Recall the description in Chapter 3 of Fayol's (1949) administrative-theory principles of management, in which planning was identified as the primary principle of effective administration. Long-range planning involves making strategic choices about the most beneficial directions for organizational activities and development. Such choices include decisions about organizational "mission, objectives, strategy, policies, programs, goals, and major resource allocations" (Grant and King, 1982, p. 3). To make such choices, organization members need pertinent environmental information. For example, to make effective long-range plans, business leaders need information about the changing economic, social, and market conditions surrounding their organization.

Planning decisions are best made proactively, utilizing the most relevant and accurate environmental information. Proactive decisions depend on organization members' abilities to forecast future constraints on organizational activities so that they can prepare the organization to overcome these upcoming problems (Simon, 1965). Forecasting is a process by which organization members reduce their uncertainty about the organization's future by compiling information that indicates potential changes in organizational conditions (Hussey, 1982). Nager and Allen (1984) refer to this process as "futures research" (p. 223), in which organization members gather environmental data to anticipate future interorganizational field conditions and climates that may affect the organization.

Planning begins with gathering relevant information. As suggested by our discussion of public-opinion and market research, gathering relevant environmental information is one of the primary functions accomplished through external organizational communication. External communication enables organization members to make contact with key representatives of the organization's environment. These representatives often can provide organization members with pertinent information for making responsible decisions about directing and innovating organizational activities.

There are many methods for gathering relevant information for long-range planning. Nager and Allen (1984) suggest the use of such research methods as the Delphi technique, in which experts are polled; scenario analysis, in which potential alternative outcomes are posed and evaluated; and cross-impact matrix analysis, in which interaction effects among anticipated events are examined. To direct long-range planning, useful environmental information can be gathered both formally through research and informally through conversations with a wide range of sources both internal and external to the organization. Grant and King (1982) identify several useful populations of information sources for long-range planning, such as employees, customers, potential customers, expert consultants, competitors, government representatives, stockholders, and creditors. Many modern organizations have hired information specialists to gather and process relevant information (Hall, 1982; Koenig and Kochoff, 1984) and have created special corporate libraries whose staffs gather, store, and disseminate relevant environmental information to organization members (White, 1984; Crum, 1970).

Grant and King (1982) identify three primary assessment activities that involve both internal and external organizational communication that should be part of organizational long-range planning.

1. Identification of *environmental opportunities and risks*, including the development of technologies, consumer demands, or competing products or services. This assessment primarily involves external communication to keep abreast of environmental changes and developments.
2. Identification of *strategic issues* that influence public attitudes and behaviors toward the organization and its products or services, such as changing societal values, government regulations, and economic conditions. This assessment primarily involves external communication to identify and understand environmental issues.
3. Identification of *organizational strengths and weaknesses* to recognize areas of organizational vulnerability as well as directions for organizational growth and development. This assessment primarily involves internal communication to gather information about the organizational structures, personnel, processes, and cultures.

These three types of assessment in strategic planning clearly indicate the need for balancing internal and external organizational communication channels to direct organizational growth and development. Organizational planning is an essential part of effective organizational innovation. In Chapter 11, we will examine in depth the interdependent roles of internal and external organizational communication in developing effective levels of organizational innovation.

ETHICAL DIMENSIONS OF EXTERNAL COMMUNICATION

Recall our discussion in Chapter 9 about the importance of ethics in internal organizational communication; it is also crucially important to observe ethical standards in external organizational communication. Ethics are specific moral constraints of a given society or culture that are used to help people make judgments about what is right and what is wrong. In Chapter 9, we identified three ideal covering principles of ethical organizational conduct: (1) honesty, (2) avoiding harm, and (3) justice. Ethical relations between an organization and its environment are honest and aboveboard, do no harm to any person or group, and are fair and equitable.

Abuses in Environmental Communication

There are many instances in the modern world where questionable ethical choices are made in guiding external organizational communication. Just pick up a daily newspaper, and you undoubtedly will be able to read stories about bribery, extortion, and collusion (all three are unethical external communication practices) in business, industrial, governmental, educational, health-care, and/or public-utility organizations. These three unethical practices are by no means an exhaustive listing of unethical external communication activities in modern organizational life. Several specific instances of potentially unethical relations between organizations and their environments include

1. industrial *espionage* and *sabotage*, in which trade secrets are stolen, and organization representatives unfairly restrain or injure competition (Mixon, 1982; Rogers and Larsen, 1984);
2. *bribery* and *coercion*, in which unfair influence is gained over those in positions of regulatory power over the organization (Sturm, 1982);
3. organizational *cooptation*, in which competitors or other members of the interorganizational field that stand in the way of an organization are absorbed and taken over by the organization (Rogers and Agarwala-Rogers, 1976; Rogers and Larsen, 1984) (cooptation can be thought of as the "Pac-man theory of management," in which the object is to consume all barriers in the path of the organization);
4. *monopoly*, in which one organization can control a market and prevent competition, or *oligopoly*, in which several organizations combine efforts to prevent free competition from other organizations (Dale, 1969);
5. *deceptive advertising*, in which false and misleading claims are made about an organization's products or services (Grunig and Hunt, 1984; Kotler and McDougal, 1982);
6. *conflict of interest*, in which decision-making organizational representatives make decisions concerning other organizations in which they accrue direct or indirect benefits through vested interests (Kreps and Thornton, 1984; Rogers and Larsen, 1984);
7. *hedging of records* and *false disclosure of information* to government and/or regulatory agencies, such as tax evasion (Sturm, 1982; Grunig and Hunt, 1984);
8. *withholding relevant information* from the public and the media to protect the organization, save face, or prevent scandal (Sturm, 1982; Grunig and Hunt, 1984);
9. *stock manipulation* to unfairly control organizational decision

making, often at the expense of other shareholders (Dale, 1969; Chatlos, 1984);

10. *overpricing* of goods and services to consumers (Hussey, 1982; Kreps, 1982b);
11. *discriminatory employment practices* against women, the aged, members of racial and ethnic minority groups, and other persons (Loy and Stewart, 1984; Kanter, 1977; Deutsch, 1979).
12. outright *thievery* of ideas, services, and products belonging to other persons or groups (Rutenberg, 1982; Sturm, 1982);
13. causing *harm, discomfort,* and/or *dangerous conditions* for organization members and for individuals outside the organization through the activities and outputs (products, services, and by-products) of the organization (Hussey, 1982; Nager and Allen, 1984; Kreps and Thornton, 1984).

These 13 potentially unethical organizational practices are not all the possible unethical external communication activities that occur in organizational life. They do represent common ethical infractions in which organizations engage. These 13 also are not always mutually exclusive. Organizational representatives may engage in several of these practices simultaneously. Evaluate each of the 13 unethical external organizational activities. How well do they live up to the three criteria for ethical conduct: honesty, avoiding harm, and justice? You probably can identify how each of the organizational practices violates at least one of the three ethical standards. Some of the practices violate all three standards.

The unethical external communication practices can be organized into three major categories of ethical issues: (1) honesty and information giving; (2) influence and control; and (3) external accountability, or the degree to which an organization lives up to its responsibilities to members of its relevant environment. Each of the practices is contained within at least one of the three categories, and some of the practices are covered by more than one category. Table 10.1 lists these three major categories.

Honesty and Information Giving

For external organizational communication to be ethical, it must be honest. It is not ethical for organization members to purposely deceive representatives of their relevant environment. (Recall the discussion of honesty in Chapter 9, where we distinguished between truth and honesty. Honesty refers to the presentation of information that is not intentionally deceptive and is true to the best knowledge of the message sender.) Practices such as false advertising, fudging of records, with-

Table 10.1

Three Major Categories of External Comminication Ethics

1. *Honesty and information giving* espionage and sabotage; deceptive advertising; hedging of records; withholding relevant information; overpricing; discriminatory employment practices; thievery.
2. *Influence and control* espionage and sabotage; bribery and coercion; cooptation; monopoly or oligopoly; conflict of interest; stock manipulation; discriminatory employment practices.
3. *External accountability* hedging of records; withholding relevant information; stock manipulation; overpricing; discriminatory employment practices; thievery; harm.

holding relevant information from government and the public, espionage and sabotage, overpricing of goods and services, unfair and discriminatory employment practices, and thievery are examples of dishonest external communication practices in organizational life.

Influence and Control

For external organizational communication to be ethical, it must be equitable. It is not ethical for organization members to exert undue and oppressive influence on representatives of the interorganizational field. Any organizational practices that unfairly restrain free trade, self-determination, and influence of individuals and other organizations, such as monopolies and oliogopolies, conflicts of interest, bribery and coercion in lobbying activities, espionage and sabotage, cooptations, stock manipulations, and discriminatory employment practices are examples of unethical external organizational communication.

External Accountability

Organizations (and their members, especially leaders) have moral and legal responsibilities to serve and do no harm to their own organization members, constituents and stockholders, customers, other organizations within their interorganizational fields, and individuals within their relevant environment. Organizations also depend on others within their relevant environments to serve and do no harm to them. The degree to which organizations live up to these mutual responsibilities and dependencies is referred to as external accountability. Rogers and Agarwala-Rogers (1976) define external accountability as "the degree to which an organization is dependent on or responsible to its environment" (p. 160).

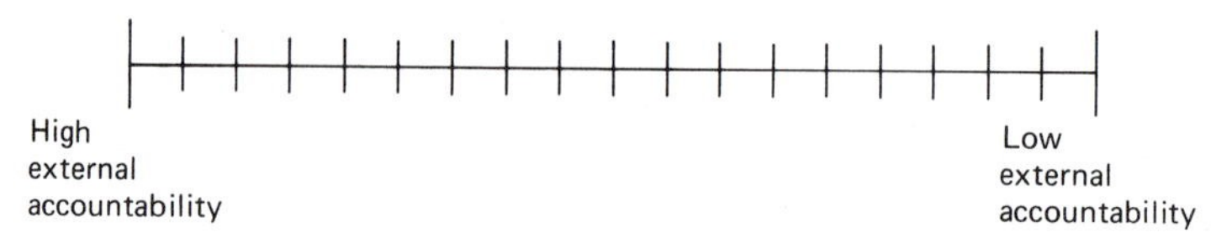

Figure 10.2 The external accountability continuum.

External accountability should not be thought of as a bipolar, on-or-off variable, where organizations are either externally accountable or not externally accountable. External accountability is a continuous variable that changes on the basis of interdependent activities of organizations and environments. It is helpful to view external accountability on a continuum from high external accountability to low external accountability (Figure 10.2).

Organizations are more or less externally accountable to the extent that they live up to the expectations of their environment and achieve the support and nurturance they expect and need from their environment. The mutuality of external accountability suggests that the effectiveness of organization–environment relations should be evaluated by the same basic criterion established in Chapter 8 for the evaluation of interpersonal relationships—the development of effective implicit contracts. Recall that effective implicit contracts are those in which relational partners clearly recognize and agree to live up to each other's expectations. As expectations change, implicit contracts must be renegotiated and updated. (The renegotiation and updating of implicit contracts between organization and environment will be related to organizational innovation in Chapter 11.) Organization members and representatives of their relevant environments, just like interpersonal-relationship partners, have mutual expectations for one another's behavior and must try to establish effective implicit contracts if their relationship is to work. Organizations are externally accountable to the extent that they establish and maintain effective implicit contracts with representatives from their relevant environment.

Failures to promote external accountability often result in unethical external organizational communication. It is not ethical for organizations to harm the larger society that surrounds them. Any organizational practice that endangers the environment decreases the organization's external accountability and violates implicit contracts between the organization and its relevant environment. For example, organizational activities such as falsifying public or government records, withholding from the public relevant information about potential or current dangers, causing harm to the environment through pollution, or usurping others' rights through discriminatory employment practices, thievery, stock manipulation, or overpricing are instances of low external accountability that are also unethical practices.

Organizations that fail to achieve and maintain effective implicit contracts (and relationships) with their relevant environments inevitably incur problems of external accountability. Such problems often result in disasters, such as the waste seepage at Love Canal (Case 10.1). Can you identify the organization that had very poor external accountability? It is not Hooker Chemical Company, which was careful to inform the local government about the dangers of the waste site and warned against construction and housing development, living up to its end of an implicit contract not to harm residents in the environment. Unhappily, the local government was not very externally accountable to the public it served, since it approved construction efforts and endangered residents' health.

When organizations are not externally accountable to the general public, the public often depends on the activities of "whistle blowers" to provide information about dangerous or unethical conditions. "Whistle-blowers are considered to be organization members who disclose employers' illegal, immoral, or illegitimate practices that are under the control of their employers to persons or organizations who may be able to affect this action" (Miceli and Near, 1984, p. 689). "Whistle blowing is based on the assumption that employees who disagree on ethical grounds with their employers about organizational policy should not quit, but should speak out" (Stewart, 1980b, p. 92). Whistle blowers often perform extremely important and noble functions for the public. They must be able to "put their duty to the public above their loyalty to the organization" (Stewart, 1980b, p. 92). Although whistle blowers run great risks and generally incur severe penalties, including reprisals and firing, they perform the key function of increasing external accountability in modern organizations (Stewart, 1980a, 1980b; Miceli and Near, 1984; Grunig and Hunt, 1984).

Whistle blowers usually attempt to influence change within their organizations to rectify problems with external accountability before divulging potentially inflammatory information to the public (Stewart, 1980b). When superiors are resistant to the upward communication of their subordinates, organization members have few outlets for exerting influence within the organization, and they must go outside the organization with the information to stimulate change. This is an organizational communication issue that is affected by problems in both internal and external organizational communication. In Chapter 11, suggestions will be offered to improve both internal and external organizational communication systems to reduce the need for whistle blowing and to increase organizational innovation and external accountability.

To improve the ethics of external organizational communication, clear moral standards for organizational behavior must be established and maintained as important themes of organizational culture. The three covering principles of ethical organizational conduct—honesty, avoiding harm, and justice—should be used as guidelines for directing and evaluating organizational communication.

Additionally, organization members should strive to develop honest and trusting relationships with representatives of their organization's relevant environment. The development of clear and flexible implicit contracts between interorganizational representatives will facilitate the development of effective and ethical relationships between organization and environment.

PART IV

CONCLUSION

In Part IV, relationships between organizational communication and organizational effectiveness are described. The information-based model of organizational communication, presented briefly in Chapter 1, is reintroduced and more fully explained. Theories and concepts described earlier are integrated into the discussion of organizational effectiveness. The coordination of internal and external channels of organizational communication is examined and applied to the ongoing development of stability and innovation in organizational life. The uses of communication to gather and interpret relevant information are explored as primary activities in enhancing innovation and organizational effectiveness. Specific strategies for promoting ongoing organizational development and innovation are suggested.

CHAPTER 11

Information and Organizational Effectiveness

COORDINATING INTERNAL AND EXTERNAL INFORMATION

The effectiveness of organizing activities is dependent on the ability of organization members to communicate and use relevant information. Organization members must be able to elicit cooperation from one another to coordinate the accomplishment of organizational activities. Organization members also must be able to adapt to and influence their organization's relevant environment to create and maintain an ongoing state of organization. In this chapter, the uses of internal and external organizational communication to seek, interpret, send, and utilize relevant information will be applied to the development of effective organization.

In Chapters 1, 9, and 10, we identified and described two primary avenues of organizational communication: (1) *internal organizational communication*, in which messages are shared among organization members; and (2) *external organizational communication*, in which messages are shared between organization members and representatives of the organization's environment. These two avenues of organizational communication perform different, yet interdependent coordinating functions in organizational life. Internal communication is used to coordinate the activities of many organization members, while external communication is used to coordinate the activities of organization members with the activities of members of organizations' relevant environments.

For organizations to be effective, organization members must be able to competently use and coordinate internal and external organizational communication. Yet because many organization members do not appreciate the importance of communication in organizational life and have not developed competent communication strategies and skills, there are many communication deficiencies in modern organizational practice (Monge, Bachman, Dillard, and Eisenberg, 1982). The failure to effectively use and coordinate internal and external organizational communication has serious repercussions for organization.

An organization whose members are able to coordinate activities with one another (effective internal communication) but are totally out of tune with the needs and constraints of the environment that the organization serves (ineffective external communication) is unlikely to meet these needs and constraints because members will not recognize or understand changing environmental conditions. Let us call this situation of good internal communication but poor external communication *type A error*. A situation of type A error is analogous to a person who is very competent at driving and handling an automobile attempting to maneuver at high speeds in heavy traffic by concentrating entirely on operating the controls of the car without looking out the windshield of the car at oncoming traffic.

Similarly, an organization whose members are very much in tune with the ever-changing constraints and needs of the environment (effective external communication) but are unable to coordinate activities very well with one another (ineffective internal communication) is also unlikely to meet the demands of the environment because members will not be able to react quickly or effectively to changing situations. Let us call this situation of good external communication but poor internal communication *type B error*. To continue the automobile example, a situation of type B error would occur when a person who had no idea about how to drive an automobile is strapped behind the steering wheel of a car traveling at 50 miles per hour looking out the car windows at heavy oncoming traffic.

Both the type A and type B error automobile examples sound like nightmares. They are! Yet many organizations fail to coordinate their internal and external communication systems, suffering from type A, type B, or, even worse, *type C error* (where organization members communicate poorly both internally and externally). Those organizations that fail to coordinate internal and external communication probably find themselves in situations that are not very different from the automobile analogies. Organization members may find themselves in situations in which they have no idea where the organization is going, where it should go, or why it should go there—type A error. They may find themselves in situations in which they know where the organization should go but are not able to get other members to coordinate activities with them to get the organization there—type B error. Or perhaps, in the most perilous of conditions, organization members may find themselves in situations in which they are totally confused about the direction of the organization and totally powerless to guide the activities of organization members in any direction—type C error. In this chapter, suggestions for effective coordination of internal and external organizational communication systems will be presented to help minimize types A, B, and C communication errors in organizational life.

Communication and Stability in Organizations

A primary goal of organization is to achieve stability and predictability in life. As discussed in Chapter 1, people organize to help them interpret, understand, and respond appropriately to difficult and complex situations. As Weick (1979) points out, organization enables people to cope with equivocality by sharing the interpretation of complexity with others and developing rules to guide their actions.

Our participation in organizational life helps us to direct our lives by providing us with organizationally designated roles, responsibilities, and jobs (activities) that we are to accomplish. The more clearly defined and understood the roles and responsibilities, the more stable and predictable organizational life becomes.

Communication is the mechanism by which rules, roles, and responsibilities are designed and presented to organization members. More specifically, internal organizational communication is used to direct and coordinate the activities of organization members. As discussed in Chapter 9, internal organizational communication is used primarily to administer organization members and manage organizational activities. Internal communication channels are used to

1. disseminate and enforce organizational goals, rules, and regulations
2. coordinate the activities of organization members in the accomplishment of organizational tasks
3. provide formal leaders with feedback about the adequacy of downward communication and the state of current organizing activities
4. socialize organization members into the culture of the organization

Each of these internal communication functions helps to increase the stability, predictability, and orderliness of organizational life (Kreps, 1983a).

Communication and Innovation in Organizations

The important need for adaptation, change, and innovation in organizational life is in striking contrast to the need for stability and order in organizations. Although organizational change happens naturally (organizations and organizational activities are continually emerging and changing), most naturally occurring change probably is not in the best interests of organization. Organizational change is generally haphazard and undirected (Weick, 1979; Cohen, March, and Olsen, 1972).

Innovation is a special type of change that is not haphazard. Innovation is planned and directed change that is designed to improve organizations and organizational life. Because of continually emerging constraints on and challenges to the accomplishment of organizational activities and goals, there is a recurring need for innovative ideas to adapt the behaviors of organization members to meet these challenges. According to the systems theory principles of openness, negative entropy, and equifinality (Chapter 5), organizations must continually adopt new input-processing strategies to accomplish advantageous outputs and enable human systems to survive.

Communication is the mechanism by which organization members can identify challenges to and constraints on organizational activities. External organizational communication enables organization members to gather relevant environmental information to inform themselves about changing environmental conditions and to direct organizational activities in adapting to changing environmental conditions. As discussed in Chapter 10, external communication helps organization members coordinate the activities of the organization with the activities of others within the relevant environment.

External communication is also used to provide persuasive information to environmental representatives about the activities, products, and/or services of the organization. Information sent through external channels can be used to influence the activities of individuals and groups in the relevant environment. Public-relations activities help organization members identify environmental risks and opportunities within the interorganizational field, inform organization leaders about needs for innovation to meet these risks and opportunities, and motivate support and action on behalf of the organization from the environment.

Balancing Innovation and Stability

An important theme that has been developed throughout this book is the need to maintain a balance between innovation and stability in organizational life. Neither innovation nor stability is an absolute good unto itself. Although each serves important functions for organizations, there is a point of diminishing return where each is also counterproductive to the goals of organizations.

Too much stability can be harmful to organization. While stability makes an organization predictable, ordered, and controlled, organizations that are too stable are dull, inflexible, and unresponsive to changing organizational needs and problems. Stability sounds like a good thing to many people, but stability can often indicate lack of growth and responsiveness. For example, it always seems strange when health-care providers report patients' conditions as being "stable." After all, the most stable human condition is death. Similarly, an overabundance of stability in organizational life undoubtedly will lead to organizational entropy and death.

Too much innovation also can be harmful to organization. While innovation helps organizations respond to problematic situations and cope with threats to survival, too much innovation can make organizational life frustratingly complex, disorienting, and unfocused. Too much organizational innovation and change can lead to a total lack of direction and anarchy among organization members and to organizational entropy. Organization members must try to establish optimal levels of innovation and stability in their organizations.

To complicate this need to establish optimal levels of innovation and stability, these two conditions tend to be negatively related in many organizations (Eisenberg, 1984; Pascale and Athos, 1981). The more stable organizations are, the more likely they are to be resistant to innovation. The more innovative organizations are, the more likely they are to have difficulty developing stability. But it is possible for organization members to balance the development of innovation and stability in organizational life. Organizations can demonstrate both innovation and stability, but it takes a great deal of effort and effective coordination of organizational communication.

Since the development of stability is related to the use of internal organizational communication, and the development of innovation is related to the use of external organizational communication, to demonstrate both innovation and stability, organization members must effectively utilize both internal and external communication channels. Ineffective use of internal communication channels will make it difficult to establish stability and implement innovative ideas. Ineffective use of external communication will make it difficult to identify directions for innovation and influence the relevant environment.

Internal communication channels and external communication channels are interrelated and interdependent, and must be coordinated in organizational life. Internal organizational activities are informed by external communication, and ideas generated through external channels are put into practice through the use of internal organizational communication. Organization members must be able to gain access to and effectively use internal and external communication channels to maintain a productive balance between innovation and stability.

In type A error, internal organizational communication channels are well utilized, and there is a high degree of stability and organization member cooperation; but external communication channels are underutilized, and there are insufficient ideas for directing organizational innovation. In type B error, external organizational communication channels are well utilized, and there are many ideas for directing organizational innovation; but internal communication channels are underutilized, and there is insufficient predictability and stability to direct coordinated action. To avoid type A or type B error and promote a balance between innovation and stability, internal and external communication must be effectively utilized together and coordinated in organizational life.

Organization leaders must recognize their roles as both internal organizational communicators and external organizational communicators. The distinction between managers and leaders, made by Bennis (1976a, 1976b) and by Zaleznik (1977) (Chapter 8), relates very closely to the dual communication functions of executives. Recall that according to Bennis's and Zaleznik's taxonomies, leaders are visionaries who direct the course of the organization, while managers are administrators who enforce rules and direct organization member activities.

According to our analysis of this distinction, leaders are effective at utilizing external communication channels, and managers are effective at utilizing internal communication channels. In Chapter 8, it was suggested that to become effective, executives should be taught to develop both leader and manager qualities. This would help combine the internal and external communication functions. Moreover, formal responsibilities for internally and externally oriented communication should be delegated to different organization members and departments. For example, the designation of a *chief executive officer* (CEO) as the executive in charge of long-range planning and external communication functions and of a *chief operating officer* (COO) as the executive in charge of day-to-day operations and internal communication functions is quite common in many large, complex organizations. This executive designation of CEO and COO clearly illustrates the dual and equally important internal and external communication functions in organizational life.

An integrating model of effective internal and external organizational communication was briefly introduced at the end of Chapter 1. Let us reintroduce that model and analyze it in light of our understand-

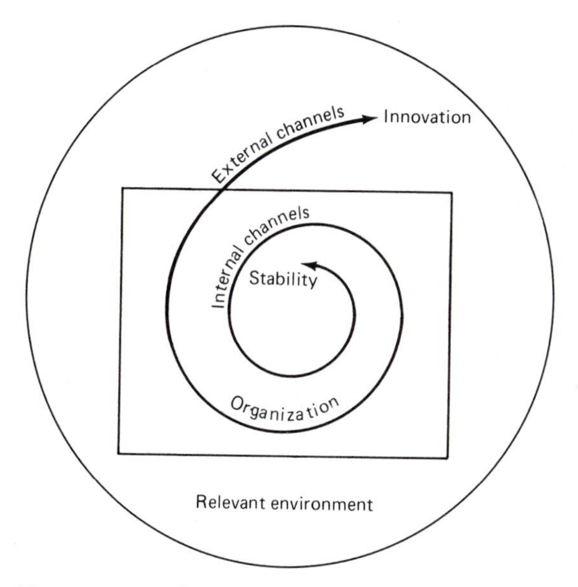

Figure 11.1 The integrating model of organizing.

ing of the interdependent organizational functions of internal and external communication (Figure 11.1). Note that in the model, internal and external channels of organizational communication are depicted by the one line of organizational communication, which illustrates that internal and external communication are interdependent and equally important aspects of organizing. The internal communication end of the organizational communication line is directed inside the organization, where it is used to administer the accomplishment of organizational processes and activities, helping to promote organizational stability. The external communication end of the organizational communication line is directed outside the organization into the relevant environment, where it is used to exchange messages between organization and environment, helping to identify directions for organizational innovation.

The line of organizational communication is coiled to represent the fact that communication activities are continually changing in response to the different information situations the organization faces. While classical theory (Chapter 3) and human-relations theory (Chapter 4) generally focused on only the internal aspects of organizational communication in promoting, respectively, order and individual growth, systems theory (Chapter 5), Weick's model (Chapter 6), and organizational-culture theory (Chapter 7) focus on the use of both internal and external organizational communication. The coiled line of organizational communication can be used to illustrate important aspects of systems theory, Weick's model, and organizational-culture theory.

Systems theory suggests that in effective organizations, members should be more open to their relevant environment in times of external turbulence and more closed to their relevant environment in times of internal turbulence. In times of external turbulence, organization members need information about how changes in the environment can influence the organization so that they can proactively plan organizational strategies for adapting to these environmental developments (Lorsch and Lawrence, 1972). "An organization is more likely to innovate when its environment is rapidly changing than when it is steady" (Rogers and Agarwala-Rogers, 1976, p. 70). In times of internal turbulence, organization members have to share information to reestablish order and elicit cooperation so that organizational activities can be accomplished. The flexibility of the coiled line of organizational communication illustrates that communication can be directed to respond to both internal and external exigencies and demands, demonstrating relative openness.

According to Weick's (1969, 1979) model, organization members adapt to information inputs from the environment through the use of appropriate organizational rules and information-processing communication cycles during the organizing phases of enactment, selection, and retention. These three phases of organizing capture the interdependence of internal and external organizational communication. Enactment is established primarily through interaction between organization members and environment (external communication), while selection and retention are accomplished primarily through communication among organization members (internal communication). The line of organizational communication in the integrating model illustrates the connection between internal and external organizational communication in enactment, selection, and retention.

Organizational culture involves the use of both internal and external channels of communication. Internal organizational communication channels are used to continually socialize new members into the cultures of the organization, while external communication channels are used to represent the cultures of the organization (public images) to individuals within the interorganizational field. The line of organizational communication in the integrating model illustrates the use of both internal and external communication in the development and dissemination of organizational culture.

Although not explicit in the model, it should be recognized that the line of internal and external communication in the integrating model of organizing assumes the development of effective interpersonal relationships in both internal and external organizational communication activities. The effective use of internal and external communication channels in organizational life is dependent on the development of meaningful and cooperative interpersonal relationships. Recall from Chapter 8 that the interpersonal relationship was identified as the basic unit of human organization. Within organizations, individual organization members must be able to establish good working relations with one another to accomplish their jobs and achieve organization. Additionally, boundary-spanning representatives of organizations must be able to establish effective relationships with individuals from their organizations' relevant environments. The establishment and maintenance of clear, updated implicit contracts are essential to the development of effective interpersonal relationships in organizational life.

Inherent within this assumption about the development of effective relationships in organizational life is the assumption that organization members will be able to use symbols strategically within both formal and informal organizational communication systems. As discussed in Chapter 9, to be effective, organizational communicators must be able to recognize the political implications of their communication. While engaging in political internal and/or external communication, organization members should use ethical standards to guide their use of message strategies (Chapters 9 and 10). They must be equally adept at communicating through formally designated channels of organizational communication and at accessing relevant information obtained through the grapevine.

Eisenberg (1984) suggests that internal and external organizational activities involve interaction in both formal and informal communication contexts, and he presents a useful categorization scheme for identifying these contexts (Figure 11.2). Formal internal communication contexts involve the activities of organizational planning and administrative functions (Chapter 3), while informal internal communication contexts involve general sharing of cultural information among organization members (Chapter 7). Formal external communication contexts involve public-relations functions, and informal external communication contexts involve the activities of establishing and maintaining politically rewarding interorganizational networks (Chapter 10).

FEEDBACK AND INNOVATION IN ORGANIZATIONS

Organization members need feedback about organizational activities to direct successful innovation within their organizations (Nadler, 1977; Rowe and Boise, 1973). Although we have discussed primarily the gathering and interpreting of information about environmental changes

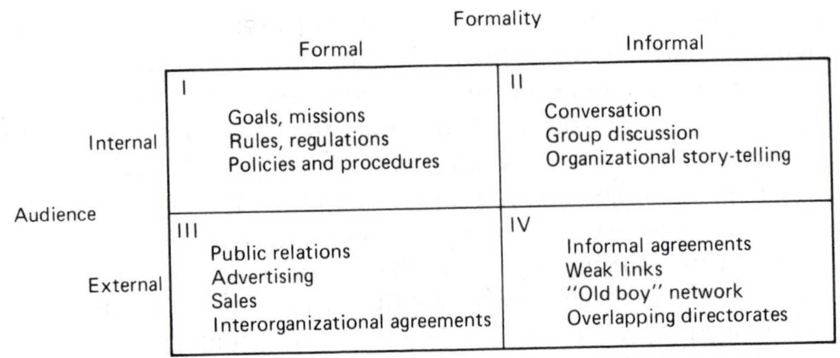

Figure 11.2 Dimensions of communication contexts. Adapted from E. M. Eisenberg, "Ambiguity as Strategy in Organizational Communication." *Communication Monographs* 51 (1984):237.

and constraints to guide organizational innovation, organizations also have to innovate in response to information about the state of internal organizational conditions. According to Greenbaum (1974), organizations have to conduct regular internal communication audits so that they can identify and diagnose potential operational difficulties. As discussed in Chapter 9, these audits typically assess organization members' perceptions about the quality of organizational operations and interpersonal relations (Brooks, Callicoat, and Siegerdt, 1979; Nadler, 1977). This internal feedback enables organization leaders to more clearly see the internal state of the organization from the point of view of the organization's membership, promoting increased *organizational reflexivity*, or the organization's ability to see itself.

As pointed out earlier, it is important for organization members to recognize emerging external constraints on organizational activities. Many external communication activities, such as public relations, lobbying and government relations, and market and public-opinion research, are designed to seek feedback and gather key information from the relevant environment. Also, organization audits and survey-research efforts often are designed to gather key environmental information (Nadler, 1977), which increases organizational reflexivity, helping organization members see their organization as members of the relevant environment see it. Such feedback is used to assess the adequacy of organizing activities and direct the course for organizational innovation.

Increased reflexivity enables organization members to recognize important *performance gaps*. "Performance gaps are discrepancies between an organization's expectations and its actual performance" (Rogers and Agarwala-Rogers, 1976, p. 70). Performance gaps occur in all situations where organizational goals are not fully accomplished. There are many kinds of performance gaps, and all organizations experience performance gaps. The farther the organization is from the accomplishment of established organizational goals, the wider the performance gap. Feedback methods are used to gather information about the nature and seriousness of organizational performance gaps.

Organizations in which relevant performance gaps are identified are better informed about directions for organizational innovation. Yet merely having relevant information about necessary changes and improvements does not mean that organizations are able to actually develop and implement innovations. Slack resources are needed to energize organizational innovation. Rogers and Agarwala-Rogers (1976) define *slack resources* as organizational "resources that are not already committed to other purposes" (p. 161). Slack resources can be personnel who are free to work on solving performance gaps, equipment or computer time that is not being utilized, or money that is not earmarked for other purposes. Organizations generally have some slack resources. To direct and implement innovations in organizations, slack resources have to be identified and mobilized.

Once slack resources are identified, they must be mobilized to direct the development and implementation of innovation strategies. Innovation strategies can be more or less novel and creative, ranging from the reinterpretation or new application of existing organizational methods, often referred to as "reinvention," to the development of totally new organizational processes and practices (Rogers and Agarwala-Rogers, 1976, p. 159). The newness of the innovation is not as important as is the fit between the strategy and the problem. The innovation strategy must match the performance gap by helping the organization address and solve the gap. For example, if an organization is operating in the red and is facing serious financial difficulties, the appropriate innovation strategy is not to hire personnel or develop new accounting procedures, but to institute revenue-generating activities to reduce the monetary deficit.

Case 11.1 relates a true story about an organizational problem and subsequent strategy for dealing with the problem.

1. Describe how feedback was used to identify performance gaps within the hospital and direct innovation in this case. What performance gaps were identified? How serious were these performance gaps for the organization and for the accomplishment of organizational goals?
2. Who were the sources of relevant information and feedback? How was the information gathered by organization members? Did the feedback increase organizational reflexivity? If not, why not; if so, in what ways?

Case 11.1

A Matter of Education*

City General Hospital was encountering an unexpected problem. A rather large number of patients at the hospital whose physicians had recommended a gastroscopy for them refused to sign the informed-consent statement and would not undergo the procedure. The gastroscopy is a fairly routine procedure that involves the use of a gastroscope to inspect the interior of the stomach. The gastroscope, a tube-like instrument with something similar to a light on its end, is inserted through the client's mouth, down the esophagus, and into the stomach. The procedure is invaluable in examining ulcers, discovering tumors of the stomach, and generally finding stomach disease.

Although the gastroscopy procedure sounds rather involved and uncomfortable, it is relatively simple and causes most clients very little discomfort. Lack of adequate information from the physician about what the patient could expect before, during, and after the procedure was expected to be the problem. After reviewing the situation, including interviews with hospital staff and clients, it was decided that a gastroscopy educational program should be developed. The hospital media department produced an informative videotape designed to describe the gastroscopy procedure and its uses. The videotape program included interviews with physicians, nurses, and those who were just recovering from the procedure. The videotape program was shown to each hospital client recommended for having a gastroscopy. Client response to the media program was extremely positive. The informed consent turn-down rate was reduced by 35 percent for those who watched the brief videotape presentation.

* *Suggested by Garland C. Elmore, "Integrating Video Technology and Organizational Communication" (Paper presented at the meeting of the Indiana Speech Association, Indianapolis, October 1981).*

3. How effective is the innovation strategy that organization members developed and implemented? How innovative is the strategy? Will the strategy solve the immediate performance gaps? Will the innovative strategies help the organization cope with future problems and performance gaps?
4. What are the different types of slack resources that were identified and mobilized to implement this innovation? Were there other slack resources that might have been used?

5. Would you describe this organization as being proactive or reactive? Why?

Communication and Organizational Development

The recognition of performance gaps and of potential performance gaps is a key step in organizational renewal and development (Pavlock, 1982; French, Bell, and Zawacki, 1978; French and Bell, 1973). Beckhard (1969, p. 4) defines organizational development (OD) as a renewal and change effort that is (1) planned, (2) organizationwide, and (3) managed from the top, to (4) increase organization effectiveness and health through (5) planned interventions in the organization's processes using behavioral-science knowledge. An OD effort involves a systematic diagnosis of the organization, the development of a strategic plan for change, and the mobilization of resources to carry out the effort. By identifying important performance gaps, an organizational-development specialist can pinpoint and diagnose specific organizational problems and difficulties and design adaptive strategies for organizational innovation.

Organizational development is a planned approach to directing organizational innovation. OD efforts perform extremely important functions for modern organizations, as well as further the development of organizational theory. Berrien (1976) contends that "no problem is more important to organizational theory than the management of change, both internal and external" (p. 47). Organization development is an applied area of study in which data are gathered and theory is built around developing strategies for directing organizational innovation.

To direct organizational innovation, OD specialists not only have to diagnose performance gaps that organizations are experiencing, but also have to identify slack resources available within organizations to use in implementing innovations. Communication is an essential tool that enables organization members to recognize the need for innovation and gather the slack resources necessary for accomplishing organizational development (Axley, 1980). It is used to gather the information and feedback needed from internal and external sources to identify performance gaps and plan organizational-development efforts (Nadler, 1977). Communication is used to gain support for OD efforts from organization leaders (Schein, 1969). Communication is essential to the mobilization of slack resources and the implementation of intervention strategies and plans into organizational operations (Nadler, 1977; Beckhard, 1969). Communication is also essential in building long-term commitment to organizational innovation (Conner and Patterson, 1982; Axley, 1980).

Rogers and Agarwala-Rogers (1976, p. 163) have identified four phases in organizational innovation. Three additional steps that we have noted seem to preface these four phases well, expanding the model to seven steps in the organizational-innovation process.

1. Identification of relevant performance gaps within the organization
2. Development of innovation strategies for addressing the performance gaps
3. Mobilization of slack resources to energize organizational innovations
4. Adoption of appropriate innovation strategies for the organization
5. Examination of the adequacy of the innovation strategies for the organization
6. Installation of the innovation strategies into the structure and activities of the organization
7. Institutionalization of the innovation strategies as integral aspects of ongoing organizational operations

Developing Proactive Organizations

The better organization members are at gathering relevant information from internal and external information sources, the better they will be at recognizing important performance gaps. Recognition of performance gaps enables organization members to diagnose current and potential organizational problems and is a first step in planning innovative OD strategies to address problems. The more effective organization members are at identifying and acting on performance gaps, the more proactive their organization will be.

Proactive organizations, as we have noted, do not wait to react to environmental influences. In proactive organizations, organization members direct innovative activities to meet upcoming problems before they hit. Organization members try to stay one step ahead of performance gaps. Proactive organization often involves influencing the relevant environment before the environment constrains organizational activities (Chapter 10). Rogers and Agarwala-Rogers (1976) claim that "organizations that seek to control their environment rather than merely adjust to it are more innovative" (p. 70).

To develop proactive organization, organization members must be trained to establish effective communication relationships with knowledgeable individuals both internal and external to the organization. By seeking relevant information and feedback from key sources, organization members can stay on top of changing environmental and internal organizational conditions. With this important information in hand, they can proactively plan innovative courses for organizational operations.

Case 11.2 relates a true story about an organizational problem and subsequent strategy for dealing with the problem.

1. Describe how communication was used to identify performance gaps within this organization, develop innovation strategies, and direct innovation. What performance gaps were identified? How serious were these performance gaps for the organization and for the accomplishment of organizational goals?
2. Who were the sources of relevant information and feedback? How was the information gathered by organization members? Did the feedback increase organizational reflexivity? If not, why not; if so, in what ways?
3. How effective is the innovation strategy developed? How effective are the implementation strategies? Can you identify the seven steps in the innovation process? Will the strategy solve the immediate performance gaps? Will the innovative strategies help the organization cope with future problems and performance gaps?
4. Would you describe this situation as an organizational-development effort? Why or why not? Does it live up to the five conditions of organizational development set by Beckhard?
5. Is this organization proactive? Why?

ORGANIZATIONAL EFFECTIVENESS

The primary theme of this book is that communication is an essential ingredient in human organization. We have seen that communication is the primary tool by which leaders inform, influence, and motivate organization members. Communication is the process by which cooperative interpersonal relationships are initiated, developed, and maintained. Communication is the binding force that promotes organizational structure and stability. Communication enables interorganizational coordination. We now will see how communication is related to the development of effective organization.

The term *effectiveness* has been used throughout the book. What is effectiveness? How do we know when an organization is or is not effective? We now turn to two primary strategies for determining effectiveness: output measures of effectiveness, and process measures of effectiveness. The argument will be made that effectiveness is a combination of high-quality output and process.

Case 11.2

Effective Communication with the Public*

Members of the State Pharmacists Association were growing more and more concerned about the ability of pharmacists within the state to influence public attitudes about pharmacy and provide the public with accurate information about pharmaceutical products and services. More specifically, they were concerned about the poor public recognition of the pharmacist as a health professional and an integral member of the health-care team, the lack of public knowledge about important health-care issues, the low job satisfaction and self-image of many pharmacists, and public misuse and abuse of medications in the state. Ernie Floyd, the education director of the Pharmacists Association, decided, in consultation with the association's administrator, that it might be a good idea for the association to develop a Pharmacy Speakers Bureau. He composed a brief questionnaire to survey the reactions of association members to the idea. Results of the survey showed that the vast majority of pharmacists who were members of the association had responded positively to the idea of a speakers bureau and strongly agreed with the need for improved information exchange with the public. Paradoxically, very few pharmacists had volunteered to be members of the speakers bureau and make public presentations.

This mixed reaction of the members, who thought that the speakers bureau was a good idea but who were not willing to actively participate in it, had Ernie confused. In the past, the association members were usually more than willing to give of their time to participate in activities that they thought to be important. Ernie was not the kind of individual to give up on an idea he believed to be important, and he pursued the idea of the speakers bureau with several local pharmacists. After several discussions with pharmacists, he discovered that the primary reason that association members were reluctant to participate in the program was their lack of confidence in their ability to speak well in public.

To help pharmacists develop confidence as effective public speakers and improve their presentational skills, Ernie arranged a workshop for association members on public speaking. He drafted a promotional pamphlet about the workshop and sent it to the association

* *Adapted from G. L. Kreps and B. C. Thornton,* Health Communication: Theory and Practice. *White Plains, N.Y.: Longman, 1984, pp. 51–52.*

membership. Local and national experts on public-communication-skills training were contacted, and arrangements were made for these experts to lead the workshop. The workshop was divided into two sessions. The first session was devoted to examining the public-communication process, including preparing the speech, presenting the speech, and answering audience questions. The second session was devoted to practicing delivering public presentations, using videotape to provide feedback for pharmacists about areas for improvement in their presentational style. Additionally, Ernie put together a speaker handbook containing tips on public speaking, how to handle questions and answers, how to publicize presentations, how to find an audience, how to outline a speech, how to utilize audiovisual materials in presentations, where to find information for presentations, and how to critique one's own presentational style.

Attendance at the workshop was good, and the workshop was very successful at helping the pharmacists apply their expertise to effective presentational communication. The handbook was distributed to all workshop participants. After the workshop, several pharmacists expressed their interest to Ernie in joining the Pharmacy Speakers Bureau. The bureau has grown in the months following the workshop, and there are many requests for speakers by different public audiences, including schools, churches, senior-citizen groups, and business organizations. The Pharmacy Speakers Bureau helps to provide these groups with important health information about such varied topics as drug costs, drug abuse, pharmacists' services, pharmacy careers, correct uses of medications, vitamins and nutrition, and alcoholism. The Pharmacy Speakers Bureau is an important part of the State Pharmacy Association that works to promote better health through improved communication.

Effectiveness and Output

An output measure of organizational effectiveness is an examination of the quantity and quality of raw-material outcomes of organizational activities. Output measures of organizational effectiveness have been extremely popular in evaluating organizational performance (Steers, 1975). The most common output measures are of organizational productivity and profit, evaluating the organization's "bottom line."

Output measures are popular because they are eminently sensible and logical. They follow the ordered, scientific, pragmatic orientations of classical theorists like Weber, Taylor, and Fayol (Chapter 3). These theorists persuasively argued that organizations are designed to achieve specific tangible goals. If an organization fails to produce the outputs it is supposed to produce, how can it be effective? If a profit-making organization continually loses money, how can it be effective? Certainly, organizations that lose money and fail to accomplish goals cannot last very long in competitive interorganizational environments. They are doomed to move toward entropy because they fail to achieve the primary production-related purposes for which they were developed.

Output measures are also popular because they are relatively straightforward to assess. Organizational output is amenable to observation and quantification. Accounting techniques, performance measures, and inventory-control methods are used to evaluate organizational profitability and productivity, and quality-control measures are used to assess the competence of material organizational outputs (Maynard, 1967).

The perspective on organizing presented in this book suggests that there is a strong positive relationship between the effectiveness of human communication and the effectiveness of organizational output. A great deal of organizational research lends support to this claim that communication has an impact on productivity (Clampitt and Downs, 1983). For example, Downs and Hain (1982), in an extensive review and interpretation of organizational communication research, suggest that effective communication in organizations is a major requirement for increasing organizational productivity. O'Reilly and Roberts (1977) found that active participation in organizational networks and effective use of organizational information were related to high work-performance ratings. Tubbs and Hain (1979) compared two production plants and found that the more productive of the two organizations had higher employee ratings of communication effectiveness. Tavernier (1980) and Tubbs and Widgery (1978) report significant productivity increases in organizations in which they implemented communication-training programs. Certainly, there have also been studies that showed little or no relationship between quality of communication and organizational output. Yet there seems to be more to organizational effectiveness than quantity and quality of output.

Effectiveness and Process

The raw-output measure of organizational effectiveness, although logical and clearly measurable, is an insufficient criterion for evaluating overall organizational effectiveness (Steers, 1975). Evaluation of raw output fails to identify many qualitative issues about the effectiveness of organizational life. Organizations can demonstrate high productivity and profits while being inhumane, coercive, and oppressive to their members and their environment (Kersten and Pickett, 1981; Deetz, 1979). Ruthless management techniques sometimes can result in increased profits. Yet these insensitive organizational activities do not lead to the development of effective relationships in organizational life. (Recall our discussion in Chapters 2 and 8 of object communication and dehumanization.) Organizational effectiveness is much more than raw output.

Effective communication is clearly related to the development of effective organization (Tubbs and Hain, 1979; Clampitt and Downs, 1983). In addition to the raw-output measure of organizational effectiveness, organizational effectiveness can be assessed by the quality of organizational communication processes. This criterion of organizational effectiveness is far more illusory, subjective, and multivariate than is the material-output measure, making it more difficult to cleanly operationalize (Steers, 1975; Downs, 1977). Organizational process cannot be measured by counting tangible products. It is evaluated by assessing organization members' interpretations about the quality of organizational life (Putnam and Pacanowsky, 1983). Process outcomes such as member satisfaction, commitment, cohesiveness, loyalty, and cultural integration are useful measures of the effectiveness of organizational communication processes.

Perhaps one of the most common measures of the quality of organizational process is organizational satisfaction (Steers, 1975; Smith, Kendall, and Hulin, 1969; Hecht, 1978). Downs (1977) reports research that suggests that the quality of communication climate, personal feedback, and relationship with supervisor is related to organization members' interpretations of job satisfaction. Albrecht's (1979) research suggests that organization members who are key communicators (actively involved in communication flows and networks within the organization) are more satisfied with organizational communication climate than are organization members who are not key communicators (not active participants in communication networks within the organization). These findings imply that high-quality communication and active participation in the communication activities of organizing is likely to lead to increased satisfaction and effectiveness of organization.

Organizations with strong supportive cultures that nurture their members and integrate them into the communication activities of organizational life demonstrate the process aspects of organizational effectiveness. These organizations help their members make sense out of the complexities of organizational life and provide them with meaningful social-support networks. These organizational cultures promote supportive communication climates and high levels of organization member cooperation and participation in organizational activities and events. Many of the characteristics of organizational life that Deal and Kennedy (1982) and Peters and Waterman (1982) suggest lead to strong organizational cultures, lead to process excellence (Chapter 7). For example, Peters and Waterman (1982) identify shared values, recognized heroes, participation in rites and rituals, and integration in communication networks as the key elements of strong cultures. These elements of communication culture also lead to process effectiveness.

Integrating High-Quality Process and Output

Organizational effectiveness is a product of both the quantity and quality of organizational outputs and the quality of organizational communication processes. Recall the discussion in Chapter 7 of convergence in organizational theory. Two approaches to understanding organization—the "rational perspective" and the "human-intuitive perspective"—were described. It was argued that there is significant merit to both of these perspectives on organization, but neither approach alone is sufficient to capture the complex multifaceted nature of organizational life. The trend suggested for organizational theory was toward convergence of these two perspectives by combining the logic of the rational approach with the experience of the human-intuitive perspective. Assessment of the quality of organization should follow the convergence model of combining the rational and the human-intuitive perspectives.

Organizational effectiveness should be conceived as the convergence of rational raw-output criteria and experiential communication-process criteria. Organizational effectiveness is the integration of high-quality organizational process and output. Pace (1983) describes effectiveness as the attainment of desirable goals. Both productivity and effective communication relationships are desired goals in enlightened organizations. The combination of output and process criteria for effectiveness allows us to combine both task and maintenance functions of organization (Chapter 8).

Besides accomplishing both task and maintenance goals, effective organizations maintain a productive balance between innovation and stability. This productive balance is achieved by effectively utilizing internal and external channels of communication. Innovation enables organizations to resolve internally and externally generated performance gaps. Stability enables organization members to establish predictable roles and relationships. Additionally, effective organizations present their members with strong, supportive, and nurturing cultures.

In summary, organizations in which members can continually accomplish ever-changing organizing tasks and goals through effective coordination and innovation, as well as establish and maintain meaningful and satisfying internal and external organizational relationships, truly demonstrate organizational effectiveness.

References

Acker, J., and D. Van Houten. "Differential Recruitment and Control: The Sex Structuring of Organizations." *Administrative Science Quarterly* 19 (1974):152–163.

Adler, R. *Communicating at Work: Principles and Practices for Business and the Professions.* New York: Random House, 1983.

Ajiferuke, M., and J. Boddewyn. "Culture and Other Explanatory Variables in Comparative Management Studies." *Academy of Management Journal* 13 (1970):153–163.

Albrecht, T. L. "The Role of Communication in Perceptions of Organizational Climate." In *Communication Yearbook 3*, edited by D. Nimmo, 343–357. New Brunswick, N.J.: Transaction Books, 1979.

———. "Coping with Occupational Stress: Relational and Individual Strategies of Nurses in Acute Health Care Settings." In *Communication Yearbook 6*, edited by M. Burgoon, 832–849. Beverly Hills, Calif.: Sage, 1982.

———. "An Over-Time Analysis of Communication Patterns and Work Perceptions among Managers." Paper presented at the meeting of the International Communication Association, San Francisco, May 1984.

Albrecht, T. L., and M. B. Adelman. "Social Support and Life Stress: New Directions for Communication Research." *Human Communication Research* 11 (1984):1–32.

Aldag, F. J., and A. P. Brief. *Task Design and Employee Motivation.* Glenview, Ill.: Scott, Foresman, 1975.

Alexander, A., and C. Camden. "Praise and Organizational Behavior: The Productivity Crisis." Paper presented at the meeting of the International Communication Association, Acapulco, Mexico, May 1980.

Allen, R. *Organizational Management Through Communication.* New York: Harper & Row, 1977.

Andrews, K., ed. *The Case Method of Teaching Human Relations and Administration.* Cambridge, Mass.: Harvard University Press, 1953.

Argyris, C. *Personality and Organization.* New York: Harper & Row, 1957.

———. *Integrating the Individual and the Organization.* New York: Wiley, 1964.

Athanassiades, J. C. "The Distortion of Upward Communication in Hierarchical Organizations." *Academy of Management Journal* 16 (1973):207–226.

Axley, S. R. "Communication's Role in Organizational Change: A Review of the Literature." Paper presented at the meeting of the International Communication Association, Acapulco, Mexico, May 1980.

Bach, B. W. "Rumor and Gossip in Organizations: A Review and Analysis." Paper presented at the meeting of the Speech Communication Association, Washington, D.C., November 1983.

Bach, G. R., and H. Goldberg. *Creative Aggression: The Art of Assertive Living.* New York: Avon Books, 1974.

Bantz, C. R., and D. H. Smith. A Critique and experimental test of Weick's model of organizing. *Communication Monographs* 44 (1974):171–184.

Barnard, C. I. *The Functions of the Executive,* anniversary edition. Cambridge, Mass.: Harvard University Press, 1968 (originally published in 1938).

Barnlund, D. C. "Therapeutic Communication." In *Interpersonal Communication: Survey and Studies,* edited by D. C. Barnlund, 613–645. Boston: Houghton Mifflin, 1968.

Bass, B., and S. Deep, eds. *Studies in Organizational Psychology.* Boston: Allyn & Bacon, 1972.

Batchelder, R. C. "Applied Management Ethics Training at Lockheed-California Company." In *Doing Ethics in Business: New Ventures in Management Development,* edited by D. G. Jones, 45–57. Cambridge, Mass.: Oelgeschlager, Gunn & Hain, 1982.

Beckhard, R. *Organization Development: Strategies and Models.* Reading, Mass.: Addison-Wesley, 1969.

———. "The Confrontation Meeting." *Harvard Business Review* 45 (1967):149–155.

Bell, M. A. "The Effects of Substantive and Affective Conflict on Problem-Solving Groups." *Speech Monographs* 41 (1974):19–23.

Benne, K., and P. Sheats. "Functional Roles of Group Members." *Journal of Social Issues* 4 (1948):41–49.

Bennis, W. "Leadership—A Beleaguered Species." *Organizational Dynamics* 5 (1976a):3–16.

———. *The Unconscious Conspiracy: Why Leaders Can't Lead.* New York: American Management Association, 1976b.

Berger, P. L., and T. Luckmann. *The Social Construction of Reality.* Garden City, N.Y.: Doubleday (Anchor Books), 1967.

Berlo, D. K. *The Process of Communication.* New York: Holt, Rinehart and Winston, 1960.

Bernthal, W. "Case Analysis in Organizational Behavior and the Practice of Management." University of Colorado, 1975. Mimeo.

Berrien, F. K. *General and Social Systems.* New Brunswick, N.J.: Rutgers University Press, 1968.

———. "A General Systems Approach to Organizations." In *Handbook of Industrial and Organizational Psychology,* edited by M. Dunnette, 41–62. Chicago: Rand McNally, 1976.

Bertalanffy, L. "General System Theory: A New Approach to the Unity of Science." *Human Biology* (December 1951): 303–361.

———. *Problems of Life: An Evaluation of Modern Biological Thought.* New York: Wiley, 1952.

———. *General System Theory.* New York: Braziller, 1968.

Bhagat, R. S., and S. J. McQuaid. "Role of Subjective Culture in Organizations: A Review and Directions for Future Research." *Journal of Applied Psychology Monographs* 67 (1982):653–685.

Blackman, J. R., and G. R. Oldham. "Motivation Through the Design of Work: Test of a Theory." *Organizational Behavior and Human Performance* 16 (1976):250–279.

Blake, R. R., and J. S. Mouton. *The Managerial Grid.* Houston: Gulf, 1964.

———. *Making Experience Work: The Grid Approach to Critique.* New York: McGraw-Hill, 1978.

Blake, R. R., J. S. Mouton, L. B. Barnes, and L. E. Greiner. "Breakthrough in Organization Development." *Harvard Business Review* 42 (1964):133–155.

Blaxall, M., and B. Reagan, eds. *Woman and the Workplace: The Implications of Occupational Segregation.* Chicago: University of Chicago Press, 1976.

Blumer, H. *Symbolic Interaction: Perspective and Method.* Englewood Cliffs, N.J.: Prentice-Hall, 1969.

Boje, D. M., D. B. Fedor, and K. M. Rowland. "Myth-Making: A Qualitative Step in OD Interventions." *Journal of Applied Behavioral Science* 18 (1982):17–28.

Bok, S. *Lying: Moral Choice in Public and Private Life.* New York: Random House, 1978.

Bormann, E. "Symbolic Convergence: Organizational Communication and Culture." In *Communication and Organizations: An Interpretive Approach*, edited by L. Putnam and M. Pacanowsky, 99–122. Beverly Hills, Calif.: Sage, 1983.

Bormann, E., W. Howell, R. Nichols, and G. Shapiro. *Interpersonal Communication in the Modern Organization*. 2d ed. Englewood Cliffs, N.J.: Prentice-Hall, 1982.

Bostrom, R. "Patterns of Communication Interaction in Small Groups." *Communication Monographs* 37 (1970):257–263.

Boulding, K. *A Reconstruction of Economics*. New York: Harper & Row, 1952.

———. "General Systems Theory: Skeleton of Science." *Management Science* 2 (1956):197–208.

Bradley, P., and J. Baird, *Communication for Business and the Professions*. Dubuque, Iowa: Brown, 1980.

Broadhurst, A., and D. K. Darnell. "Introduction to Cybernetics and Information Theory." *Quarterly Journal of Speech* 51 (1965):442–453.

Brod, C. *Technostress: The Human Cost of the Computer Revolution*. Reading, Mass.: Addison-Wesley, 1984.

Brooks, K., J. Callicoat, and G. Siegerdt. "The ICA Communication Audit and Perceived Communication Effectiveness Changes in 16 Audited Organizations." *Human Communication Research* 5 (1979):130–137.

Brown, I. C. *Understanding Other Cultures*. Englewood Cliffs, N.J.: Prentice-Hall, 1963.

Browning, L. D., and J. A. Gilchrest. "Negotiating for Organizational Direction: The Effect of Politics on Men and Women in Leadership Positions." Paper presented at the meeting of the International Communication Association, Acapulco, Mexico, May 1980.

Brownmiller, S. *Against Our Will*. New York: Simon and Schuster, 1975.

Buchanan, B. "Building Organizational Commitment: The Socialization of Managers in Work Organizations." *Administrative Science Quarterly* 18 (1974):533–546.

Burack, E. *Organization Analysis: Theory and Applications*. Hinsdale, Ill.: Dryden Press, 1975.

Burke, W., ed. *Contemporary Organization Development: Conceptual Orientations and Interventions*. Washington, D.C.: National Training Labs, 1972.

Burrell, G., and G. Morgan. *Sociological Paradigms and Organizational Analysis*. London: Heinemann, 1979.

Calise, P. F., and M. Locke. "Office Automation: Who's in Control." *Management World* 13 (1984):17–19.

Campbell, D. T. "Variations and Selective Retention in Socio-Cultural Evolution." In *Social Change in Developing Areas: A Reinterpretation of Evolu-*

tionary Theory, edited by H. R. Barringer, G. I. Blanksten, and R. W. Mack. Cambridge, Mass.: Schenkman, 1965.

Cantor, B., ed. *Experts in Action: Inside Public Relations*. New York: Longman, 1984.

Caplow, T. *Principles of Organization*. New York: Harcourt Brace Jovanovich, 1964.

Carney, T. F. "Currents in Organizational Communication." *Journal of Communication* 29 (1979):200–211.

Castaneda, C. *A Separate Reality*. New York: Simon & Schuster, 1971.

"Changing a Corporate Culture: Can Johnson & Johnson Go from Band-Aids to High Tech?" *Business Week*, 14 May 1984, 130–138.

Chase, A. B. "How to Make Downward Communication Work." *Personnel Journal* 49 (1970):478–483.

Chatlos, W. E. "Investor Relations." In *Experts in Action: Inside Public Relations*, edited by B. Cantor, 84–101. New York: Longman, 1984.

Churchman, C. W. *The Systems Approach*. New York: Dell, 1968.

Cicourel, A. V. *The Social Organization of Juvenile Justice*. New York: Wiley, 1968.

Clampitt, P. G., and C. W. Downs. "Communication and Productivity." Paper presented at the meeting of the Speech Communication Association, Washington, D.C., November 1983.

Cobb, S. "Social Support as a Moderator of Life Stress." *Psychosomatic Medicine* 38 (1976):300–314.

Cohen, M. D., J. G. March, and J. P. Olson. "A Garbage Can Model of Organizational Choice." *Administrative Science Quarterly* 17 (1972):1–25.

Conner, D. R., and R. W. Patterson. "Building Commitment to Organizational Change." *Training and Development Journal* 36 (1982):18–30.

"Corporate Culture: The Hard to Change Value that Spells Success." *Business Week*, 17 October 1980, 148–160.

Cousins, N. *Anatomy of an Illness as Perceived by the Patient*. New York: Norton, 1979.

Cox, W. R. "Government Relations." In *Experts in Action: Inside Public Relations*, edited by B. Cantor, 7–30. New York: Longman, 1984.

Crum, N. "Head Librarian and Manager: Dynamics of a Creative Relationship." *Special Libraries* 61 (1970):486–491.

Cummings, H. W., L. Long, and M. Lewis. *Managing Communication in Organizations*. Dubuque, Ia.: Gorsuch Scarisbrick, 1983.

Cussella, L. P. "The Effects of Feedback on Intrinsic Motivation: A Propositional Extension of Cognitive Evaluation Theory from an Organizational Communication Perspective." In *Communication Yearbook* 4, edited by D.

Nimmo, 367–387. New Brunswick, N.J.: Transaction Books/International Communication Association, 1980.

Dale, E. *Management: Theory and Practice.* 2d ed. New York: McGraw-Hill, 1969.

Dalton, G. W., and P. R. Lawrence. *Motivation and Control in Organizations.* Homewood, Ill.: Irwin, 1971.

Dandridge, T. C., I. I. Mitroff, and W. Joyce. "Organizational Symbolism: A Topic to Expand Organizational Analysis." *Academy of Management Review* 5 (1980): 248–256.

Darnell, D. K. "Information Theory: An Approach to Human Communication." In *Approaches to Human Communication,* edited by R. W. Budd and B. D. Ruben, 156–169. Rochelle Park, N.J.: Hayden, 1972.

Darwin, C. *The Origin of Species.* 1859. Reprint. New York: Random House (Modern Library), 1948.

Davis, K. "Management Communication and the Grapevine." *Harvard Business Review* 31 (1953):43–49.

———. "The Organization that's Not on the Chart." In *Readings in Interpersonal and Organizational Communication,* edited by R. C. Huseman, C. M. Logue, and D. L. Freshley, 2d ed., 149–154. Boston: Holbrook Press, 1973.

Davis, K., and J. Newstrom, eds. *Organizational Behavior.* 6th ed. New York: McGraw-Hill, 1981.

Davis, S., and P. Lawrence. *Matrix.* Reading, Mass.: Addison-Wesley, 1977.

Davis, W., and J. R. O'Connor. "Serial Transmission of Information: A Study of the Grapevine." *Journal of Applied Communication Research* 5 (1977):61–72.

Deal, T. E., and A. A. Kennedy. *Corporate Cultures: The Rites and Rituals of Corporate Life.* Reading, Mass.: Addison-Wesley, 1982.

Deci, E. L. *Intrinsic Motivation.* New York: Plenum, 1975.

Deetz, S. "Social Well-Being and the Development of an Appropriate Organizational Response to De-Institutionalization and Legitimation Crises." *Journal of Applied Communication Research* 7 (1979):45–54.

———. "Critical Interpretive Research in Organizational Communication." *Western Journal of Speech Communication* 46 (1982):131–149.

Dervin, B., and M. Voight, eds. *Progress in Communication Sciences.* Volume 2. Norwood, N.J.: Ablex, 1980.

Deutsch, A. *The Human Resources Revolution: Communicate or Litigate.* New York: McGraw-Hill, 1979.

Deutsch, M. *Nationalism and Social Communication—An Inquiry into the Foundation of Nationalism.* Cambridge, Mass.: M.I.T. Press, 1966.

———. "Conflicts: Productive and Destructive." *Journal of Social Issues* 25 (1969):7–41.

DeWine, S., and F. Barone. "Employee Communication and Role Stress: Enhancement or Sabotage of the Organizational Climate." Paper presented at the meeting of the International Communication Association, San Francisco, May 1984.

DiSalvo, V. S. "A Summary of Current Research Identifying Communication Skills in Various Organizational Contexts." *Communication Education* 29 (1980):283–290.

Dooher, J., and V. Marquis, eds. *Effective Communication on the Job*. New York: American Management Association, 1956.

Dooley, A. R., and W. Skinner. "Casing Case-Method Methods." *Academy of Management Review* 2 (1977):277–289.

Downs, A. *Inside Bureaucracy*. Boston: Little, Brown, 1967.

Downs, C. W. "The Relationship Between Communication and Job Satisfaction." In *Readings in Interpersonal and Organizational Communication*, edited by R. C. Huseman, C. M. Logue, and D. L. Freshley, 3d ed., 363–376. Boston: Holbrook Press, 1977.

Downs, C. W., D. Berg, and W. Linkugel. *The Organizational Communicator*. New York: Harper & Row, 1977.

Downs, C. W., and T. Hain. "Productivity and Communication." In *Communication Yearbook* 5, edited by M. Burgoon, 435–453. New Brunswick, N.J.: Transaction Books, 1982.

Drake, M. A. "Information and Corporate Cultures." *Special Libraries* 75 (1984):263–269.

Drucker, P. *The Practice of Management*. New York: Harper & Row, 1954.

Duncan, H. D. *Symbols in Society*. Oxford: Oxford University Press, 1968.

Dunn, D. M. "Interpersonal Communication Training in Professional Organizations." Paper presented at the meeting of the Indiana Speech Association, Indianapolis, October 1981.

Eddy, W., W. Burke, V. Dupre, and O. South, eds. *Behavioral Science and the Manager's Role*. Washington, D.C.: National Training Labs, 1969.

Eisenberg, E. M. "Ambiguity as Strategy in Organizational Communication." *Communication Monographs* 51 (1984):227–242.

Elliston, F. A. "Anonymity and Whistle Blowing." *Journal of Business Ethics* 1 (1982):167–177.

Elmore, G. C. "Integrating Video Technology and Organizational Communication." Paper presented at the meeting of the Indiana Speech Association, Indianapolis, October 1981.

Emery, E., P. H. Ault, and W. K. Agee. *Introduction to Mass Communications*. 2d ed. New York: Dodd, Mead, 1968.

Etzioni, A. *Modern Organizations*. Englewood Cliffs, N.J.: Prentice-Hall, 1964.

———. *A Comparative Analysis of Complex Organizations*. 2d ed. New York: Free Press, 1971.

———, ed. *Readings on Modern Organizations*. Englewood Cliffs, N.J.: Prentice-Hall, 1969.

Evered, R., and M. Louis. "Alternative Perspectives in the Organizational Sciences: Inquiry from the Inside and Inquiry from the Outside." *Academy of Management Review* 6 (1981):385–396.

Everett, J. E., B. W. Stening, and P. A. Longton. "Some Evidence for an International Managerial Culture." *Journal of Management Studies* 19 (1982):153–162.

Ewbank, H. *Meeting Management*. Dubuque, Ia.: Brown, 1968.

Fairhurst, G. T., and B. K. Snavely. "A Test of the Social Isolation of Male Tokens." *Academy of Management Journal* 26 (1983):353–361.

Farace, R., P. Monge, and H. Russell. *Communicating and Organizing*. Reading, Mass.: Addison-Wesley, 1977.

Fay, T. J. "Corporate Advertising." In *Experts in Action: Inside Public Relations*, edited by B. Cantor, 159–174. New York: Longman, 1984.

Fayol, H. *General and Industrial Management*. 1916. Reprint. London: Pitman, 1949.

Ferguson, S., and S. D. Ferguson, eds. *Intercom: Readings in Organizational Communication*. Rochelle Park, N.J.: Hayden, 1980.

Fest, T. "Basic Guidelines for a Managerial Communication System." University of Colorado, 1975. Typescript.

Festinger, L. *A Theory of Cognitive Dissonance*. Stanford, Calif.: Stanford University Press, 1957.

Filoromo, T., and D. Ziff. *Nurse Recruitment: Strategies For Success*. Rockville, Md.: Aspen Systems, 1980.

Finn, P., and M. Harrity. "Research." In *Experts in Action: Inside Public Relations*, edited by B. Cantor, 273–288. New York: Longman, 1984.

Fisher, B. A. *Small Group Decision Making: Communication and Process*. New York: McGraw-Hill, 1974.

———. *Perspectives on Human Communication*. New York: Macmillan, 1978.

Fisher, D. *Communication in Organizations*. St. Paul, Minn.: West, 1981.

Fleming, W. *Art, Music, and Ideas*. New York: Holt, Rinehart and Winston, 1975.

Fletcher, J. *Morals and Medicine*. Boston: Beacon Press, 1954.

Folger, J. P., and M. S. Poole. *Working Through Human Conflict*. Glenview, Ill.: Scott, Foresman, 1984.

Follett, M. P. "The Giving of Orders." 1925. Reprint in *Organization Theory*, edited by D. S. Pugh. Baltimore: Penguin, 1971.

Fournies, F. *Coaching for Improved Work Experience*. New York: Van Nostrand Reinhold, 1978.

Frank, A. *Communicating on the Job*. Glenview, Ill.: Scott, Foresman, 1982.

Frankel, L., and A. Fleisher. *The Human Factor in Industry*. New York: Macmillan, 1920.

French, R. P., and B. Raven. "The Bases of Social Power." In *Group Dynamics*, edited by D. Cartwright and A. Zander, 601–623. New York: Harper & Row, 1960.

French, W. L., and C. Bell, eds. *Organization Development: Behavioral Science Interventions for Organization Improvement*. Englewood Cliffs, N.J.: Prentice-Hall, 1973.

French, W. L., C. Bell, and R. Zawacki, eds. *Organization Development: Theory, Practice, and Research*. Dallas: Business Publications, 1978.

French, W. L., and R. W. Hollmann. "Management by Objectives: The Team Approach." *California Management Review* 17 (1973):13–22.

Frost, J., and W. Wilmot. *Interpersonal Conflict*. Dubuque, Ia.: Brown, 1978.

Frost, P. "Toward a Radical Framework for Practicing Organizational Science." *Academy of Management Review* 5 (1980):501–508.

Garfinkel, H. "Suicide for All Practical Purposes." In *Studies in Ethnomethodology*, edited by H. Garfinkel, 11–18. Englewood Cliffs, N.J.: Prentice-Hall, 1967.

Geertz, C. *The Interpretation of Cultures*. New York: Basic Books, 1973.

Georgopoulos, B. S., G. M. Mahoney, and N. W. Jones. "A Path-Goal Approach to Productivity." *Journal of Applied Psychology* 41 (1957):345–353.

Gerth, H. H., and C. W. Mills, eds. *From Max Weber: Essays in Sociology*. New York: Oxford University Press, 1946.

Gibb, J. R. "Defensive Communication." *Journal of Communication* 11 (1961):141–148.

Giddens, A. *New Rules of Sociological Method*. New York: Basic Books, 1976.

Gieselman, R. D. "Applying Survey Methods to Employee Communication." *Journal of Business Communication* 6 (1968):13–23.

Gilbreth, L. *The Quest for the One Best Way*. New York: Clark, 1915.

Gilchrest, J. A., and L. D. Browning. "The Impact of Loose Coupling Theory on Organizational Communication." Paper presented at the meeting of the Speech Communication Association, Chicago, November 1984.

Gildea, J., and P. Haas, eds. *Case Studies in Organizational Communication*. New York: Industrial Communication Council/Towers, Perrin, Forster, & Crosby, 1975.

Glover, J. D., and R. M. Hower. "Some Comments on Teaching by the Case Method." In *The Case Method of Teaching Human Relations and Adminis-*

tration, edited by K. Andrews, 13–24. Cambridge, Mass.: Harvard University Press, 1953.

Glover, J. D., R. M. Hower, and R. Tagiuri. *The Administrator: Cases on Human Aspects of Management*. 5th ed. Homewood, Ill.: Irwin, 1973.

Glueck, W. *Personnel: A Diagnostic Approach*. 2d ed. Dallas: Business Publications, 1978.

Goffman, E. *Asylums*. Garden City, N.Y.: Doubleday (Anchor Books), 1961.

Goldhaber, G. M. "The ICA Communication Audit: Rationale and Development." Paper presented at the meeting of the Academy of Management, Kansas City, Missouri, August 1976.

———. *Organizational Communication*. 3rd ed. Dubuque, Ia.: Brown, 1983.

Goldhaber, G. M., H. Dennis, G. Richetto, and O. Wiio. *Information Strategies: New Pathways to Corporate Power*. rev. ed. Norwood, N.J.: Ablex, 1984.

Goldhaber, G. M., M. P. Yates, D. T. Porter, and R. Lesniak. "Organizational Communication: 1978." *Human Communication Research* 5 (1978):76–96.

Gordon, M. E., and S. J. Miller. "Grievances: A Review of the Literature." *Personnel Psychology* 37 (1984):117–146.

Granovetter, M. "The Strength of Weak Ties." *American Journal of Sociology* 78 (1973):1360–1380.

Grant, J. H., and W. R. King. *The Logic of Strategic Planning*. Boston: Little, Brown, 1982.

Gray, R. K. "Lobbying." In *Experts in Action: Inside Public Relations*, edited by B. Cantor, 192–195. New York: Longman, 1984.

Greenbaum, H. H. "The Audit of Organizational Communication." *Academy of Management Journal* 17 (1974):750–752.

Grunig, J. E., and T. Hunt. *Managing Public Relations*. New York: Holt, Rinehart and Winston, 1984.

Hage, J., and M. Aiken. *Social Change in Complex Organizations*. New York: Random House, 1970.

Hagen, R., and A. Kahn. "Discrimination Against Competent Women." *Journal of Applied Social Psychology* 5 (1975):362–376.

Hall, D. E. "Winning at Office Politics." *Credit and Financial Management* 86 (1984):20–23.

Hall, E. T. *The Silent Language*. Garden City, N.Y.: Doubleday, 1959.

Hall, H. J. "Services for the Analysis and Evaluation of Information." Final report for the National Science Foundation Division of Information Science and Technology, Rutgers University, School of Communication, Information, and Library Studies, 1982.

Haney, W. *Communication and Organizational Behavior: Text and Cases*. 3d ed. Homewood, Ill.: Irwin, 1972.

Harragan, B. L. *Games Mother Never Taught You: Corporate Gamesmanship for Women*. New York: Warner, 1977.

Harrison, R. "Understanding Your Organization's Character." *Harvard Business Review* 5 (1972):119–128.

Harvard Business School. "Case Development at the School." *Harvard Business School Bulletin* (January–February 1965):9.

———, ed. *On Human Relations*. New York: Harper & Row, 1979.

Hawes, L. C. "Information Overload and the Organization of 1984." *Western Speech* 35 (1971):191–198.

———. "Social Collectives as Communication: Perspectives on Organizational Behavior." *Quarterly Journal of Speech* 60 (1974):497–502.

———. "Toward a Hermeneutic Phenomenology of Communication." *Communication Quarterly* 25 (1977):38–41.

Hawes, L. C., and D. H. Smith. "A Critique of the Assumptions Underlying the Study of Communication in Conflict." *Quarterly Journal of Speech* 59 (1973):423–435.

Hayakawa, S. I. *Language in Thought and Action*. 3d ed. New York: Harcourt Brace Jovanovich, 1972.

Hecht, M. L. "Measure of Communication Satisfaction." *Human Communication Research* 4 (1978):350–368.

Heilman, M. E. "Information as a Deterrent Against Sex Discrimination: The Effects of Applicant Sex and Information Type on Preliminary Employment Decisions." *Organizational Behavior and Human Performance* 33 (1984):174–186.

Heilman, M. E., and H. Hornstein. *Managing Human Forces in Organizations*. Homewood, Ill.: Irwin, 1982.

Hellriegal, D., and J. Slocum. "Organizational Climate: Measures, Research, and Contingencies." *Academy of Management Journal* 17 (1974):255–280.

Hennig, M., and A. Jardin. *The Managerial Woman*. Garden City, N.Y.: Doubleday (Anchor Books), 1977a.

———. "Women Executives in the Old-Boy Network." *Psychology Today* 10 (1977b):76–81.

Hertzberg, F. *Work and the Nature of Man*. New York: Collins, 1966.

———. "One More Time: How Do You Motivate Employees?" *Harvard Business Review* 46 (1968):53–62.

Hicks, H., and C. R. Gullett. *Organizations: Theory and Behavior*. New York: McGraw-Hill, 1975.

House, R. J. "A Path-Goal Theory of Leader Effectiveness." *Administrative Science Quarterly* 16 (1971):321–338.

House, R. J., and G. Dessler. "The Path-Goal Theory of Leadership: Some Post Hoc and A Priori Tests." In *Contingency Approaches to Leadership*, edited by J. G. Hunt and L. L. Larson, 29–55. Carbondale: Southern Illinois University Press, 1974.

Hrebiniak, L. G., and W. F. Joyce. *Implementing Strategy*. New York: Macmillan, 1984.

Hunt, G. T. *Communication Skills in the Organization*. Englewood Cliffs, N.J.: Prentice-Hall, 1980.

Hunt, G. T., and C. Lee. "Organizational Climate." Paper presented at the meeting of the International Communication Association, Portland, May 1976.

Hunt, J. G., and J. W. Hill. "A New Look in Motivation Theory for Organizational Research." *Human Organization* 28 (1969):100–109.

Huseman, R. C., C. M. Logue, and D. L. Freshley, eds. *Readings in Interpersonal and Organizational Communication*. 2d ed. Boston: Holbrook Press, 1973.

Hussey, D. *Corporate Planning: Theory and Practice*. 2d ed. New York: Pergamon Press, 1982.

Ivantcho, B., ed. *Position Descriptions in Special Libraries: A Collection of Examples*. New York: Special Libraries Association, 1983.

Jacobson, W. D. *Power and Interpersonal Relations*. Belmont, Calif.: Wadsworth, 1972.

Janis, I. *Victims of Groupthink: A Psychological Study of Foreign Decisions and Fiascos*. Boston: Houghton Mifflin, 1967.

———. "Groupthink." *Psychology Today* 4 (1971):43–46, 74–76.

Jaques, E. *The Changing Culture of a Factory*. New York: Dryden Press, 1952.

Johanesson, R. E. "Job Satisfaction and Perceptually Measured Organizational Climate: Redundancy and Confusion." In *New Developments in Management and Organizational Theory: Proceedings of the Eighth Annual Conference*, edited by P. Frey, 27–37. New York: Eastern Academy of Management, 1971.

Johnson, B. M. *Communication: The Process of Organizing*. Boston: Allyn & Bacon, 1977.

———. *Getting the Job Done*. Glenview, Ill.: Scott, Foresman, 1984.

Johnson, B. M., and L. D. Browning. "Extended Relationships: It's Who You Know that Counts." Paper presented at the meeting of the Speech Communication Association, Philadelphia, November 1979.

Jones, D. G., ed. *Doing Ethics in Business: New Ventures in Management Development*. Cambridge, Mass.: Oelgeschlager, Gunn & Hain, 1982.

Jourard, S. "An Exploratory Study of Body Accessibility." *British Journal of Social and Clinical Psychology* 5 (1966):221–231.

Kanter, R. M. *Men and Women of the Corporation*. New York: Basic Books, 1977.

Kassarjian, H., and T. Robertson, eds. *Perspectives in Consumer Behavior*. 2d ed. Glenview, Ill.: Scott, Foresman, 1973.

Kast, F., and J. Rosenweig, eds. *Contingency Views of Organization and Management*. Chicago: Science Research Associates, 1973.

Katz, D., and R. Kahn. *The Social Psychology of Organizations*. 2d ed. New York: Wiley, 1978.

Keichel, W. "Corporate Strategies Under Fire." *Fortune*, 27 December 1982, 35–39.

Kelly, J. W. "The Culture of High Technology: Is It Female Friendly?" Paper presented at the meeting of the International Communication Association, San Francisco, May 1984.

Kennedy, J. F. "To Keep the Lobbyist Within Bounds." *New York Times Magazine*, 19 February 1956, 11, 40, 42, 44, 47.

Kersten, A., and T. Pickett. "A Critical Interpretive Theory of Organizational Communication." Paper presented at the meeting of the International Communication Association/Speech Communication Association, Alta, Utah, August 1981.

Kilmann, R., and K. Thomas. "Interpersonal Conflict-Handling Behavior as a Reflection of Jungian Personality Dimensions." *Psychological Reports* 37 (1975):971–980.

Klos, L. A. "Measure Your Leadership with the Managerial Grid." *Supervisory Management* 19 (1974):10–47.

Knapp, M. *Nonverbal Communication in Human Interaction*. 2d ed. New York: Holt, Rinehart and Winston, 1978.

Knight, K., and R. McDaniel. *Organizations: An Information Systems Perspective*. Belmont, Calif.: Wadsworth, 1979.

Koch, S., and S. Deetz. "Metaphor Analysis of Social Reality in Organizations." *Journal of Applied Communication Research* 9 (1981):1–15.

Koehler, J., K. Anatol, and R. Applbaum. *Organizational Communication: Behavioral Perspectives*. 2d ed. New York: Holt, Rinehart and Winston, 1981.

Koenig, M. E. D., and S. T. Kochoff. "The Emerging Role for the Librarian in Data Administration." *Special Libraries* 75 (1984):238–246.

Kolb, D., I. Rubin, and J. McIntyre. *Organizational Psychology: An Experiential Approach*. 2d ed. Englewood Cliffs, N.J.: Prentice-Hall, 1974.

Korzybski, A. *Science and Sanity: An Introduction to Non-Aristotelian Systems and General Semantics*. 3d ed. Lakeville, Conn.: International Non-Aristotelian Library, 1948.

Kotler, P., and G. McDougal. *Principles of Marketing*. Englewood Cliffs, N.J.: Prentice-Hall, 1982.

Kreps, G. L. "Human Communication and Weick's Model of Organizing: A

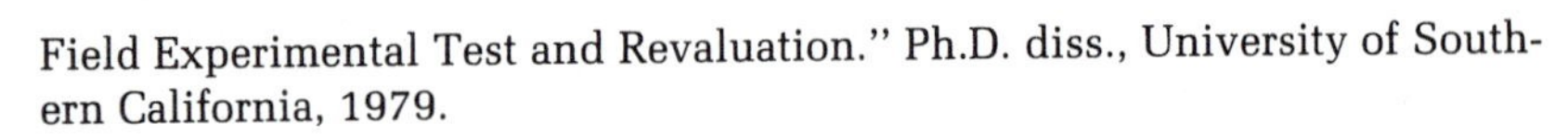
Field Experimental Test and Revaluation." Ph.D. diss., University of Southern California, 1979.

———. "A Field Experimental Test and Revaluation of Weick's Model of Organizing." In *Communication Yearbook* 4, edited by D. Nimmo, 389–398. New Brunswick, N.J.: Transaction Books/International Communication Association, 1980.

———. "Communication and Gerontology: Health Communication Training for Providers of Health Services to the Elderly." Paper presented at the Speech Communication Association Summer Conference on Communication and Gerontology, Edwardsville, Illinois, July 1981a.

———. "Therapeutic Communication and the Interview Process." Paper presented at the meeting of the Indiana Speech Association, Indianapolis, October 1981b.

———. "Organizational Culture as an Equivocality Reducing Mechanism." Paper presented at the meeting of the Speech Communication Association, Louisville, November 1982a.

———. "Humanizing Organizational Communication for Elderly Health Care Recipients." Paper presented at the meeting of the Speech Communication Association, Louisville, November 1982b.

———. "The Use of Interpretive Research to Develop a Socialization Program at RCA." In *Communication and Organizations: An Interpretive Approach*, edited by L. Putnam and M. Pacanowsky, 243–256. Beverly Hills, Calif.: Sage, 1983a.

———. "Organizational Communication and Organizational Culture: A Weickian Perspective." Paper presented at the meeting of the Academy of Management, Dallas, August 1983b.

———. "Health Communication and Aging: An Overview." Paper presented at the meeting of the International Communication Association, Dallas, May 1983c.

———. "Communication Training for Health Care Employees: Implications for Higher Education and the Health Care Industry." In *Proceedings of Partnerships for Employee Training: Implications for Education and Business and Industry*. Volume 2, 175–192. Manhattan, Kans.: National Issues in Higher Education, 1984a.

———. "Using the Case Study Method in Organizational Communication Classes: Developing Students' Insight, Knowledge, and Creativity." Paper presented at the meeting of the International Communication Association, San Francisco, May 1984b.

———. "Organizational Sexism in Health Care." In *Communication, Gender and Sex Roles in Diverse Interaction Contexts*, edited by L. P. Stewart and S. Ting-Toomey. Norwood, N.J.: Ablex, 1985a.

———. "A Field Research and Development Study of Nurse Turnover and Retention in a Large Urban Health Care Organization." Paper presented at the meeting of the International Communication Association, Honolulu, May 1985b.

Kreps, G. L., and B. C. Thornton. *Health Communication: Theory and Practice.* New York: Longman, 1984.

Krivonos, P. D. "Distortion of Subordinate to Superior Communication." Paper presented at the meeting of the International Communication Association, Portland, May 1976.

———. "The Relationship of Intrinsic–Extrinsic Motivation and Communication Climate in Organizations." *Journal of Business Communication* 15 (1978):53–65.

Kuhn, T. S. *The Structure of Scientific Revolutions.* 2d ed. Chicago: University of Chicago Press, 1970.

Ladendorf, J. "Information Service Evaluation: The Gap Between the Ideal and the Possible." *Special Libraries* 64 (1973):273–279.

Larkin, T. J. "Network Analysis as an Investigative Tool for Organizational Communication." Paper presented at the meeting of the International Communication Association, Acapulco, Mexico, May 1980.

Lawrence, P. "The Preparation of Case Material." In *The Case Method of Teaching Human Relations and Administration,* edited by K. Andrews, 215–224. Cambridge, Mass.: Harvard University Press, 1953.

Lawrence, P., and J. W. Lorsch. *Organization and Environment: Managing Differentiation and Integration.* Cambridge, Mass.: Harvard University Press, 1967.

———. *Developing Organizations: Diagnosis and Action.* Reading, Mass.: Addison-Wesley, 1969.

———. *Organization and Environment.* Homewood, Ill.: Irwin, 1969.

Leavitt, H. J. *Managerial Psychology.* 3d ed. Chicago: University of Chicago Press, 1972.

Leavitt, H. J., and R. A. H. Mueller. "Some Effects of Feedback on Communication." *Human Relations* 4 (1951):401–410.

Lederman, L. C. "Communication, Information, and Alienation: The Impact of Information Systems and High Technology on Human Interaction." Paper presented at the meeting of the Eastern Communication Association, Philadelphia, May 1984.

Lee, M. B., and W. L. Zwerman. "Developing a Facilitation System for Horizontal and Diagonal Communication in Organizations." *Personnel Journal* 54 (1975):400–401, 407.

Leon, M. "Tylenol Fights Back." *Public Relations Journal* 39 (1983):10–14.

Levinson, H. "Asinine Attitudes Toward Motivation." *Harvard Business Review* 51 (1973):70–76.

Lewis, P., and J. Williams, eds. *Readings in Organizational Communication.* Columbus, Ohio: Grid Publishing, 1980.

Lightcap, K. "Marketing Support." In *Experts in Action: Inside Public Relations,* edited by B. Cantor, 124–129. New York: Longman, 1984.

Likert, R. *New Patterns of Management.* New York: McGraw-Hill, 1961.

Lippitt, G. *Visualizing Change: Model Building and the Change Process.* Fairfax, Va.: National Training Labs/Learning Resources, 1973.

Lippitt, R., and R. White. "An Experimental Study of Leadership and Group Life." In *Readings in Social Psychology,* edited by G. E. Swanson, T. Newcomb, and E. Tartley, rev. ed., 340–355. New York: Holt, Rinehart and Winston, 1952.

Litwak, E., and L. F. Hylton. "Interorganizational Analysis: A Hypothesis on Co-ordinating Agencies." *Administrative Science Quarterly* 10 (1962):395–420.

Liu, W., and R. Duff. "The Strength of Weak Ties." *Public Opinion Quarterly* 36 (1972):361–366.

Lorey, W. "Mutual Trust Is the Key to Open Communications." *Administrative Management* 37 (1976):70–72, 74, 92.

Lorsch, J. W., and P. Lawrence. *Organization Planning: Cases and Concepts.* Homewood, Ill.: Irwin, 1972.

Louis, M. R. "Surprise and Sense Making: What Newcomers Experience when Entering Unfamiliar Organizational Settings." *Administrative Science Quarterly* 23 (1980):225–251.

Loy, P. H., and L. P. Stewart. "The Extent and Effects of Sexual Harassment of Working Women." *Sociological Focus* 17 (1984):31–43.

Lynch, D. "MIS: Conceptual Framework, Criticisms, and Major Requirements for Success." *Journal of Business Communication* 21 (1984):19–31.

McClellan, M. A., G. R. Heald, and C. W. Edney. "The Attributed Effects of Communication Feedback and Threats of Punishment on Intrinsic Motivation." Paper presented at the meeting of the International Communication Association, Acapulco, Mexico, May 1980.

Maccoby, M. *The Gamesman: The New Corporate Leaders.* New York: Simon and Schuster, 1976.

MacDonald, D. "Communication Roles and Communication Networks in a Formal Organization." *Human Communication Research* 3 (1976):365–375.

McGregor, D. *The Human Side of Enterprise.* New York: McGraw-Hill, 1960.

McLean, A. A. *Work Stress.* Reading, Mass.: Addison-Wesley, 1979.

McMurry, R. N. "Clear Communications for Chief Executives." *Harvard Business Review* 43 (1965):131–147.

McNair, M., and A. Hersum, eds. *The Case Method at the Harvard Business School.* New York: McGraw-Hill, 1954.

Makris, P. "Informatics in Health Care Delivery Systems." *Information Age* 5 (1983):205–209.

Malin, M. H. "Protecting the Whistle-Blower from Retaliatory Discharge." *University of Michigan Journal of Law Reform* 16 (1983):277–318.

March, J. G., and J. P. Olsen. "The Uncertainty of the Past: Organizational Learning Under Ambiguity." *European Journal of Political Research* 3 (1975):147–171.

———. *Ambiguity and Choice in Organizations.* Bergen, Norway: Universitetsforlaget, 1976.

March, J. G., and H. A. Simon. *Organizations.* New York: Wiley, 1958.

Maslow, A. H. "A Theory of Human Motivation." *Psychology Review* 50 (1943):370–396.

———. *Motivation and Personality.* New York: Harper & Row, 1954.

Maynard, H. B., ed. *Handbook of Business Administration.* New York: McGraw-Hill, 1967.

Mayo, E. *The Human Problems of Industrial Civilization.* New York: Macmillan, 1933.

Mead, G. H. *Mind, Self, and Society.* Chicago: University of Chicago Press, 1934.

Measell, J. S. "Public Relations and Speech Communication: Partners in the 80s?" Paper presented at the meeting of the Speech Communication Association, New York, November 1980.

Mehan, H., and H. Wood. *The Reality of Ethnomethodology.* New York: Wiley, 1975.

Melcher, A. *Structure and Process of Organizations: A Systems Approach.* Englewood Cliffs, N.J.: Prentice-Hall, 1976.

Meyer, A. "How Ideologies Supplant Formal Structures and Shape Responses to Environments." *Journal of Management Studies* 19 (1981):45–61.

Meyer, H. M., E. Kay, and J. R. P. French. "Split Roles in Performance Appraisals." *Harvard Business Review* 43 (1965):123–129.

Miceli, M. P., and J. P. Near. "The Relationships among Beliefs, Organizational Position, and Whistle Blowing Status: A Discriminant Analysis." *Academy of Management Journal* 27 (1984):687–705.

Mier, D. "From Concepts to Practices: Student Case Study Work in Organizational Communication." *Communication Education* 31 (1982):151–154.

Miller, J. G. "Living Systems: The Organization." *Behavioral Science* 17 (1972):1–182.

Millstein, I. M., and S. M. Katsh. *The Limits of Corporate Power.* New York: Macmillan, 1981.

Milmoe, S., R. Rosenthal, H. T. Blane, M. E. Chafetz, and I. Wolf. "The Doctor's

Voice: Postdictor of Successful Referral of Alcoholic Patients." *Journal of Abnormal Psychology* 72 (1967):78–84.

Mitroff, I. I., and R. H. Kilmann. "On Organization Stories: An Approach to the Design and Analysis of Organizations Through Myths and Stories." In *The Management of Organization Design: Strategies and Implementation*, edited by R. H. Kilmann, L. R. Pondy, and D. P. Slevin. New York: Elsevier, 1976.

Mixon, P. "Industrial Espionage." In *Organizational Reality: Reports from the Firing Line*, edited by P. J. Frost, V. F. Mitchell, and W. R. Nord, 2d ed., 541–545. Glenview, Ill.: Scott, Foresman, 1982.

Mobley, W. *Employee Turnover: Causes, Consequences, and Control*. Reading, Mass.: Addison-Wesley, 1982.

Mockler, R. J. "Situational Theory of Management." *Harvard Business Review* 49 (1971):146–154.

Monge, P. R., S. Bachman, J. P. Dillard, and E. M. Eisenberg. "Communication Competence in the Workplace: Model Testing and Scale Development." In *Communication Yearbook* 5, edited by M. Burgoon, 505–528. New Brunswick, N.J.: Transaction Books, 1982.

Monge, P. R., J. M. Boismier, A. L. Cook, P. D. Day, J. A. Edwards, and K. K. Kirste. "Determinants of Communication Structure in Large Organizations." Paper presented at the meeting of the International Communication Association, Portland, May 1976.

Montagu, A. *Touching: The Human Significance of the Skin*. New York: Columbia University Press, 1971.

Morgan, G., and L. Smirchich. "The Case for Qualitative Research." *Academy of Management Review* 5 (1980):491–500.

Mount, E. *Special Libraries and Information Centers: An Introductory Text*. New York: Special Libraries Association, 1983.

Murdick, R. G., and J. E. Ross. *Information Systems for Modern Management*. 2d ed. Englewood Cliffs, N.J.: Prentice-Hall, 1975.

Nader, R., P. J. Petkas, and K. Blackwell, eds. *Whistle Blowing: The Report of the Conference on Professional Responsibility*. New York: Grossman, 1972.

Nadler, D. R. *Feedback and Organization Development: Using Data-Based Methods*. Reading, Mass.: Addison-Wesley, 1977.

Nager, N., and T. H. Allen. *Public Relations: Management by Objectives*. New York: Longman, 1984.

Nason, A. *Essentials of Modern Biology*. New York: Wiley, 1968.

Near, J. P., and T. C. Jenson. "The Whistle-Blowing Process: Retaliation and Perceived Effectiveness." *Work and Occupations* 10 (1983):3–28.

O'Connell, S. *The Manager as Communicator*. New York: Harper & Row, 1979.

Offor, C. "Changing Patterns of Information Use and Supply." *ASLIB Proceedings* 30 (1978):35–45.

Opler, M. E. "Themes as Dynamic Forces in Culture." *American Journal of Sociology* 51 (1945):198–206.

O'Reilly, C. A., and K. H. Roberts. "Communication and Performance in Organizations." Paper presented at the meeting of the Academy of Management, Orlando, August 1977.

Ornstein, R. E. *The Psychology of Consciousness.* San Francisco: Freeman, 1972.

Owen, J., P. Page, and G. Zimmerman, eds. *Communication in Organizations.* St. Paul, Minn.: West, 1976.

Pacanowsky, M., and N. O'Donnell-Trujillo. "Communication and Organizational Cultures." *Western Journal of Speech Communication* 41 (1982):115–130.

———. "Organizational Communication as Cultural Performances." *Communication Monographs* 50 (1983):126–147.

Pace, R. W. *Organizational Communication: Foundations for Human Resource Development.* Englewood Cliffs, N.J.: Prentice-Hall, 1983.

Pace, R. W., and R. F. Ross. "The Basic Course in Organizational Communication." *Communication Education* 32 (1983):402–412.

Paisley, W. "Information and Work." In *Progress in Communication Sciences,* edited by B. Dervin and M. Voight, Volume 2, 113–165. Norwood, N.J.: Ablex, 1980.

Parkinson, C. N., and N. Rowe. *Communicate: Parkinson's Formula for Business Survival.* Englewood Cliffs, N.J.: Prentice-Hall, 1977.

Parsons, T. *Structure and Process in Modern Societies.* Glencoe, Ill.: Free Press, 1963.

Pascale, R. T., and A. G. Athos. *The Art of Japanese Management.* New York: Simon and Schuster, 1981.

Patterson, W. P. "Corporations in Crisis: Coming to Grips with the Information Age." *Industry Week,* 5 March 1984, 57–61.

Pavlock, E. J., ed. *Organization Development: Managing Transitions.* Washington, D.C.: American Society for Training and Development, 1982.

Pelz, D. C. "Influence: A Key to Effective Leadership in the First-Line Supervisor." *Personnel* 29 (1952):3–11.

Perrill, N. K., and S. L. Bueschel. "Selection and Appraisal in Ninety-Seven Organizations: Relationships Between Criteria Used and Relationships Between Size and Interview Structure." Paper presented at the meeting of the International Communication Association, Acapulco, Mexico, May 1980.

Perrill, N. K., and C. D. Stopek. "Organizational Selection and Appraisal Criteria: A Field Test of a New Data-Gathering Instrument in a Continuing Study." Paper presented at the meeting of the International Communication Association, Minneapolis, May 1981.

Peters, C., and T. Branch. *Blowing the Whistle: Dissent in the Public's Interest.* New York: Praeger, 1972.

Peters, T. J. "Symbols, Patterns and Settings: An Optimistic Case for Getting Things Done." *Organizational Dynamics* 7 (1978):3–23.

Peters, T. J., and R. H. Waterman. *In Search of Excellence.* New York: Harper & Row, 1982.

Pettegrew, L. S. "Organizational Communication and the S.O.B. Theory of Management." *Western Journal of Speech Communication* 46 (1982):179–191.

Pettigrew, A. M. "On Studying Organizational Cultures." *Administrative Science Quarterly* 24 (1979):570–581.

Pfeffer, J. "Management as Symbolic Action: The Creation and Maintenance of Organizational Paradigms." In *Research in Organizational Behavior,* edited by B. M. Staw, Volume 1, 3–39. Greenwich, Conn.: JAI Press, 1979.

Phillips, G. *Communicating in Organizations.* New York: Macmillan, 1982.

Pilotta, J., ed. *Women in Organizations.* Prospect Heights, Ill.: Waveland Press, 1983.

Pondy, L. R., P. J. Frost, G. Morgan, and T. C. Dandridge, eds. *Organizational Symbolism.* Greenwich, Conn.: JAI Press, 1983.

Pondy, L. R., and I. I. Mitroff. "Beyond Open System Models of Organization." In *Research in Organizational Behavior,* edited by B. M. Staw, Volume 1. Greenwich, Conn.: JAI Press, 1979.

Preston, P. *Communication for Managers.* Englewood Cliffs, N.J.: Prentice-Hall, 1979.

Pritchard, R. E., and R. W. Karasick, "The Effects of Organizational Climate on Managerial Job Performance and Job Satisfaction." *Organizational Behavior and Human Performance* 9 (1973):126–146.

Putman, L. "The Interpretive Perspective: An Alternative to Functionalism." In *Communication and Organizations: An Interpretive Approach,* edited by L. Putnam and M. Pacanowsky, 13–30. Beverly Hills, Calif. Sage, 1983.

Putnam, L., and M. Pacanowsky, eds. *Communication and Organizations: An Interpretive Approach.* Beverly Hills, Calif.: Sage, 1983.

Read, W. H. "Upward Communication in Industrial Hierarchies." *Human Relations* 15 (1962):3–15.

Redding, W. C. "Human Communication Behavior in Complex Organizations: Some Fallacies Revisited." In *Perspectives on Communication,* edited by C. E. Larson and F. E. X. Dance, 99–112. Shorewood, Wis.: Helix Press, 1970.

———. *Communication Within the Organization: An Interpretive Review of Theory and Research.* New York: Industrial Communication Council, 1972.

———. *The Corporate Manager's Guide to Better Communication.* Glenview, Ill.: Scott, Foresman, 1984.

Redding, W. C., and G. Sanborn, eds. *Business and Industrial Communication: A Source Book*. New York: Harper & Row, 1964.

Reuss, C., and D. Silvis, eds. *Inside Organizational Communication*. New York: Longman, 1981.

Reuter, E. B. "Race and Culture." In *Principles of Sociology*, edited by A. M. Lee, 2d ed. New York: Barnes & Noble Books, 1955.

Rice, R. E., W. D. Richards, and C. Cavalcanti. "Communication Network Analysis Methods." Paper presented at the meeting of the International Communication Association, Acapulco, Mexico, May 1980.

Richards, W. D. *A Manual for Network Analysis Using the NEGOPY Program*. Stanford, Calif.: Institute for Communication Research, 1975.

———. "A Cognitive Constructivist Approach to Communication Network Analysis." Paper presented at the meeting of the Learned Societies, Montreal, 1981.

Richmond, V. P., L. M. Davis, K. Saylor, and J. C. McCroskey. "Power Strategies in Organizations: Communication Techniques and Messages." *Human Communication Research* 11 (1984):85–108.

Rion, M. R. "Training for Ethical Management at Cummins Engine." In *Doing Ethics in Business: New Ventures in Management Development*, edited by D. G. Jones, 27–44. Cambridge, Mass.: Oelgeschlager, Gunn & Hain, 1982.

Roberts, K. H., and C. A. O'Reilly, "Failures in Upward Communication in Organizations: Three Possible Culprits." *Academy of Management Journal* 17 (1974):205–215.

Robinson, E. *Public Relations and Survey Research*. New York: Appleton-Century-Crofts, 1969.

Roethlisberger, F. J. *Management and Morale*. Cambridge, Mass.: Harvard University Press, 1956.

Roethlisberger, F. J., and W. J. Dickson. *Management and the Worker*. Cambridge, Mass.: Harvard University Press, 1939.

Rogers, C. "The Necessary and Sufficient Conditions of Psychotherapeutic Change." *Journal of Consulting Psychology* 21 (1957):95–103.

Rogers, E., and R. Agarwala-Rogers. *Communication in Organizations*. New York: Free Press, 1976.

Rogers, E., and J. Larsen. *Silicon Valley Fever*. New York: Basic Books, 1984.

Rosen, B., and T. Jerdee. "On-the-Job Sex Bias: Increasing Managerial Awareness." *The Personnel Administrator* 22 (1977):15–18.

Rosen, S. *Long-Range Planning: A Presidential Perspective*. New York: Presidents Association, 1973.

Rossiter, C. M., and W. B. Pearce. *Communicating Personally: A Theory of Interpersonal Communication and Human Relationships*. Indianapolis: Bobbs-Merrill, 1975.

Rowe, L., and W. Boise, eds. *Organizational and Managerial Innovation*. Pacific Palisades, Calif.: Goodyear, 1973.

Roy, D. F. "Banana Time: Job Satisfaction and Informal Interaction." *Human Organization* 18 (1960):156–168.

Ruben, B. D. *Communication and Human Behavior*. New York: Macmillan, 1983.

Ruben, B. D., and J. Kim, eds. *General Systems Theory and Human Communication*. Rochelle Park, N.J.: Hayden, 1975.

Rudolph, E. E. "Informal Human Communication Systems in a Large Organization." *Journal of Applied Communication Research* 1 (1973):7–23.

Ruesch, J. *Disturbed Communication*. New York: Norton, 1957.

———. *Therapeutic Communication*. New York: Norton, 1961.

Rusk, H. A. "Fund Raising." In *Experts in Action: Inside Public Relations*, edited by B. Cantor, 262–271. New York: Longman, 1984.

Rutenberg, S. "How Computer Criminals Can Get Rich Quick." In *Organizational Reality: Reports from the Firing Line*, edited by P. J. Frost, V. F. Mitchell, and W. R. Nord, 2d ed., 545–549. Glenview, Ill.: Scott, Foresman, 1982.

Schein, E. H. *Process Consultation: Its Role in Organization Development*. Reading, Mass.: Addison-Wesley, 1969.

———. *Organizational Psychology*. 2d ed. Englewood Cliffs, N. J.: Prentice-Hall, 1970.

Schmidt, M., and O. Lipstreu. "The Case Method." University of Colorado, 1975. Mimeo.

Schneider, A., W. Donaghy, and P. Newman. *Organizational Communication*. New York: McGraw-Hill, 1975.

Schnelle, K. *Case Analysis and Business Problem Solving*. New York: McGraw-Hill, 1967.

Schuler, R. S. "Definition and Conceptualization of Stress in Organizations." *Organizational Behavior and Human Performance* 25 (1980):184–215.

Schultz, R. "How to Handle Grievances." *Supervision* 28 (1966):10–12.

Schutz, W. C. *Firo: A Three-Dimensional Theory of Interpersonal Behavior*. New York: Holt, Rinehart and Winston, 1958.

Schwartz, H., and S. Davis. "Matching Corporate Culture and Business Strategy." *Organizational Dynamics* 10 (1981):30–48.

Selame, E., and J. Selame. *Developing a Corporate Identity: How to Stand Out from the Crowd*. New York: Chain Store Books, 1975.

Selye, H. *Stress Without Distress*. Philadelphia: Lippincott, 1974.

Shannon, C. E., and W. Weaver. *The Mathematical Theory of Communication*. Urbana: University of Illinois Press, 1949.

Sherwin, D. S. "Strategy for Winning Employee Commitment." *Harvard Business Review* 50 (1972):37–47.

Shire, D. "Age Discrimination in Employment." *The Personnel Administrator* 20 (1975):28–30, 54–55.

Sigband, N. B. "Needed: Corporate Policies on Communications." *Advanced Management Journal* 34 (1969):61–67.

———. "What's Happened to Employee Commitment?" *Personnel Journal* 53 (1974):131–135

Silberman, C. *Crisis in Black and White*. New York: Random House, 1964.

Silverman, D. *The Theory of Organisations*. New York: Basic Books, 1971.

Simon, H. A. "On the Concept of Organizational Goal." *Administrative Science Quarterly* 9 (1964):1–22.

Simon, R. *Public Relations: Concepts and Practices*. 2d ed. Columbus, Ohio: Grid, 1980.

Sincoff, M. Z., D. A. Williams, and C. E. T. Rohm. "Steps in Performing a Communication Audit." Paper presented at the meeting of the International Communication Association, Portland, May 1976.

Sink, D. S. "State of the Art Approaches to the Problem of Unlocking Employee Potential." *Industrial Engineering* 19 (1983):65–70.

Smircich, L. "Concepts of Culture and Organizational Analysis." *Administrative Science Quarterly* 28 (1983):257–273.

Smircich, L., and G. Morgan. "Leadership: The Management of Meaning." *Journal of Applied Behavioral Science* 18 (1982): 257–273.

Smith, D. H. "Communication Research and the Idea of Process." *Speech Monographs* 39 (1972):174–182.

Smith, P. C., L. M. Kendall, and C. L. Hulin. *The Measurement of Satisfaction in Work and Retirement: A Strategy for the Study of Attitudes*. Chicago: Rand McNally, 1969.

Snow, C. P. *The Two Cultures: And a Second Look*. New York: Cambridge University Press, 1963.

Sommer, R. *Personal Space*. Englewood Cliffs, N.J.: Prentice-Hall, 1969.

Spradley, J. P., and D. W. McCurdy. *The Cultural Experience: Ethnography in Complex Society*. Chicago: Science Research Associates, 1972.

Spriegel, W. R., and C. E. Myers, eds. *The Writings of the Gilbreths*. Homewood, Ill.: Irwin, 1953.

Staw, B., and G. Salancik, eds. *New Directions in Organizational Behavior*. Chicago: St. Clair Press, 1977.

Steers, R. M. "Problems in the Measurement of Organizational Effectiveness." *Administrative Science Quarterly* 20 (1975):546–558.

Stewart, L. P. "Whistle Blowing: Implications for Organizational Communication Scholars." Paper presented at the meeting of the International Communication Association, Acapulco, Mexico, May 1980a.

———. "Whistle Blowing; Implications for Organizational Communication." *Journal of Communication* 30 (1980b):90–101.

Stewart, L. P., and S. Ting-Toomey, eds. *Communication, Gender and Sex Roles in Diverse Interaction Contexts*. Norwood, N.J.: Ablex, 1985.

Stinson, J. E., and T. W. Johnson. "The Path-Goal Theory of Leadership: A Partial Test and Suggested Refinement." *Academy of Management Journal* 18 (1975):242–252.

Stodgill, R. M., and A. E. Coons, eds. *Leader Behavior: Its Description and Measurement*. Columbus: Ohio State University Bureau of Business Research, 1957.

Sturm, D. "Assessing the Sun Company's Ethical Condition: Voices from Within." In *Doing Ethics in Business: New Ventures in Management Development*, edited by D. G. Jones, 73–113. Cambridge, Mass.: Oelgeschlager, Gunn & Hain, 1982.

Sudnow, D. *Passing On: The Social Organization of Dying*. Englewood Cliffs, N.J.: Prentice-Hall, 1967.

Tabris, M. D. "Crisis Management." In *Experts in Action: Inside Public Relations*, edited by B. Cantor, 57–73. New York: Longman, 1984.

Tavernier, G. "Using Employee Communication to Support Corporate Objectives." *Management Review* 69 (1980):8–13.

Taylor, F. *Scientific Management*. New York: Harper & Row, 1911.

Taylor, J. A., and R. V. Farace. "The Referential Function of Informal Communication Groups in Complex Organizations." Paper presented at the meeting of the International Communication Association, Portland, May 1976.

Terkel, S. *Working*. New York: Random House, 1972.

Thayer, L., ed. *Communication and Communication Systems*. Homewood, Ill.: Irwin, 1968.

Thompson, J. D. *Organizations in Action*. New York: McGraw-Hill, 1967.

Thompson, V. A. *Bureaucracy and the Modern World*. Morristown, N.J.: General Learning Press, 1976.

Timm, P. *Managerial Communication: A Finger on the Pulse*. Englewood Cliffs, N.J.: Prentice-Hall, 1980.

Tompkins, P. "Management Qua Communication in Rocket Research and Development." *Communication Monographs* 44 (1977):1–26.

———. "Organizational Metamorphosis in Space Research and Development." *Communication Monographs* 45 (1978):110–118

———. *Communication as Action*. Belmont, Calif.: Wadsworth, 1982.

———. "The Functions of Human Communication in Organization." In *Hand-*

book of Rhetorical and Communication Theory, edited by C. C. Arnold and J. W. Bowers, 659–719. Boston: Allyn & Bacon, 1984.

Tompkins, P., and G. Cheney. "Account Analysis of Organizational Decision Making and Identification." In *Communication and Organizations: An Interpretive Approach*, edited by L. Putnam and M. Pacanowsky, 123–146. Beverly Hills, Calif.: Sage, 1983.

Tortoriello, T., S. Blatt, and S. DeWine. *Communication in the Organization: An Applied Approach*. New York: McGraw-Hill, 1978.

Tosi, H., ed. *Readings in Management: Contingencies, Structure, and Process*. Chicago: St. Clair Press, 1976.

Townsend, L. A. "A Corporate President's View of the Internal Communication Function." *Journal of Communication* 15 (1965):208–215.

Trei, A. "What I Am Learning at HBS." *Harvard Business School Bulletin* (June 1958): 20.

Truax, C., and R. Carkhuff. *Toward Effective Counseling in Psychotherapy: Training and Practice*. Chicago: Aldine, 1967.

Tubbs, S., and T. Hain. "Management Communication and Its Relationship to Total Organizational Effectiveness." Paper presented at the meeting of the Academy of Management, Atlanta, August 1979.

Tubbs, S., and R. N. Widgery. "When Productivity Lags, Are Key Managers Really Communicating?" *Management Review* 67 (1978):20–25.

Turk, H. "Comparative Urban Structure from an Interorganizational Perspective." *Administrative Science Quarterly* 18 (1973):37–55.

Turner, B. A. *Exploring the Industrial Subculture*. London: Macmillan, 1971.

Turner, S. P. "Complex Organizations as Savage Tribes." *Journal for the Theory of Social Behavior* 7 (1983):99–125.

Tushman, M. L., and T. J. Scanlan. "Characteristics and External Orientations of Boundary-Spanning Individuals." *Academy of Management Journal* 24 (1981):83–98.

Ulrich, D. N. "The Case Method." In *The Case Method of Teaching Human Relations and Administration*, edited by K. Andrews, 25–34. Cambridge, Mass.: Harvard University Press, 1953.

Uttal, B. "The Corporate Culture Vultures." *Fortune*, 17 October 1983, 66–70, 72.

Velasquez, M. "Teaching Business Ethics: Aims and Methods." In *Doing Ethics in Business: New Ventures in Management Development*, edited by D. G. Jones, 137–152. Cambridge, Mass.: Oelgeschlager, Gunn & Hain, 1982.

Velmans, L. A. "Public Relations—What It Is and What it Does: An Overview." In *Experts in Action: Inside Public Relations*, edited by B. Cantor, 1–6. New York: Longman, 1984.

Vladeck, B. C. *Unloving Care: The Nursing Home Tragedy*. New York: Basic Books, 1980.

Vogel, A. "Why Don't Employees Speak Up?" *Personnel Administration* 30 (1967):18–24.

Vroom, V. H. *Work and Motivation*. New York: Wiley, 1964.

Wager, L. W. "Organizational Linking Pins: Hierarchy Status and Communicative Roles in Interlevel Conferences." *Human Relations* 25 (1972):307–326.

Wallace, R. K., and H. Benson. "The Physiology of Meditation." *Scientific American* 226 (1972):84–90.

Walters, K. D. "Your Employees' Right to Blow the Whistle." *Harvard Business Review* 53 (1975):26–34, 161–162.

Walton, E. "How Effective Is the Grapevine?" *Personnel Journal* 38 (1961):45–49.

Walton, R. E. *Interpersonal Peacemaking: Confrontations and Third-Party Consultation*. Reading, Mass.: Addison-Wesley, 1969.

Warren, R. L. "The Interorganizational Field as a Focus for Investigation." *Administrative Science Quarterly* 12 (1967):396–419.

Watzlawick, P., J. Beavin, and D. Jackson. *Pragmatics of Human Communication*. New York: Norton, 1967.

Weber, M. *The Theory of Social and Economic Organization*. 1909. Reprint, translated by A. Henderson and T. Parsons. New York: Oxford University Press, 1948.

Webster, F. E. *Marketing Communication: Modern Promotional Strategy*. New York: Ronald Press, 1971.

Weick, K. *The Social Psychology of Organizing*. Reading, Mass.: Addison-Wesley, 1969.

———. "Amendments to Organizational Theorizing." *Academy of Management Journal* 17 (1974):487–502.

———. "Educational Organizations as Loosely Coupled Systems." *Administrative Science Quarterly* 21 (1976):1–19.

———. *The Social Psychology of Organizing*. 2d ed. Reading, Mass.: Addison-Wesley, 1979.

Weiman, C. "A Study of Occupational Stressors and the Incidence of Disease/Risk." *Journal of Occupational Medicine* 19 (1977):119–122.

White, D., and H. W. Vroman. *Action in Organizations*. 2d ed. Boston: Allyn & Bacon, 1982.

White, H. S. "Special Libraries and the Corporate Political Process." *Special Libraries* 75 (1984):81–86.

White, R., and R. Lippitt. *Autocracy and Democracy*. New York: Harper & Row, 1960.

———. "Leader Behavior and Member Reaction in Three Social Climates." In *Group Dynamics*, edited by D. Cartwright and A. Zander, 318–336. New York: Harper & Row, 1968.

Whorton, J. W., and J. A. Worthley. "A Perspective for the Challenge of Public Management: Environmental Paradox and Organizational Culture." *Academy of Management Review* 6 (1981):357–363.

Whyte, W. F. *Street Corner Society*. Chicago: University of Chicago Press, 1955.

Wiener, N. *Cybernetics*. Cambridge, Mass.: M.I.T. Press, 1948.

Wigand, R. T. "Communication and Interorganizational Relationships among Complex Organizations in Social Service Settings." Paper presented at the meeting of the International Communication Association, Portland, May 1976.

Williams, L. K., J. W. Seybolt, and C. C. Pinder. "On Administering Questionnaires in Organizational Settings." *Personnel Journal* 28 (1975):93–103.

Williams, T. R. *Field Methods in the Study of Culture*. New York: Holt, Rinehart and Winston, 1967.

Wilmot, W. W. *Dyadic Communication*. 2d ed. Reading, Mass.: Addison-Wesley, 1980.

Wren, D. A. *The Evolution of Management Thought*. New York: Ronald Press, 1972.

Zaleznik, A. "Managers and Leaders: Are They Different?" *Harvard Business Review* 55 (May–June 1977): 67–78.

APPENDIX

Using the Case-Study Method in Organizational Communication Classes

Developing Students' Insight, Knowledge, and Creativity

Introduction to the Case-Study Method

The case-study method is a technique for examining realistic organizational problems through systematic analysis. Typically, in the case-study method, a description of a potentially problematic real-life phenomenon (in organizational communication classes, a description of a troublesome situation that organization members are encountering) is presented to students. This description is referred to as the case or the case history and is generally presented in written form, although cases may be presented orally or through use of media. Students are encouraged to perform the critical role of case-study analyst. Case analysis involves the identification and examination of salient issues causing

Adapted from G. L. Kreps, "Using the Case Study Method in Organizational Communication Classes: Developing Students' Insight, Knowledge, and Creativity" (paper presented to the meeting of the International Communication Association, San Francisco, 1984).

the problems that organization members are experiencing in the case, as well as the development of strategies for addressing and rectifying the case issues and problems identified. The case-study analyst must demonstrate a combination of insight, knowledge, and creativity in identifying relevant issues causing organizational distress in the case under examination, analyzing these issues in light of relevant (organizational communication) research and theory and devising realistic and appropriate strategies for helping organization members cope with the problematic situation presented in the case (Schnelle, 1967; Mier, 1982).

The quality of case analysis is largely dependent on the quality of the case history that is presented. The case history provides the analyst with critical information about the organization under examination. It is the task of the analyst to examine and interpret the evidence presented in the case history. Good case histories provide students with intriguing data that leads them to in-depth study and potentially heuristic analysis. Lawrence (1953) describes the benefits of selecting high-quality cases for analysis:

> A good case is the vehicle by which a chunk of reality is brought into the classroom to be worked over by the class and the instructor. A good case keeps the class discussion grounded upon some of the stubborn facts that must be faced up to in real-life situations. It is the anchor on academic flights of speculation. It is the record of complex situations that must be literally pulled apart and put together again before the situations can be understood (p. 215)

The selection of appropriate cases to present to students for analysis is crucial. The case must be carefully selected (or prepared) to reflect course information and demonstrate important theoretical issues in organizational communication. Case histories that provide realistic problem situations that reflect important theories and concepts of organizational communication enable the student analysts to apply their studies to strategic organizational problem identification and solution.

Case studies can be integrated into organizational communication classes using several instructional strategies. For example, the instructor can have students read a case history and then present the class with his or her own case analysis. This is an especially useful strategy when first initiating case analysis as a class instructional method. By presenting the class with his or her own analysis of the case, the instructor demonstrates the proper manner for conducting case analyses and gives class members examples of how organizational theory can be applied to case analyses. Cases also can be analyzed by the group aloud in class by both students and instructor through class discussion. After students have some experience with case studies and are familiar with the case-study method, it is often beneficial for the instructor to assign students a case to analyze on their own and have them develop their own case-study reports. Case-study reports may be assigned as written class work and turned in to the instructor for evaluation, or they can be assigned to individual students or student teams for oral class presentation. Oral presentations of case analyses can be a good stimulator for in-depth group discussion and critique.

The instructor should facilitate effective in-class case study analysis as a discussion leader. Schmidt and Lipstreu (1975) suggest that the role of the effective case-analysis-discussion leader includes drawing attention to neglected facts, asking questions about points raised by participants, questioning the impact of different courses of action suggested, encouraging the group to ask questions and provide detailed commentary, and discouraging vague generalizations and ready-made solutions. The discussion leader also can raise the level of case analysis by clearly identifying and exemplifying the crucial role of organizational theory and research in analyzing case histories and developing strategies for organizational innovation. Case-study work is most productive when the instructor helps the students integrate case examples with course information. The instructor should also help process student interpretations of cases, recognizing that there is no one correct evaluation of any case history but many different viable perspectives on case analysis. The instructor should emphasize to students that the best case-study analyses are methodical, reasoned, and substantiated by organizational theory and research.

The case-study method is by no means a totally new educational method (Dooley and Skinner, 1977). It has its roots in the Socratic method of education, in which the instructor tells students a story about a problematic situation and queries them about how they might solve the problem. Case-study work provides students with many questions. Learning is accomplished by attempting to answer the questions. The case method has been extensively used in business, medical, library, social-work, and legal education. The strength of the case method for organizational communication instruction is that it is particularly well suited for helping students to learn about complex organizational phenomena. For example, the case-study method has a long and productive history of use in management education at the Harvard Business School, where it has helped prepare students to become effective organizational analysts and decision makers (McNair and Hersum, 1954; Andrews, 1953, Trei, 1958; Harvard Business School, 1965). The case study has been used as an instructional tool in many textbooks concerning organizations, where case histories and/or case analyses have been included to illustrate theories about organizational behavior (White and Vroman, 1982; Kreps and Thornton, 1984; Glover, Hower, and Tagiuri, 1973; Gildea and Haas, 1975; Haney, 1972). In recent years, several authors have written popular books about organizations that present real case histories to validate their perspectives about organizational life (Peters and Waterman, 1982; Deal and Kennedy, 1982; Terkel, 1972; Harragan, 1977). The extensive utilization of the case method would seem to indicate that the case method offers substantial benefits in education.

Instructional Rationale

Organizational communication education is an applied area of study that examines theory and research about the role of human interaction in organizational life (Carney, 1979; Pace and Ross, 1983). Organizational communication study is rooted in the actual communication behaviors performed by organization members in the accomplishment of organizational tasks. Case-study analysis is an instructional method that encourages students' application of relevant organizational communication theory to organizational practice. Case studies bring organizational communication theory to life by enabling the student to visualize how the theory relates to organizational analysis, organizational problem solving, and improvement of organizational performance.

Case studies can help organizational communication students recognize the role of communication in effective organizational functioning. Gildea and Haas (1975) described how case studies illuminate the uses of organizational communication when they wrote that "case studies are presented to show how others initiated or enhanced their organization's commitment to an ongoing program of effective communication" (p. 4). Additionally, the use of case studies in organizational communication courses can provide many pedagogical benefits for both instructors and students. For example, Mier (1982) suggests that the case method can be used in organizational communication courses to help accomplish the following three instructional goals.

1. To help formulate key concepts introduced in textbook readings and classroom lectures
2. To help reinforce learning through application of key concepts covered in lectures, readings, films, and textbook cases (student case studies)
3. To help students pinpoint the communication issue as it relates to other organizational contingencies (textbook cases and student cases). (p. 151)

Further pedagogical functions of the case-study method in organizational communication instruction include

1. helping instructors generate class discussion by presenting meaningful situations for class exploration and posing questions about case analysis and problem solving;
2. helping instructors illustrate and clarify important organizational communication concepts by relating these concepts to examples from case analyses;
3. helping to expand students' knowledge of organizational communication research and theory by encouraging students to search for explanatory research and theory in diagnosing case problems;
4. helping to promote students' recognition of the uses of organizational communication theory and research by demonstrating that theory can be effectively used to analyze case problems and direct strategies for helping organization members cope with case problems;
5. helping to foster student's analytical insight in the nature of organizational process by encouraging them to examine organizational activities, diagnose the sources of organizational problems, and develop strategies for organizational innovation;
6. helping to facilitate students' ability to demonstrate creativity in making decisions about solving organizational problems; past research has demonstrated that the ability to make decisions and solve organizational problems is one of the most valuable communication-related skills that organization members can possess (DiSalvo, 1980); and
7. providing students with experience in business writing and professional presentations in the preparation of written and oral case-study reports.

Schmidt and Lipstreu (1975) identify five additional benefits of the case method as an effective learning device.

1. Provides a satisfying learning opportunity because it combines two essentials—realism and participation
2. Provides opportunities for the development of social skills; of respect for the opinions of others; of effective participation in a group; of improved understanding of why people act as they do
3. Bridges the gap between knowledge and skills
4. Acquaints individuals with the elusiveness of wisdom and truth and the complexities of administrative situations
5. Provides opportunities for effective role-playing, in which a role player may see himself as others see him
6. Offers experiences in which people, in varying degrees, learn to modify or get rid of some of their prejudices because they must take into account the different views presented. (p. 2)

The case-study method has many potential benefits for organizational communication education, if used properly.

Guidelines For Using Case Studies

Glover and Hower (1953) claim that the most important prerequisite for case analysis is the instructor's ability to set a conducive atmosphere for case analysis. The instructor's ability to establish rapport with students will help establish a favorable climate for case analysis. A favorable climate for case analysis is one in which students feel free to answer questions, present their idiosyncratic points of view, and creatively analyze the case under review.

> This means a permissive atmosphere in which they [students] feel free to put forth their ideas and their questions without the instructor's reacting in the form of rejection, derision, blame or authoritarian injunctions to think along certain other lines preferred by the instructor at that moment. This free atmosphere will be fostered if the instructor makes up his mind to hear and try to understand what students have to say, and encourages others to do the same. (Glover and Hower, 1953, p. 14)

Gibb's (1961) notion of developing a supportive climate by stressing communication behaviors that are nonjudgmental, cooperative, empathic, and spontaneous seems to provide a viable model for establishing a communication climate in the organizational communication class that is conducive to productive case-study analysis.

As mentioned earlier, the selection of an appropriate case for analysis is an important criterion for effective use of the case-study method. An appropriate case provides the analyst with enough information to provide the organizational communication student with sufficient clues as to the underlying problems that the organization under examination is experiencing, without analyzing the situation for the student. Additionally, a good case should illustrate concepts that are relevant to the research and theory being covered in the organizational communication class. Cases should be as realistic as possible, including background information about characters in the case, the organizations examined, and the relationships among characters. The most enriching cases describe "the process by which actions take place" and may include conversations among characters "recorded as nearly verbatim as possible" (Ulrich, 1953, p. 31). The richer the case selected for case-study analysis, the more likely the case study is to be an effective pedagogical tool in organizational communication classes.

Case-study reports must be well organized and must explain the nature of problems confronting the organization. The case-study report lends itself to a conventional three-part analytic structure: (1) problem identification, (2) analysis, and (3) recommendation (Bernthal, 1975). In the problem-identification section, analysts emamine the case history and, based on the evidence presented, diagnose different key issues that are causing the organizational difficulties. In the analysis section, the case-study analyst examines why the problems are occurring and describes current knowledge about the organizational issues identified. Finally, in the recommendation section, the analyst devises strategies for relieving the problems facing the organization.

In identifying relevant issues in a case history, there must be a systematic search for important evidence within the case, identifying the underlying issues confronting organizations as well as the more readily evident problems. Analysts must recognize the mutual influence of different systems, subsystems, and both internal organizational and environmental factors in identifying key issues confronting organizations. Once key issues are identified, they are ranked in terms of the strength of each issue's influence on the organization and on the problematic situation in which the organization finds itself. The analyst must be able to distinguish among primary issues, subissues, and mere symptoms of issues confronting the organization. Furthermore, the analyst should be able to demonstrate pertinent evidence presented in the case history that led to the identification of problem issues.

In the analysis section of the case-study report, the analyst must examine the issues and problems diagnosed previously in the problem-identification section of the report and describe why these issues cause problems for organizations. An important factor in the analysis section is that relevant organizational theory and research must be applied to the case study. The analyst must explore the issues confronting the organization in the case in light of his or her knowledge of organizational theory and research. It is organizational theory that enables the analyst to fully analyze the case history. Organizational theory helps the analyst address such questions as: Why are these issues arising? What negative influences do these issues have on organizational functioning now, and what negative affects might they produce in the future? What are some of the productive ways that organizations (in general) can deal with the issues identified? How do these productive organizational strategies relate to the specific organization under examination? The more complete the analyst's search and application of relevant organizational research and theory to the case, the more enlightening the case-study analysis.

In the recommendations section of the case-study report, the analyst examines the issues identified and analyzed in the first two sections of the report to shed light on how organization members might redirect organizational activities to help relieve the problems incurred in the case. If actors in the case have already taken action, the analyst should evaluate the actions taken and suggest alternative courses of action. The analyst must be careful to devise recommendations that address each of the issues identified in the problem-identification section. Furthermore, the organizational-innovation strategies that the analyst suggests must be consistent with the issue analysis and theoretical evaluations presented in the analysis section. For example, if the case-study analyst identifies a defensive communication climate as being a key issue causing problems in an organizational case history and describes some of the communication behaviors that lead to and reduce defensiveness in organizations in the analysis section, then the recommendations that the analyst suggests must deal specifically with the defensive-climate issue and follow the theoretical guidelines for dealing with defensive climates presented in the case-analysis section. Case-study analysts should be concerned with developing both short-range strategies, for relieving organizational problems immediately, and long-range strategies, for preventing similar problems from recurring. In this manner, the analyst reacts appropriately to the present organizational situation and devises strategies for helping organization members become more proactive in preventing and defusing potential organizational difficulties.

Case analysis, then, begins with identification of salient issues contributing to organizational difficulties, next examines the nature of these issues with regard to organizational research and theory, and finally develops strategies for helping organization members resolve these problems. Bernthal (1975) echos many of the guidelines for case analysis that have been identified here when he specifies that effective case-study analyses should be systematic, recognize the interdependence of organizational systems and subsystems, be realistic and explanatory, and be research and theory based. In the following section, I will provide an example of a typical case-study-report assignment that follows the guidelines presented above.

Sample Case-Study-Report Assignment

The case-study report should be written in a professional manner and typed, double-spaced, as though you were a consultant hired by the organization to help solve the problems described in the case. There should be three major sections in the case-study report.

First, *statement of the problem(s)* Succinctly state what you decide are the most pressing problems facing the individuals (and the organization) in the case. Explain why you think these are the major issues in this situation. What information presented in the case leads you to identify these issues? (Be careful to look for the root issues causing problems in the case. Often the most obvious problems in a case are merely symptoms of more basic underlying problems. You may want to identify both main issues and subissues.)

Second, *Analysis* Based on your knowledge of the nature of organizational communication, explain why you think the problems you have identified (in the first section) are occurring. Shed some insight into the reasons that problems such as the ones in this case occur in organizations. How do the issues you identify affect organizations in general? How should the organizational communication concepts be utilized effectively? (Be sure to relate your analysis to organizational communication theory.)

Third, *Recommendations* Develop realistic strategies for alleviating the problems you have identified and analyzed (in the first two sections). Indicate how the recommendations you suggest may be implemented within the organization. (Be sure to differentiate between short-term strategies to help the organization cope with the existing problems and long-term plans designed to keep these problems from emerging again. Short-term strategies are generally reactive, while long-term strategies are more proactive.) What specific activities should organization members engage in to initiate the recommendations you suggest?

Conclusion

The case-study method is a potentially useful pedagogical tool that can be successfully used in organizational communication classes. Case work is most productive when cases are openly discussed in class. Student involvement and creativity in case-study discussions should be encouraged. Effective use of case studies can promote the development of students' insight, knowledge, and creativity. Case-study work helps cultivate students' insight by providing them with experience in recognizing and diagnosing organizational problems. Case-study work can expand students' knowledge of organizational theory by demonstrating how to apply relevant research and theory to organizational analysis and problem solving. Case-study work also can help develop students' creativity by providing them with the opportunity to examine and interpret case histories, identify salient facts and issues emerging out of the case histories, and develop organizational development strategies for helping organization members cope with organizational difficulties.

Name Index

Subject Index